Mike Denial is the main author of the enormously successful O-level textbook *Investigating Chemistry* and joint author of two related books. Currently Principal Lecturer at Norton Tertiary College, Sheffield, he has wide experience of Chemistry teaching and examining, having taught in both grammar and comprehensive schools and been head of department in three of them.

Pan Study Aids for GCSE include:

Accounting

Biology

Chemistry

Commerce

Computer Studies

Economics

English Language

French

Geography 1

Geography 2

German

History 1: World History since 1914

History 2: Britain and Europe since 1700

Human Biology

Mathematics

Physics

Sociology

Study Skills

PAN STUDY AIDS

CHEMISTRY

Mike Denial

A Pan Original
Pan Books   London and Sydney

First published 1987 by Pan Books Ltd,
Cavaye Place, London SW10 9PG

9 8 7 6 5 4 3

© M. J. Denial 1987

ISBN 0 330 29938 7

Text design by Peter Ward
Text illustration by M L Design
Photoset by Parker Typesetting Service, Leicester
Printed and bound in Spain by
Mateu Cromo SA, Madrid

CONTENTS

Contents

24 NEA Questions included.

PREFACE; USING THIS STUDY GUIDE

It is important that you read this. Otherwise, you will not obtain full benefit from the book.

This Study Guide will help anyone to prepare for a GCSE examination in chemistry, no matter which syllabus is being followed. It can be used during the teaching programme to help with understanding, the organization of facts and ideas, and to practise/reinforce what is needed in the examination. Equally, it can be used towards the end of the course, in preparation for the final examination. The book provides more than a summary of all the important facts and ideas: it is a complete guide on how to prepare for an examination in GCSE chemistry.

All of the necessary facts have been shown in clear and simple form. The main ideas are thoroughly discussed and linked together, so that patterns are emphasised. Common misunderstandings and examination mistakes have been stressed, and advice is given on answering different types of examination question. All of the important ideas are reinforced by 'Check your understanding' sections. The differences between syllabuses have been shown, and checklists are provided at the end of each chapter.

Students will need to understand the following points when using the book.

1 HOW DO I KNOW WHICH FACTS AND IDEAS ARE NOT INCLUDED IN MY PARTICULAR SYLLABUS?

The Guide covers all of the GCSE chemistry syllabuses, but they differ in content. Most students will recognise items which they have not studied in school or college, and ignore them. The chart on p.13 should also help. If there is any doubt about syllabus content, a teacher or lecturer should be asked for advice. Alternatively (or in addition) a copy of the syllabus produced by the examining board is usually available through a local bookseller, or direct from the offices of the board, or perhaps through your school or college. The addresses of the boards are given on p.10. A syllabus is very useful; it also acts as a detailed checklist during the revision programme.

You will also need to remember that usually there are different examination papers for each chemistry syllabus. One, or perhaps two, papers are usually taken by all students and can lead to the award of certain grades (typically grades C to G). Another paper is usually only taken by those students considered to be capable of gaining the highest grades (grades A, B or C). If your examination system is different from this, it will have been explained to you. The important point is that if you are going to take only the basic papers, you will not need to revise the more difficult ideas covered in this book.

To make it easier for you to organise your revision, the basic, important facts and ideas are set in type the same size as this setting. You should first concentrate on learning, understanding and practising these. They are likely to be common to most syllabuses. More difficult ideas are shown in the sans serif type such as this. These passages are also marked with a vertical, yellow rule. However, *some* of this more difficult material is still needed for the basic papers. Each syllabus differs in the material which is examined only for the higher grades. You should be able to recognise, from your notes, which, if any, of the more difficult ideas you should revise. The chart on p.13 should also help. As always, the advice of a teacher/lecturer and a copy of the syllabus should be obtained.

2 THE STUDY GUIDE DOES NOT GIVE DETAILS OF ALL THE EXPERIMENTS I HAVE DONE. DOES THIS MATTER?

No! It is assumed that students will have followed a course involving laboratory work, and that they have a notebook describing this work. All students taking GCSE chemistry have their practical work assessed by the teacher/lecturer throughout the course. The marks obtained for practical skills contribute at least 20% of the total marks available in the examination. Your mark for practical work depends entirely on how you have performed experiments in the laboratory, and it cannot be influenced by this book.

However, questions in the written papers could require a description of an experiment, or you could be asked to plan an experiment to solve a problem, or you could be given some results from an experiment and be asked to use them in some way. Advice about these points is given throughout the book, and many questions are provided for practice. By far the most difficult demands of a chemistry course are the abilities to link ideas together, to recognise patterns, and to be able to use an idea in a new or different situation. The Study Guide helps you to improve these abilities, for although the experiments you will have done are usually relatively easy to understand, their conclusions and applications are more difficult, and it is these which are emphasised in the book.

To make it easier for you to recognise how practical work links with the ideas and facts in the book, typical experiments which you may have used are mentioned briefly. Such experiments are *typical* only. Individual teachers and lecturers will have their own ways of developing practical work. It is up to the student to link his or her practical work with the topics in this book. This is very important.

This exercise alone will guarantee a greater understanding of chemistry, and help you to link ideas together and to use them in new situations. The individual experiments may differ, but the conclusions and ideas obtained from them will always be the same, and they are all in this book.

3 DO I NEED TO LEARN ALL THE FACTS I HAVE DISCUSSED?

No! One of the most important features of GCSE is that there is much more emphasis on *using* and *understanding* facts, rather than on learning them. For example, you may be allowed to use a Data Book, and almost certainly a copy of the Periodic Table, in the examinations, so that you can look up facts when you need them. Also, some examination questions will give you facts and information which you then have to use, but do not need to remember. You should regard some of the facts that you have used during your course, and also some of those in this Guide, as being there for reference only, and not to be learned.

The 'Check your understanding' sections have been specially designed to give you practice in *using* facts, and this is far more important than learning them. This is a very important feature of the Study Guide. You must become confident in your ability to use information sensibly if you are to obtain a good grade. If you use the questions successfully (answers are provided) you will be making yourself think in the way you have to for GCSE chemistry.

However, you will have to learn *some* facts and ideas. Each syllabus varies considerably in what you have to learn and in what will be given to you. You must use your own notes, a copy of the syllabus and advice in order to be sure. Note that the 'Check your understanding' sections are not intended to be like examination questions. Some of them are, but they are designed to help you use ideas and not to ask you to recall facts. *Some* examination questions will ask you to recall facts, as well as to use them. A good selection of examination questions is provided at the end of each chapter. To obtain full benefit from the book, you must use both the 'Check your understanding' and specimen examination questions.

There is a separate book in this series which is all about Study Skills. This will help you to prepare for a GCSE examination in any subject.

ACKNOWLEDGMENTS .

THE GCSE BOARDS

The specimen examination questions which are used in this Study Guide are reproduced by kind permission of the GCSE boards. Details and addresses are given below. The codes used for each board, and further details about some of the papers, are given on pages 49 and 50.

LONDON AND EAST ANGLIAN GROUP (LEAG)

(a)   East Anglian Examinations Board, The Lindens, Lexden Road, Colchester, CO3 3RL. Tel (0206) 549595
(b)   London Regional Examining Board, Lyon House, 104 Wandsworth High Street, London, SW18 4LF. Tel (01) 870 2144
(c)   University of London School Examinations Board, Stewart House, 32 Russell Square, London, WC1B 5DP. Tel (01) 636 8000

MIDLAND EXAMINING GROUP (MEG)

(a)   East Midland Regional Examinations Board, Robins Wood House, Robins Wood Road, Aspley, Nottingham, NG8 3NR. Tel (0602) 296021
(b)   Oxford and Cambridge Schools Examinations Board, 10 Trumpington Street, Cambridge, CB2 1QB. Tel (0223) 64326
(c)   Oxford and Cambridge Schools Examinations Board, Elsfield Way, Oxford, OX2 8EP. Tel (0865) 54421
(d)   Southern Universities Joint Board, Cotham Road, Cotham, Bristol, BS6 6DD. Tel (0272) 736042
(e)   The West Midlands Examinations Board, Norfolk House, Smallbrook Queensway, Birmingham, B5 4NJ. Tel (021) 643 2081
(f)   University of Cambridge Local Examinations Syndicate, Syndicate Buildings, 1 Hills Road, Cambridge, CB1 2EU. Tel (0223) 61111

NORTHERN EXAMINING ASSOCIATION (NEA)

(a)   Associated Lancashire Schools Examining Board, 12 Harter Street, Manchester, M1 6HL. Tel (061) 228 0084
(b)   Joint Matriculation Board, Manchester, M15 6EU. Tel (061) 273 2565
(c)   Northern Regional Examinations Board, Wheatfield Road, Westerhope, Newcastle upon Tyne, NE5 5JZ. Tel (091) 286 2711

(*d*)　　　North West Regional Examinations Board, Orbit House, Albert Street, Eccles, Manchester, M30 0WL. Tel (061) 788 9521

(*e*)　　　Yorkshire and Humberside Regional Examinations Board, 31–33 Springfield Avenue, Harrogate, North Yorkshire, HG1 2HW. Tel (0423) 66991

(*f*)　　　Yorkshire and Humberside Regional Examinations Board, Scarsdale House, 136 Derbyshire Lane, Sheffield, S8 8SE. Tel (0742) 557436

NORTHERN IRELAND SCHOOLS EXAMINATIONS COUNCIL (NISEC)

Northern Ireland Schools Examinations Council, Beechill House, 42 Beechill Road, Belfast, BT8 4RS. Tel (0232) 704666

SOUTHERN EXAMINING GROUP (SEG)

(*a*)　　　Associated Examining Board, Stag Hill House, Guildford, Surrey, GU2 5XJ. Tel (0483) 506506

(*b*)　　　South East Regional Examinations Board, 2–10 Mount Ephraim Road, Tunbridge Wells, Kent, TN1 1EU. Tel (0892) 35311/2/3/4

(*c*)　　　Southern Regional Examination Board, Avondale House, 33 Carlton Crescent, Southampton, SO9 4YL. Tel (0703) 32312

(*d*)　　　The South Western Examinations Board, 23–29 Marsh Street, Bristol, BS1 4BP. Tel (0272) 273434

(*e*)　　　University of Oxford Delegacy of Local Examinations, Ewert Place, Banbury Road, Summertown, Oxford, OX2 7BZ. Tel (0865) 54291

WELSH JOINT EDUCATION COMMITTEE (WJEC)

Welsh Joint Education Committee, 245 Western Avenue, Cardiff, CF5 2YX. Tel (0222) 561231

SYLLABUS DETAILS

The following codes are used in the grid:
- •   basic or full treatment needed for all papers
- ○   limited treatment needed for all papers
- √   some material needed only for alternative papers which are set for the highest grades

Note that these codes are used for **guidance only**. They cannot be used to show *all* the details which each syllabus requires. A blank entry does not *necessarily* mean that the material is not in the syllabus, but only that it is not specifically referred to. Some syllabuses contain much more detailed information than others.

NOTES

1   The symbol √ is not used in the grid for the MEG and MEG (Salters) syllabuses. Examination papers cover *all* of the work in these syllabuses, but the alternative papers (for higher grades) are more demanding than the basic papers.

2   The following social aspects of chemistry are unique to the MEG (Salters) syllabus or are briefly referred to in one or two others, and they have not been referred to in the Study Guide: smokes and mists, food tests, classification of fibres, cotton, linen, wool, silk, types of fire extinguisher, physical properties of wood and its uses, building materials, hormone treatment (food and medical), electrostatic precipitation, emulsions.

	LEAG (A)	LEAG (B) (Nuffield)	MEG	MEG Alternative (Nuffield)	MEG (Salters)	NEA (A) ✗	NEA (B) (Nuffield)	SEG	SEG Alternative (Nuffield)	NISEC	WJEC
Contribution from internal assessment	20%	25%	20%	25%	40%	20%	25%	20%	20%	20%	10%
Number of papers (+ internal assessment)	3	3	3	2	2	2	2	2	3	3	2
Alternative paper for higher grades	Paper 3	Paper 3	Paper 3	Paper 2	Paper 2	Paper 2	Paper 2	Paper 3 (P2 is internal)	Paper 4 (P3 is internal)	Paper 3	Paper 2
CHAPTER 1 Atoms, molecules, ions	●	●	●	●	●	●	●	●	●	●	●
Atomic structure	● ✓	● ✓	●	●	●	● ✓	●	● ✓	● ✓	● ✓	● ✓
Bonding	● ✓	●	●	●	●	● ✓	●	●	○	● ✓	● ✓
Radioactivity and nuclear power	○	○	○		○	●	● ✓		●	● ✓	● ✓
CHAPTER 2 States of matter, change of state	●	●	●	●	●	●	●	●	●		●
Diffusion	●	○	●	●		●	●	○		●	●
CHAPTER 3 Elements, compounds, mixtures	●	●	●		●	●	●	●	●	●	●
Metals and non-metals	●	●	●	●	●	●	● ✓		●	●	●
Purification methods	●	●	●	●	●	●		●	●	●	●
Testing purity	●	●	●			● ✓			●		●
CHAPTER 4 Activity Series – reactions with air, acids, water, displacement	●	●	●	●	●	● ✓	●	● ✓	●	● ✓	●
Other reactions/applications of Activity Series	●	●	●	●	○	● ✓	○	●	●	●	●
Simple cells	●			●	○	● ✓	●		●		●
CHAPTER 5 Basic ideas on electrolysis	●	●	●	● ✓		●	●	●	●	●	●
Specific examples: CuCl$_2$ (aq)						●		●	●		●
HCl (aq)								●			
NaCl (aq)			●	●	●	● ✓	○	● ✓		● ✓	●
CuSO$_4$ (aq) with C electrodes				●		●		✓	●		
CuSO$_4$ (aq) with Cu electrodes				●	○	○				● ✓	
H$_2$SO$_4$ (acidified water)				●		●				● ✓	
NaCl (l)				●		○	●	●			
Al$_2$O$_3$ (l)	●	●	●		●	● ✓	●	●	●	●	●
Molten PbBr$_2$ and/or LiCl							●			● ✓	●
Other examples not specified	●	●	●	●	○	●					
Prediction of products	✓			●				● ✓	○		
Anodising aluminium		○			●	●					
Electroplating	●	○			●		○				●
Purification of copper	●	○		●	●		○			●	

Syllabus details

	LEAG (A)	LEAG (B) (Nuffield)	MEG	MEG Alternative (Nuffield)	MEG (Salters)	NEA (A)	NEA (B) (Nuffield)	SEG	SEG Alternative (Nuffield)	NISEC	WJEC
CHAPTER 6											
Oxidation/reduction with loss/gain O	●	●	●	●	●	●	●	●	●	●	●
Oxidation/reduction with loss/gain H				●							●
Oxidation/reduction with loss/gain electrons				●		✓		✓	●	✓	
General points about using resources, siting industry, etc	●	●	●	●	●	●✓	●	●	●	●	●
Manufacture of iron	●	●	●		●	●	●	●	●	●	●
Steel and other alloys	●		○		○	●	●	●	●	●	●
Recycling	○	●	●		●	●	●	○	●		
Corrosion and its prevention	●	●	●	●	●	●✓	●	●	●	●✓	●
CHAPTER 7 *Note:* In this chapter, ○ usually refers to compounds, not the metal											
Na and its compounds	●	○	○	○	○	●	○	●	●	●	●
K and its compounds	○	○			○	○	○	○	○	○	○
Ca and its compounds	●	○	●		●	●✓	○	○	○	○	○
Mg and its compounds	○	○	○	○	○	○✓	○	○	○	○	○
Zn and its compounds	○	○	○	○	○	○	○	○	○	●	○
Al and its compounds	○	○	○	○	○	○	○	○	○	○	○
Fe and its compounds	○	○	○	○	○	●✓	○	○	○	○✓	○
Cu and its compounds	○	○	○	○	○	●✓	○	○	○	●	○
Pb and its compounds			○		○			○	○	○	○
Use of hydroxides to identify metal compounds	●		●		●	✓				●✓	●
Amphoteric nature $Al_2O_3/Al(OH)_3$			○			✓				●✓	○
Amphoteric nature $ZnO/Zn(OH)_2$			○						●	✓	○
Tests for sulphate, chloride, carbonate	●				○	●✓		●		●✓	●
Test for ammonium compounds	●		●	●	●			●		●	●
Flame tests	●				●						●
Test for nitrates					●						●
Tests for common gases	●	●	●	●	○	●	●	●	●	●	●
CHAPTER 8											
Properties of acids, bases, alkalis	●	●	●		●	●	●	●	●	●	●
Acids/bases as proton acceptors etc				●		✓	✓	✓	●✓		
Strong/weak acids and bases	○	○	○	○	●	●✓		✓	○	○	○
Preparing soluble salts: acids and metals, carbonates, bases, alkalis	●	●	●	●	○	●	●	●	●	●	●
Preparing insoluble salts		○	●			●	○			●	
Preparing salts by direct combination						●			✓		○
pH scale and neutralisation	●	●	●	●	●	●✓		●✓	●✓	●	●

	LEAG (A)	LEAG (B) (Nuffield)	MEG	MEG Alternative (Nuffield)	MEG (Salters)	NEA (A)	NEA (B) (Nuffield)	SEG	SEG Alternative (Nuffield)	NISEC	WJEC
CHAPTER 9											
General principles, preparing/collecting gases	●		○		○	●				●	
The air	●	●	●	●	●	●	●	●	●	●	●
Oxygen, etc from liquid air	●			●		●			●	●	○
Processes which produce/use up O_2	●	○	●	●	○	●	●		●	●	●
CO_2/O_2 balance. Greenhouse effect	○	○	○		○	●	○		○		○
Air pollution	●	●	●	●	●	●	●	●	●	●	●
Preparation, properties, uses of O_2	●	●	●	○	○	●	○	●	○	●	●
Types of oxide	○		●	●		●✓	●	○	●✓	●	●
Preparation, properties, uses of H_2	●	○	●	○	○	●	○	●	○	●	○
CHAPTER 10											
Water cycle, treatment, purification	●	●	●		●	●	●		●	●	●
Properties and test for water	●	●	●	●	○	●	●	●	●	●	●
Hard water, methods of softening	●	○	●		●	●✓	●	●	○	●	●
Solvent properties of water	●	●	○	●	●	●	●	●	●	●	●
Water pollution	●	●	●	○	●	●	●	●	●	●	●
CHAPTER 11											
Using the Periodic Table – details vary	●	●	●	●✓	●	●✓	●	●	●	●	●
Some history of the Periodic Table									○	●	
Transition metals and compounds	●			●✓			●	✓	●		
Simple relationships in Group 4							●	●			
Displacement reactions of halogens	●	●	●	●		✓			●	●	●
Structure – details vary	●	●	●	●	○	●✓	●		●✓	●	●
Other structural types, eg metals (in detail) or $SiSO_2$				✓	○		○	✓	✓	●	
CHAPTER 12											
Formula (molecular) mass	●	●	●		●	●	●	●	●	●	●
Equations (words, formulae, ionic)	●✓	●✓	●✓	●✓	●	●✓	●	●✓	●✓	●✓	●✓
Calculating masses from equations	●		●	●✓							
The mole	✓	●	●	✓		✓		✓	●	●	●
Calculations on volumes of gases	✓		●	●		✓	✓		●	✓	
% composition by mass	●					●		●	●		
Calculations to find emperical and molecular formulae	○✓		●	✓		✓			○		●
Concentrations of solutions, titrations	○		●	✓	○	✓	✓		○	●✓	○
Avogadro constant	✓			✓					●	✓	

	LEAG (A)	LEAG (B) (Nuffield)	MEG	MEG Alternative (Nuffield)	MEG (Salters)	NEA (A)	NEA (B) (Nuffield)	SEG	SEG Alternative (Nuffield)	NISEC	WJEC
CHAPTER 13											
Carbon, CO_2, CO, properties, uses	●	○	●	○	●	● √	○	●	○	●	●
Carbon cycle	●					●		●	●		
Sulphur, SO_2, properties, uses	○	○	○	○	○	●	○	●		○	●
Frasch process										●	
Contact process	●		●		●	●	●	●	●	●	●
Concentrated H_2SO_4 – properties	○		●	○		●			√	●	●
Dilute sulphuric/hydrochloric acids	●	●	●	●	●	●	●	●	●	●	●
Nitrogen, ammonia – properties, uses	●	●	●	○	●	● √	○	●	○	●	●
Haber process	●	●	●	●	●	●	●	●	●	●	●
Manufacture of nitric acid		●						●		√	
Nitrogen cycle, fertilisers	●	●	●	●	●	●	● √	●	●	●	●
Chlorine: properties, uses	●	○	●	●	●	●	●	●	○	● √	○
Hydrogen chloride (the gas)	●									●	
CHAPTER 14											
Alkanes – properties, names, formulae of first few	●	●	●	○	●	●	●	●	○	●	●
Alkenes – „	○	●	●	●	●	● √		● √	●	●	●
Isomerism			●			√					
Saturated, unsaturated, addition, substitution			●	●	○	●	○		●		
Plastics – (varies)	●		○	●	●	●		● √	●	● √	●
Alcohols – fermentation, properties	●	●	●	●	●	● √		●	●	●	●
Alcholic drinks	○	○		○	○	● √	○			○	○
Ethanoic acid									√	√	○
Starch, carbohydrates				○	●		●		●		
Esters										√	
CHAPTER 15											
Endothermic, exothermic, ΔH	○ ●	●	○	● √	●	● √	● √	○	● √	○	○
Bond-making, bond-breaking		●		●	●	○	●				
Flash points, ignition temperatures					●	●					●
Calculations on energy changes		○		● √	○	√	√				
Fuels: properties, problems	●				○	●	●	●	●	●	●
Petroleum: distillation, fractions, cracking	●	●	●	●	●	● √		●	●	●	●
Natural gas and coal	●		●		●	●	○	●	●	●	●
Destructive distillation of coal		○				○			○	●	
Alternative energy sources (vary)	●	●	●	○	○	●		●	● √	●	●
Energy calculations on charge of state				√							

	LEAG (A)	LEAG (B) (Nuffield)	MEG	MEG Alternative (Nuffield)	MEG (Salters)	NEA (A)	NEA (B) (Nuffield)	SEG	SEG Alternative (Nuffield)	NISEC	WJEC
CHAPTER 16 Speeds of reaction – experiments, graphs on surface area, concentration, temperature, pressure, catalysts	●	●	●	●	●	●✓	●	●✓	●	●	●
Light – effect on reactions						●			○		
Equilibrium. How to change equilibrium position				✓					✓		
The 'salt' and 'limestone' industries	●	●		●	●	●	●	●	●	●	
Applications of speeds of reaction in industry	●	○	●	●✓	○	●		○	○	○	○
Reversible reactions	●	●	○	●	●	○	●	✓	●	●	●
Food preservatives		○	○	○	●		●		○		○

ATOMIC STRUCTURE AND BONDING. RADIOACTIVITY AND NUCLEAR POWER

CONTENTS

1.1 ATOMS, MOLECULES AND IONS

Students often make mistakes when using these terms. For example, they often write 'atom' when they should use either molecule or ion. Free atoms are very rare. In fact, only the noble gases (p261) exist naturally as simple, free atoms. Most substances are made up of either molecules or ions. Each of these words has a special meaning, and it is important to use them correctly. It will be easier to use the words correctly if you understand bonding (p30) and structure (p264). If in doubt, write 'particles'. This is a general word which can mean atoms, molecules or ions. If you are using the SEG (Alt) syllabus, you may need to understand a simple experiment to estimate particle size.

ATOMS

An atom is the smallest particle into which an element can be split up and still keep its properties.

There are only about 100 different kinds of atom, but all the substances around us are made up from these atoms. The differences between substances depend on which atoms are used to make them, how many atoms are used, the order in which they are joined together, the way they are joined together, and the way they are packed together. Chemists normally show which atoms are in a substance by writing the *formula* or *symbol* of the substance. The formula also tells us the proportions of the different atoms in the substance. For example, the formula of sulphuric acid is H_2SO_4. This tells us that particles (molecules) of sulphuric acid each contain 2 atoms of hydrogen, 1 atom of sulphur and 4 atoms of oxygen.

MOLECULES

A molecule is a group of atoms which are *joined* together and which can exist as a separate unit.

We need this special word because most substances cannot exist as free atoms. Instead, the atoms join with one or more other atoms to form a group of atoms called a molecule. The atoms in a molecule may be of the same kind, e.g. two chlorine atoms in the molecule Cl_2. Equally, the atoms in a molecule may be different, e.g. a molecule of water, H_2O, contains two different kinds of atom. A molecule of sulphuric acid, H_2SO_4, contains three different kinds of atom (Fig 1.1).

Fig 1.1 Atoms and molecules

An atom of hydrogen, symbol H, which does not exist on its own at ordinary temperatures and pressures

A molecule of hydrogen, formula H_2, which can exist on its own

A simple way of representing a molecule of hydrogen (i.e. two hydrogen atoms bonded together)

A molecule of water, formula H_2O. This molecule contains two atoms of hydrogen and one atom of oxygen, i.e. three atoms altogether. In simple form this is shown

H O H

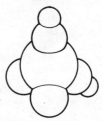

A molecule of sulphuric acid, formula H_2SO_4. This molecule contains seven atoms, four of oxygen, two of hydrogen, and one of sulphur. Tha atoms are arranged:

H O O H
  S
O   O

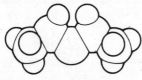

A molecule of ethoxyethane, formula $C_4H_{10}O$. This contains fifteen atoms, four of carbon, ten of hydrogen, and one of oxygen. In simple form this is shown as

H—C—C—O—C—C—H

Note that we do not write 2Cl for a chlorine molecule. 2Cl means two free atoms of chlorine, but Cl_2 means two atoms of chlorine *joined* together to make a molecule. A molecule of a certain substance always has the same formula, e.g. a molecule of chlorine is always Cl_2 but never Cl_3 or Cl_4.

IONS

An ion is a *charged* particle formed from an atom (or group of atoms) by the loss or gain of electrons.

Atoms and molecules are always *neutral*, but ions are always either *negatively charged* or *positively charged*. (See ionic bonding, p30). The symbol for an ion always has the charge written alongside it, e.g.

Cl^- (a chloride ion, which has a single negative charge);
Mg^{2+} (a magnesium ion, which has two positive charges).

Atoms of metals always form **positive** ions.

Atoms of non-metals always form **negative** ions (Except hydrogen, H^+).

SUMMARY; ATOMS, MOLECULES AND IONS USING CHLORINE AS THE EXAMPLE

Symbol or formula	Meanings
Cl	One atom of the element chlorine
$2Cl$	Two separate atoms of chlorine
Cl_2	A molecule of chlorine (two atoms joined together)
$2Cl_2$	Two separate molecules of chlorine
Cl^-	An ion of chlorine (chloride ion)
$2Cl^-$	Two separate chloride ions

CHARGES ON IONS. RADICALS

Note that the number of charge units on an ion (e.g. whether it is 1+, 2+, 1– or 2–, etc.) depends on the *valency* or *combining power* of the element (p42). The valency is normally either the number of electrons in the outer energy level of the atom (for metals) or 8 minus that number (for non-metals). The valency can also be worked out from the position of the element in the Periodic Table (p255).

Sometimes atoms form a group which stay together during a chemical reaction, but cannot exist on its own without a partner. Such groups of atoms are called **radicals**. Most radicals can act as the 'non-metal part' of a compound and therefore most radicals form negative ions. An important exception is the ammonium radical, which forms a positive ion. Some common radicals are listed below. Their charges are included.

SO_4^{2-}	sulphate	CO_3^{2-}	carbonate
OH^-	hydroxide	NO_3^-	nitrate
HCO_3^-	hydrogencarbonate		

Note the differences between a radical and a molecule. Molecules *can* exist on their own (e.g. H_2O) but radicals cannot. For example, we cannot have a bottle of 'sulphate' – the radical must have a partner, e.g. copper sulphate.

EVIDENCE FOR THE EXISTENCE OF PARTICLES

It is not possible in a simple laboratory to *prove* that atoms, molecules or ions exist, but many experiments or facts are different to explain in any other way. For example, coloured solutions can be diluted many times until only a very small proportion of the original substance is left, but the colour is still there, and it is spread evenly throughout the solution. You may have done this by diluting a solution of potassium manganate (VII) until the purple colour is almost invisible. We can explain this 'equal splitting up' of a substance if we believe that the original substance consists of many tiny, exactly similar, particles.

Some of these are present (in ever decreasing concentrations) in each of the diluted solutions.

Diffusion experiments (p59) are impossible to explain unless we believe that substances consist of large numbers of identical particles, which can spread out evenly when given chance to do so.

Most substances can exist in three different states. For example, water can exist as *solid* ice, *liquid* water or the *gas* steam. We can understand this if we imagine that the substance in each state consists of the same particles, but they move differently and are packed differently according to the temperature and pressure (p57). You could be asked to describe an experiment which has helped to convince you that substances are made of particles.

CHECK YOUR UNDERSTANDING (Answers on p405)

1   Which of the following means one or more *separate* atoms?
           I Cl_2 I_2 Br Br_2 2Br SO_4 NO_3
           $2NO_3$ 2I

2   Which of the following are molecules?
           H_2O SO_2 O Cl_2 Cl I_2 Br Br_2 Na
           H_2SO_4 HNO_3 Pb
    (You may find it helpful to check some of these with the symbols for elements given on p41).

3   Using the table of symbols on p41, write the correct symbol or formula for each of the following:
    (*a*)   an atom of zinc;
    (*b*)   two atoms of copper;
    (*c*)   a molecule of nitrogen (which contains two nitrogen atoms);
    (*d*)   a molecule of carbon monoxide (which contains one carbon atom and one oxygen atom);
    (*e*)   two molecules of nitrogen (see part (*c*)).

4   Which of the following would form negative ions? (How did you decide?)
           sodium   chlorine   sulphur   magnesium   iron   copper
           potassium   oxygen   hydrogen   nitrogen

1.2 ATOMIC STRUCTURE

All atoms contain a very small, very dense **nucleus**. The nucleus is at the centre of the atom. Inside the nucleus there is at least one tiny particle called a **proton**. Protons have a positive charge. (Note 'p' for proton and 'p' for positive.) All of the atoms in a particular element have the same number of protons. Atoms of different elements have different numbers of protons.

The atomic number of an atom is the number of protons in the atom.

Another useful way of thinking about atomic number is: **the atomic number of an element is its position in the periodic Table** (see p253).

|| The atomic number of an element is often given the symbol Z. ||

Also found inside the nucleus are tiny particles called **neutrons**. Neutrons have no electrical charge; they are neutral. All atoms except most atoms of hydrogen contain at least one neutron. (Note 'n' for neutron, and 'n' for neutral).

Outside the nucleus we find even smaller particles called **electrons**. Electrons have a negative charge. An atom always has an equal number of electrons and protons, and is therefore electrically neutral. (As explained on p31, ions do not have an equal number of electrons and protons, and this is why ions always have a charge.) Electrons move around the atom in fixed **energy levels** (sometimes called shells or orbits).

Each energy level can hold up to a certain number of electrons:

Energy level	Maximum number of electrons
1	2
2	8
3	8 (for the elements in your syllabus)

The tiny particles inside an atom are so small that we need a special 'mass scale' to compare their masses. A proton has a mass of 1 **atomic mass unit**. A neutron has almost the same mass as a proton. An electron is so tiny that it has a mass of only about $\frac{1}{2000}$ of the mass of a proton or neutron. Almost all of the mass of an atom, therefore, is due to the mass of the protons and the mass of the neutrons. Putting this another way, almost all the mass of an atom is in the nucleus, which is where the protons and neutrons are found.

The mass number of an atom is the total number of neutrons and protons in the atom. (This is the same as the total number of particles in the nucleus).

The mass number of an atom is often given the symbol A.

Particle	Approximate mass (atomic mass units)	Charge
proton	1.0	+1
neutron	1.0	0
electron	1/1840 _negligible_	−1

DRAWING ATOMIC STRUCTURES

We need to know two things about an atom before we can draw its structure:

(*a*)   the mass number, and

(*b*)   the atomic number.

Each kind of atom has different numbers, but there is no need to learn them. The information is given, when needed, like this: $^{4}_{2}He$. He is the symbol for an atom of helium. The numbers tell us that an atom of helium has a mass number of 4 and an atomic number of 2. Note that the top number is the mass number, and the bottom one the atomic number. (If in doubt, the larger of the two numbers is always the mass number.)

We can work out the numbers of electrons, protons and neutrons in an atom from these numbers.

Atomic number = number of protons
Atomic number = number of electrons (if it is a neutral atom)
Mass number − atomic number = number of neutrons

An atom of $^{35}_{17}Cl$ thus consists of 17 electrons and 17 protons (because the atomic number is 17) and also 18 neutrons (because mass number − atomic number = 18), arranged as shown in Fig 1.2.

Fig 1.2 Atom of $^{35}_{17}Cl$

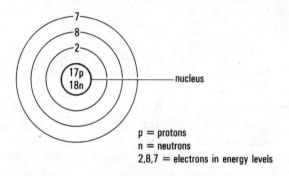

p = protons
n = neutrons
2,8,7 = electrons in energy levels

Note When drawing atomic structures *always* label your diagram or use a key.

Sometimes, instead of drawing a diagram to show the arrangement of electrons, we can use a series of numbers separated by commas. For example, an atom of sodium, $_{11}Na$, has 11 electrons. These are arranged 2 in the first energy level, 8 in the second, and 1 in the third. We can show this by writing 2,8,1. Similarly, the electron structure of an atom of chlorine, $_{17}Cl$, can be shown as 2,8,7.

CHECK YOUR UNDERSTANDING (Answers on p405)

1 How many protons are there in each of the following atoms?
(a) ^7_3Li (b) $^{16}_8O$ (c) $^{20}_{10}Ne$ (d) $^{27}_{13}Al$ (e) $^{39}_{19}K$

2 How many neutrons are in each of the following atoms?
(a) ^9_4Be (b) $^{12}_6C$ (c) $^{19}_9F$ (d) $^{31}_{15}P$ (e) $^{40}_{20}Ca$

3 How many electrons are there in each of the following atoms?
(a) $^{11}_5B$ (b) $^{14}_7N$ (c) $^{28}_{14}Si$ (d) $^{32}_{16}S$ (e) $^{22}_{18}Ar$

4 Summarise each of the following statements by using the symbol for the atom and two numbers, e.g. ^4_2He (refer to the table of symbols on p41 if necessary):
(a)   an atom of sodium has atomic number 11 and mass number 23;

(b)   an atom of magnesium has atomic number 12 and mass number 24;

(c)   an atom of chlorine has atomic number 17 and mass number 35. ‒ Periodic Table.

5   Use the information on p424 to answer the following:

(a)   which atoms are 'two times as heavy' as atoms of neon?;

(b)   which atoms are 'half as heavy' as atoms of silicon?;

(c)   suppose that you can choose any two *different* atoms to make a pair of atoms, e.g. H+Ne = a pair of atoms. How many pairs of different atoms can you find which *together* weigh the same as *one* atom of sodium?

6   What is incorrect about each of the following?

(a)   an atom of $^{16}_{8}O$ can be shown as in Fig 1.3.

Fig 1.3 Atom of $^{16}_{8}O$ (diagram contains deliberate mistake(s))

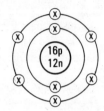

(b)   an atom of $^{32}_{16}S$ can be shown as in Fig 1.4:

Fig 1.4 Atom of $^{32}_{16}S$ (diagram contains deliberate mistake(s))

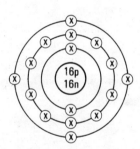

(c)   Fig 1.5 shows the structure of an atom:

Fig 1.5 Structure of an atom (diagram contains deliberate mistake(s))

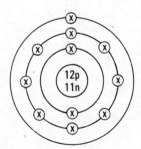

7   Make sure that you can draw the structure of an atom of any of the first 20 elements, if you are given the atomic number and the mass

number. (You can use the data on p424 to check this. Compare your answers with the drawings in your notebook).

ISOTOPES

All neutral *atoms* of a particular element must have the same number of electrons and protons. For example, the atomic number of oxygen is 8. All atoms of oxygen **must** contain 8 protons and 8 electrons. *Ions* are not neutral, however, and do not contain equal numbers of protons and electrons. An ion of oxygen contains 8 protons and 10 electrons. Note that atoms *and* ions of a particular element must contain a fixed number of *protons*. In the case of oxygen this fixed number is 8. If an atom or ion contains any other number of protons, it cannot be an atom or ion of oxygen. The atomic number, therefore, is *always* equal to the number of *protons*. It is also equal to the number of electrons in an *atom*, but this is not true for an *ion*.

However, it is still possible for some atoms of a particular element to be different from some other atoms of the *same* element. This happens because it is possible to vary the number of **neutrons** in the nucleus while keeping a fixed number of protons and electrons. The number of neutrons only affects the mass of an atom: it has no effect on its chemical properties.

Isotopes are atoms of the same element which contain different numbers of neutrons. They have the same atomic number but different mass numbers.

All of the isotopes of one element have the same chemical properties, because they have the same number of electrons and protons. A common example is chlorine, which has two main isotopes. One is $^{37}_{17}Cl$ and the other is $^{35}_{17}Cl$. They both contain 17 electrons and 17 protons, but $^{37}_{17}Cl$ contains 20 neutrons and $^{35}_{17}Cl$ contains 18 neutrons (see Fig 1.6). Figure 1.7 also shows the isotopes of hydrogen. The most common atoms of hydrogen are the only atoms which do not contain any neutrons. The other isotopes of hydrogen, which form a *very* small proportion of ordinary hydrogen, do have neutrons.

Fig 1.6 The isotopes of chlorine

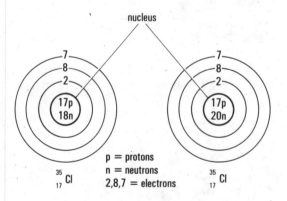

Many elements consist of several isotopes (e.g. tin has 10), but a few do not have any naturally occurring isotopes. It is now possible to produce *artificial* isotopes of all the elements. Some isotopes are **stable** (they do not decompose naturally), but others are unstable (**radioactive**) and decompose naturally.

Fig 1.7 The isotopes of hydrogen

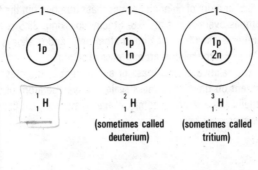

Fig 1.8 Stable and unstable isotopes

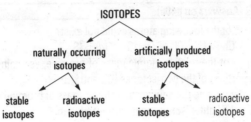

RELATIVE ATOMIC MASS

The mass number of an atom refers only to one particular kind of atom. If an element consists of several isotopes, each isotope has a different mass number. An element can therefore have atoms with different mass numbers, but they must all have the same atomic number. In most cases we can ignore the fact that atoms of the same element can have different mass numbers, because *most* of the atoms usually have the same mass number. For example, oxygen has isotopes but *most* atoms of oxygen have the mass number 16. In the table on p424 the mass number of oxygen is given as 16; we ignore the fact that a *few* oxygen atoms have other mass numbers.

Sometimes, however, two or more isotopes occur in significant proportions. Chlorine consists of 75% $^{35}_{17}Cl$ and 25% $^{35}_{17}Cl$. To put this another way, chlorine atoms occur in the ratio 3 ($^{35}_{17}Cl$):1 ($^{37}_{17}Cl$); out of every four atoms of chlorine, on average 3 have a mass of 35 units and 1 has a mass of 37 units. In cases like this it would be quite wrong to say that chlorine has a mass number of 35. True, most chlorine atoms have a mass of 35 units, but a reasonably high proportion have a mass of 37 units. We allow for this by referring to an 'average' atom of chlorine. We can work this out as follows.

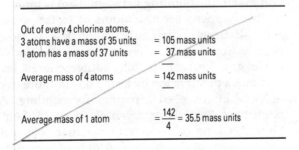

Out of every 4 chlorine atoms,
3 atoms have a mass of 35 units = 105 mass units
1 atom has a mass of 37 units = 37 mass units

Average mass of 4 atoms = 142 mass units

Average mass of 1 atom $= \dfrac{142}{4} = 35.5$ mass units

This is why, in the table on p424, the 'mass number' of chlorine is given as 35.5. No

Also Hydrogen
Copper.

particular atom of chlorine has this mass number, but the mass numbers of the different isotopes average out at 35.5. Strictly speaking, 35.5 is not a mass number. A mass number is used for *one* kind of atom only, and is always a whole number (e.g. ^{37}Cl or ^{35}Cl). 35.5 is the **relative atomic mass** of chlorine.

The relative atomic mass of an element is the mass of an 'average' atom of the element on the atomic mass scale. An average atom of chlorine (mass 35.5) does not actually exist. Chlorine atoms *behave* on average as if they all had such a mass number, however.

CHECK YOUR UNDERSTANDING (Answers on p406)

1 Which of the following atoms could not exist?
   (a) $^{37.5}_{17}Cl$ (b) $^{37}_{17}Cl$ (c) $^{14}_{6}C$ (d) $^{32.3}_{16}S$
2 Work out the relative atomic mass of bromine, assuming that it is a made up of equal proportions of the two isotopes $^{79}_{35}Br$ and $^{81}_{35}Br$.
3 What would be the new relative atomic mass of bromine if the isotopes occurred in a 2:1 ratio, the lighter isotope being more abundant?
4 Look at the table of information in question 3 on p39. Which of the particles could be isotopes of the same element?

1.3 BONDING

The only atoms which exist as *separate* atoms are those of the noble gases. All other atoms combine together (bond together) to make larger groups of particles.

Atoms of the noble gases do not easily bond with other atoms because they have *fully filled electron shells*. Other atoms bond together so that they, too, can gain fully filled electron shells. There are two main kinds of bonding. When atoms form ions in order to combine, the bonding is **ionic**. When atoms *share* electrons in order to combine together, the bonding is **covalent**.

IONIC BONDING

When an atom of a metal is joined to one or more atoms of a non-metal, the bonding between them is ionic.

This happens because atoms of metals usually have one, two or three electrons in their outer energy levels. Atoms of metals therefore *lose* electrons so that they can have the electron arrangement of a noble gas, i.e. a fully filled outer energy level. The metal atom becomes a **positive ion** by losing one or more electrons (see Fig 1.9).

Metal atoms need a partner for bonding. Atoms of non-metals often have five, six or seven electrons in their outer energy levels. They need to *gain* electrons so that they can have the electron arrangement of a noble gas. Atoms of non-metals can become **negative ions** by gaining one or more electrons (see Fig 1.9). Atoms of metals and atoms of non-metals are ideal partners for ionic bonding.

They are held together by the opposite electrical charges of the ions produced.

Fig 1.9 The formation of positive and negative ions

(a)   The formation of positive ions

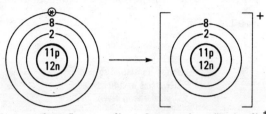

Structure of a sodium atom, Na

$$^{23}_{11}\text{Na}$$

Note:
Inner electrons shown by numbers
Outer electrons shown individually
Neutral because no. of protons =
no. of electrons

Structure of a sodium ion, Na$^+$

Ion has a positive charge of
1 unit because there is now
1 more proton than electrons.
Ion has fully filled outer
energy level

(b)   The formation of negative ions

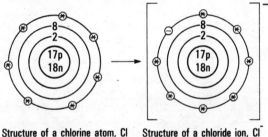

Structure of a chlorine atom, Cl

$$^{35}_{17}\text{Cl}$$

Notes as for sodium atom

Structure of a chloride ion, Cl$^-$

Ion has a negative charge of
1 unit because there is now
1 more electron than protons

Extra electron shown $\ominus$

Ion has fully filled outer
energy level

SUMMARY

- Metal+non-metal = ionic bonding
- Atoms join together in order to end up with the fully filled electron shells of a noble gas
- Metal atoms form positive ions
- Non-metal atoms form negative ions
- The degree of charge on an ion depends upon the number of electrons lost or gained.

e.g. 1 electron *lost*   = 1 *positive* charge on ion (+1)
    2 electrons *lost* = 2 *positive* charges on ion (+2)
    1 electron *gained* = 1 *negative* charge on ion (−1), etc.

AN EXAMPLE OF IONIC BONDING: SODIUM CHLORIDE, NaCl

See Fig 1.10.

Fig 1.10 The bonding in sodium chloride

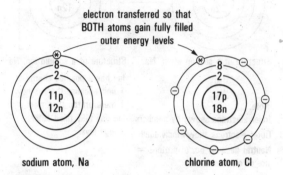

electron transferred so that
BOTH atoms gain fully filled
outer energy levels

sodium atom, Na   chlorine atom, Cl

Note: It is not necessary to show the neutrons and protons in a bonding diagram. The nucleus of a sodium atom can be shown Na and the nucleus of a chlorine atom Cl.

These become:

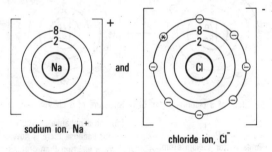

sodium ion. Na⁺   and   chloride ion, Cl⁻

which are held together by opposite charges to form sodium chloride, NaCl.

OTHER SIMPLE EXAMPLES OF IONIC BONDING

Several other pairs of elements combine in exactly the same way as sodium and chlorine. Sodium is in Group 1 of the Periodic Table and therefore its atoms have one electron in their outer energy levels (p253). Chlorine is in Group 7 of the Periodic Table, and therefore its atoms have seven electrons in their outer energy levels. When *any* element from Group 1 (Na, K, Li) bonds with *any* element from Group 7 (e.g. Cl,F,Br,I), they bond together ionically in *exactly* the same way as sodium and chlorine. To make sure that you understand, draw diagrams like Fig 1.10 to show how atoms of $^{23}_{11}$Na and $^{19}_{9}$F bond to form sodium fluoride, NaF, and how atoms of $^{39}_{19}K$ and $^{35}_{17}Cl$ bond to form potassium chloride, KCl. In each example, the metal atom should form a positive ion, of charge +1, and the non-metal atom should form a negative ion, of charge −1.

SOME MORE COMPLICATED EXAMPLES OF IONIC BONDING

In the examples used so far, *one* atom of a metal has joined with *one* atom of a non-metal to form the compound. Other examples of this type occur when *any* element from Group 2 of the Periodic Table (e.g. Ca,Mg) combines with *any* element from Group 6 of the Periodic Table (e.g. O,S). Atoms of Group 2 elements each need to *lose* two electrons to have filled outer energy levels, and atoms of Group 6 elements each need to *gain* two electrons. To make sure that you understand this, draw diagrams like Fig 1.10 to show how $^{24}_{12}Mg$ combines with $^{16}_{8}O$, and how $^{40}_{20}Ca$ combines with $^{16}_{8}O$. In each example, you should need one atom of each type, each metal atom should form a 2+ ion, and each non-metal atom should form a 2− ion.

Some examples of ionic bonding involve *two* atoms of a metal bonding with just *one* atom of a non-metal. This happens when any element from Group 1 of the Periodic Table combines with any element from Group 6 of the Periodic Table. Draw a diagram to show how $^{23}_{11}Na$ combines with $^{16}_{8}O$. Your diagram should show two ions of charge +1 bonding with one ion of charge −2.

Similarly, when any element from Group 2 of the Periodic Table combines with any element from Group 7 of the Table, 1 metal ion combines with two non-metal ions. Show how $^{24}_{12}Mg$ combines with $^{35}_{17}Cl$.

PROPERTIES OF IONIC COMPOUNDS

1   Ionically bonded substances contain large numbers of negatively charged and positively charged ions. The oppositely charged ions attract each other and form a large, three-dimensional giant structure (p269). The structure is held together by strong 'bonds' in all directions. A large amount of energy is needed to separate the ions, and so ionic compounds usually have high melting points and boiling points.

2   They are solids at room temperature, because of high melting points. (The solids are usually *crystalline*, i.e. they are found as crystals, each solid forming crystals of a particular fixed shape.)

3   Many ionic compounds dissolve in water, but they do not usually dissolve in organic solvents such as ethanol.

4   When ionic compounds are dissolved in water, or are melted, the ions separate from each other and become free to move. The liquids formed are electrolytes (p107).

COVALENT BONDING

If atoms of two or more non-metals join together, the bonding is likely to be covalent.

Non-metals need to gain electrons to have filled outer energy levels. This time there is no metal atom to provide any electrons. The non-metal atoms therefore have to *share* electrons to help each other gain filled outer energy levels. They are bonded together by the shared electrons. A group of atoms held together by sharing electrons (i.e. by covalent bonding) is called a molecule.

The simplest kind of covalent bond is formed when two atoms each provide one electron for sharing. The bond is then *one pair* of shared electrons (one electron from each atom). Such a bond is called a **single covalent bond**. This is sometimes shown by a single line between the symbols of the atoms, e.g. Cl-Cl. This means a single covalent bond between two chlorine atoms.

Sometimes two atoms share *two pairs* of electrons (two electrons from each atom). This is called a **double covalent bond**. A double covalent bond between two carbon atoms could be shown as C=C. When two atoms share *three pairs* of electrons, the bond is called a **triple covalent bond**. These are comparatively rare. The bonding in a nitrogen atom is triple covalent. This could be shown as N≡N.

SIMPLE EXAMPLES OF COVALENT BONDING BETWEEN TWO ATOMS OF THE SAME KIND

(a) The hydrogen molecule, H_2

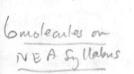
6 molecules on NEA Syllabus

Fig 1.11 The hydrogen molecule

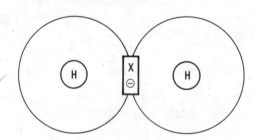

X = electron from 1st H atom
⊖ = electron from 2nd H atom

Summary: H–H

The 'box' (Fig 1.11) contains shared electrons. This is the covalent bond. It consists of one pair of electrons and so is a single covalent bond. Note that as the electrons inside the 'box' are shared by both atoms, it appears as if each atom has two electrons in its outer energy level. The first energy level can only hold up to two electrons, and so each atom appears to have a filled outer energy level. The shared electrons act like 'glue' and hold the atoms together.

(b) The chlorine molecule, Cl_2

Chlorine has an atomic number of 17; each atom has 17 electrons. The electrons are arranged 2,8,7. The bonding is shown in Fig 1.12.

The 'box' (covalent bond) contains one shared pair of electrons. It is a single covalent bond.

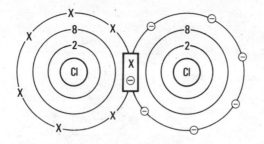

Fig 1.12 The chlorine molecule

X = electrons from 1st Cl atom
⊖ = electrons from 2nd Cl atom
Summary: Cl — Cl

Note It is usual in these diagrams to show the outer electrons *individually*, and to show the inner electrons by numbers only. Make sure that you understand how the arrangement appears to give each chlorine atom a filled outer energy level.

(c) The oxygen molecule, O_2

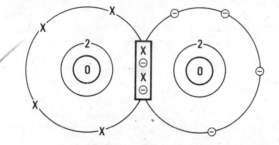

Fig 1.13 The oxygen molecule

OXYGEN has atomic number 8
X = electron from 1st O atom
⊖ = electron from 2nd O atom
Summary: O = O

The covalent bond this time consists of *two* pairs of shared electrons. It is a *double* covalent bond.

EXAMPLES OF COVALENT BONDING IN MOLECULES CONTAINING TWO DIFFERENT KINDS OF ATOM

(a) The hydrogen chloride molecule, HCl

The hydrogen chloride molecule contains a single covalent bond and can be summarised H-Cl.

Fig 1.14 The hydrogen
chloride molecule

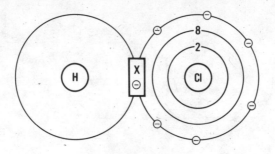

HYDROGEN has atomic number 1
CHLORINE has atomic number 17

X = electron from H atom
⊖ = electron from Cl atom
Summary: H–Cl

(b) The water molecule, H₂O

Fig 1.15 The water
molecule

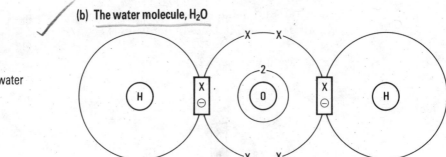

HYDROGEN has atomic number 1
OXYGEN has atomic number 8

⊖ = electron from H atom
X = electron from O atom
Summary: H–O–H

Each water molecule contains two, separate, single covalent bonds.
Its bonding can be summarized as as H-O-H.

(c) The ammonia molecule, NH₃
The ammonia molecule contains three, separate, single covalent
bonds. Its bonding can be summarised as shown in Fig 1.17.

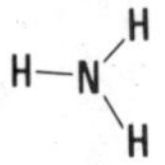

$$H-N\begin{matrix} H \\ \\ H \end{matrix}$$

Fig 1.16 Bonding in ammonia molecule

Fig 1.17 The ammonia
molecule

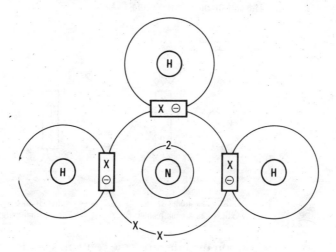

NITROGEN has atomic number 7   ⊖ = electron from H atom
HYDROGEN has atomic number 1   X = electron from N atom

(d) The methane molecule, CH₄

Fig 1.18 The methane
molecule

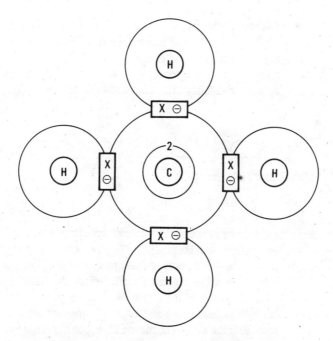

CARBON has atomic number 6   X = electron from C atom
HYDROGEN has atomic number 1   ⊖ = electron from H atom

Fig 1.19 Bonding in
methane molecule

Each methane molecule contains four, separate, single covalent
bonds. Its bonding can be summarised as shown in Fig 1.19.

(e) The carbon dioxide molecule, CO_2

Fig 1.20 The carbon dioxide molecule

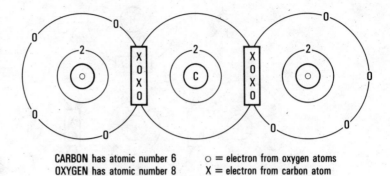

CARBON has atomic number 6
OXYGEN has atomic number 8

o = electron from oxygen atoms
X = electron from carbon atom

The carbon dioxide molecule contains two double covalent bonds. Its bonding can be summarised as O=C=O.

PROPERTIES OF COVALENTLY BONDED SUBSTANCES

1 Covalently bonded substances are often insoluble in water, but do dissolve in organic solvents such as ethanol.
2 They do not conduct electricity when melted or when dissolved in water, i.e. they are not electrolytes.
3 The covalent bonds *inside* each molecule are very strong and cannot easily be broken. (These bonds are called **intramolecular bonds**.) However, when the molecules are close together in the solid state, there are some other 'bonds', *between* the molecules, which hold the molecules together. (These are called **intermolecular bonds**.) The bonds between molecules are fairly weak and easy to break.

Fig 1.21 A simple example of the bonding in the molecular solid iodine

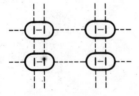

Solid iodine consists of simple, separate, I_2 molecules. The bonds *inside* each molecule are strong covalent bonds. Bonds *between* molecules (dotted lines) are weak. When solid iodine is heated, the weak bonds break, and the molecules separate. A substance which consists of simple molecules is called *molecular*. Not all covalently bonded substances are molecular (see the structures of diamond and graphite, p267). As the 'bonds' between molecules in a molecular substance are easily broken, molecular substances have fairly low melting points and boiling points. When heated, the 'bonds' *between* the molecules break, the molecules separate, and the substance melts. Even at room temperature, many molecular substances have 'already melted', in which case they are liquids. Many have also 'already boiled' at room temperature, so that they are found as gases. If a molecular substance is a solid at room temperature, it is usually easy to change it into a liquid; it will have a low melting point.

Some molecular substances which are gases at room temperature	Some molecular substances which are liquids at room temperature	Some molecular substances which are solids at room temperature
Gases such as O_2, H_2, Cl_2, N_2, NH_3, HCl, CO_2. Organic substances such as methane, CH_4, ethane, C_2H_6.	Water, H_2O Ethanol, C_2H_5OH	Iodine, I_2 Sulphur, S_8

CHECK YOUR UNDERSTANDING

(Use data on p424 if necessary. Answers on p406.)

1   What do a chloride *ion* and an argon *atom* have in common? Why is a chloride ion not called an argon atom?

2   All but *two* of the <u>following</u> substances have the same kind of bonding:

   (a)   Which kind of bonding do most of the substances have?
   (b)   How did you decide your answer?
   (c)   Which are the two exceptions?

   potassium chloride; potassium fluoride; sulphur chloride; sodium oxide; calcium fluoride; magnesium oxide; carbon dioxide; aluminium fluoride.

3   The table below shows the numbers of electrons, protons and neutrons in five different particles labelled A to E. Use the information to answer the questions which follow. If you cannot answer any of the questions, some hints are given. Do not use the hints unless you have to.

	Electrons	Protons	Neutrons
A	10	10	10
B	11	10	12
C	12	12	12
D	17	17	18
E	17	17	20

   (a)   Which particle is an atom of a metal?
   (b)   Which particle is an ion of a metal?
   (c)   Which particle is an atom of an inert (noble) gas?

HINTS

(a)   The particles could be atoms or ions. How do you decide which of them are *atoms*? (See p28.) How do you decide which of them is an atom of a *metal*? (See p30.)

(b)   How do you decide which of the particles are ions? (See p31.) How do you then decide which of them are ions of *metals*? Your answer may be connected with the *charge* on the ion (p31) or you may prefer to work out whether the ion has been formed from an atom which has *lost* electrons or *gained* electrons (p30).

(c)   What do all atoms of noble gases have in common? (p30).

4   All but *two* of the following substances have the same kind of bonding:

(a)   Which kind of bonding do most of the substances have?

(b)   How did you decide your answer?

(c)   Which are the two exceptions?

calcium fluoride; a hydrogen molecule; an oxygen molecule; a nitrogen molecule; potassium oxide; hydrogen chloride; water; methane, CH_4; ethane, C_2H_6; carbon dioxide; trichloromethane, $CHCl_3$.

5   The table below shows some information about three compounds labelled W, X and Y. Use the information to answer the questions.

Substance	Melting point (°C)	Does it conduct electricity when melted or dissolved in water?	Compound is formed by joining
W	42	No	?
X	?	Yes	a metal+a non-metal
Y	602	?	a metal+a non-metal

(a)   What kind of bonding would you expect in W?

(b)   Suggest what should appear in the last column for W.

(c)   What kind of bonding would you expect in X?

(d)   Would you expect X to have a low melting point or a high one?

(e)   What kind of bonding would you expect in Y?

(f)   Would you expect Y to behave as an electrolyte when melted or dissolved in water?

6   Describe what is incorrect about each of the following:

(a)   There are two single covalent bonds in a water molecule. The bonding can be summarized as H-H-O.

(b)   The atomic number of fluorine, F, is 9. The bonding in a fluorine molecule, F_2, is shown in Fig 1.22.

Fig 1.22 Bonding in a fluorine molecule (incorrect)

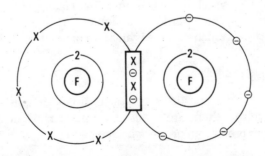

(b)   When a covalent bond consists of two shared electrons, it is a double covalent bond.

7 The elements W,X,Y and Z have atomic numbers respectively of 7,9,10 and 11. Write the formula for the substance you would expect to form between each of the following pairs of elements, and state the kind of bonding you would expect in each case.
(a) W and X   (b) X and Z   (c) X and X   (d) Y and Y

8 Try to work out bonding diagrams for:
(a) carbon dioxide, CO_2 (b) tetrachloromethane, CCl_4 (c) a nitrogen molecule, N_2
(d) a molecule of ethene, C_2H_4 (the two carbon atoms are joined together, and two hydrogen atoms are joined to each carbon atom.)

WORKING OUT THE FORMULA OF A SUBSTANCE

All compounds have a formula, e.g. sodium chloride has the formula NaCl. Sodium chloride always has this formula; it cannot be Na_2Cl or $NaCl_2$, etc. We must always write the correct formula for a particular substance. Many compounds consist of a 'metal' part joined to a 'non-metal' part or radical.

Table 1.1: Symbols and combining powers of the common elements and radicals

(a) Those with combining power of 1 *Valency*	Symbol	ion formed
chlorine (chloride)	Cl	Cl^-
bromine (bromide)	Br	Br^-
iodine (iodide)	I	I^-
hydroxide	OH	OH^-
hydrogencarbonate	HCO_3	HCO_3^-
nitrate	NO_3	NO_3^-
silver	Ag	Ag^+
potassium	K	K^+
ammonium	NH_4	NH_4^+
hydrogen	H	H^+

(b) Those with combining power of 2 *Valency*		
oxygen (oxide)	O	O^{2-}
sulphate	SO_4	SO_4^{2-}
carbonate	CO_3	CO_3^{2-}
sulphur (sulphide)	S	S^{2-}
lead(II)	Pb	Pb^{2+}
zinc	Zn	Zn^{2+}
magnesium	Mg	Mg^{2+}
calcium	Ca	Ca^{2+}
copper(II)	Cu	Cu^{2+}
iron(II)	Fe	Fe^{2+}

(c) Those with combining power of 3		
aluminium	Al	Al^{3+}
iron(III)	Fe	Fe^{3+}

(d) Those with combining power of 4		
carbon	C	no ion

You will have learned many common formulas during your chemistry course. It is also useful to be able to *work out* a formula if necessary. The following section reminds us how to do this.

Elements and radicals (p23) can be given one or more special numbers called their *valencies* or *combining powers*. For example, sodium has a combining power of 1. The combining power of an element is usually the number of electrons an atom of the element must lose or gain in order to have a complete outer shell of electrons. This explanation is not the complete answer, however, for some elements have more than one combining power. The combining powers of the common elements and radicals are given in Table 1.1.

A chemical formula can be worked out if the appropriate symbols and combining powers are known. The steps (using aluminium oxide as the example) are as follows:

1   Write down the symbols involved, putting the metal (if present) first, and leaving a small gap between them:

Al   O

2   Write the combining power of the *first* symbol *after* the *second* symbol. In the example, the combining power of aluminium is 3 so we write the figure 3 after the other symbol, which in this example is O for oxide. Similarly, the combining power of oxygen or oxide is 2, and so the figure 2 is added after the first symbol. The formula of aluminium oxide is thus Al_2O_3. In effect, the two combining powers have been 'swapped over'.

Notes
(*a*)   It is not necessary to write the number 1 in any formula; just leave it out. For example, write $MgCl_2$ rather than Mg_1Cl_2.

(*b*)   If a radical is present, brackets may be needed to avoid confusion. Suppose we need to write the formula of aluminium sulphate. If you use the steps described above, you may write the formula as Al_2SO_{43}. This is completely wrong; it does not mean '2 aluminium groups' joined to '3 sulphate groups', which is what we should be describing. The correct formula is $Al_2(SO_4)_3$. Similarly, the correct formula for magnesium hydroxide is $Mg(OH)_2$, not $MgOH_2$. Make sure that you understand the difference between these formulas. Incorrect use of brackets is very common.

(*c*)   When a metal has more than one combining power, difficulties arise when we write the *name* of one of its compounds. For example, iron has two combining powers, 2 and 3. If we write the name 'iron sulphate' it is not very helpful; it does not tell us which combining power of iron is being used. In these cases we put the combining power **in Roman numbers** inside a bracket after the metal name. For example, iron(II) sulphate tells us that the iron is using a combining power of 2. Iron(III) sulphate tells us that iron is using a combining power of 3.

(*d*)   Remember that this method of 'swapping the combining powers' to obtain a formula has no scientific base. You will understand what is really happening when you fully understand atomic structure, bonding and the Periodic Table.

40!

CHECK YOUR UNDERSTANDING (Answers on p407)

1   Copy the following table into your notebook. You will have 48 spaces in which to write the formulas of different substances. Work out the formulas, and write your answers in the appropriate spaces. Check your answers by looking up the formulas in appropriate parts of the book.

	Sulphate	Chloride	Oxide	Nitrate	Hydroxide
Sodium					
Iron(II)					
Aluminium					
Magnesium					
Calcium					
Potassium					
Copper(II)					
Iron(III)					

2   What is wrong about each of the following formulas?
(a) $AlOH_3$ (b) $Fe(III)Cl_3$ (c) OMg (d) $(Na)_2O$

3   Copy out and complete the following table.

Name of compound	Combining power of metal in compound	Combining powers of other element or radical	Formula of compound
Copper(II) sulphate			
Copper(II) oxide			
Copper(II) hydroxide			
Copper(I) oxide			
Iron(II) sulphate			
Iron(III) sulphate			

4 What is wrong with each of the following:
   (a) The formula of iron 3 chloride is $FeCl_3$
   (b) The formula of Sodium(II) oxide is NaO
   (c) The formula of iron(II) nitrate is Fe_2NO_3

1.4 RADIOACTIVITY AND NUCLEAR POWER

Marie Curie first used the word *radioactive* to describe some sub-stances which give out 'rays'. We now know that this happens because the nuclei of some atoms are **unstable**. They can become more stable by giving out these rays. The rays may be small particles, or 'packets' of energy, or both. These unstable atoms give out these rays or radioactivity *spontaneously*. In other words, it happens quite automatically and continuously; there is no need to do anything like heating the substance, and it cannot be stopped. It just keeps happening.

There are three main kinds of ray or radioactivity: β-particles (beta particles), α-particles (alpha particles) and γ rays (gamma rays) (Table 1.2). These rays can be detected by using a Geiger Counter or by photographic film.

Table 1.2 A summary of the main properties of the different types of radioactivity

	β-particles	α-particles	γ rays
What are they?	Fast electrons. Originate in nucleus. A neutron changes into a proton+an electron. (Note, they do not come from electron shells)	2 neutrons+2 protons joined together. This is the same as a helium nucleus.	radiation (energy) of very short wavelength.
Charge?	Negative (−1)	Positive (+2)	0
Mass in atomic mass units	Approx $\frac{1}{2000}$	4	0
Penetrating power	Paper has little effect. Slower ones stopped by thin sheets of aluminium, but sheets 35 mm thick needed to stop most	Poor, e.g. stopped by sheet of paper.	Great. Paper and aluminium have little effect. Lead of considerable thickness needed to stop this kind of radiation.

WHAT HAPPENS TO AN ATOM WHEN IT DECOMPOSES BY GIVING OUT RADIOACTIVITY?

An unstable atom 'rearranges' its nucleus by giving out particles and/or energy. An atom of this kind is sometimes called a **radio-isotope**. The particles and energy given out are called **radiation**. Some radioisotopes occur naturally, e.g. ^{235}U and ^{14}C. (These are sometimes shown as U-235 and C-14.) Others are by-products of the reactions which occur in a nuclear reactor, e.g. isotopes of plutonium and radio-iodine.

When a radioisotope gives out radiation we say it **decays**. The speed at which a particular radioisotope decays is fixed for that particular substance. It cannot be changed by any of the methods normally used to speed up reactions, e.g. by heating, or by using a catalyst. We measure the speed of decay by referring to its **half life**. This is the time taken for half of the atoms present at any moment to decay. Half lives vary from fractions of a second for some radioisotopes, to millions of years for others. For example, the half life of an isotope of thorium is 24 days. This means that if we start with eight million atoms of the thorium isotope, we would be left with four million atoms after 24 days. After the next 24 days (48 altogether) there would be two million atoms left, and after the next 24 days, one million, etc. A radioisotope with a half life of one year would decay as follows.

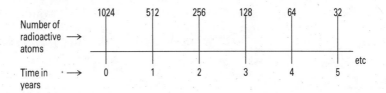

USES OF RADIOACTIVITY AND RADIOACTIVE ISOTOPES

1 MEDICAL, E.G. CONTROLLING SOME KINDS OF CANCER

A radioactive substance was first used outside the laboratory when it was found that radium stopped the growth of certain kinds of cancer cells. Other radioactive substances are now used for this purpose, but the technique is not easy. Cancers often occur deep in the body, and unfortunately radioactivity also damages healthy cells. It is therefore difficult to treat a small area of the body without damaging healthy cells, but modern technology is constantly improving the technique.

2 TRACERS

A radioactive atom of a certain element has exactly the same chemical properties as a stable atom of the same element. If some radioactive iodine, for example, is allowed to enter the body, the body cannot tell the difference from ordinary iodine, and treats the radioactive iodine in exactly the same way. However, we can tell exactly where the radioactive iodine is, even if it is present in only very tiny amounts, because of the radioactivity. The radioactive atoms give out 'signals', i.e. radiation. This can be detected by a Geiger Counter, for example. We can therefore 'trace' how the body uses iodine. This can help to answer medical problems, e.g. whether a patient can transport certain minerals round the body, to where they are needed. Tracers are used in both living and non-living systems, in a wide variety of ways.

3 CARBON DATING

The air contains carbon dioxide, which is constantly 'recycled' by living things (p308). Most of the carbon atoms in the carbon dioxide are the normal, stable atoms of ^{12}C. A very small fraction of the carbon atoms are unstable. These are radioactive ^{14}C atoms. The ratio of the two kinds of atom is constant in all *living* things, as the carbon inside them is constantly recycled. As soon as the living thing dies, the ratio starts to change. This happens because no 'fresh' carbon dioxide takes part in any further exchange. Instead, any radioactive carbon atoms inside the dead animal or plant decay steadily. The number of radioactive carbon atoms starts to decrease, but the number of normal carbon atoms stays the same. The longer this goes on, the smaller is the ratio between the radioactive carbon atoms and the stable carbon atoms. This can be used to decide how many years have passed since the object died. For example, the wood in a prehistoric canoe can be examined in this way, and so the canoe can be dated. We are able to date objects which were in existence up to fifty thousand years ago.

4 OTHER USES

You may have discussed uses such as thickness gauging, the sterilisation of medical instruments, and the detection of leaks and flaws.

NUCLEAR POWER

Some 'heavy' unstable atoms become more stable by splitting to form 1 or more smaller, more stable atoms. When they do this, energy and radiation are given out. This kind of reaction is called **atomic fission**. The energy changes are enormous, many times greater than those produced from similar masses of substances in chemical reactions. A substance which can take part in a fission process is called **fissile**. The best known fissile material is an isotope of uranium, ^{235}U.

The process taking place inside a nuclear reactor can be summarised as shown in Fig 1.23.

Fig 1.23 Process within a nuclear reactor

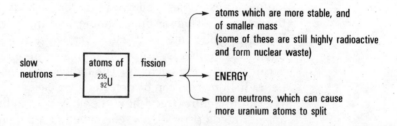

The energy is given out inside the reactor as heat. This is removed by a coolant such as carbon dioxide gas. The hot gas changes water into steam. The steam is then used to drive electricity generators, in exactly the same way as electricity is produced in a coal-fired, gas-fired or oil-fired power station.

You may have studied nuclear power in more detail. You may know what a **chain reaction** is, how carbon **moderators** make it possible to have a chain reaction in natural uranium, and how **control rods** keep the reaction under control. The early reactors used **uranium** as a fuel, and later ones use natural uranium enriched with **plutonium**. The plutonium does not occur in nature, but is a by-product from other nuclear reactors. The coolant in later reactors is sometimes liquid sodium metal.

SOME DISADVANTAGES OF USING RADIOACTIVE ISOTOPES

The use of radioactive isotopes is like any other scientific development: it offers new and perhaps more efficient processes, but at the same time it brings potential dangers and problems. The difficulty is always the same: do the potential advantages count more than the potential disadvantages?

Some of the advantages of using radioactive isotopes have been mentioned already. In addition, approximately 16% of Britain's electricity is now produced from nuclear power stations. You will have discussed the advantages of this process in your chemistry course, and compared it with the production of electricity from the burning of coal and oil. For example, you may have discussed points such as:

(a)   Nuclear power uses fuel which is not required for any other purpose, unlike petroleum which is also needed to produce organic chemicals and plastics, etc.

(b)   No smoke, soot or 'acid rain' is produced by nuclear power stations.

(c)   It is cheaper to generate electricity by nuclear power than by burning coal, oil or gas.

(d)   An advanced gas-cooled reactor can make as much electricity from 1 kg of enriched uranium fuel as could be produced from about 60 tonnes of coal.

(e)   Development of fast reactors would enable current stocks of uranium in Britain to provide as much energy as our entire coal reserves.

However, the potential dangers in using radioactive isotopes and nuclear power have been well publicised. The main dangers arise from the effect of radiation on living things. We are all exposed to a small amount of *natural* radioactivity. If a living organism is exposed to higher levels of radiation, all sorts of effects are possible, the more serious including various forms of cancer, and sterility. The accident with a nuclear power station at Chernobyl, Russia, in 1986 showed what can happen. Radioactive isotopes were carried by winds to all parts of Europe. Increased radioactivity was detected in grass, milk, drinking water and meat. Some people died immediately, some within a week or two because of radiation effects, and an unknown number will be affected over a longer period of time. There is also the theoretical risk of an accidental nuclear explosion at a nuclear power station. However, it is argued that more research has been done on nuclear power than on any other kind of fuel, and that the statistical risk of a *member of the public* dying as a result of an accident at a nuclear power station is less than that of being struck by lightning. It is also true that people are killed mining coal and producing oil. Nevertheless, accidents continue to happen. Some people argue that the potential risks are so great, we should not further develop nuclear power.

The disposal of radioactive waste material is also very difficult. The waste may be the comparatively small amounts from medical applications in hospitals, for example, or the relatively large amounts produced in nuclear power stations. The waste also has to be transported safely. Unlike most chemical waste, it cannot be neutralised by chemical reaction, nor can its rate of decay be slowed down. Many isotopes have very long half lives, and so they have to be stored safely for many years. This in turn means that they have to be placed in areas safe from the public, away from food and water supplies, and in containers which will not rot, or leak, or be damaged accidently for a long time. An additional problem is that the radiation given off has great penetrating power, especially the γ rays which can travel through thick metal sheets. It is not safe to go anywhere near such material without special protection; containers have to be handled with robots, for example. A recent technique of disposal is to seal nuclear waste in special glass 'marbles' which are then dropped into very deep water. Some waste which is only slightly radioactive is discharged into the sea, but there is concern that this may then effect seafood rather more than expected.

CHECK YOUR UNDERSTANDING (Answers on p407)

1   A radioactive substance has a half life of 15 minutes. If 2 grams of the substance are available at the start of the experiment, how much will be left at the end of an hour?

2   If a radioisotope loses an alpha particle, what happens to
   (a)   its mass number, and
   (b)   its atomic number?

3   If a radioisotope gives out a β particle, what happens to
   (a)   its mass number, and
   (b)   its atomic number?

4   $^{232}_{90}$Th gives out alpha particles and forms an element X which decays by emitting beta particles to form element Y. Y decays by beta emission to form the element Z.
   (a)   Complete the following by writing the mass numbers and atomic numbers in front of the elements X, Y and Z.

   $$^{232}_{90}\text{Th} \xrightarrow{\alpha} \text{X} \xrightarrow{\beta} \text{Y} \xrightarrow{\beta} \text{Z}$$

   (b)   How are Z and thorium related?

| CHECK LIST ▶ | REMEMBER THAT SOME OF THESE POINTS MAY NOT BE RELEVANT FOR THE PARTICULAR SYLLABUS YOU ARE FOLLOWING. |

YOU SHOULD UNDERSTAND THE FOLLOWING POINTS.

1 ▶ The differences between an atom, a molecule, and an ion.

2 ▶ Which kind of elements form positive ions, and which form negative ions.

3 ▶ The difference between (for example) Cl, 2Cl, Cl_2, Cl^- and $2Cl^-$.

4 ▶ The basic facts about electrons, protons and neutrons. Where they are found, their relative masses, their charges.

5 ▶ Atomic mass and mass number. How to work out the structure of an atom if given these two numbers.

6 ▶ Isotopes.

7 ▶ Relative atomic mass. Why a relative atomic mass is sometimes not a whole number, e.g. (35.5), whereas a mass number always is a whole number.

8 ▶ Which kind of elements join together by ionic bonding.

9 ▶ How to draw diagrams to show how some common elements combine by ionic bonding, if you are told the atomic numbers (or the position in the Periodic Table) of the elements.

10 ▶ The properties you would expect a typical ionically bonded compound to have.

11 ▶ The properties a typical covalently bonded compound might have.

12 ▶ Which kind of elements join together by covalent bonding.

13 ▶ How to draw diagrams to show how some common molecules are formed by covalent bonding.

14 ▶ The difference between single, double and triple covalent bonds.

15 ▶ Why simple molecular substances have low melting and boiling points, but ionically bonded substances have much higher ones.

16 ▶ How to work out the formula of a substance, if you are given either the symbols and charges on the ions, or the combining powers (valencies) of the elements.

17 ▶ What radioactivity means. Alpha, beta and gamma rays.

18 ▶ What a half life means.

19 ▶ Some advantages and disadvantages of using radioactive isotopes and nuclear power.

20 ▶ The basic idea of how a nuclear reactor produces electricity; what fission means.

SPECIMEN EXAMINATION QUESTIONS

Remember that the most difficult questions will be in a separate examination paper. These papers are NEA Syllabus A, Paper 2; SEG, Paper 3; SEG, alternative syllabus, Paper 4; LEA, Syllabus A, Paper 3; LEA, Syllabus B, Paper 3; NISEC, Paper 3; MEG, Paper 3; MEG, Nuffield Syllabus, Paper 2; WJEC, Paper 2. This should help you to decide which of the questions are intended to be more difficult, e.g. for obtaining Grades A and B in the examination. Questions from these papers are marked with the symbol †.

CODES USED WITH EXAMINATION QUESTIONS THROUGHOUT THE BOOK

spec   Specimen examination question.
NEA   Northern Examining Association
SEG   Southern Examining Group
LEA   London and East Anglian Group
NISEC Northern Ireland Schools Examinations Council
MEG   Midland Examining Group
WJEC Welsh Joint Education Committee
A number (1, 2 etc) is used to show the examination paper from which the questions are taken.
Where alternative syllabuses are available from an examination board, the syllabus is shown by a letter (A or B), or by the term (Alt) which means alternative syllabus.
Where a group of questions is taken from the same paper, only one acknowledgment is given, at the end of the group.
REMEMBER THAT YOU MAY BE ALLOWED TO USE YOUR DATA BOOK IN THE EXAMINATION.

Homework.
qu. 1 – 12 inclusive

Questions 1 to 4
Use your Data Book to help you to answer the following questions, using the list A to D given below.
A 1   B 2   C 3   D 4
1   The value of a positive charge on a calcium ion.
2   The numbers of atoms joined together to make a nitrate ion.
3   The number of magnesium ions in the formula of magnesium hydrogencarbonate.
4   The number of sulphate ions in the formula of aluminium sulphate.
[*NEA* spec (A), 1]

5   What elements are present in $MgHPO_4$?
    A   Hydrogen, magnesium, oxygen, potassium
    B   Hydrogen, magnesium, oxygen, phosphorus
    C   Hydrogen, manganese, oxygen, phosphorus
    D   Hydrogen, manganese, oxygen, potassium
6   The isotope $^{35}_{17}X$ contains
    A 17 neutrons   B 17 protons   C 35 neutrons
    D 35 protons
[*SEG* spec (Alt), 1)]

7   An atom or group of atoms possessing an electrical charge is known as
    A an ion   B a molecule   C a neutron   D an electron
    E an electrode   [*LEA* spec (A), 1]
8   The nucleus of an atom contains
    A neutrons only   B electrons only   C electrons and neutrons   D neutrons and protons   E electrons, protons and neutrons
9   Which ONE of the following pairs of ions does calcium bromide contain?
    A Ca^{2+} and Br^- B Ca^+ and Br^{2-} C Ca^{2+} and Br^{2-}
    D Ca^- and Br^+ E Ca^{2-} and Br^+

10 When a copper ion (Cu^{2+}) is changed into a copper atom, the copper ion

   A loses two electrons   B loses two protons   C gains two electrons   D gains one electron   E gains two neutrons

                        [Qu 8–10, *NISEC* spec 1]

11 A metal forms an ion X^{3+}. The formula of its sulphate is

   A XSO_4 B $X(SO_4)_3$ C X_2SO_4 D X_3SO_4 E $X_2(SO_4)_3$

12 When a sodium atom becomes a sodium ion

   A   it loses one electron

   B   its atomic number changes by one unit

   C   it shares its electrons with other atoms

   D   it gains one electron

   E   its relative atomic mass decreases

                    [Qu 11–12 *LEA* spec (B), 1]

13 (*a*)   Nuclear power stations have been producing electricity from radioactive elements for about 30 years.

    (i) Name one radioactive metal which is used in nuclear power stations after extracting it from ores found in the earth's crust.

    (ii) Name another metal from which nuclear power can be obtained and which is made in nuclear reactors.

    (iii) State one of the dangers which must be avoided in nuclear power stations and describe the precaution which is taken to avoid that danger.

(*b*)   The half life period of carbon-14 (^{14}C) is 5736 years. What does the term 'half life period' mean?

(*c*)   State two other sources of energy which do not depend on the burning of fuels or the use of radioisotopes and which can be used to make electricity.   [*NEA* spec (A), 1]

14 (*a*)   Name two types of particle contained in an atom as well as the electron.

(*b*)   In what part of the atom are they found?

(*c*)   Show by means of a diagram how the electrons are arranged in an atom of aluminium. (Atomic number of aluminium is 13.)

(*d*)   State how many of each of the three particles are contained in an atom of fluorine (atomic number of fluorine is 9, mass number is 19).

(*e*)   State how a fluoride ion differs from a fluorine atom.

(*f*)   Draw a diagram to show how the electrons are arranged in the covalent compound NH_3.

(*g*)   Show by means of a diagram how the electrons are arranged in the ionic compound potassium chloride (KCl).

(*j*)   Describe two ways in which covalent compounds usually differ from ionic compounds in their physical or chemical properties.

                    [*NISEC* spec 2]

THE KINETIC THEORY. STATES OF MATTER

CONTENTS

2.1 THE KINETIC THEORY

All particles (atoms, molecules or ions) have **energy**. This energy causes the particles to **move**. This idea (theory) of energy and movement is called the **kinetic theory**. Energy in the form of movement is called **kinetic energy**. The kinetic energy can be in different forms of movement, e.g. molecules can vibrate, rotate, or move from place to place. The amount of kinetic energy in a group of particles depends upon the temperature. As the temperature increases, so does the amount of kinetic energy in the particles, and so the particles can move more quickly and in more ways. If the temperature falls, the kinetic energy falls, and the particles slow down.

2.2 STATES OF MATTER

Most substances can exist in three different forms called **states of matter**. These states are **solid, liquid** and **gas**. One state can be changed to another by changing the temperature or the pressure. Sometimes it is necessary to change both temperature and pressure before a substance can change state, but usually just a change in temperature is enough. Each change has a special name as shown in Fig 2.1.

Fig 2.1 Changes in states of matter

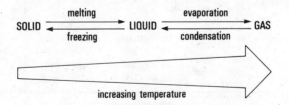

(Some solids miss out the liquid stage when heated.
They change straight from solid to gas, ie, they SUBLIME)

In a *solid* the particles are packed close together. Solids usually have a definite shape of their own because of this. The kinetic energy of the particles is mainly in the form of vibrations; the particles do not have enough energy to move from place to place. If a solid is heated, the particles gain more and more kinetic energy and their movement increases. Eventually, at the **melting point**, the particles have enough energy to separate from each other and move from place to place. At this point the solid melts. This happens to a block of ice when it is heated; it melts to form liquid water.

In a *liquid* the particles are still close together, but now they move about. This means that a liquid has no shape of its own, but its particles 'flow' or 'spread out' to take up the same shape as the container. When a liquid is heated, its particles gain more and more energy until some have so much energy that they can escape from the *surface* of the liquid and become a gas. This is called **evaporation**. Evaporation is not the same as boiling. Liquids can evaporate at temperatures well below their boiling points. For example, a puddle of water can evaporate rapidly on a hot day, but the temperature of the water does not reach anywhere near its boiling point of 100°C.

If the liquid is heated further, particles evaporate more rapidly. Eventually, at the **boiling point**, a special situation is reached. The particles then change into gas so rapidly that it happens even *inside* the liquid. (Evaporation only occurs at the surface.) This causes bubbling inside the liquid.

The liquid **boils**. Each *pure* substance has a *fixed* melting point and a *fixed* boiling point (at normal air pressure).

In a *gas* the particles move very rapidly indeed and are much further apart. A gas has no shape of its own – it spreads out to fill its container. When a liquid changes into a gas, it expands to approximately 1,700 times the volume it had as a liquid. This clearly shows how the particles of a gas are much more 'spread out' than those of a liquid (Fig 2.2).

Fig 2.2 The states of matter

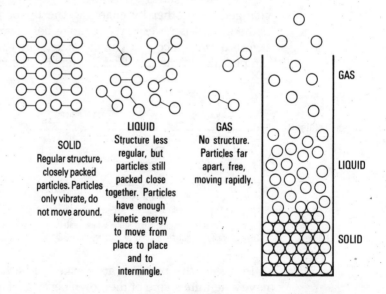

SOLID
Regular structure, closely packed particles. Particles only vibrate, do not move around.

LIQUID
Structure less regular, but particles still packed close together. Particles have enough kinetic energy to move from place to place and to intermingle.

GAS
No structure. Particles far apart, free, moving rapidly.

GAS

LIQUID

SOLID

You could be given lists of melting points and boiling points for different substances and be asked whether each of them would be a solid, a liquid or a gas at a certain temperature. If a substance is at a temperature **below its melting point**, then it has not yet melted and it will be solid. If a substance is **above its melting point but below its**

boiling point, then it will have melted into a liquid but it will not yet have boiled and changed into a gas. Therefore it will be a liquid. If a substance is at a temperature **above its boiling point** then it will be a gas (Fig 2.3).

Fig 2.3 Relationship between the state of a substance and its melting point and boiling point

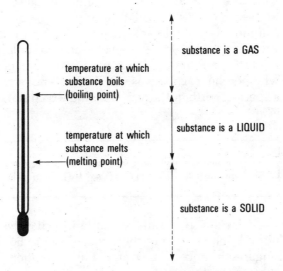

Note that once a pure liquid has reached its boiling point the temperature will not rise any further (unless the pressure is changed). Any heat energy still being provided (e.g. from a Bunsen burner) is being used to separate the particles in the liquid from each other and to change them into the gas state. No matter how many Bunsen burners are used, or for how long, the temperature of the boiling liquid will not rise. Pure liquids, therefore, have a fixed boiling point at a particular atmospheric pressure.

CHANGING A GAS INTO A LIQUID

Most gases can be changed into liquids. We can do this by **cooling** them, or by **increasing the pressure** on them, or by using both methods at the same time. If we cool a gas, we take out some of its kinetic energy and the particles start to slow down. If we continue to cool the gas, eventually the particles slow down so much that they do not have enough energy to move apart from each other. They stay close together and form a liquid (**condense**).

If we put pressure on a gas (i.e. if we **compress** it), we 'squeeze' the particles closer together and again they eventually form a liquid. We have to cool some gases down to *very* low temperatures, and compress them at the same time, before they *liquefy* (change into a liquid). (See the liquefaction of air, p205.)

In the same way, most liquids can be changed into solids by cooling and/or by using pressure. Even air can be changed into a solid. (**Note** We can make a gas take up a much smaller volume by compressing it. We cannot compress a liquid very much because its particles are already very close together, and most solids are even more diffcult to compress for the same reason.)

2.3 STATE SYMBOLS IN EQUATIONS

Sometimes we see a particular substance in only *one* state of matter. For example, you will probably only see oxygen as a gas, and never as a liquid or a solid. There are many substances, however, which you will see in two or even all three states of matter. For example, water is common as a solid (ice), liquid water, or the gas form called water vapour or steam. Water has the same formula in all three states, i.e. H_2O. If the formula H_2O is used in an equation, we may not know whether the reaction was with ice, water or steam. We therefore need a special shorthand way of showing which state of matter a substance is in.

> If the substance is in the form of a SOLID we add (s) after its formula, e.g. $H_2O(s)$. Similarly, we use (l) if it is a LIQUID, e.g. $H_2O(l)$, and (g) if it is a GAS, e.g. $H_2O(g)$.

You will also use many substances **dissolved** in water as a **solution**. A solution is not the same as a pure liquid. A pure liquid is a single substance, e.g. water, but a solution contains at least *two* substances. Sugar dissolved in water is a solution. Sugar solution contains both sugar and water. The properties of a substance often change when it is made into a solution. It is important, therefore, to know whether a substance in an equation is taking part in the reaction in solution. Solutions are not a fourth state of matter, but we do have a shorthand symbol for them. We use (aq). This comes from the Latin, aqua, meaning water.

> If a substance is in solution in water we add (aq) after its formula, e.g. $NaCl(aq)$.

2.4 GAS PRESSURE

The particles of a gas move around very rapidly and constantly hit the walls of whatever container it is in. These hits cause the *pressure* of the gas.

There are two ways of increasing the pressure of a gas inside a container. The first is to increase the temperature of the gas. The particles of the gas then gain more kinetic energy, move more rapidly, and hit the walls of the container more often and at greater speeds. The pressure therefore increases. The second way is to reduce the volume of the container. The same number of gas particles is then concentrated into a smaller volume. The number of particles hitting any part of the wall of the container is increased, and so the pressure goes up.

Fig 2.4 Effect on pressure when volume is decreased

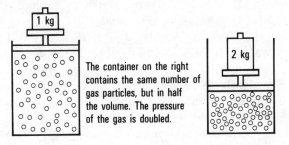

The container on the right contains the same number of gas particles, but in half the volume. The pressure of the gas is doubled.

THE EFFECT OF AIR PRESSURE ON A BOILING POINT

When a liquid boils, the particles which change into gas must have enough energy to escape from the liquid *and* to push their way through the air molecules above the liquid. If the air pressure is higher than normal, the escaping particles have to 'fight' harder to escape and push their way between the air molecules. They therefore need more kinetic energy before they can escape, and the liquid must therefore be heated to a higher temperature before it boils. The boiling point of a liquid thus depends upon the air pressure.

> A liquid has a fixed boiling point at a fixed atmospheric pressure (usually taken at 1 atmosphere pressure).
> If the air pressure is **lower**, then the boiling point goes **down**.
> If the air pressure is **higher**, then the boiling point goes **up**.

This explains how a pressure cooker cooks food more quickly than in an open pan. In an open pan, water cannot be made to boil at much more than 100°C because the air pressure does not change very much. Inside a pressure cooker, the pressure is much higher than the air pressure outside. The boiling point of the water inside is therefore well above 100°C, and the food can be cooked at a higher temperature. You may have done an experiment to show how the boiling point of a liquid is dependent on the air pressure. If so, make sure that you can explain the experiment.

2.5 HOW DO WE KNOW THAT PARTICLES EXIST, AND THAT THEY MOVE ABOUT?

> **Diffusion** is the spreading out of particles from a region where they are concentrated.

You should be able to describe and explain experiments you have done on diffusion. Diffusion occurs rapidly in gases. For example, a drop of liquid bromine in a gas jar evaporates rapidly and then spreads out (diffuses) to fill the gas jar. After a short time, the colour of the bromine is the same throughout the gas jar. It has spread evenly.

Diffusion occurs more slowly in a liquid. For example a crystal of purple potassium manganate(VII) dissolves in water and then the purple colour spreads through the liquid. It is some time before all the water has the same shade of purple. Some liquids take several days to 'mix evenly'. Separate layers of copper(II) sulphate solution and water have a clear boundary between them at first, but the two liquids become 'evenly blue' after a few days. Solids, on the other hand, diffuse very slowly indeed, if at all.

As these 'mixing' processes take place without any heating or shaking, they help us to understand that particles in the gases or liquids are moving. In other words, they have kinetic energy. As the particles always spread out evenly, it helps us to understand that the particles of a particular substance are all exactly the same. As the spreading (diffusion) is much faster in gases than in liquids, it helps us to believe that the particles in a gas move much faster than those in a liquid. As solids do not diffuse much at all, it suggests that the particles in a solid do not move from place to place – they are 'locked together'. Revise any experiments you have done on diffusion, and make sure that you can explain them.

OMIT for NEA.

Some syllabuses include **brownian motion** as further evidence for the movement of particles. You may have observed, through a microscope, the movement of smoke particles in a smoke cell, or small solid particles 'dancing' about on the surface of a liquid. If so you should understand how we explain this – by the bombardment of the *visible* pieces of solid (e.g. carbon in smoke) by *invisible*, moving air or water molecules.

GAS MOLECULES MOVE AT DIFFERENT SPEEDS

You may have seen one or more experiments which show that one gas diffuses more quickly than another. If so, make sure that you can explain the results. You may have used a porous pot to show that hydrogen diffuses more rapidly than air, or that carbon dioxide diffuses more slowly than air.

Another typical experiment uses a glass tube (see Fig 2.5).

Fig 2.5 Comparing the rate of movement of two gases

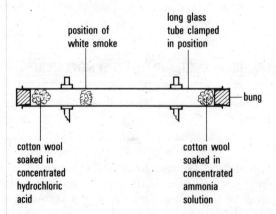

Ammonia gas (NH_3) diffuses down the tube from one end (by evaporating from a concentrated solution of the gas in water). Hydrogen chloride gas (HCl) diffuses down the tube from the other end (by evaporating from a concentrated solution of the gas in water, i.e. concentrated hydrochloric acid). When the two gases meet, a white smoke of ammonium chloride is formed.

$$Ammonia (g) + Hydrogen\ chloride (g) \rightarrow Ammonium\ chloride (s)$$
$$NH_3 (g) \quad + \quad HCl(g) \quad \rightarrow \quad NH_4Cl (s)$$

The two gases do not meet in the middle of the tube. They meet nearer to the hydrogen chloride end. The ammonia gas therefore travels further than the hydrogen chloride gas in the same time. Ammonia diffuses more rapidly than hydrogen chloride.

Three main factors influence the rate of diffusion of a gas. The **lighter** a molecule is, the more **rapidly** it diffuses. (Ammonia molecules are lighter than hydrogen chloride molecules.) Molecules diffuse **more rapidly** if they are **heated**. (They then gain more kinetic energy.)

Molecules diffuse more **rapidly** in a vacuum, but more slowly if they have to 'fight' their way through other molecules (e.g. air molecules).

CHECK YOUR UNDERSTANDING (Answers on p407)

Ask

1   Which state of matter does each of the following statements describe?
   (a)   The particles are packed very tightly together.
   (b)   The particles are far apart.
   (c)   The particles are moving very rapidly.
   (d)   It is almost impossible to compress the particles.
   (e)   The particles move to take up the same shape as the container.

2   Write the formula of sodium chloride, NaCl, to show that it is being used in
   (a)   the solid state,
   (b)   in solution,
   (c)   as a molten liquid, and
   (d)   as a gas.

3   The pressure in a car tyre is taken at 8 a.m. when the car is standing in the shade. It is taken later at 12 noon, when the car is standing in the sun. How would you expect the two readings to compare? Explain your answer.

4   What is wrong with the statement that substance X has a boiling point of 35°C and a melting point of 65°C?

5   A gas takes 2 minutes to diffuse 3 metres through the air in a glass tube. What would happen to the time taken if
   (a)   the temperature was increased, and
   (b)   there was a vacuum in the tube?

6 Substance	Melting point (°C)	Boiling point (°C)
A	−20	80
B	−150	−14
C	−143	−33
D	43	125
E	19	160

The table shows the melting points and boiling points of five substances labelled A to E.

(a)   Which of the substances has the lowest melting point?
(b)   Which of the substances has the highest boiling point?
(c)   Which of the substances would be in the solid state at 25°C?
(d)   Which of the substances would be in the gas state at 60°C?
(e)   Which of the substances would be in the gas state at −50°C?
(f)   Which of the substances would be in the liquid state at 130°C?
(g)   A mixture of A and B is kept in the liquid state at −20°C. The mixture is slowly warmed. Which of the two substances would boil first, and therefore separate from the other as a gas?

7   Use your understanding of relative molecular masses (p279) to decide which gas in each of the following groups would diffuse most rapidly:
(a) H_2 CO O_2 (b) Cl_2 HCl SO_2 (c) CO_2 N_2 O_2

8   Which of the following gases would you expect to diffuse at the *same rate*, at the same temperature? O_2 N_2 H_2 CO

9   Why does water boil at about 70°C near the top of Mount Everest?

10   An experiment was set up as shown in Fig 2.6.

Fig 2.6 A diffusion experiment. The porous pot allows gases to diffuse through it

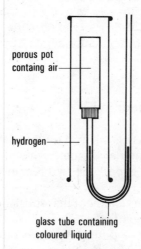

porous pot containg air

hydrogen

glass tube containing coloured liquid

(a)   What would you expect to happen to the liquid in the glass tube? Explain your answer.
(b)   What further change would you expect to see if the gas jar was then taken away? Explain your answer.
(c)   What would you expect to see happen if the experiment was repeated using carbon dioxide instead of hydrogen?

11   An experiment was set up as shown in part (a) of Fig 2.7.

Fig 2.7 The mysterious
flask of water

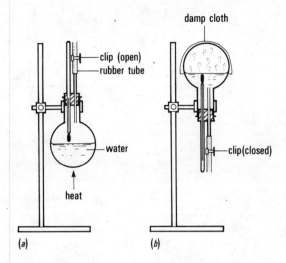

The water was boiled. (It boiled at 100°C.) Steam was allowed to escape for several minutes. The clip was then closed, heating stopped, and the flask turned over as in (b). When a cold damp cloth was placed over the flask as shown, the water inside suddenly started to boil again. It boiled at 97°C. Can you explain this?

CHECK LIST ▶

REMEMBER THAT SOME OF THESE POINTS MAY NOT BE RELEVANT TO THE PARTICULAR SYLLABUS YOU ARE FOLLOWING.

YOU SHOULD UNDERSTAND THE FOLLOWING POINTS.

1 ▶ Kinetic energy. How it is affected by temperature changes.
2 ▶ The states of matter. How one form can be changed into another. How they differ in movement and packing of particles.
3 ▶ The words which describe each change of state.
4 ▶ Use of melting point/boiling point data to decide which state a substance is in at a particular temperature.
5 ▶ State symbols in equations; why they are needed.
6 ▶ What causes gas pressure. How it is affected by temperature and volume changes.
7 ▶ The effect of air pressure on the boiling point of a liquid.
8 ▶ Evidence for the movement of particles – diffusion experiments, and perhaps Brownian motion.
9 ▶ Why gases diffuse more quickly than liquids.
10 ▶ All gases diffuse quickly, but some more quickly than others.

ELEMENTS, COMPOUNDS AND MIXTURES. PURIFICATION

CONTENTS

3.1 ELEMENTS, COMPOUNDS AND MIXTURES

ELEMENTS

Over 7 million different chemical substances have been discovered but they are all made up from approximately one hundred simple substances called **elements**. Elements are the building bricks from which all chemicals are made. They are like the letters of the alphabet. In the same way that we can make up thousands of different words from only 26 letters, it is possible to make thousands of different substances from one hundred or so elements.

> An element is a substance which cannot be made simpler by any chemical process. All of the atoms within it have the same atomic number.

It is also useful to think of an element as being one of the substances listed in the Periodic Table. For example, copper(II) sulphate, $CuSO_4$, is not an element. Copper(II) sulphate can be further simplified into copper (Cu), sulphur (S), and oxygen (O). Copper(II) sulphate contains three different kinds of atom (Cu, S and O). However, we cannot simplify further copper, or sulphur, or oxygen. Each of these is an element. Each contains only one kind of atom. Each is listed in the Periodic Table.

METALS AND NON-METALS

The elements can be divided into two main groups. Most of the elements (about 80%) are **metals**. A smaller number are **non-metals**. The main differences between metals and non-metals are summarised in Table 3.1. However, although *most* metals will show *most* of the properties of metals, there are always exceptions. Some elements have properties of both metals and non-metals. (You may have called these **semi-metals**). If only one or two tests are carried out on a substance, the information provided is not normally enough to decide whether the substance is a metal or a non-metal. For example, although carbon is a non-metal, in the form of graphite it is a very good conductor of electricity, and all its forms have very high melting points. Similarly, although mercury is a metal, it is a liquid at room temperature. To make sure that you understand these points, imagine that you are given an 'unknown' substance, and asked to find out whether it is a metal or a non-metal. How would you do it? Remember: your tests must be *safe* (the substance could be danger-ous, or very reactive, or poisonous), they must be *sensible* (easy, quick, use small quantities and simple apparatus) and they must be sufficient in number to allow for some exceptions (see Table 3.1).

Table 3.1 Differences between metals and non-metals

Learn

Metals	Non-Metals
Differences in physical properties	
1 Good conductors of electricity	Poor conductors of electricity, except carbon in the form of graphite
2 Good conductors of heat	Poor conductors of heat
3 When freshly cut, have a shiny surface	Are often dull, even when freshly cut
4 Can be beaten into shape (are **malleable**) and drawn into wire (are **ductile**)	Usually shatter or break when treated in this way, i.e. are **brittle**
Differences in chemical properties	
5 Sometimes react with dilute acids to form hydrogen	Never react with dilute acids to form hydrogen
6 Usually have 1,2 or 3 electrons in outer energy levels of their atoms	Usually have 5,6,7 or 8 electrons in outer energy levels of their atoms
7 Always form positive ions	Never form positive ions except for H+
8 Always formed at the negative electrode in electrolysis	Formed at the positive electrode in electrolysis, except for H+
9 Compounds are usually ionic	Compounds may be ionic (e.g. when a non-metal combines with a metal) or covalent (when two non-metals combine)
10 Oxides usually basic	Oxides never basic, usually acidic or neutral

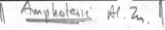 Amphoteric Al. Zn.

BONDING IN METALS

The properties of metals are very different from those of other ele-ments, and also from those of compounds. This is largely because metals have a different kind of bonding. All metals are good conduc-tors of heat and electricity, because they all have this special kind of bonding.

In simple terms we can imagine that in a piece of metal, each metal atom has 'given up' its outer electrons. These electrons form a 'pool' of electrons which are free to move around between the atoms. For example, in a piece of sodium metal (see Fig 3.1) each sodium atom (electron structure 2,8,1) loses its outer electron to leave a positively charged sodium ion. The electron joins others in forming a pool of electrons which are free to move around but hold the whole structure together. This is like thinking of the bricks of a wall (the sodium ions) held together by mortar (the pool of electrons).

Metals are sometimes described as consisting of 'islands of positive ions surrounded by a mobile sea of electrons'.

Fig 3.1 Bonding in sodium metal

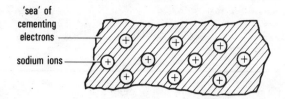

Metals are good conductors of electricity because of the 'moving sea' of electrons within them. If electrons (i.e. electric current) enter a metal at one side, a similar number of electrons are 'pushed out' at the other side, and the metal conducts (see Fig 3.2). Similarly, metals are good conductors of heat because the 'mobile electrons' can spread heat energy quickly. *Solids* with other forms of bonding do not conduct electricity (except graphite) because they do not have these 'mobile electrons', or any other charged particles which are free to move.

Fig 3.2 Electrical conduction by a metal

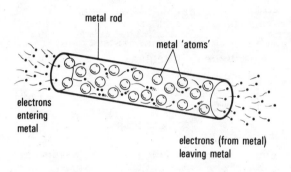

COMPOUNDS

A compound is a substance which contains two or more elements which are *joined* together.

Many of the chemicals you have used in the laboratory are compounds. Because the elements in a compound are *joined* together, they cannot be separated by *physical* methods (p72) such as dissolving, filtering, chromatography, using a magnet, distillation, etc. The elements in a compound can only be separated by using more drastic, *chemical* methods, such as electrolysis. For example, we cannot obtain copper on its own from blue crystals of copper(II) sulphate by physical methods, nor can we separate hydrogen and oxygen in water (H_2O) by physical methods. Copper(II) sulphate, $CuSO_4$, and water, H_2O, are compounds. The elements within them are *joined* together.

Note Be especially careful when mentioning alloys, such as bronze, brass, stainless steel and solder. Many students think of alloys as being elements, or as compounds. They are in fact mixtures.

MIXTURES

> A mixture contains two or more different substances which are not chemically joined together, and which can be easily separated by physical methods.

The key points here are that the substances in a mixture are *not joined*, and are (usually) easy to separate. A mixture can be of elements (e.g. brass contains zinc and copper), or of compounds (e.g. copper(II) sulphate solution contains water and copper(II) sulphate), or both (e.g. zinc and copper(II) sulphate is a mixture of an element plus a compound). Mixtures can also be of solids only (e.g. salt and sand), or of gases (e.g. the air is a mixture of oxygen, nitrogen and other gases), or of solids in a liquid (e.g. sea water is a mixture of solids such as sodium chloride dissolved in water), or of liquids only (e.g. crude oil or petroleum is a mixture of hundreds of liquids).

These points are summarised below where atoms of four different elements are represented by the symbols:

The 'sticks' between the atoms in the figure are simply used to show which atoms are joined together to form molecules. Note that these very simple diagrams do not show real molecules. Also, some compounds do not contain molecules.

Fig 3.3 A simple representation of elements, compounds and mixtures

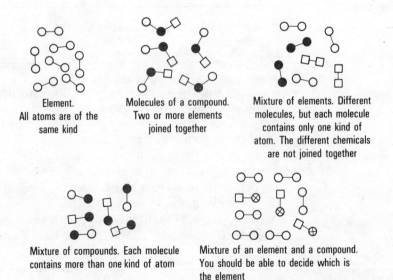

Element. All atoms are of the same kind

Molecules of a compound. Two or more elements joined together

Mixture of elements. Different molecules, but each molecule contains only one kind of atom. The different chemicals are not joined together

Mixture of compounds. Each molecule contains more than one kind of atom

Mixture of an element and a compound. You should be able to decide which is the element

SOME IMPORTANT DIFFERENCES BETWEEN COMPOUNDS AND MIXTURES

Important changes take place when elements *join* together to form a compound. For example, a *mixture* of sodium and chlorine (Na and Cl_2) is completely different from the *compound* sodium chloride (NaCl) formed when the two elements join. Table 3.2 summarises the main differences.

Table 3.2 Differences between compounds and mixtures

Compound	Mixture
1 Each sample looks exactly the same as any other sample, and each sample is uniform, (the same all over)	It may be uniform (e.g. a mixture of two colourless liquids or two colourless gases), but it may be possible to see the separate components (e.g. in a mixture of iron and sulphur)
2 Always contains the same elements in fixed proportions (e.g. water always contains the same % of hydrogen and oxygen)	Can have any composition, e.g. from 1% sulphur and 99% iron, to 99% sulphur and 1% iron
3 Melting and boiling points are fixed for any pure compound (although boiling point varies with air pressure)	Melting and boiling points depend upon the composition of the mixture. A mixture of 1% X and 99% Y could be called 'impure Y' and will have a melting point below that of pure Y. A mixture of 3% X and 97% Y will have an even lower melting point
4 Cannot be split up into separate components by physical processes	Separation possible by physical processes, such as purification techniques
5 Its properties are totally unlike those of the elements within it	The substances in the mixture keep their own properties, and the mixture has all of these properties

Point 5 in the table is particularly important. Using the earlier example of sodium and chlorine, we know that sodium is a soft, grey metal, which reacts rapidly with water. Chlorine is a dangerous, poisonous gas. It reacts with water to produce an acid solution. However, when these two elements join to form the compound sodium chloride, everything changes. Sodium chloride (common salt) shows no metallic properties, does not react with water, and we 'eat' it every day with our food. As soon as elements join, they seem to lose their own properties, and the compound formed has properties of its own.

You may have seen changes like this demonstrated, perhaps using sodium and chlorine. You may have used other chemicals to make the same point, e.g. by comparing the properties of the elements iron and sulphur with the properties of the compound iron(II) sulphide (FeS) made by heating a mixture of iron and sulphur. The chemicals used as examples may vary, but the important difference between compounds and mixtures will be the same. You must be able to describe the differences between elements, mixtures and compounds using any appropriate example. You will be expected to know whether the common chemicals you have used are elements, compounds or mixtures.

PHYSICAL AND CHEMICAL CHANGES

The *physical properties* of a substance tell us what a substance looks like (e.g. its colour, smell, appearance). Physical properties also include facts such as the melting point, boiling point, whether a substance is toxic, its solubility in water and its density. Note that all of these describe the substance itself and not what it does. In noting or measuring any of these points, the substance does not change from one chemical to another. For example, if we take the melting point of ice, the water formed is still the same chemical as the ice from which it came. *Physical changes* do not involve a substance changing into something else. For this reason, physical changes are easily reversed. They include melting, boiling and using a magnet. In each case, the substance is not changing chemically (its chemical formula does not change), and the change is easily reversed, (melted water can easily be frozen again).

Chemical changes involve chemical reactions in which substances change into something else. They are not easily reversed. Chemical changes also usually take place with very obvious energy changes. For example, the burning of magnesium in air is a chemical change. The magnesium changes chemically (from the grey metal, Mg, to the white compound, magnesium oxide, MgO); the process cannot easily be reversed (magnesium oxide does not change back into magnesium when it cools); the reaction takes place with a large change of energy – light and heat are given out. When elements are *mixed* together there is no chemical change. When they *join* together to form a compound, there is a chemical change, as is summarised by point 5 in Table 3.2.

Physical changes	Chemical changes
1 Easily reversed	Usually very difficult to reverse
2 No new substance formed	New substance formed
3 Energy changes usually small and not obvious	Energy changes usually considerable and obvious

CHECK YOUR UNDERSTANDING (Answers on p408)

(*f*) water   (*g*) air   (*h*) chromium   (*i*) a drink of tea   (*j*) milk
(*k*) magnesium chloride   (*l*) sea water   (*m*) iodine

1   In the parts (*a*) to (*e*) letters are used as symbols for atoms, but they

are not the normal symbols. 'Sticks' are used to show which atoms are joined together. For each part, decide whether the symbols show an element, a compound, or a mixture. If your answer is a mixture, decide whether it is a mixture of elements, or a mixture of compounds, or a mixture of both elements and compounds.

2 Four of the following substances have something in common. Which is the odd one out?

A Nickel   B Sulphur   C Sodium   D Copper   E Silver

3 Is it true that most metals are magnetic? Explain your answer.

4 How would you obtain a pure sample of iron from a mixture of iron and sulphur? (You should be able to suggest two ways.)

5 A student was asked to prove that hydrochloric acid, HCl, contains hydrogen. The student suggested testing a sample of the acid for hydrogen by using the 'pop' test (p168). What is wrong with this suggestion?

6 The following table compares some of the properties of five substances labelled A to E. Which of them could not be a pure compound?

	Melting point (°C)	Appearance	Observations when water is added	Effect of a magnet
A	0	colourless liquid	colourless solution formed	none
B	varies	yellow grains and grey grains	yellow solid floats on top, grey solid sinks	grey solid attracted to magnet
C	860	dark grey solid	no change	attracted to magnet
D	varies	colourless gas	some gas dissolves	none
E	44	yellow solid	insoluble	none

7 When asked to suggest other exceptions to the general points given in Table 3.1, a group of students suggested that an exception to point 3 is glass (which is shiny, but not a metal), and an exception to point 4 was plastic (which can be drawn into thin strands but is not a metal). Another student said that these were not exceptions because they did not even belong in the table. Who was right?

3.2 PURIFICATION TECHNIQUES

Most chemicals which you use from a reagent bottle in the laboratory are pure. However, it is almost certain that they were not found naturally in a pure state. Most substances are found mixed with others; they are *impure*. This is also true of most of the chemicals you will have made in a laboratory; at some stage in the preparation they will be impure, i.e. they will be mixtures. If you make crystals of the salt copper(II) sulphate, for example, the crystals will not at first be pure. No matter how careful you have been, the crystals will contain small amounts of other substances, such as water. (Many students do not think of water as being an impurity, but it can be. Pure copper(II) sulphate is a dry solid, so if it is wet, the substance is not pure!)

You must understand some of the methods chemists use to purify substances. You should be familiar with the following techniques. You should also be able to decide which technique you should use in a particular situation. If you understand the differences between physical and chemical changes (p72) you will realize that methods of purification are usually *physical* changes, so that we do not change the substances we are separating.

1 METHODS USED TO SEPARATE OR PURIFY MIXTURES OF SOLIDS

(a) SOLUTION, FOLLOWED BY FILTRATION AND THEN CRYSTALLISATION

When you describe a process of this type, try to use as many key words (in bold type) as possible.

This method can be used only if *one* of the mixed solids will dissolve in a liquid, but the other or others will not. You may have used this method to separate pure salt (sodium chloride) from rock salt.

A suitable liquid is chosen (the **solvent**) which will **dissolve** one of the substances in the mixture. (The substance which dissolves is the **solute**.) It may be necessary to warm the solvent before it will dissolve enough solid. The remaining solid or solids do not dissolve because they are **insoluble** in the solvent. The undissolved solids float in the liquid and form a **suspension**. The mixture is **filtered**. The **solution** containing the dissolved substance passes through the filter paper. It is collected in a container and is called the **filtrate**. The suspended, undissolved solid is trapped on the filter paper. It is called the **residue**.

Instead of filtering, a centrifuge can be used. This 'spins down' the suspended, undissolved solid so that it forms a residue at the bottom of a special test tube. A clear liquid (the solution) is left above the residue. The liquid can be poured off (**decanted**) from the solid. A centrifuge is better than filtration if only small quantities are being used.

What happens next depends upon whether you want to end up with the solid which has dissolved, or with the insoluble solid which is the residue. If you want the dissolved solid, the filtrate is heated to **evaporate** *some* of the solvent (usually about half of the volume). The concentrated solution is then left to cool. The dissolved solid then **crystallizes** out, and can be separated from the liquid. The crystals can be washed with a *little* solvent and then allowed to **dry**. (See the use of a desiccator, p.78.)

If the residue is needed, it is washed with solvent and then allowed to dry.

The sequence of steps is summarised in Fig 3.4. **Note** This is a *general* method. The solvent does not have to be water. If another solvent is used, it may be flammable, and so great care is needed when it is heated. For example, the solution or solvent must not be heated directly with a naked flame. Electrical heating, or heating over a water bath, is much safer.

Fig 3.4 One way of separating a solid from a mixture of solids

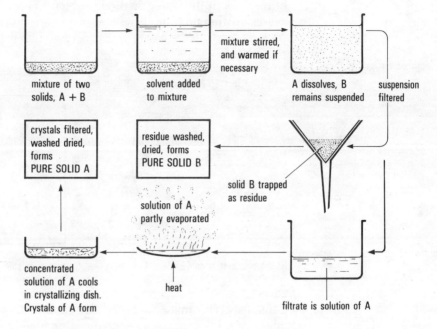

(b) CHROMATOGRAPHY

You may have used this technique to separate *coloured* substances from each other, e.g. the substances in the leaves of a plant, or artificial food colourings, or the coloured substances in inks. The method can be used to separate any mixture if the various substances all dissolve in a suitable solvent.

The simplest method is to place a circle of filter paper across the top of a beaker. A *few*, small drops of the concentrated dissolved mixture are added to the centre of the paper. Drops of solvent are then added slowly to the original spot, so that the solvent spreads out towards the edge of the filter paper. The different substances in the mixture spread differently. Some dissolve easily in the solvent and are 'washed' towards the outer edge of the circle by the solvent. Other substances do not dissolve well in the solvent and do not move far from their place in the original centre spot. The different substances are therefore separated into bands across the paper. The technique is generally used for *coloured* substances, so that the different bands can be seen easily. However, it can be used for *colourless* substances. They will still be separated, and it may be possible to find out where each has moved to on the paper by using a spray which forms a colour with one or more of the substances.

You may have used a slightly different method in which spots of mixture are placed near the bottom of a *strip* of paper. The paper is then allowed to stand in a small volume of solvent in a bottle or gas jar. The solvent rises up the paper, and separates the substances in each spot of mixture. In this case, separate *spots* are produced, instead of *bands* as in the other method. In either case, the finished paper is called a **chromatogram** (Fig 3.5).

Fig 3.5 Chromatograms

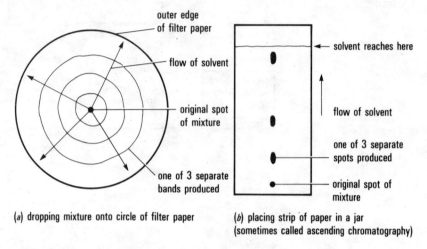

(a) dropping mixture onto circle of filter paper

(b) placing strip of paper in a jar
(sometimes called ascending chromatography)

Obviously, chromatography is only suitable for separating *very small* quantities. Its main uses are (*a*) deciding whether a substance is pure or not, and (*b*) deciding what a substance is. In (*a*), a spot will separate into two or more substances if it contains a mixture, but it will produce only one spot or band if it is a single, pure substance. In (*b*), the *position* of the spot or band on the paper tells us what the substance is. For example, a dye used in food colourings can be identified by chromatographing it alongside some pure, known dyes.

Fig 3.6 Analysing a dye by paper chromatography

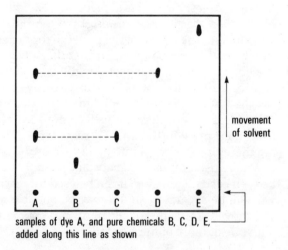

samples of dye A, and pure chemicals B, C, D, E, added along this line as shown

In this way a public analyst can find out whether a dye used in food is a permitted one or an 'illegal' one. The idea is illustrated in Fig 3.6. The figure shows that dye A is a mixture, and that it contains dyes C and D.

If necessary, each of the separated substances in a chromatogram can be obtained in a pure state. This is done by cutting out the appropriate spot or band on the paper. If the piece of paper is then stood in a solvent, the substance on it dissolves into the solvent. The solvent can then be evaporated to leave the pure substance.

2 METHODS USED TO SEPARATE OR PURIFY A MIXTURE OF A SOLID AND A LIQUID

(a) CRYSTALLISATION

This can be used only if the *solid* is required in the pure state, and it is *dissolved* in the liquid. Method as described towards the end of 1(*a*) (p74). Typical examples of this method are used in the crystallisation of soluble salts.

(b) FILTRATION, OR CENTRIFUGING

These can be used only if the solid does *not* dissolve in the solvent. For example, a suspension of chalk (calcium carbonate) in water can be separated in this way. Note that the method produces *both* the pure solid *and* the pure solvent, unlike (*a*). In (*a*), the solvent is 'lost' because it evaporates.

(c) SIMPLE DISTILLATION

This method is normally used when a solid is dissolved in a solvent, and the *solvent* is required in the pure state. For example, it could be used to separate pure water from a solution of copper(II) sulphate in water, or pure water from the dissolved impurities in sea water.

Distillation is the boiling of a solution in a special apparatus. The vapour is **condensed** and collected in a *separate* container from the original solution. The condensed vapour which is collected in this way is called the **distillate**. When the mixture (solution) is heated, the solvent evaporates but the dissolved solid does not do so.

You will have used some simple, small scale apparatus to distil solutions. You will also realise that if the process is to be efficient, a **Liebig condenser** should be used. Some examples of distillation apparatus are shown in Fig 3.7.

Notes (1) When a Liebig condenser is used, the cooling water must enter the condenser at the lower opening and leave at the upper opening. Do you understand why? (2) Normally, a thermometer is not placed inside the liquid, but opposite to where the vapour leaves the apparatus, as in Fig 3.7. We are interested in the temperature of the vapour (which is the same as the boiling point of the *distillate*) and not that of the mixture, which will keep changing as its composition changes.

Fig 3.7 Distillation
apparatus

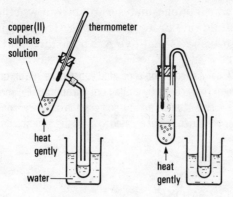

(a) Two examples of simple apparatus
which can be used to obtain pure water from
copper(II) sulphate solution

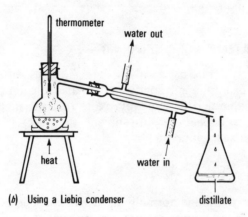

(b) Using a Liebig condenser

(d) DRYING

If a solid is wet it can often be dried fairly well by simply leaving it in
the air, for the water to evaporate. It may *look* dry afterwards, but it is
likely that it will still contain water because the air always contains
water vapour. Some solids can be dried by gentle heating in an oven,
provided that they do not decompose when heated.

Solids are often best dried in a **desiccator**. A desiccator is also often
used to *keep* solids which have been dried. The solid is placed in a
container, which is then stood on a wire gauze 'shelf' in the desiccator. A drying agent is placed below the gauze. Suitable drying
agents include anhydrous calcium chloride, calcium oxide, and silica
gel. The lid of the desiccator makes an air-tight seal.

3 METHODS USED TO SEPARATE OR PURIFY A MIXTURE OF LIQUIDS

If water and ethanol are mixed together, it is impossible to tell one liquid from the other in the mixture. The two liquids mix completely. They are **miscible**. Two liquids which will not mix are called **immiscible**. Oil and water are immiscible. No matter how much we shake such a mixture, the oil and water will separate again. Different methods are used to separate mixtures of liquids, according to whether the liquids are miscible or immiscible.

Note You should not describe *one* liquid as being immiscible. The word is used ony for a named *pair* of liquids. For example, water is miscible with ethanol, but water is immiscible with oil.

(a) IMMISCIBLE LIQUIDS

A separating funnel (Fig 3.8) is used to separate immiscible liquids. If you have used one for this purpose, make sure that you can describe how to use it to separate two immiscible liquids.

Fig 3.8 Separation of two immiscible liquids

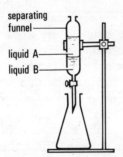

separating funnel

liquid A

liquid B

(b) SIMPLE DISTILLATION

This is used only to separate a mixture of *miscible* liquids. Usually *one* of the liquids evaporates more easily than the others, and so its molecules escape first when the mixture is heated. (A substance which evaporates easily is called **volatile**. The more volatile liquid evaporates first from a mixture.) Its molecules can be condensed separately and collected in a container away from the rest of the liquid.

However, simple distillation is not always reliable in separating a mixture of liquids. *Some* molecules of *all* the liquids also evaporate when they are heated. The vapour coming off may contain *mainly* molecules of one kind (from the most volatile liquid) but it will also contain some molecules from the others. The condensed liquid (distillate) may not, therefore, be pure. When a mixture of ethanol (boiling point 78°C) and water (boiling point 100°C) is distilled, the distillate contains both ethanol and water. However, the ethanol is much more concentrated in the distillate than it is in the starting mixture. Simple distillation works best if the liquids in the mixture have *very different* boiling points. There is then more chance that the vapour which evaporates will consist almost entirely of one kind of molecule only. Simple distillation is also useful for *concentrating* a liquid in a mixture, as in the water/ethanol example above.

(c) FRACTIONAL DISTILLATION

This is an 'improvement' on simple distillation for mixtures of liquids. It is used to separate a pure liquid from another if their boiling points are relatively close, or to separate one liquid from a mixture of several liquids, or to simplify a very complex mixture of liquids such as crude oil (petroleum).

A fractionating column is used, e.g. in the laboratory as in Fig 3.9. In industry, a fractionating column is much more complicated and on a larger scale, e.g. to simplify crude oil (p365) or to separate liquid air. In the laboratory, the fractionating column is usually packed with glass beads or some other unreactive (*inert*) material. Molecules escape from the mixture of liquids when it is heated, and they rise up the column. The vapour which leaves the liquid is likely to contain several different kinds of molecule, although one kind may make up most of the vapour. The temperature inside the column gradually decreases from bottom to top. (The column is hottest at the bottom because it is nearer to the heating system.) As the molecules rise up the column, they collide with glass beads which are gradually getting cooler as the molecules move further away from the heat. Some molecules will condense back into liquids, which trickle back down the column. Eventually, only molecules of *one* kind 'survive' as vapour all the way up the column. These then escape to be condensed and collected separately, as a pure liquid.

Fig 3.9 Fractional distillation of a mixture of two miscible liquids

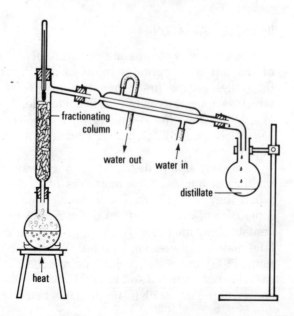

When all the molecules of one kind have escaped, the temperature at the top of the column rises until it reaches the boiling point of the 'next' liquid. Molecules of this liquid can then 'survive' as vapour all the way up the column and escape as a vapour. They can be condensed, and collected in a *different* container from the first one. The process is illustrated in Fig. 3.10.

Fig 3.10 An illustration of how a fractionating column works

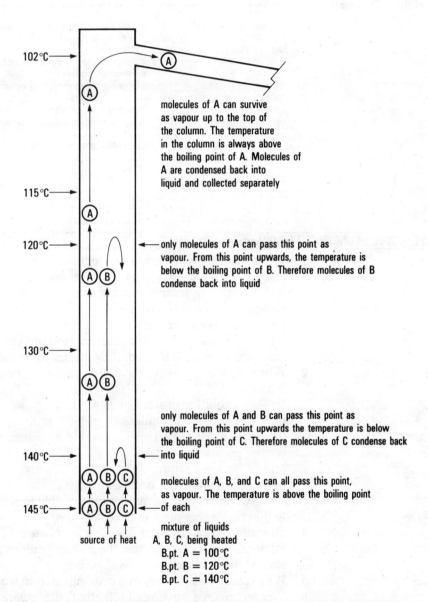

102 °C

molecules of A can survive as vapour up to the top of the column. The temperature in the column is always above the boiling point of A. Molecules of A are condensed back into liquid and collected separately

115 °C

120 °C

only molecules of A can pass this point as vapour. From this point upwards, the temperature is below the boiling point of B. Therefore molecules of B condense back into liquid

130 °C

only molecules of A and B can pass this point as vapour. From this point upwards the temperature is below the boiling point of C. Therefore molecules of C condense back into liquid

140 °C

molecules of A, B, and C can all pass this point, as vapour. The temperature is above the boiling point of each

145 °C

source of heat

mixture of liquids A, B, C, being heated
B.pt. A = 100 °C
B.pt. B = 120 °C
B.pt. C = 140 °C

Each separate liquid collected in this way is called a **fraction**. You may have used the idea to obtain almost pure ethanol from a mixture of ethanol and water. Similarly, you may have separated crude oil into fractions (p366).

(Note that in very complicated mixtures such as crude oil, which contains many liquids, each fraction obtained in the first distillation is still a mixture.)

SUMMARY OF PURIFICATION METHODS

Method	What it separates
Solution and filtration	An insoluble substance from a soluble one
Crystallisation	A solid from its solution
Separating funnel	Immiscible liquids
Simple distillation	A liquid from one or more dissolved solids, or two liquids with widely different boiling points
Fractional distillation	Liquids with boiling points close together, and a better separation of other liquid mixtures
Chromatography	Many mixtures; particularly useful if one or more parts coloured
Use of a drying agent	Water from a (nearly dry) solid or organic liquid. Typical drying agents such as calcium oxide, silica gel and anhydrous calcium chloride are used in desiccators to dry solids.

CHECK YOUR UNDERSTANDING (Answers on p409)

1   What is wrong with each of the following?
(a)   Sand can be crystallised from sea water.
(b)   When a teaspoon of sugar is stirred into a cup filled with hot water, a suspension is formed.
(c)   Oil is an immiscible liquid.
(d)   If a mixture of salt solution (sodium chloride) and copper(II) sulphate solution is filtered, the filtrate will be salt solution.

2   Which of the following mixtures could be separated by *simple* distillation?
(a)   a solution of salt in water,
(b)   a mixture of liquid A (b.p. 100°C) and liquid B (b.p. 115°C),
(c)   a mixture of two immiscible liquids with widely separated boiling points,
(d)   salt and sand,
(e)   two liquids, b.p. 60°C and 210°C.

3   Write down as many examples as possible in which a process similar to 'filtering' takes place in everyday life.

4   Suppose that you were distilling a mixture of water and another liquid,X, and that you know the boiling point of pure X is 55°C. What should the first sample of distillate be?

5   Why would you not separate cooking oil from water by distillation?

6   You are given a mixture of dimethylbenzene and a dilute solution of potassium chloride in water. Dimethylbenzene is a liquid which boils at 140°C and is immiscible with water.
(a)   How many substances are present in the mixture?
(b)   Which of the following methods would be a very quick way of separating one of the substances from the mixture?

A filtration   B use a separating funnel   C distillation
D chromatography

(c)   What would you do then to complete the separation of pure water?

7   Study the chromatogram in Fig 3.11 and then answer the questions.

Fig 3.11

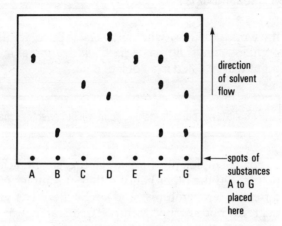

direction
of solvent
flow

spots of
substances
A to G
placed
here

(a)   Which two substances are exactly the same?
(b)   Which substances are not mixtures?
(c)   Which substances do not contain A?
(d)   Which substances do contain C?
(e)   What can you conclude about substance F?
(f)   What can you conclude about substance G?

8   From the following methods of separation (filtration, evaporation, fractional distillation, chromatography) choose the one most suitable for separation of each of the following mixtures.

A   petrol and paraffin
B   the various colours in red rose petals
C   sea water, to obtain salt

9   Name the method of purification you would use in each of the following:

(a)   to remove the 'cloudiness' from lime water
(b)   to obtain pure water from sea water
(c)   to separate a mixture of paraffin and water

10   Explain *briefly* how you would do each of the following separations. (The names of the techniques, or a few words, will be enough explanation for each step.) You may need to use chemical methods for some separations, and you may need to look up some solubilities.

(a)   To obtain pure water from copper sulphate solution.
(b)   To obtain iron from a mixture with copper.
(c)   To obtain copper from a mixture of iron and copper, using a different method than in (c).
(d)   To obtain pure samples of sodium chloride and calcium carbonate from a mixture of the two.
(e)   To obtain copper from a mixture of copper and calcium.

(f)   To obtain both copper sulphate and calcium sulphate from a mixture of the two.

3.3 HOW DO WE DECIDE THAT A SUBSTANCE IS PURE?

(a) FINDING THE MELTING POINT OF A SOLID

If we need to know whether a *solid* is pure, we usually take its melting point. A *pure* solid has a *fixed and sharp* melting point. This melting point will be listed in a book of data.

> If a solid is not pure, its melting point will be **lower** than that of the pure solid.

For example, pure ice and pure stearic acid have fixed melting points. On the other hand, different samples of paraffin wax melt at different temperatures, and each one melts gradually over several degrees, not sharply within 1°C. Paraffin wax is a *mixture*, and its composition varies.

One way of finding an accurate melting point is shown in Fig 3.12. Make sure that you can describe the technique if you have used it, e.g. to find the melting point of a solid such as stearic acid.

Another way involves plotting a graph called a **cooling curve**. For example, a solid such as stearic acid can be melted as shown in Fig 3.13. When it has completely melted, it is allowed to rise in temperature for a further 5°C or so. It is then allowed to cool. The temperature of the substance is taken every half minute, or every minute. This is done until the liquid has changed back to a solid and the temperature has fallen a further 5°C or so below the melting point. The results are plotted on a graph as in Fig 3.14.

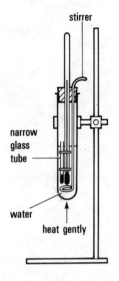

Fig 3.12 Melting point determination

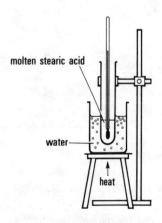

Fig 3.13 Apparatus for determining the cooling curve for stearic acid

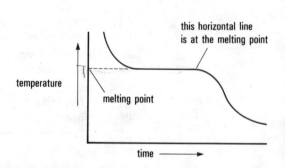

Fig 3.14 A typical cooling curve

The important part of the cooling curve is the 'horizontal' part where the temperature *stops* falling for a time. This happens when the liquid changes back into a solid. This is the freezing point (or melting point) of the substance.

Note that a melting point is also a useful way of finding out what an unknown solid is, as well as checking on its purity. Each pure solid has its own fixed melting point, which can be found in a book of data.

(b) FINDING THE BOILING POINT OF A LIQUID

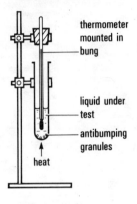

Fig 3.15 Finding the boiling point of a liquid

If we need to test the purity of a *liquid*, we usually take its boiling point. A boiling point is not quite so useful as a melting point, because it also depends upon the atmospheric pressure.

> A pure liquid has a fixed boiling point at a fixed atmospheric pressure. If the liquid is impure, the boiling point will be **higher** than that of the pure liquid.

The simplest way of finding a boiling point is shown in Fig 3.15. The antibumping granules help to make sure that the liquid boils smoothly. The liquid is heated *gently* to boiling. The steady boiling point is then noted. This method **must not** be used if the liquid is flammable. A much safer method for flammable liquids is to use a distillation apparatus (p78), but placing the thermometer bulb in the liquid rather than in the vapour. The vapour, and the distillate, are kept safely away from the source of heat.

CHECK YOUR UNDERSTANDING (Answers on p409)

1   What change or changes would you make to the apparatus in Fig 3.12 if you were finding the melting point of a solid which melts at approximately 140°C?

2   A student checked the boiling point of some pure water and found that it was not 100°C. A friend suggested that the thermometer was not being read properly, or that there was a fault in the thermometer. Can you suggest another possible explanation?

3   A student did a boiling point test on a liquid, and found the boiling point to be 102°C. The student concluded that the liquid was impure water. A friend suggested that there *could* be two other explanations. What are they? (The thermometer was not faulty, and the student had used it correctly.)

4   In winter, antifreeze is added to the water in a car cooling system. This helps to prevent the water in the radiator freezing. If the water did freeze, the radiator would burst.
   (*a*)   Why would the radiator burst if the water froze?
   (*b*)   Why does the addition of antifreeze help to prevent the water freezing?

5   Salt is often added to the roads in the winter months. This helps to prevent ice forming on the roads. Can you give a *brief*, scientific explanation of how this works?

6   A student took the melting point of an 'unknown' solid, and found it to be 57°C. The test was done accurately, and with reliable apparatus. The student looked up some melting points in a book of data. They are shown below. The student concluded that the unknown solid was probably the same as substance C, as this had the nearest melting point to 57°. Do you agree with this conclusion? If not, suggest alternative explanations.

Substance	Melting point (°C)
A	43
B	51
C	59
D	66
E	75

CHECK LIST ▶   REMEMBER THAT SOME OF THESE POINTS MAY NOT BE RELEVANT TO THE SYLLABUS YOU ARE FOLLOWING.

YOU SHOULD UNDERSTAND THE FOLLOWING POINTS.

1 ▶   What an element is. You must know which of the substances you have studied are elements.

2 ▶   The main differences between metallic elements and non-metallic elements. How to test whether an 'unknown' element is a metal or a non-metal.

3 ▶   How metal atoms are bonded together. How this explains good conductivity.

4 ▶   What compounds and mixtures are. You should know which of the substances you have studied are mixtures and compounds.

5 ▶   Compounds have very different properties from the properties of the elements within them.

6 ▶   Physical and chemical changes.

7 ▶   How to purify substances by: solution; filtration; crystallisation; chromatography; simple distillation; use of dessiccator; use of separating funnel; fractional distillation.

8 ▶   You could be given data about unfamiliar substances and asked how you would separate them or purify them.

9 ▶   You should be able to use key words such as : **solvent, solute, insoluble, solution, suspension, filtrate, residue, evaporate, crystallise, chromatogram, immiscible, miscible, condense, distillate, fraction.**

10 ▶   How to find a melting point or a boiling point by experiment, either (*a*) to check the purity of a substance, or (*b*) to help find out what something is.

11 ▶   The effect of impurities on the melting and boiling points of a substance.

12 ▶   The shape of a typical cooling curve. How to obtain data for it, how to plot it, and what information can be obtained from it.

SEE GENERAL NOTE BEFORE QUESTIONS ON pp.49 AND 50. REMEMBER THAT YOU MAY BE ALLOWED TO USE A DATA BOOK IN THE EXAMINATION.

Questions 1–3

From the list A to D below

A condensation   B distillation   C evaporation   D filtration

select the process which

1 Can be used to separate sand from water most quickly and cheaply.
2 Causes water to collect on classroom windows in cold weather.
3 Involves the change of a liquid to a gas and of the gas back to a liquid.

[Qu 1–3, *NEA* spec (A),1]

4 Which one of the following changes produces a new substance?
  A   Burning powdered sulphur
  B   Condensing ethanol vapour
  C   Melting paraffin wax
  D   Vaporising iodine crystals
5 Which one of the following could be obtained by simple distillation?
  A   Chlorine from sea water
  B   Glucose from a mixture of glucose and maltose
  C   Propanone from a mixture of propanone and water
  D   Water from sea water   [Qu 4,5, *SEG* spec (Alt), 1]

Questions 6–9 concern the following practical methods:

A Chromatography   B Crystallisation   C Distillation
D Electrolysis   E Filtration

Choose, from A to E, the method which would be used to

6 Isolate nitrogen from liquid air.
7 Separate coloured substances in a sample of coloured soft drink.
8 Separate petrol from crude oil.
9 Separate a drug which has been precipitated from a solution.
10 Sugar dissolves in tea to form a mixture. The sugar is the
  A solvent   B solution   C solute   D filtrate
  E precipitate   [Qu 6–10, *LEA* spec (A), 1]
11 Which one of the following is an element?
  A brass   B bronze   C glass   D zinc   E wood
       [*NISEC* spec, 1]
12 (See Fig 3.16).
  (*a*)   The contents of which tube could be separated by
           (i) filtration
           (ii) distillation?
  (*b*)   (i) Give *one* use of salt which is related to the food industry.
           (ii) Give one harmful effect of drinking alcoholic beverages.
       [*MEA* spec 2]
       NEA?

Fig 3.16 Diagram for
question 12

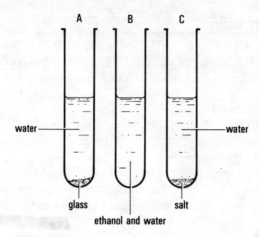

13 Paper chromatography was used by a forensic scientist to find out
which one of four ball-point pens (labelled A,B,C and D) was used to
write a 'poison-pen' letter.

  A small amount of ink from the note was dissolved in ethanol and
the solution made more concentrated. A drop of the concentrated
solution and a drop of each of the four inks from pens A–D were put
onto a piece of filter paper and the experiment carried out. The results
are shown in Fig 3.17.

Fig 3.17 Diagram for
question 13

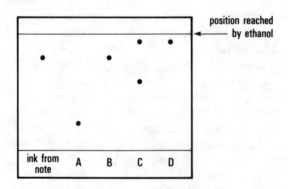

(a)   What is a 'forensic scientist'?
(b)   Why was ethanol used rather than water in this experiment?
(c)   Explain how the solution of ink in ethanol could *safely* be
concentrated.
(d)   Which pen (A,B,C or D) was used to write the note?
Explain your answer.
(e)   Which ink contains a mixture of two dyes? Explain your
answer.
(f)   Draw a labelled diagram to show how a sample of ethanol
could be recovered from a solution of ink in ethanol.

[*LEA* spec (B), 2]

THE ACTIVITY SERIES

CONTENTS

Chemistry has several *classification systems*. Substances are placed in order in a list, or are placed in certain groups, according to their properties. You should be able to use the main classifications as follows:

(*a*)   To predict what properties a substance would be expected to have if you know where it belongs in a classification system. You should be able to do this even if you have never used the substance;

(*b*)   to do the opposite of (*a*). If you are told some of the properties of a substance, you should be able to say where the substance should fit in a classification system.

The main classification systems you will use are the Activity Series, metals and non-metals, the Periodic Table, ionically bonded substances, molecular substances, types of oxide, and elements, compounds and mixtures. This chapter deals with the Activity Series and it is to this that we now turn.

The metals vary in their reactivity. Some are very reactive; they react easily and rapidly with many other elements. Some are very unreactive. It is possible to arrange them in order of their reactivity. Such a series, in which the most reactive metals are placed at the top, is called an **Activity Series**. For example, sodium and potassium are the most reactive common metals. They are so reactive that they have to be stored in oil, because otherwise they would react with oxygen and water vapour in the air. These metals are found at the top of the series. On the other hand, gold and platinum are very unreactive, and they are found at the bottom.

Table 4.1 lists some common elements in an Activity Series. Note the following points.

(i) You may not need to learn the table. You may be given any information you need to use it. It is more important that you understand how to *use* the list.

(ii) Table 4.1 includes two non-metals, carbon and hydrogen. It is sometimes useful to know which metal oxides these elements will react with (p98).

(iii) Table 4.1 includes some metals which are not used in all syllabuses.

Table 4.1 An Activity Series of metals (plus carbon and hydrogen)

K	potassium
Na	sodium
Li	lithium
Ca	calcium
Mg	magnesium
[Al]	aluminium (see note)
[C]	carbon (non-metal
Zn	zinc
Fe	iron
Sn	tin
Pb	lead
[H]	hydrogen (non-metal)
Cu	copper
Ag	silver
Au	gold
Pt	platinum

Note The relative positions can be affected by the temperature. For example, hydrogen is higher in the series at high temperatures.

The 'true' position of aluminium is explained below.

4.1 EXPERIMENTS USED TO PLACE METALS IN AN ACTIVITY SERIES

1 REACTIONS OF THE METALS WITH OXYGEN

A small sample of the metal is usually placed on a combustion spoon and heated in a Bunsen flame. Some metals burn almost immediately and the spoon is then removed from the flame. Others may not *burn* at all, even when strongly heated. A metal can still *react* with oxygen, without burning, however. For example, copper becomes coated with a layer of black copper(II) oxide when heated. The metals can also be heated and then placed in a gas jar or tube of oxygen. Typical results are shown in Table 4.2. The results clearly show the differences in reactivity.

Note that the position of aluminium in the series needs some explanation. From most of its reactions, you would place it fairly low in the activity series. However, the metal is really quite reactive. It *instantly* forms an oxide coating with oxygen. This coating, although thin, is very tough and difficult to break. It protects the metal underneath, preventing it from showing its true chemical reactivity.

increasing chemical reactivity	metal	reaction	
	Sodium	Metal instantly forms oxide layer in cold. Burns easily when heated, with yellow flame. Off-white solid formed	sodium + oxygen ⟶ sodium oxide $2Na(s) + O_2(g) \longrightarrow Na_2O_2$
	Calcium	Rapidly covered with oxide layer in the cold. Sometimes difficult to burn because of this. Fresh specimens burn easily when heated, with brick red flame. White solid formed	calcium + oxygen ⟶ calcium oxide $2Ca(s) + O_2(g) \longrightarrow 2CaO(s)$
	Magnesium	Oxide layer formed slowly when cold. Burns easily when heated, with dazzling white flame. White solid formed	magnesium + oxygen ⟶ magnesium oxide $2Mg(s) + O_2(g) \longrightarrow 2MgO(s)$
	Aluminium	Oxide layer formed instantly in cold. Layer difficult to penetrate – protects metal beneath, which does not burn (unless in powder form) even when heated strongly	aluminium + oxygen ⟶ aluminium oxide $4Al(s) + 3O_2(g) \longrightarrow 2Al_2O_3(s)$
	Zinc	Oxide layer formed in cold. Turnings and pieces will not burn when heated, but the powder burns when heated, with blue-white flame. Oxide yellow when hot, white when cold	zinc + oxygen ⟶ zinc oxide $2Zn(s) + O_2(g) \longrightarrow 2ZnO(s)$
	Iron	Reacts in cold with water *and* oxygen (i.e. rusts) so not really comparable with the others. Heated *powder* sparkles as it oxidises but does not really burn	iron + oxygen ⟶ iron oxide $3Fe(s) + 2O_2(g) \longrightarrow Fe_3O_4(s)$
	Lead	Oxide layer formed in the cold, but does not burn when heated	lead + oxygen ⟶ lead(II) oxide $2Pb(s) + O_2(g) \longrightarrow 2PbO(s)$
	Copper	Does not form any appreciable oxide layer in cold, although may react with gases in the air to form a green layer. Forms black oxide coating when heated, but this protects the metal below, which does not burn	copper + oxygen ⟶ copper(II) oxide $2Cu(s) + O_2(g) \longrightarrow 2CuO(s)$
	Silver Gold }	no oxide layer, even when heated	

Table 4.2 The reactions of common metals with oxygen in the air

2 REACTIONS OF THE METALS WITH DILUTE ACIDS

The *typical* dilute acids used are usually dilute hydrochloric acid and dilute sulphuric acid. Dilute nitric acid is *not* typical of most acids in the way it reacts with metals. The main details of the reactions are given in Table 4.3.

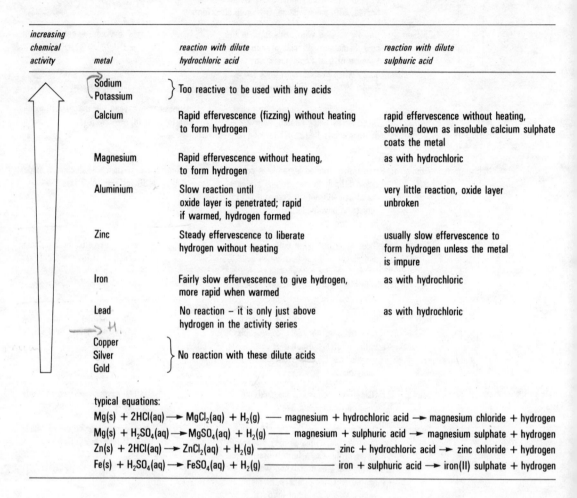

increasing chemical activity	metal	reaction with dilute hydrochloric acid	reaction with dilute sulphuric acid
	Sodium Potassium	} Too reactive to be used with any acids	
	Calcium	Rapid effervescence (fizzing) without heating to form hydrogen	rapid effervescence without heating, slowing down as insoluble calcium sulphate coats the metal
	Magnesium	Rapid effervescence without heating, to form hydrogen	as with hydrochloric
	Aluminium	Slow reaction until oxide layer is penetrated; rapid if warmed, hydrogen formed	very little reaction, oxide layer unbroken
	Zinc	Steady effervescence to liberate hydrogen without heating	usually slow effervescence to form hydrogen unless the metal is impure
	Iron	Fairly slow effervescence to give hydrogen, more rapid when warmed	as with hydrochloric
	Lead	No reaction – it is only just above hydrogen in the activity series	as with hydrochloric
	Copper Silver Gold	} No reaction with these dilute acids	

typical equations:

$Mg(s) + 2HCl(aq) \longrightarrow MgCl_2(aq) + H_2(g)$ —— magnesium + hydrochloric acid → magnesium chloride + hydrogen

$Mg(s) + H_2SO_4(aq) \longrightarrow MgSO_4(aq) + H_2(g)$ —— magnesium + sulphuric acid → magnesium sulphate + hydrogen

$Zn(s) + 2HCl(aq) \longrightarrow ZnCl_2(aq) + H_2(g)$ —————— zinc + hydrochloric acid → zinc chloride + hydrogen

$Fe(s) + H_2SO_4(aq) \longrightarrow FeSO_4(aq) + H_2(g)$ —————— iron + sulphuric acid → iron(II) sulphate + hydrogen

Table 4.3 The reactions of metals with typical acids

Note the following.

(i) There is a group of very active metals (too reactive to add to acids), a group of fairly reactive metals all of which react in a similar way, and a group of unreactive metals.

(ii) Those metals which do react always form a *metal salt* and *hydrogen*. The salt is a **chloride** if hydro**chloric** acid is used, or a **sulphate** if **sulph**uric acid is used.

(iii) Aluminium only shows its 'true' activity if the oxide layer is broken.

3 REACTIONS OF THE METALS WITH WATER OR STEAM

The reactivity of the metals can also be compared by testing small samples of each (a) in cold water, and, if no reaction, (b) by heating the metal in steam. A typical way of doing stage (b) is shown in Fig 4.1. If it is necessary to *collect* any gas formed, the apparatus is changed as shown.

Fig 4.1 The reaction of magnesium with steam

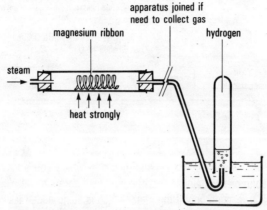

If the gas is collected, great care is needed to prevent 'sucking back'. This can happen if the flame is removed from the test tube while the delivery tube is still under water. The gas in the test tube then contracts, the pressure inside the system falls, and air pressure forces cold water up the delivery tube and perhaps into the hot tube, which may crack.

Typical results are shown in Table 4.4. Note again that the metals follow the same order of reactivity. You may not need all of the details in the Table.

Table 4.4: The reactions of the metals with water or steam

Metal	Reaction
Potassium	Reacts very rapidly with cold water. Metal melts, floats, darts about. Hydrogen gas formed – catches fire (lilac flame) because of heat given out in reaction. Solution of potassium hydroxide formed – turns red litmus blue. POTASSIUM+WATER →POTASSIUM HYDROXIDE+HYDROGEN $2K(l)+2H_2O(l) \rightarrow 2KOH(aq)+H_2(g)$
Sodium	Very similar to potassium, not quite so reactive. Hydrogen formed but does not usually burn. Solution of sodium hydroxide formed. SODIUM+WATER →SODIUM HYDROXIDE+HYDROGEN $2Na(l)+2H_2O(l) \rightarrow 2NaOH(aq)+H_2(g)$
Calcium	Fairly rapid reaction in cold water. Calcium hydroxide formed – some dissolves (lime water), some makes solution cloudy. Solution alkaline. CALCIUM+WATER →CALCIUM HYDROXIDE+HYDROGEN $Ca(s)+2H_2O(l) \rightarrow Ca(OH)_2+H_2(g)$
Magnesium	Very slow in cold water, rapid when heated in steam. MAGNESIUM+STEAM →MAGNESIUM OXIDE+HYDROGEN $Mg(s)+H_2O(g) \rightarrow MgO(s)+H_2(g)$

Metal	Reaction
Aluminium	No reaction (water or steam) due to oxide coat.
Zinc	No reaction unless heated in steam, then fairly rapid. Oxide formed – equation as for Mg.
Iron	Reacts slowly when heated in steam. Unusual oxide formed. (This happens slowly in iron radiators.) IRON+STEAM →IRON OXIDE+HYDROGEN $3Fe(s)+4H_2O(g) \rightleftharpoons Fe_3O_4(s)+4H_2(g)$
Lead, silver, copper, gold }	No reaction in water or steam.

4 REACTIONS OF THE METALS WITH SOLUTIONS OF COMPOUNDS OF OTHER METALS (DISPLACEMENT REACTIONS)

You may have done experiments in which you added small samples of metals to solutions containing a compound of a different metal. You should have found that there is a reaction only if the metal which is being added (as an *element*) is above the other metal (which is in solution as one of its *compounds*), in the Activity Series. The two metals then 'swap' places. The metal which is added **displaces** the other metal from its compound. For example, if magnesium metal is added to a solution of copper(II) sulphate there is a reaction, because magnesium is above copper in the series. Magnesium displaces copper from copper(II) sulphate solution. The magnesium 'dissolves', and copper metal 'precipitates'. The solution slowly changes from blue copper(II) sulphate to colourless magnesium sulphate.

Magnesium+copper(II) sulphate →copper+magnesium sulphate
$Mg(s)+CuSO_4(aq) \rightarrow Cu(s)+MgSO_4(aq)$

Or, if you have studied **ionic equations** (p285):

$Mg(s)+Cu^{2+}(aq) \rightarrow Mg^{2+}(aq)+Cu(s)$

Note that if copper is added to magnesium sulphate solution there is no reaction. Can you explain why not?

Typical displacement reactions are shown below.

$Mg(s)+ZnSO_4(aq) \rightarrow MgSO_4(aq)+Zn(s)$
$Mg(s)+Zn^{2+}(aq) \rightarrow Mg^{2+}(aq)+Zn(s)$

(No colour change.)

$Mg(s)+FeSO_4(aq) \rightarrow MgSO_4(aq)+Fe(s)$
$Mg(s)+Fe^{2+}(aq) \rightarrow Mg^{2+}(aq)+Fe(s)$

(Green colour of iron salt changes to colourless.)

$Zn(s)+FeSO_4(aq) \rightarrow ZnSO_4(aq)+Fe(s)$
$Zn(s)+Fe^{2+}(aq) \rightarrow Zn^{2+}(aq)+Fe(s)$

(Green colour of iron salt changes to colourless.)

$$Zn(s)+CuSO_4(aq) \rightarrow ZnSO_4(aq)+Cu(s)$$
$$Zn(s)+Cu^{2+}(aq) \rightarrow Zn^{2+}(aq)+Cu(s)$$

(Blue colour of copper salt changes to colourless.)

$$Fe(s)+CuSO_4(aq) \rightarrow FeSO_4(aq)+Cu(s)$$
$$Fe(s)+Cu^{2+}(aq) \rightarrow Fe^{2+}(aq)+Cu(s)$$

(Blue colour of copper salt changes to pale green.)

Note the following points.

(i) In the above examples, magnesium shows the most number of displacements because it is highest in the reactivity table. As copper is the least reactive of the metals used, it will not displace any of the others.

(ii) Aluminium does not take part in these reactions because its oxide layer protects it.

(iii) Sodium, potassium, lithium and calcium are not used in displacement reactions. They are so reactive that they also react with the *water* in the solutions, and this complicates the reactions.

4.2 OTHER APPLICATIONS OF THE ACTIVITY SERIES

1 THE REACTIVITY OF THE COMPOUNDS OF THE METALS

You may also have done experiments in which you have compared the reactivity of *compounds* of metals. For example, you may have compared how easily some compounds of metals break up (decompose) when heated. A reaction in which a substance breaks down when it is heated, and the products do not recombine on cooling, is called a **thermal decomposition**. Carbonates and nitrates of metals are often compared in this way.

Compounds of the *reactive* metals are the *least reactive* when heated. A reactive metal forms very stable compounds which are very difficult to decompose. For example, the carbonate of sodium does not decompose when heated (although the hydrated compound will give off water vapour). Calcium carbonate will decompose, but not easily; calcium is lower in the series. Copper, very low in the series, forms a carbonate which decomposes very quickly when heated. The green powder changes to a black solid (copper(II) oxide) and colourless carbon dioxide gas is given off.

$$CaCO_3(s) \rightarrow CaO(s)+CO_2(g) \text{ (No colour change.)}$$
Calcium carbonate $\rightarrow$ Calcium oxide+carbon dioxide
$$CuCO_3(s) \rightarrow CuO(s)+CO_2(g)$$
Copper(II) carbonate $\rightarrow$ copper(II) oxide+carbon dioxide
     (green)   (black)   (colourless)

A similar pattern occurs with the nitrates of metals. **Note**:

(i) When nitrates of metals are heated, small samples are placed in test tubes, which are heated in a *fume cupboard*. Nitrogen dioxide gas, NO_2, may be given off, and it is toxic. It is not necessary to use a fume cupboard with carbonates.

(ii) When **nitr**ates decompose, the brown gas **nitr**ogen dioxide is usually formed. When **carbon**ates decompose, **carbon** dioxide gas is usually formed.

2 THE LINK BETWEEN THE POSITION OF A METAL IN THE ACTIVITY SERIES AND THE METHOD USED IN INDUSTRY TO EXTRACT IT

The Activity Series is almost the reverse of the order in which metals have been discovered and used. Gold and silver are so unreactive with oxygen and water that they are found **native** (as the free element). Either metal is comparatively easy to separate from earth or rock. Gold and silver were thus discovered early in history and used by the earliest civilisations.

Most other metals do not occur as the free element. They are more reactive, and combine with oxygen and other substances to form compounds. These compounds (**minerals** or **ores**) are found mixed with rock, etc. The compound (mineral) has to be separated from the rock, in exactly the same way that native gold has to be separated. Then, however, comes an extra step. This is the chemical reaction needed to break down the compound to form the free element. Sometimes several such steps are needed.

Many minerals are oxides, or are easily made into oxides. The extra step is therefore often a reaction in which oxygen is removed from the oxide to form the metal; the reaction is a **reduction** (p129).

Metal oxide + substance to → free metal + waste products
(mineral, or remove oxygen
formed from (reducing
mineral) agent)

This extra step (reduction) is relatively easy, and requires comparatively little energy, if the metal is fairly low in, or near the centre of, the Activity Series. Compounds of less reactive metals are easy to decompose. The reduction is more difficult and costs more in energy if the metal is high in the series. Compounds of the reactive metals are very difficult to decompose, and methods such as electrolysis have to be used. Metals such as sodium were not discovered until comparatively recently; electrolysis could not be used to extract metals until the nineteenth century.

3 CARBON AND HYDROGEN IN THE ACTIVITY SERIES

These two *non-metals* can be placed in the series. It is useful to know their positions for the following reasons.

(i) Metals are often formed by reducing their oxides. Hydrogen and carbon can be used as reducing agents, e.g.:

lead(II) oxide + hydrogen → lead metal + steam
$PbO(s)$ + $H_2(g)$ → $Pb(s)$ + $H_2O(g)$
lead(II) oxide + carbon → lead metal + carbon monoxide
$PbO(s)$ + $C(s)$ → $Pb(s)$ + $CO(g)$

Hydrogen and carbon will only remove oxygen from oxides of metals which are below them in the series. You may have seen an experiment in which an oxide of lead is placed on a carbon block, in a fume cupboard, and then heated strongly from above. Silvery beads of molten lead are formed as the oxide is reduced to lead by the carbon. You may also have seen an experiment in which copper(II) oxide is heated in a stream of hydrogen gas. The hydrogen reduces the copper(II) oxide to copper metal.

(ii) A metal above hydrogen in the series will displace hydrogen from dilute acids, which are compounds containing hydrogen. Metals below hydrogen, such as copper, do not react with dilute acids to liberate hydrogen (Table 4.3). The only apparent exception is lead, which is shown above hydrogen in the series and yet does not displace it from acids. In fact, lead is so close to hydrogen in the series that they almost share the same place.

4 REACTIONS BETWEEN A METAL AND AN OXIDE OF A METAL

Metals themselves can also be used as reducing agents. If magnesium metal is mixed with copper oxide and the mixture is then heated, the following reaction takes place:

$$\text{magnesium} + \text{copper oxide} \rightarrow \text{magnesium oxide} + \text{copper}$$
$$\text{Mg(s)} \quad + \quad \text{CuO(s)} \qquad \text{MgO(s)} \qquad + \text{Cu(s)}$$

A metal can only reduce an oxide of another metal if it is above the other metal in the series. The opposite reaction to that shown above could not happen; copper could not reduce magnesium oxide to magnesium. It may be helpful to think of this kind of reaction as a 'battle' for oxygen; the more reactive metal wins the battle. You may have seen a demonstration of the 'thermite reaction' in which aluminium reduces iron oxide to iron, giving out a great deal of heat energy in the process.

5 ELECTRICITY FROM CHEMICAL REACTIONS. SIMPLE CELLS

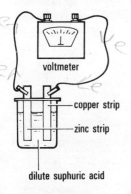

voltmeter

copper strip

zinc strip

dilute suphuric acid

Fig 4.2 A chemical reaction produces an electric current

You may have used apparatus connected as in Fig 4.2. Strips of two different metals (or a metal strip and a carbon rod) are placed in an electrolyte such as a dilute acid. The two **electrodes** are joined by wire through a voltmeter. A current flows between the electrodes, and a voltage is registered on the meter. This will hapopen only if two *different* metals are used, or if a metal and carbon are used as electrodes. Also, the liquid must be an *electrolyte* (p107). This is like the reverse of electrolysis. In electrolysis, electricity is used to cause chemical changes. Here, chemical changes are used to produce electricity.

The current is formed because one of the two electrodes is made of a substance which is a better 'giver of electrons' than the other. It passes electrons through the wire to the other electrode. This flow of electrons is an electric current, and the electrolyte completes the circuit by allowing ions to move between the electrodes. The voltage shown on the meter depends upon the electrodes being used. Metals high in the Activity Series are very good 'givers' of electrons. Metals near the bottom of the series are poor at 'giving' electrons. If the electrodes consist of a metal near the top of the series (e.g. magnesium) and a metal near the bottom (e.g. copper), the voltage is comparatively high. The closer together the two electrodes in the series, the smaller the voltage produced.

Arrangements such as those just described are known as **simple cells**. The Daniell Cell uses zinc and copper as 'electrodes', and copper(II) sulphate solution as the electrolyte. Simple cells like these are rarely used as sources of electricity, because they are not convenient to carry around, they are large and they soon 'run out' of chemicals and stop producing electricity. They led, however, to the common torch battery or **dry cell**, as shown in Fig 4.3. The 'electrodes' in this are zinc (the case) and a carbon rod. The electrolyte is a paste. You may also have studied a storage battery, such as the lead/sulphuric acid batteries used in cars.

Fig 4.3 A dry cell

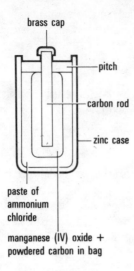

1   Say whether each of the following statements is true or false.
(*a*)   Iron will react with dilute hydrochloric acid to form hydrogen gas.
(*b*)   Copper will react with dilute sulphuric acid to form hydrogen gas.
(*c*)   Copper burns when heated in oxygen.
(*d*)   Nitric acid reacts with metals in the same general way as dilute hydrochloric and dilute sulphuric acids.
(*e*)   If magnesium metal is reacted with dilute sulphuric acid, the salt magnesium sulphate will be formed.
(*f*)   Aluminium reacts when heated in steam.

2   Some reactions of four elements, A,B,C and D are summarised below. Place the elements in an Activity Series.

	Reaction with cold water	Reaction with steam	Reaction when heated in air	Reaction with dilute acid
A	none	reacts when hot to form oxide+hydrogen	does not burn; covered with oxide layer	steady reaction to form hydrogen
B	none	none	does not burn; covered with oxide layer	very slow reaction when warm
C	rapid reaction	not tried	burns to form yellow oxide	rapid reaction to form hydrogen
D	none	none	none	none

3   Gas sometimes collects at the top inside cast iron radiators in central heating systems. The gas is a mixture. Part of it is air, which has been dissolved in the water.
(*a*)   Explain why the dissolved air comes out of solution.

(b)   Using your knowledge of the Activity Series, suggest another gas which may be present, and explain how it could be formed.

4   A carbonate of a metal decomposes rapidly when heated, and gives off carbon dioxide. Where in the Activity Series would you expect the metal to be placed?

5   The oxides of four metals, A,B,C and D are heated separately with carbon. Carbon removes oxygen from the oxides of A,B and C but does not react with the oxide of D. Metal C is then heated with the oxides of the other metals. C will remove oxygen from the oxide of A, but does not react with the oxide of B.

List the metals A,B,C and D in order of reactivity, putting the most reactive first.

6   Decide whether each of the following statements is true or false.

(a)   Hydrogen can be used to reduce iron oxide to iron.
(b)   Zinc will reduce magnesium oxide to magnesium.
(c)   Iron will displace copper from a solution of copper sulphate.
(d)   In a simple cell, a bigger voltage is produced if magnesium and carbon are used as electrodes instead of zinc and carbon.

CHECK LIST ▶   YOU SHOULD UNDERSTAND THE FOLLOWING POINTS.

1 ▶   How to place metals in an activity series, according to how they react with dilute acids, oxygen, water or steam, and by their displacement reactions. (It is not necessary to learn all of the factual details.)

2 ▶   You could be asked to plan some experiments to find where an 'unknown metal' would be placed in the series.

3 ▶   You will almost certainly need to understand some *other* reactions or applications of the Activity Series, as in the second part of the chapter. These vary considerably from one syllabus to another (one syllabus includes all of them). It is very important that you check carefully which of these reactions you are likely to need.

SPECIMEN EXAMINATION QUESTIONS

SEE GENERAL NOTE BEFORE QUESTIONS ON pp.49 AND 50. REMEMBER THAT YOU MAY BE ALLOWED TO USE A DATA BOOK IN THE EXAMINATION.

1   Which one of the following metals reacts most vigorously with water?
A calcium   B magnesium   C potassium   D sodium
[NEA spec (A), 1]

2   A simple cell can be made by dipping two metal strips into dilute sulphuric acid. Which of the following (Fig 4.4) would produce the

Fig 4.4 Diagram for question 2

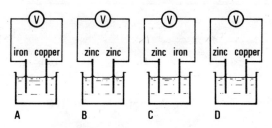

greatest voltage? (In the reactivity series zinc is above iron, and iron is above copper.)

3 In which one of the following sets are all the metals so reactive that they have to be extracted by electrolysis?

A   calcium, copper, silver
B   calcium, magnesium, sodium
C   copper, iron, magnesium
D   iron, magnesium, silver   [Qu 2,3, *SEG* spec (Alt), 1]

4 The following metals are arranged in order of their reactivity: magnesium (most reactive), zinc, iron, copper. Between which of the following pairs of substances will a reaction occur?

A   copper and zinc sulphate
B   magnesium and copper(II) sulphate
C   copper and iron(II) sulphate
D   iron and zinc sulphate
E   zinc and magnesium sulphate   [*LEA* spec (B), 1]

5 (*a*)   From the reactivity series in the data booklet choose
        (i) an element that can occur uncombined in the earth's crust;
        (ii) an element that reacts vigorously with cold water.
    (*b*)   A gas may be made by passing steam over heated zinc using the apparatus shown in Fig 4.5.

Fig 4.5 Diagram for
question 5

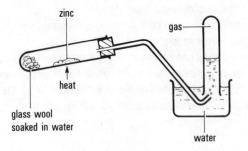

(i) Name the gas collected.
(ii) Name the other product of the reaction.
(iii) Write an equation for the reaction.
(iv) Name one metal that should *not* be reacted with steam in this way. Explain your choice.   [*SEG* spec 1]

6 The table below shows how four metals (W,X,Y and Z) react with dilute hydrochloric acid. (W,X,Y and Z are *not* the chemical symbols.)

Metal	Reaction with dilute hydrochloric acid
W	Slow production of hydrogen
X	Rapid production of hydrogen. Solution gets warm
Y	No reaction
Z	Very fast production of hydrogen. Solution gets hot

(*a*)   Describe a suitable test for hydrogen.

(b)   Arrange the four metals in order of reactivity with the most
reactive metal first.

(c)   When a piece of W is added to copper(II) sulphate solution, a
reaction takes place very slowly. A brown deposit forms on the metal
and the solution turns colourless.

(i) What is the brown deposit formed?

(ii) What type of reaction is taking place?

(iii) What difference would you expect if an equal mass of
powdered metal W was used in place of the single piece of
metal? Explain your answer.   [*LEA* spec (B), 2]

1

1
1
2
6

18 to be

ELECTROLYSIS

CONTENTS

5.1 WHAT IS ELECTROLYSIS? COMMON EXAMPLES

INTRODUCTION

An electric current is a flow of charged particles. This can be either a flow of electrons (in a solid) or a flow of ions (in a liquid). The only substances which conduct electricity in the *solid* state are all the metals, plus carbon (in the form of graphite). These substances are called **conductors.** Conductors do not change chemically when they conduct. A substance which is used to prevent the flow of electricity is called an **insulator.**

Some *solutions* or *pure liquids* also conduct electricity. These are called **electrolytes.** An electrolyte will not conduct when it is in the solid state. Electrolytes (unlike conductors) *do change chemically* when they conduct. (Remember that a solution is not the same as a pure liquid.) You can think of this chemical change as the 'splitting up' of the electrolyte by the electricity. Splitting a solution or pure liquid by electricity is called **electrolysis.**

Rods made of metal or carbon are used to pass electricity into (and out of) an electrolyte. Such rods are called **electrodes.** Electrons leave the battery or power pack and travel through the wire to one of the electrodes. They 'pile up' on this electrode and make it negatively charged. This electrode is called the **negative electrode** or **cathode.** The other electrode is the **positive electrode** or **anode.** To complete the circuit, electrons have to be 'taken off' the negative electrode and an equal number of electrons have to be 'added to' the positive electrode. They then pass up the positive electrode, and go back to the battery or power pack. The ions in the liquid or solution have a job to do: to make the circuit complete. Some ions take electrons off from the negative electrode. Ions of a different kind give up electrons at the positive electrode.

A liquid or solution can only be an electrolyte if it contains **ions.** A compound formed between a metal and a non-metal will contain ions (p30), and be an electrolyte. These ions have to be free to *move* about between the electrodes before they can carry a current. This is why a solid electrolyte cannot conduct; its ions are not free to move about. When the ions are dissolved in water or when they are melted to form a pure liquid, they can then move around. The ions, being charged, are attracted by the charges on the two electrodes. Positively charged ions are attracted to the negative electrode (cathode). Such ions are sometimes called **cations.** Negatively charged ions are attracted to the positive electrode (anode). Such ions are sometimes called **anions.**

A liquid or solution which contains only *molecules* cannot act as an electrolyte. The bonds inside such a substance are covalent (p33). There are no charged particles inside such a liquid to help transfer electrons from one electrode to the other. A substance which consists of non-metals only (e.g. ethanol, C_2H_5OH) will contain covalent bonds and cannot be an electrolyte. Electrolysis is evidence for the existence of ions.

An apparatus used to pass electricity through a solution or liquid is called an **electrolysis cell.** There are various kinds, such as those shown in Fig 5.1.

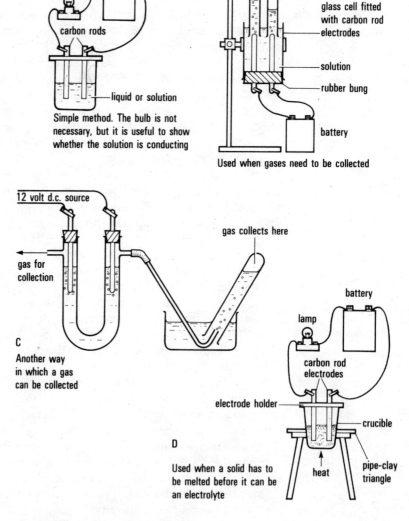

Fig 5.1 Different kinds of electrolysis cell

SUMMARY

For a substance to act as an electrolyte:
(*a*) it must contain ions; and
(*b*) it must be dissolved in water, or melted.
When a low voltage direct current is then used:
(*a*) the electrolyte conducts electricity; and
(*b*) chemical changes take place at both electrodes.
In general, metals (or hydrogen) are formed at the negative electrode (cathode). Non-metals (except hydrogen) are formed at the positive electrode (anode).

Note A *low voltage, direct current* is used in electrolysis. This is completely different from using mains electricity, which is at a higher voltage (e.g. 240 volts) and is alternating current (a.c.).

A MORE DETAILED EXPLANATION OF WHAT HAPPENS IN ELECTROLYSIS

Let us consider what happens when melted sodium chloride (common salt) is electrolysed. This reaction is used on a large scale in industry to make sodium metal (p116). It is used here as an example because there are only two kinds of particle present: sodium ions and chloride ions.

The ions present from the sodium chloride are Na^+ and Cl^-. We show this by writing: $NaCl(s) \rightarrow Na^+(l) + Cl^-(l)$.

Electrons from the battery (an electric current) go to one electrode (the cathode) and make it negatively charged. This attracts the positively charged sodium ions, Na^+. Positively charged ions are atoms which have lost electrons (p32). They therefore have a 'vacancy' for electrons. The sodium ions each take one electron from the cathode and change back into neutral sodium atoms. We show this by writing: $Na^+ + e^- \rightarrow Na$. A change like this *always* happens at the negatively charged electrode; positively charged ions gain electrons and become atoms. The electrode *loses* electrons. A chemical change always takes place; in this example, sodium metal is formed. Remember, however, that some metal ions each need to gain two or three electrons in order to change back into neutral atoms, e.g.:

$$Cu^{2+} + 2e^- \rightarrow Cu$$
$$Al^{3+} + 3e^- \rightarrow Al$$

All metal ions and hydrogen ions are positively charged, so they can be **discharged** at the cathode and change back into neutral atoms.

The negatively charged chloride ions, Cl^-, are attracted to the positively charged electrode (anode). Negatively charged ions are atoms which have gained extra electrons. The chloride ions which arrive at the positively charged electrode are discharged by each losing its 'extra' electron. The electrons which are 'given up' go into the electrode and pass back to the battery to complete the circuit. The chloride ions become neutral chlorine atoms. As chlorine atoms 'go around' in pairs, they each find a partner and form a chlorine molecule, Cl_2. Chlorine gas is thus formed at the electrode and bubbles off. We show the change at the electrode as:

$$Cl^- - e^- \rightarrow Cl \text{ (or } Cl^- \rightarrow Cl + e^-)$$
$$2Cl \rightarrow Cl_2$$

A change similar to this always happens at the anode. Negatively charged ions *lose* electrons and become *atoms*. In most cases, these will be atoms of a gas, and they join together in pairs to form molecules. The gas bubbles off. A chemical change therefore takes place at the electrode. The electrons which are given up by the ions go back to the battery and complete the circuit.

Note that electrons do not actually pass through the liquid. They appear to do so, however, as the battery continuously sends electrons down to the negatively charged electrode and receives an *equal* number back from the positive electrode. (see Fig 5.2).

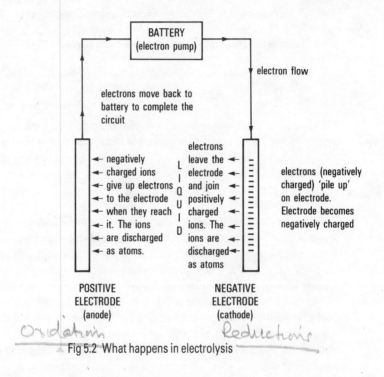

Fig 5.2 What happens in electrolysis

Note the following points. They are often confused.

1 Negative ions *lose* electrons when they are discharged at an electrode.
2 Positive ions *gain* electrons when they are discharged at an electrode.
3 Gas atoms normally join in pairs to form molecules. For example, it is incorrect to suggest that chlorine atoms, Cl, are the *final* products at an electrode, but correct to state that chlorine molecules, Cl_2, are formed.
4 Each ion loses or gains the *same* number of electrons as the *charge* on it, when it is discharged at an electrode (see examples which follow).

COMMON EXAMPLES OF ELECTRODE REACTIONS IN ELECTROLYSIS

Learn

(a) AT THE NEGATIVE ELECTRODE (CATHODE)

$$H^+ + e^- \rightarrow H, \text{ and then } 2H \rightarrow H_2.$$

(The hydrogen ions usually come from a dilute acid, or from water in the solution.)

$$Na^+ + e^- \rightarrow Na. \quad 23g$$

(Sodium ions are usually discharged only when they come from a *melted* sodium compound.)

$$Cu^{2+} + 2e^- \rightarrow Cu.$$

(The copper ions come from solutions of copper compounds.)

$$Al^{3+} + 3e^- \rightarrow Al. \quad 27g$$

(b) AT THE POSITIVE ELECTRODE (ANODE)

$$Cl^- - e^- \rightarrow Cl (\text{or } Cl^- \rightarrow Cl + e^-), \text{ and then } 2Cl \rightarrow Cl_2.$$

(The choloride ions can come from *dissolved* or *melted* ionic chlorides, such as NaCl.)

$$O^{2-} - 2e^- \rightarrow O, \text{ and then } 2O \rightarrow O_2.$$

(See p.118.)

$$OH^- - e^- \rightarrow OH, \text{ and then } 4OH \rightarrow 2H_2O + O_2.$$

(The hydroxide ions can come from *dissolved* or *melted* ionic hydroxides such as NaOH, or from the water present in a solution.)

SOME TYPICAL ELECTROLYSIS EXPERIMENTS

Note: ions from water

Although water consists of *molecules*, H_2O, and is *covalently* bonded, a *few* of these molecules split into ions:

$$H_2O \rightarrow H^+ + OH^-.$$

These ions are always present in any solution in water, in addition to any ions which may come from the dissolved substance. The ions from water often take part in electrolysis reactions, and are discharged at the electrodes. Only a few water molecules at any moment split up like this, but as soon as one is discharged at an electrode, another forms to take its place.

Note that examples of electrolysis may vary from one syllabus to another. Make sure that you understand the ones you have used in your course. Examples not included in this book are copper (II) sulphate *with copper electrodes* (and its application in industry to the purification of copper), molten lead bromide, and molten lithium chloride.

(a) THE ELECTROLYSIS OF COPPER(II) CHLORIDE SOLUTION, USING CARBON ELECTRODES

In this example the ions from the water in the solution take no part in the reactions at the electrodes. The only ions involved are the copper ions, Cu^{2+}, and the chloride ions, Cl^-, from the dissolved copper(II) chloride, $CuCl_2$.

$$CuCl_2 \rightarrow Cu^{2+} + 2Cl^-$$

blue

At the negative electrode (cathode)

Copper ions are attracted and discharged. They change chemically into copper metal. The copper coats the electrode to form a pink-brown coating.

$$Cu^{2+} + 2e^- \rightarrow Cu$$

blue

At the positive electrode (anode)

Chloride ions are attracted and discharged. They change chemically into chlorine gas, which bubbles off.

$$Cl^- - e^- \rightarrow Cl \text{ (or } Cl^- \rightarrow Cl + e^-\text{), and then } 2Cl \rightarrow Cl_2$$

Changes in the solution

As the electrolysis continues, the blue colour of the solution gradually fades as the copper ions are removed.

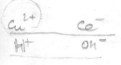

(b) THE ELECTROLYSIS OF DILUTE HYDROCHLORIC ACID, USING CARBON ELECTRODES

OMIT for NEA.

In this example, the ions from the water in the solution appear to take no part in the reactions at the electrodes. The ions involved come from the hydrochloric acid.

$$HCl(aq) \rightarrow H^+(aq) + Cl^-(aq)$$

At the negative electrode (cathode)

Hydrogen ions are attracted and discharged. They change chemically into hydrogen gas, which bubbles off.

$$H^+ + e^- \rightarrow H, \text{ and then } 2H \rightarrow H_2.$$

At the positive electrode (anode)

Chloride ions are attracted and discharged. They change chemically into chlorine gas, which bubbles off:

$$Cl^- - e^- \rightarrow Cl \text{ (or } Cl^- \rightarrow Cl + e^-\text{), and then } 2Cl \rightarrow Cl_2.$$

Changes in the solution

No visible changes. Acid gradually becomes dilute and electrolysis stops when ions are 'used up'.

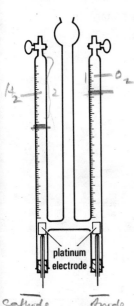

cathode   Anode

Fig 5.3 Another electrolysis cell – the Hofmann voltameter

(c) ELECTROLYSIS OF 'ACIDIFIED WATER' (DILUTE SULPHURIC ACID)

In this example, it *appears* as if only ions from the water take part in the reactions at the electrodes. The ions from the acid *appear* not to take part. The Hofmann voltameter (Fig 5.3) is normally used for this experiment, with platinum electrodes.

Ions from the acid: $H_2SO_4 \rightarrow 2H^+ + SO_4^{2-}$
Ions from water: $H_2O \rightarrow 2H^+ + OH^-$

At the negative electrode (cathode)

Hydrogen ions are attracted and discharged. They change chemically into hydrogen gas, which bubbles off.

$H^+ + e^- \rightarrow H$, and then $2H \rightarrow H_2$.

(Some of these hydrogen ions come from the acid, and some from the water, but the *effect* is as if they all come from water.)

At the positive electrode (anode)

Hydroxide ions are attracted and discharged. They change chemically into hydroxide radicals, which instantly form water molecules and oxygen gas. The oxygen bubbles off.

$OH^- - e^- \rightarrow OH$ (or $OH^- \rightarrow OH + e^-$), and then $4OH \rightarrow 2H_2O + O_2$.

The sulphate ions remain unchanged in the solution.

Note If there are two different kinds of positively charged ions, or two different kinds of negatively charged ions, both types are attracted to the appropriate electrode, but only *one* type is discharged. In this example, sulphate ions (as well as hydroxide ions) are attracted to the positive electrode, but only hydroxide ions are discharged.

If a Hofmann voltameter is used for this experiment, the volumes of the gases can be measured. The volume of hydrogen collected at the cathode is almost exactly double the volume of oxygen collected at the anode. (It would be exactly double if the two gases were equally soluble in water. Oxygen is slightly more soluble than hydrogen, so that more of it dissolves in the electrolyte, and its volume is less than that of the hydrogen.) This experiment is sometimes used to show that water is made by joining two volumes of hydrogen with one volume of oxygen, because water appears to 'split up' to produce volumes of the two gases in this ratio.

Changes in the solution

The electrolyte behaves as if only water is being 'split up'. The ions from the acid effectively remain unchanged. As the reaction proceeds, the acid becomes more and more concentrated.

OM IT
for NEA

(d) ELECTROLYSIS OF COPPER (II) SULPHATE SOLUTION WITH CARBON OR PLATINUM ELECTRODES

Ions come from both the dissolved copper sulphate and water:

$$CuSO_4(s) \rightarrow Cu^{2+}(aq) + SO_4^{2-}(aq)$$
$$H_2O(l) \rightarrow 2H^+(aq) + OH^-(aq)$$

At the negative electrode (cathode)
Copper ions are attracted and discharged. They change chemically and become copper metal, which coats the electrode.

$$Cu^{2+} + 2e^- \rightarrow Cu$$

At the positive electrode (anode)
Hydroxide ions are attracted and discharged. They change chemically and become hydroxide radicals, which instantly form water molecules and oxygen gas. The oxygen bubbles off.

$$OH^- - e^- \rightarrow OH, \text{ and then } 4OH \rightarrow 2H_2O + O_2.$$

Changes in the solution
The 'other' ions in the solution (H^+ and SO_4^{2-}) gradually become more concentrated as the Cu^{2+} and OH^- ions are discharged. The solution gradually becomes dilute sulphuric acid. The blue colour fades as the copper ions are used up.

(e) ELECTROLYSIS OF SODIUM CHLORIDE SOLUTION (BRINE) USING CARBON ELECTRODES

Ions come from both the dissolved sodium chloride and water:

$$NaCl(s) \rightarrow Na^+(aq) + Cl^-(aq)$$
$$H_2O(l) \rightarrow H^+(aq) + OH^-(aq)$$

At the negative electrode (cathode)
Hydrogen ions are attracted and discharged. They change chemically into hydrogen gas, which bubbles off.

$$H^+ + e^- \rightarrow H, \text{ and then } 2H \rightarrow H_2.$$

At the positive electrode (anode)
Chloride ions are attracted and discharged. They change chemically into chlorine gas, which bubbles off.

$$Cl^- - e^- \rightarrow Cl \text{ (or } Cl^- \rightarrow Cl + e^-\text{), and then } 2Cl \rightarrow Cl_2.$$

Note If *melted* sodium chloride is electrolysed (p116), the products are different.

Changes in the solution
As H^+ and Cl^- ions are discharged, the 'other' ions (Na^+ and OH^-) gradually become more concentrated in solution. The solution gradually changes to dilute sodium hydroxide solution.

PREDICTING WHAT WILL BE FORMED IN AN ELECTROLYSIS

Remember: only *ionically* bonded substances can act as electrolytes.

If the substance is *melted*, it is easy to predict what the products will be. There will be only two types of ion present. The negatively charged ones will be discharged at the anode usually to form a gas. The positively charged ions will be discharged at the cathode, usually to form a metal or hydrogen.

If the substance is in solution, up to four different types of ion will be present. There will be H^+ and OH^- from the water, and other ions from the dissolved substance. Only *one* kind of ion will be discharged at each electrode. If the negatively charged ions include Cl^-, this will nearly always be discharged in preference to any others. If chloride ions (or other halide ions) are not present, usually hydroxide ions from the water are discharged. Radicals such as SO_4^{2-} and NO_3^- are not discharged.

If one of the positively charged ions is formed from a metal low in the Activity Series (e.g. Cu^{2+}), usually it will be discharged in preference to any other. Otherwise, H^+ ions from the water are normally discharged. These are only very general guidelines, because the concentration of each kind of ion is also important.

Mass changes in electrolysis. The faraday constant

One or two syllabuses include experiments and calculations on the quantity of electricity involved in the formation of a certain mass of product at an electrode. You may have used a unit called the **faraday** constant in this connection, and related the quantity of electricity needed to the charge on the ion being discharged. Revise this work if necessary.

CHECK YOUR UNDERSTANDING (Answers on p410)

1 Name six substances which will conduct in the solid state.

2 Sodium chloride cannot act as an electrolyte when it is in the solid state. Why not?

3 W and X are metals. Y and Z are non-metals. Which of the following compounds would be expected to act as an electrolyte?
WX_2 W_2Y YZ XZ

4 Which of the following substances could act as electrolytes? Ethanol, C_2H_5OH; sodium hydroxide, $NaOH$; potassium bromide, KBr; sulphur chloride, SCl_2; water, H_2O; sugar, $C_6H_{12}O_6$.

5 What *kinds* of substance are usually formed at the positive electrode in electrolysis?

6 Copper ions, Cu^{2+}, are attracted to an electrode during an electrolysis experiment.
(*a*)   Which electrode are they attracted towards?
(*b*)   Will copper ions *lose* electrons, or will they *gain* electrons, when they are discharged at the electrode?
(*c*)   How many electrons will each copper ion lose or gain?
(*d*)   Show what happens at the electrode by writing an 'equation'.

7 Ask yourself the same questions as in question 6, but this time about chloride ions, not copper ions. (A chloride ion is Cl^-.)

$Cu^{2+} + 2e \rightarrow Cu_{(s)}$

$Cl^- - e \rightarrow Cl$
$2Cl \rightarrow Cl_2$

8 What is wrong with each of the following?

(a) Chlorine atoms bubble off at the positive electrode when a solution of sodium chloride (brine) is electrolysed.

(b) $Al^{3+} + 2e^- \rightarrow Al$

(c) $Br^- + e^- \rightarrow Br$

9 An electric current was passed through an unknown solution. Two gases were formed. The gas formed at the positive electrode bleached damp blue litmus paper, and had a sharp smell. The gas formed at the negative electrode burned with a squeaky pop. The solution was probably

A sodium hydroxide   B hydrochloric acid   C nitric acid

D sulphuric acid   E copper(II) sulphate.

10 Predict the likely products at each electrode when each of the following substances is electrolysed. Also, predict any changes which should occur within the electrolyte as each reaction takes place.

(a) copper(II) bromide solution, ($CuBr_2$)

(b) sodium iodide solution, (NaI)

(c) melted potassium bromide, (KBr)

(d) copper(II) nitrate solution, ($Cu(NO_3)_2$).

11 When copper sulphate solution is electrolysed, the blue colour gradually fades and the solution becomes acidic. Explain these changes.

12 When dilute hydrochloric acid is electrolysed,

(i) equal volumes of hydrogen and chlorine are produced, but

(ii) the volume of hydrogen collected is usually greater than the volume of chlorine collected. Can you explain *each* of these apparently contradictory statements?

5.2 USES OF ELECTROLYSIS

1 PRODUCTION OF METALS IN INDUSTRY

Metals near to the top of the Activity Series are more difficult to separate from their compounds than those lower in the Series (p98). Also, more energy is needed to make the separation. Sodium and aluminium are metals near the top of the Activity Series. They have to be separated from their compounds by electrolysis.

(a) THE PRODUCTION OF SODIUM METAL

Sodium is manufactured in the Downs Cell (Fig 5.4; the details in the diagram do not have to be learned). The electrolyte is *molten* sodium chloride (to which some calcium chloride is added). The only ions which take part in the reaction are from the sodium chloride:

$$NaCl(s) \rightarrow Na^+(l) + Cl^-(l).$$

Sodium forms at the negative electrode (cathode):

$$Na^+ + e^- \rightarrow Na.$$

Fig 5.4 The Downs cell for the production of sodium

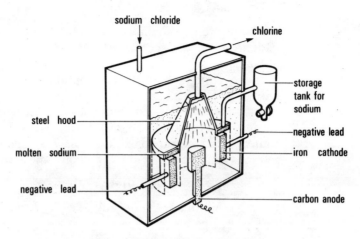

Note that the steel hood prevents the chlorine from coming into contact with the sodium metal. (They would react.) It also prevents sodium from reacting with the air.

Chlorine gas forms at the positive electrode (anode):

$$Cl^- - e^- \rightarrow Cl \text{ (or } Cl^- \rightarrow Cl + e^-), \text{ and then } 2Cl \rightarrow Cl_2.$$

Economic and environmental points

(i) Sodium chloride has a fairly high melting point (801°C). It would take a great deal of heat energy to melt it and to keep it molten. The melting point is lowered to about 600°C by adding some calcium chloride. This acts as an 'impurity' to the sodium chloride and lowers the melting point (p84), but does not affect the reaction. This allows a considerable saving on energy needed to heat the electrolyte.

(ii) *Both* products (sodium and chlorine) have important uses. Both can therefore be sold, which helps to make the process economical.

(iii) The raw material, sodium chloride, is readily available in Britain, and comparatively cheap. It can be 'mined' without causing serious environmental problems (p394).

(iv) There are no waste materials, and no other pollution problems which could affect the environment.

(v) In spite of all these good economic points, the process still has high running costs, because of the electrical energy needed. Some of this is used to keep the electrolyte molten, and the rest is used for the electrolysis.

(b) THE PRODUCTION OF ALUMINIUM METAL

The main ore of aluminium is **bauxite,** which is impure aluminium oxide, Al_2O_3. This is not found in Britain. It is obtained from Australia and Jamaica, where it is purified and then shipped.

The electrolyte is purified aluminium oxide, which is mixed with another (melted) aluminium compound commonly called **cryolite.** A typical industrial cell is shown in Fig 5.5; the details do not have to be learned. The carbon lining of the tank acts as the negative electrode (cathode), and the carbon blocks act as the positive electrode (anode). The only ions which take part in the reaction come from the aluminium oxide:

$$Al_2O_3(s) \rightarrow 2Al^{3+}(l) + 3O^{2-}(l)$$

Aluminium forms at the negative electrode, where it melts because of the high temperature:

$$Al^{3+} + 3e^- \rightarrow Al.$$

Oxygen is formed at the positive electrode:

$$O^{2-} - 2e^- \rightarrow O \text{ (or } O^{2-} \rightarrow O + 2e^-\text{), and then } 2O \rightarrow O_2.$$

Fig 5.5 The extraction of aluminium by electrolysis

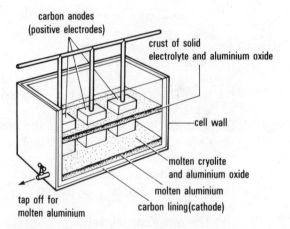

Economic and environmental points

(i) Aluminium oxide has a high melting point (around 2050°C). However, it can be dissolved in molten cryolite at around 900°C. The solution formed is an electrolyte. This greatly reduces the heat energy needed.

(ii) The carbon anodes are rapidly worn away because they react with the oxygen to form carbon dioxide. They need to be replaced regularly, and this is expensive. Typically, a set is replaced each day. This reaction also causes another problem. The oxygen cannot be sold, because it is mixed with carbon dioxide, carbon monoxide and fluoride fumes. The process thus produces only one useful product, unlike the electrolysis of molten sodium chloride.

(iii) There is no solid waste, and the main by-products, oxygen and carbon dioxide, do not cause pollution.

(iv) The main cost of the process is the large amount of electricity it uses. Each Al^{3+} ion needs three electrons to be changed into an aluminium atom, compared with only one electron per sodium ion in the previous process. In addition, about one-third of the electrical energy is used to keep the electrolyte molten.

(v) Another expense is the cost of transporting the ore. For this reason, and the previous one, aluminium smelters are built on sites where transport costs are kept to a minimum (e.g. near a port) and where electricity is easily available (e.g. near a source of hydroelectric power, or near a special power station).

(vi) Aluminium is the most abundant metal in the earth's crust. All clays and many rocks contain the metal as a compound. At the moment, however, only bauxite can be used to extract the metal economically. The world's supplies of bauxite are large but they will not last for ever. The recycling of aluminium (p140) is very important.

2. THE PRODUCTION OF SODIUM HYDROXIDE AND CHLORINE

Both of these substances are produced by the electrolysis of sodium chloride solution (brine). The products are very important industrial chemicals, and the process is important on a large scale. Various types of electrolysis cell are used, all designed to produce good yields of pure products. If you have studied one of the cells in detail, make sure that you understand how it works.

Hydrogen is formed at the negative electrode (cathode), and chlorine gas at the positive electrode (anode). As the hydrogen and chloride ions are removed from the electrolyte, sodium ions (from the sodium chloride) and hydroxide ions (from the water) gradually become more concentrated. Eventually, the solution becomes sodium hydroxide with a little sodium chloride. The sodium chloride is removed to leave fairly pure sodium hydroxide. See p.114 for the equations and the basic process.

Economic and environmental points

(i) Three products are obtained, all of which can be sold, and this greatly helps the economics of the process. Chlorine has many uses (p321), hydrogen is in demand (p220), and sodium hydroxide is a very important alkali (p156).

(ii) The starting material, sodium chloride, is readily available in Britain, and relatively cheap.

(iii) There is no solid waste, and no pollutant gases should enter the atmosphere.

(iv) Less energy is needed per tonne of product than for extracting sodium or aluminium.

ELECTROPLATING

This is the process of coating an object (usually made of metal) with a thin layer of a different metal by electrolysis. This is a useful way of protecting a metal from corrosion, e.g. by plating steel (which easily rusts) with a layer of nickel, chromium or gold. The process is also used to make a metal object more attractive.

The object which is to be plated is cleaned very thoroughly and then used as the negative electrode (cathode) in an electrolysis cell. The electrolyte is a solution of a compound which contains the 'plating' metal, e.g. copper(II) sulphate solution (for plating with copper) or nickel sulphate solution (for plating with nickel). The positive electrode (anode) is usually made of carbon, or of the same metal which is being plated on to the object. The positively charged metal ions in the electrolyte (e.g. Cu^{2+} or Ni^{2+}) are attracted to the negatively charged 'object'. The metal ions receive electrons, are discharged, form metal atoms, and coat the object with a layer of metal.

4. ANODISING

Aluminium metal is normally very unreactive because it is protected by a thin but strong layer of aluminium oxide (p92). If the layer of oxide can be made thicker than usual, it protects the metal even more, and it has another advantage. The oxide layer can be dyed (most pure metals cannot be dyed). Also, the dyed surface is very strong, and does not wear easily. Objects made of this 'special' aluminium are resistant to attack by chemicals, they will not corrode, and they can be attractively coloured, e.g. saucepans. This extra layer of oxide is made by a process called **anodising.** The aluminium is made the positive electrode (anode) in an electrolysis cell. The electrolyte is chosen to make sure that oxygen gas is formed at the positive electrode. (Sulphuric acid is commonly used as the electrolyte.) The oxygen reacts with the aluminium to produce a thicker layer of oxide on the metal.

CHECK LIST ▶

REMEMBER THAT SOME OF THESE POINTS MAY NOT BE RELEVANT FOR THE PARTICULAR SYLLABUS YOU ARE FOLLOWING.
YOU SHOULD UNDERSTAND THE FOLLOWING POINTS.

1 ▶ How to use apparatus to decide whether a solution/liquid is an electrolyte (e.g. Fig 5.1A), and whether a solid is a conductor (by modifying the apparatus).

2 ▶ The meaning of any special words used in your syllabus, such as electrode, anode, cathode, anion, cation, discharge.

3 ▶ The difference between conduction of electricity in a solid and in a solution/liquid.

4 ▶ A substance can only be an electrolyte if it contains *ions* and is *dissolved* or *melted*. It changes chemically when it conducts.

5 ▶ Apparatus used to do electrolysis experiments.

6 ▶ Metals (and hydrogen) are formed at the negative electrode (cathode). Non-metals (except hydrogen) are formed at the positive electrode (anode). Most non-metals discharged in

electrolysis are gases, which first form as atoms, but these immediately 'double up' to form molecules.

7 ▶ Examples of electrolysis as used in your syllabus.

8 ▶ Examples of how electrolysis is used in industry.

9 ▶ If you intend to aim for a high grade, you will be expected to have a clear understanding of what happens in electrolysis, to write equations for what happens at each electrode, and to predict what will happen in unfamiliar examples.

SPECIMEN EXAMINATION QUESTIONS

SEE GENERAL NOTE BEFORE QUESTIONS ON pp.49 AND 50. REMEMBER THAT YOU MAY BE ALLOWED TO USE A DATA BOOK IN THE EXAMINATION.

1 Which one of the following will conduct electricity?

A ethanol   B hexane   C sodium chloride crystals

D molten alumina

2 The reaction taking place at the negative electrode during the electroplating of copper can be represented by the equation:

A $Cu \rightarrow Cu^{2+} + 2e^-$ B $Cu^{2+} + e^- \rightarrow Cu$

C $Cu^{2+} + 2e^- \rightarrow Cu$ D $Cu^{2+} + 2e^- \rightarrow 2Cu$

[NEA spec (A), 1]

3 When dilute sulphuric acid is electrolysed using carbon electrodes, the gases produced at each electrode are

	Cathode	Anode
A	CO_2	CO_2
B	O_2	H_2
C	CO_2	H_2
D	H_2	O_2
E	H_2	CO_2

[LEA spec (B), 1]

4 Which one of the following elements forms at the cathode when a mixture of sodium chloride and potassium chloride is electrolysed?

A chlorine   B hydrogen   C potassium   D sodium

[SEG spec (Alt), 1]

5 A chemical reaction occurs when

A   an electric current is passed through a copper wire

B   salt solution is heated

C   crude oil is distilled

D   dilute hydrochloric acid is added to magnesium ribbon at room temperature

E   ice melts to form water

6 Aluminium is obtained industrially by

A   reaction of aluminium oxide with carbon in a blast furnace

B   reaction of aluminium oxide with carbon monoxide in a blast furnace

C   electrolysis using aluminium chloride

D   electrolysis using aluminium sulphate

E   electrolysis using aluminium oxide   [LEA spec (A), 1]

7   Which *one* of the following substances will conduct an electric current without undergoing chemical change?

A sodium chloride solution   B distilled water   C copper foil

D molten lithium chloride   E dilute hydrochloric acid

8   In the electrolytic refining of copper the cathode is made of

A carbon   B copper   C iron   D platinum   E zinc

[*NISEC* spec 1]

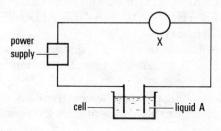

Fig 5.6 Diagram for question 9

9   Liquid A is to be electrolysed (Fig 5.6).

(*a*)   What type of power supply is suitable for this purpose?

(*b*)   What piece of apparatus could be connected at X to show that liquid A is a conductor?

(*c*)   Give the name of the charged particles which conduct the electric current in

(i) the connecting wires,

(ii) the electrolyte.

(*d*)   A metal kettle is to be coated with copper using electrolysis. State what you would use in the cell as

(i) anode,

(ii) cathode,

(iii) electrolyte.   [*LEA* spec (A), 2]

10   Read the following passage carefully. Using the information it contains, and your knowledge of chemistry, answer questions (a) to (k) which follow it.

Sodium and its extraction

Of the many salts dissolved in sea water, common salt (sodium chloride) is the most abundant, comprising some 3% of mass of the world's oceans. In England, deposits of sodium chloride are found in Cheshire, Lancashire and Durham.

The production of sodium requires a high energy process. It is produced by the electrolysis of molten sodium chloride in the Downs cell. Here the molten sodium chloride contains calcium chloride to lower its melting point. Once the process has been started, the very high current used keeps the electrolyte in the molten state. Sodium metal is produced at the cathode.

Very little waste material is produced from this process. The by-product of the reaction, chlorine, is of great commercial importance. It is, in fact, in greater demand than sodium itself!

Compared to some metals like aluminium, metallic sodium has relatively few uses. The annual world production of aluminium is about 14 million tonnes, while 0.2 million tonnes of sodium is produced each year. Sodium is used as a coolant in some nuclear reactors, in sodium vapour street lamps, and in the manufacture of sodium salts.

(a)   Name the chief natural source of the metal sodium.

(b)   By what method is sodium obtained from this source?

(c)   State how the sodium chloride is kept in the molten state during the process.

(d)   Explain why it is desirable to lower the melting point of the sodium chloride.

(e)   Give the formula of the substance used to lower the melting point.

(f)   State one advantage of this process from a pollution point of view and also one commercial advantage.

(g)   Give two uses of the by-product.

(h)   The electrodes used in the production of sodium must be capable of withstanding very high temperatures and must not react at all with any of the substances present (i.e. be inert). Name a substance which would be suitable to act as an electrode.

(i)   Sodium is a very reactive metal which will react explosively with many other elements. Name two elements which must be kept away from the sodium while it is being formed and stored.

(j)   Suggest two reasons why sodium is suitable as a coolant in nuclear reactors.

(k)   Many street lamps give out yellow light. Explain why this tells you that sodium is present in these lamps. [NISEC spec 2]

†11   Fig 5.7 shows the electrolysis of sodium chloride solution.

Fig 5.7 Diagram for question 11

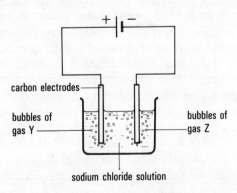

(a)   Name the gases Y and Z.

(b)   If a few drops of universal indicator are added to the solution before electrolysis starts, the indicator is green. As electrolysis happens, the indicator gradually turns blue.

(i) What is the pH of the solution when the indicator is green?

(ii) Explain why the electrolysis causes the indicator to go blue.

(iii) Name a compound produced on an industrial scale by electrolysis of sodium chloride solution.

(c)   In the electrolysis of copper(II) chloride solution the electron transfer at the negative electrode is shown by the following equation: $Cu^{2+}(aq)+2e^- \rightarrow Cu(s)$.

(i) What does (aq) stand for?

(ii) What would you expect to *see* at the negative electrode during the electrolysis?

(d)   The table gives information about three substances A,B and C when they are solid and when they are molten.

Solid substance			Molten substance		
Substance	Appearance of solid	Does the solid conduct electricity?	Does the melt conduct electricity?	Product at + electrode	Product at – electrode
A	white solid	no	yes	bromine	lead metal
B	yellow solid	no	no		(does not conduct)
C	grey solid	yes	yes	none	none

(i) Suggest possible identities for substances A and B.

(ii) What type of bonding does solid B have?

(iii)What type of bonding does solid C have?

(iv) When the melted substance A conducts electricity what particles are carrying the current?

(e)   (i) Predict the products of the electrolysis of an aqueous solution of aluminium sulphate using inert electrodes. Explain how you arrive at your answer.

(ii) Why is cryolite added to aluminium oxide during the electrolytic manufacture of aluminium?   [*SEG* spec 3]

†12   When copper(II) sulphate solution is electrolysed between platinum electrodes, the equation for the overall changes taking place can be written as:

$$2CuSO_4(aq)+2H_2O(l) \rightarrow 2Cu(s)+O_2(g)+2H_2SO_4(aq)$$

(a)   (i) Describe what you would **see** at the cathode.

(ii) Write an ionic half-equation for the reaction occurring at the cathode.

(b)   (i) Describe what you would **see** at the anode.

(ii) Describe a test for the anode product.

(iii) Write an ionic half-equation for the reaction occurring at the anode.

(c)   If 1.27 g of copper are produced, calculate the volume of oxygen, measured at room temperature and atmospheric pressure, that would be produced in the same time. (Relative atomic mass: Cu = 63.5; 1 mole of any gas at room temperature and atmospheric pressure occupies 24 000 cm³)

(d)   Copper is purified on a large scale electrolytically. What economic and environmental issues might influence the siting of the purification plant?

(e)   State what material is used as the
(i) cathode,
(ii) anode,
(iii) electrolyte.

(f)   (i) During the process a slime or sludge forms under one electrode. Give the name of the electrode under which it forms.
(ii) Suggest a reason why a part of the slime may be valuable.

[LEA spec (A), 3]

†13 The following results were obtained during the electrolysis of 500 cm³ of aqueous copper(II) sulphate using carbon electrodes.

Total mass of copper deposited on the cathode/g	Time current was passed
0.70	30 minutes
1.40	1 hour
2.75	2 hours
3.00	2½ hours
3.00	3 hours
3.00	3½ hours

(a)   Draw a labelled diagram of the apparatus you could use, including the electrical circuit, in order to carry out this electrolysis.

(b)   (i) Plot the results on the graph (Fig 5.8)

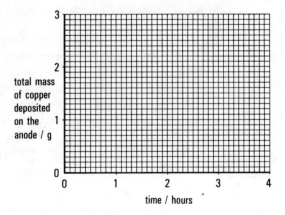

Fig 5.8 Graph for question 13

(ii) What is the total mass of copper deposited on the cathode after the current has passed for 1½ hours?

(iii) Calculate the concentration, in mol/dm³, of the original aqueous copper(II) sulphate.

(iv) Suggest **two** reasons why some metal objects are copper plated. [(MEG, spec 3]

†14　The apparatus (Fig 5.9) was used to find the charge on a chromium ion.

Fig 5.9 Diagram for question 14

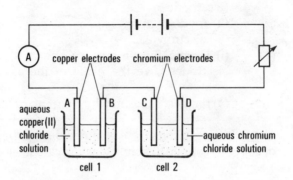

(a)　Why must a d.c. supply of electricity be used for the experiment?

(b)　At which electrode (A, B, C or D) will copper be deposited?

(c)　Chlorine gas may be formed in both cells. Describe a test to confirm the presence of chlorine gas.

(d)　How could the experiment be changed to avoid the formation of poisonous fumes?

(e)　In the experiment described above a current of 0.5 amps was passed through the circuit for 3 hours 15 minutes.

(i) What is the purpose of the variable resistor in the circuit?

(ii) Calculate the number of coulombs of electricity used in the experiment.

(iii) At the end of the experiment it was found that 1.04 g of chromium metal had been deposited in cell 2. Calculate the charge on a chromium ion.

The relative atomic mass of chromium is 52. In your calculation, take 1 faraday as 96 000 coulombs.

(iv) Write an ionic half-equation, including state symbols, for the formation of chromium metal in cell 2.

(v) Calculate the mass of copper metal deposited in cell 1 during the same experiment. (The relative atomic mass of copper is 64.)

(f)　Give **one** industrial application of the process taking place in cell 2. [SEG spec (Alt), 4]

OXIDATION AND REDUCTION. METALS AND ALLOYS. RECYCLING AND CORROSION

CONTENTS

6.1 OXIDATION AND REDUCTION

The words **oxidation** and **reduction** are used to describe some common and important chemical reactions. A chemical is *oxidised* if it *gains oxygen* in a reaction. For example, when magnesium metal burns in air or oxygen, magnesium oxide is formed.

$$\text{Magnesium} + \text{oxygen} \rightarrow \text{magnesium oxide}$$
$$2Mg(s) + O_2(g) \rightarrow 2MgO(s)$$

The magnesium has been oxidised to magnesium oxide because it has gained oxygen. The reaction is an **oxidation.**

The opposite of oxidation is **reduction.** A chemical is *reduced* if it *loses oxygen* in a reaction. For example, if copper(II) oxide is heated in a stream of hydrogen gas, copper metal and steam are formed:

$$\text{Copper(II) oxide} + \text{hydrogen} \rightarrow \text{copper} + \text{steam}$$
$$CuO(s) + H_2(g) \rightarrow Cu(s) + H_2O(g).$$

The copper(II) oxide has been reduced to copper because it has lost oxygen. (You may also have discussed how the loss/gain of hydrogen can be called oxidation and reduction.)

Some very important reactions are reductions. For example, many metals are extracted from their oxides. The change from metal oxide to metal is a reduction; the metal oxide loses oxygen.

If you are given an equation, in words or symbols, you should be able to decide whether any substance is being oxidised or reduced. Make sure that you can do this.

OXIDISING AGENTS

A substance which oxidises another substance is called an **oxidising agent.** Common examples are oxygen itself, hydrogen peroxide, chlorine, and concentrated sulphuric and nitric acids.

REDUCING AGENTS

A substance which removes oxygen from another substance is called a **reducing agent.** Common examples are hydrogen, carbon, and carbon monoxide. Usually, the substance being reduced is heated with one of these reducing agents. These reducing agents are used in industry, for example to reduce metal oxides to the metal.

Hydrogen will reduce metal oxides if the metal is below hydrogen in the Activity Series (p98). Carbon will reduce metal oxides if the metal is below carbon in the Activity Series. Carbon monoxide is used in industry to remove oxygen from iron oxide (i.e. to reduce iron oxide) in the manufacture of iron (p134).

Note that an oxidising agent is itself *reduced* as it reacts. It gives oxygen to the other substance, but loses oxygen itself. Similarly, a reducing agent is itself *oxidised* as it reacts. It removes oxygen from the other substance, but gains oxygen itself. Eg:

$$CuO(s) + H_2(g) \rightarrow Cu(s) + H_2O(g)$$

The copper(II) oxide is reduced to copper by the hydrogen, which is a reducing agent. The reducing agent, hydrogen, is oxidised to steam (by gaining oxygen) in the process. These points are frequently confused.

Note also that in a full chemical equation, reduction cannot take place without another substance being oxidised. Equally, oxidation cannot take place without another substance being reduced. Such reactions are called **redox** reactions (**red**uction and **ox**idation).

OTHER EXAMPLES OF OXIDATION AND REDUCTION

"OIL RIG"

Oxidation is loss (of e)

Reduction is gain (of e)

The word oxidation is also used to describe a reaction when a substance *loses* one or more *electrons.* For example, if a metal atom loses electrons to become an ion, it is being oxidised:

$$Fe - 2e^- \rightarrow Fe^{2+} \text{ (or } Fe \rightarrow Fe^{2+} + 2e^-\text{)}$$

Iron atoms are oxidised to iron(II) ions because they lose electrons.

Similarly, if a substance *gains* one or more *electrons* it is being reduced.

$$Fe^{2+} + 2e^- \rightarrow Fe$$

The iron(II) ions are reduced to iron atoms because they gain electrons.

Oxidation or reduction reactions which involve electrons are easy to recognise in 'half equations' such as those which show what happens at an electrode in electrolysis. For example, all discharges at a *negative* electrode are *reductions*, because the ion being discharged gains electrons. The addition of electrons is included in the 'half equation', e.g.:

$$Cu^{2+} + 2e^- \rightarrow Cu.$$

Similarly, all discharges at a *positive* electrode are *oxidations*, because the ion being discharged loses electrons. The loss of the electrons is shown in the 'half equation', e.g.:

$$Cl^- - e^- \rightarrow Cl, \text{ (or } Cl^- \rightarrow Cl + e^-\text{)}$$

It is also easy to recognise electron transfer reactions in displacement reactions, such as those in the Activity Series (p96) and with the halogens (p260). However, in the ionic equations for these reactions, the electrons are not included. These reactions are redox reactions because they involve electron transfers, but the electrons are not shown in the equation because they are 'cancelled out' on each side of the equation. In displacement reactions the reactive metal loses electrons and forces the other metal ion to gain electrons. The reactive metal acts as a reducing agent; the metal ion in solution is reduced, e.g.:

$$Mg(s) + Cu^{2+}(aq) \rightarrow Mg^{2+}(aq) + Cu(s)$$

It should be obvious from the equation that the magnesium atoms are losing electrons, and that the copper ions are gaining them, even though no electrons are shown in the euqation. If the equation is divided into two 'half-reactions' the electron transfer is then more obvious still:

$$Mg - 2e^- \rightarrow Mg^{2+} \text{ (or } Mg \rightarrow Mg^{2+} + 2e^-)$$
$$Cu^{2+} + 2e^- \rightarrow Cu$$

When these two 'halves' are added together to obtain the full equation, the electrons cancel out and are not shown.

When chlorine gas is passed over heated iron(II) chloride, a reaction takes place to form iron(III) chloride. This is a redox reaction involving electron transfer, but this time it is much more difficult to recognise what is happening. The clue to this kind of electron transfer is that there is a valency (combining power) change. Look at the equation:

$$2FeCl_2 + Cl_2 \rightarrow 2FeCl_3.$$

The iron(II) has changed to iron(III). In other words, Fe^{2+} ions have changed into Fe^{3+} ions. To do so, each Fe^{2+} ion must lose an electron. The iron(II) ions are therefore being oxidised. As this is a complete equation, some reduction must also be taking place. Some chlorine atoms are being reduced by gaining electrons and becoming chloride ions. *Whenever an atom becomes an ion (or vice versa), and whenever an ion changes its charge, there is always a transfer of one or more electrons. Such reactions are always either oxidations or reductions.*

CHECK YOUR UNDERSTANDING (Answers on p411)

Study the following equations carefully and decide which substances are being oxidised and which are being reduced. Give reasons for your answers.

1 $2Ca(s) + O_2(g) \rightarrow 2CaO(s)$
2 $Fe_2O_3(s) + 3CO(g) \rightarrow 2Fe(l) + 3CO_2$
(The substances are iron(III) oxide, carbon monoxide, iron metal, and carbon dioxide.)
3 $C(s) + H_2O(g) \rightarrow CO(g) + H_2(g)$
4 $CuO(s) + H_2(g) \rightarrow Cu(s) + H_2O(g)$
5 $Cu(s) - 2e^- \rightarrow Cu^{2+}(aq)$
6 $2Ag^+(aq) + Mg(s) \rightarrow 2Ag(s) + Mg^{2+}(aq)$
7 $2FeSO_4(s) \rightarrow Fe_2O_3(s) + SO_2(g) + SO_3(g)$
8 $Fe(s) + CuSO_4(aq) \rightarrow FeSO_4(aq) + Cu(s)$
9 $Cl_2(g) + 2KBr(aq) \rightarrow 2KCl(aq) + Br_2(aq)$
10 $2Na(s) + Cl_2(g) \rightarrow 2NaCl(s)$

6.2 THE INDUSTRIAL EXTRACTION OF METALS

Soil or rock which contains a metal or a compound of a metal is called a **mineral** or **ore**. Sometimes the metal may be found as the element itself, *mixed* with rock, etc. (e.g. metals near the bottom of the Activity Series, such as gold). More often, the metal is *joined* to other substances to form a compound, which is itself mixed with rock or soil. (For more details, see the Activity Series, p98.) The main steps in extracting a metal can be summarised as in Fig 6.1:

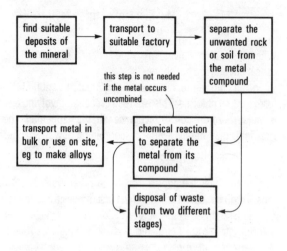

Fig 6.1 Main steps in extracting a metal

The extraction of metals is just one branch of the chemical industry. The chemical industry extracts and uses **raw materials.** The main raw materials are energy, water, air, minerals and hydrocarbons. Apart from metals and alloys, products include fertilisers, soaps, detergents, drugs, solvents, dyes, explosives, adhesives, plastics, insecticides and paints. Some people think of the chemical industry as smelly factories, pouring out pollutants and making substances with strange names and complicated formulas, which have nothing to do with daily life; factories where valuable materials are taken from the environment and replaced by heaps of solid waste. These impressions of industry are not balanced ones.

There are many areas of the world where natural activities pour more pollutants into the air than industry does (e.g. when a volcano erupts). Standards of pollution control in industry are now much improved, and they are getting better. Our present standard of living depends upon the chemical industry. We need and use metals and alloys in our daily lives, and yet we cannot just extract a metal without causing problems. We have to strike the correct balance between the benefits the metal brings to us, and the difficulties caused by making it. This is true of any industrial process. Remember, too, that some of the advantages may not at first be obvious. They include employment for many people, not only in the mining and extraction stages, but in transport and in the manufacture of many objects from the finished metal.

CHOOSING A SUITABLE SITE

The summary of the main steps in extracting a metal included finding a 'suitable' deposit. This means a plentiful amount of mineral in one area, and if possible the metal compound should form a good fraction of the whole mineral. If possible, the mineral should be easy to 'get at', and without causing problems to the countryside, pollution, or disturbing the local way of life. Minerals are found at different depths, and a mine may be necessary. This will disturb various layers of soil, and the plant and animal life which lives there. Even if the mineral is near the surface, and we can use **open-cast mining**, there is still waste to dispose. Again, the development could cause people to leave their houses, or farmers to lose valuable agricultural land. Note also that pollution has many forms, including noise, as well as the more obvious examples of toxic solids, toxic gases and toxic liquids. Also, the deposit should be close to good transport systems, which could include motorways, ports, or rail connections, depending upon what is to happen to the mineral.

Many of the points about a 'suitable' deposit also apply to a 'suitable' factory. A suitable factory might be one which is specially built to deal with the deposit (e.g. near to it), or, if not, the most appropriate one taking account of transport, nearness of energy supplies, whether it is well placed to distribute the product, and so on. Disposal of solid and other waste, the local labour force, government grants, and water supplies could also affect the choice of site.

It is important to realise that some mineral deposits are plentiful and widespread, but others may be rare and localised. The world supplies of some minerals will exist for many years to come (e.g. sodium chloride). However, supplies of other minerals are already running out, e.g. for tin and mercury. Some minerals contain a high proportion of the metal, but others contain only traces. Similarly, the extraction of some metals causes very little waste, but the extraction of others creates problems of waste disposal. Each situation is different, therefore, and requires different methods. If you are given some information about a mineral, you should be able to make sensible comments about the problems which have to be faced in using it.

You should understand the importance of recycling metals, particularly those in short supply (p138). You should also understand that as time goes on, two things will affect which deposits of ores we can use. As technology improves, we can use deposits which were thought to be 'unsuitable' a few years earlier. Again, as some metals run out, we will be forced to use deposits which contain only small amounts of metal, or which are difficult to extract (e.g. from the bottom of the sea).

HOW CAN THE ENVIRONMENT BE RESTORED AFTER A MINING DEVELOPMENT?

Usually, some disturbance to the environment is unavoidable when a mineral is extracted. Every effort is made to restore the site as quickly as possible. For example, large quarries can be filled in (perhaps with non-toxic waste from the same development) and re-planted. Agriculture, perhaps, can be restored. Alternatively, a quarry can be filled with water and used for recreation or leisure (e.g. sailing). New scientific discoveries help us to improve methods of disposal. For example, some toxic wastes could not be used to fill quarries because they killed plants, etc. We can now breed special plants and grasses which are not killed by these wastes, and large, unpleasant 'holes in the countryside' are now being filled in and replanted. Unfortunately, of course, humans could still be affected by the toxic waste if we were to eat any plants grown on them. Similarly, in the past, such newly created soils were not good for growing plants because the soil could not hold on to plant foods – they were washed out by rain. Now we can plant nitrogen-fixing plants (p317), which helps to overcome this problem.

SOME IMPORTANT EXAMPLES OF THE INDUSTRIAL EXTRACTION OF METALS

Apart from the general points in the previous section, see also under the Activity Series, p98. You may have done or seen experiments in which metals are produced from their compounds. Examples might be:

(*a*)   Heating copper(II) carbonate, copper(II) hydroxide or copper(II) nitrate to form copper(II) oxide, and then *reducing* the copper(II) oxide to copper by heating it in hydrogen (p98).

(*b*)   Heating an oxide of lead on a charcoal block in a fume cupboard. The hot carbon *reduces* the lead oxide to lead (p98).

These two examples (a and b) are not used on a large scale in industry, but the same *idea* is ofen used. We often *reduce a metal oxide* to produce a metal in industry, although we may use different reducing agents.

(*c*)   You may also have seen metals such as copper being formed at the negative electrode in an electrolysis. The electrolyte is a compound of the metal. This idea is the other main way in which metals are produced in industry, but of course some of the industrial processes use hot, melted electrolytes instead of the solutions used in a laboratory.

1 THE EXTRACTION OF IRON IN THE BLAST FURNACE

Iron is extracted from **iron ore**, which is usually impure iron(III) oxide, Fe_2O_3. The common name for this kind of iron ore is **haematite.** The oxide is *reduced* to the metal inside a large tower called a **blast furnace** (see Fig 6.2). The reduction can be summarised:

Iron(III) oxide − oxygen → iron metal

$$Fe_2O_3 - 3[O] \rightarrow 2Fe.$$

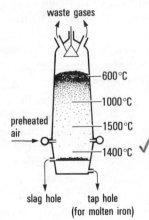

waste gases

preheated air

600 °C
1000 °C
1500 °C
1400 °C

slag hole   tap hole
(for molten iron)

Fig 6.2 The blast furnace

Other reactions inside the furnace include:

(a)   a reaction to produce the reducing agent,
(b)   reactions to remove some of the impurities in the ore,
(c)   reactions to give out heat to keep the contents at a high temperature.

The main changes can be summarised as in Fig 6.3.

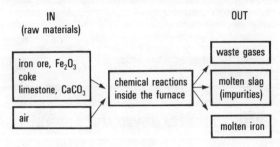

Fig 6.3 Changes inside the blast furnace

Some more detailed information

1   The solid raw materials are added at the top of the furnace. The air (which is warmed first) is 'blasted in' near the bottom.

2   Carbon monoxide is the main reducing agent which changes the iron oxide into iron. The carbon monoxide is formed by two steps:

(a)   Hot coke burns to form carbon dioxide

$$C(s)+O_2(g) \rightarrow CO_2(g)$$

(b)   The carbon dioxide then reacts with more hot coke to form carbon monoxide.

$$CO_2(g)+C(s) \rightarrow 2CO(g)$$

(c)   The carbon monoxide then reduces the iron(III) oxide.

$$Fe_2O_3(s)+3CO(g) \rightarrow 2Fe(l)+3CO_2(g)$$

3   The waste products are gases (mainly nitrogen and oxides of carbon, which escape at the top), and liquid slag. The slag is formed as follows. The limestone decomposes at the high temperature to form calcium oxide.

$$CaCO_3(s) \rightarrow CaO(s)+CO_2(g)$$

The calcium oxide then reacts with silicon impurities (sand-like, and clay-like substances) to produce slag (molten calcium silicate) which floats on top of the molten iron.

$$CaO(s)+SiO_2(s) \rightarrow CaSiO_3(l)$$

The slag is 'tapped off' from time to time.

4   The dense, molten iron forms a layer at the bottom of the furnace and it is tapped off at the appropriate time. The product is called **cast iron** or **pig iron.** It is not pure. It contains a significant proportion of carbon, and is very brittle. Most of the iron produced is immediately changed into steel (p137).

Economic and environmental points

Environmental points	Energy points
The extraction of iron is a 'dirty' process – uses large quantities of solids, so dust and smoke are problems. Toxic gases also formed, e.g. sulphur dioxide from the coke (p212). Large quantities of solid waste – slag. Process now very much cleaner than it used to be. Dust and smoke almost no problem any more. Waste gases are cleaned (scrubbed) before being allowed to enter the air. Slag no longer 'dumped' to spoil environment – used instead in road-making, for filling-in quarries, etc.	Once started, reactions are exothermic (p357) and so no heat energy needed to keep it going. Furnace normally operated for two/three years before process stopped and lining replaced. Heat energy produced is not wasted – used to warm up the cold air before it is blasted into the furnace. Main running cost is the fuel (coke), which is also needed to produce the carbon monoxide which is the reducing agent.

2 THE EXTRACTION OF ALUMINIUM BY ELECTROLYSIS (p118)

3. THE EXTRACTION OF SODIUM BY ELECTROLYSIS (p116)

6.3 ALLOYS. THE EARTH'S RESOURCES. RECYCLING

ALLOYS

An alloy is a mixture of two or more metals, or of a metal and a non-metal. Alloys are used more often than *pure* metals. Most of a modern car, for example, is made of metal, but only a small proportion of this is pure metal. Most of the metal parts of a car are alloys, such as mild steel (the body), different alloy steels (moving parts), tin alloys (bearings) brass (radiators), nickel alloys (spark plugs), etc. We use more alloys than pure metals because it is possible to produce thousands of alloys, each with its own special properties, from less than 80 pure metals. Many alloys are more useful than the parent metals from which they are made. For example, the alloy brass is much harder than its parent elements such as copper. Duralumin is much stronger than aluminium. Stainless steel will not corrode, but iron (the parent metal) corrodes rapidly. Cupro-nickel looks silvery, completely different from copper.

The properties of a metal can be changed by the addition of only a *small* amount of another element. In particular, it is easy to 'improve' upon the properties of a metal, especially its strength and ability to resist corrosion. Titanium alloys have been developed for artificial joints, because they do not react with blood or tissues, they are non-toxic, they are strong, and they resist wear. It would be very difficult to find a pure metal which has all these properties and is economical to use. Some common alloys are summarised in Table 6.1.

Table 6.1 Some common alloys

Alloy	Elements within it	Uses
Brass	copper (mainly) + zinc	ornaments, many others
Bronze	copper (mainly)+tin	many
Coinage bronze	copper (mainly)+tin+zinc	'copper' coins
Cupronickel	copper (mainly)+nickel	'silver' coins
Duralumin	aluminium (mainly)+copper+ magnesium	strong but light – aircraft bodies
Solder	tin (mainly)+lead	low melting point – electrical connections
Steel	iron (mainly)+carbon (perhaps+ other metals)	railway lines, bridges, cutlery, car bodies, etc.
Stainless steel	iron (mainly)+chromium+nickel +carbon	objects which resist corrosion

STEEL

Steel is an alloy. Its parent metal is iron. There are many different steels, but they all contain iron, a small amount of carbon, and perhaps small quantities of other metals such as chromium, manganese, vanadium and nickel. The cast iron produced by the blast furnace contains about 4% carbon, and this is reduced to between 0.15% and 1.5% carbon in steel. Steel is the most used alloy in the world. Its properties can be changed by altering the amount of carbon, by adding other metals, and by heat treatment. Its main disadvantage is that it corrodes easily (except stainless steel).

How steel is made

Most of the cast iron made in a blast furnace is immediately changed into steel, while it is still molten. The iron contains several impurities, particularly carbon, sulphur and phosphorus. In order to change the crude iron into steel, three steps may be needed.

(i) All of the sulphur and phosphorus must be removed.

(ii) Most of the carbon must be removed (but not all: steel still contains some carbon).

(iii) Other metals are mixed in, if necessary.

Steps (i) and (ii) are done together by oxidising the sulphur, phosphorus and carbon into their oxides. These then escape as gases, or form a slag which is removed later. When all the impurities have been 'burned out' except for a small proportion of carbon, other metals are added if necessary.

Most steel is made by the **basic oxygen process.** The process is given this name because a **base** (calcium oxide) is added to form a slag with some of the impurities, and **oxygen** is used to oxidise the impurities. There are many versions of the process. A typical example is shown in Fig 6.4.

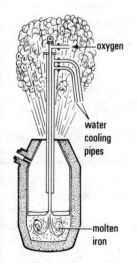

oxygen

water cooling pipes

molten iron

Fig 6.4 A typical steel-making process

THE EARTH'S RESOURCES

Resources are substances found in nature which can be processed to provide the things we need and use in daily life. The resources are found in the lakes, rivers and seas (the **hydrosphere**); in the air (the **atmosphere**), and in the solid part of the Earth (the **lithosphere**). The main resources are:

WATER (p227)	THE AIR (p203) from which we obtain oxygen, nitrogen, etc.	FOSSIL FUELS (p364) like oil, coal, gas, from which we obtain energy and organic chemicals	MINERALS (salt, metal ores, sand, limestone, china clay, etc.) from which we obtain metals, non-metals, and many compounds

The seas are as yet relatively unused, but they do contain minerals. You may have discussed how magnesium, bromine and sodium chloride can be extracted from sea water.

Some resources are **renewable**, which means that they can be remade. An example is oxygen in the air. The fraction of oxygen in the air does not change very much, even though we are constantly using it for breathing and burning, because photosynthesis keeps oxygen and carbon dioxide in balance (p208). Another renewable resource is a tree, but this takes a long time to grow to maturity. Other resources are **finite.** Once they have been used, they have 'gone for ever'. They will not be renewed, or at least they cannot be renewed quickly enough. Fossil fuels and metal ores are examples of finite resources. It took millions of years to produce deposits of natural gas and crude oil, and yet we will use up many of these deposits in a time period of about 100 years. (Crude oil was not used on a large scale until about 100 years ago.) Supplies of these cannot last for ever.

SOME SOLUTIONS TO THE PROBLEM OF 'SHRINKING' METAL ORES

1 Recycle used objects, to save on the amount of new metal needed.
2 Change of attitude: use an object for a longer period of time before throwing it away – stop wanting new things before the old ones are really worn out.
3 Try to find artificial substitutes for some things, in the same way that artificial rubber is often used instead of natural rubber. The artificial material may not use a resource which is in short supply.

RECYCLING

This is the re-using of waste material. Recycling occurs in nature, e.g. the carbon (p308), nitrogen (p316), and water (p229) cycles. Industrial cycles can never return *all* waste material for reprocessing; some is always lost.

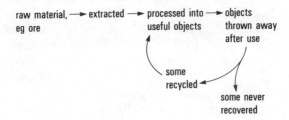

Fig 6.5 Industrial recycling

Recycling has several advantages:

1 Less need for new material, therefore the resource (e.g. mineral) is not used up so quickly.

2 Less waste to dispose of.

3 Recycled objects do not have to go through the extraction stage, i.e. obtaining the metal from the ore. The extraction often needs a great deal of energy (e.g. the blast furnace to extract iron) and so there is a saving on energy. To make 1 tonne of copper from copper ore needs ten times the energy to produce 1 tonne of copper from scrap.

4 It is very difficult to produce a *pure* metal from scrap, because scrap will include alloys, which are mixtures. However, pure metals are used only rarely. Most metals are used as alloys. It is not difficult to produce a new steel alloy of known composition from a complicated mixture of different types of scrap steel. The first step is the separation of the scrap steel from other materials. The scrap is then melted. Instruments show the exact percentages of all the substances present in the mixture. It is then relatively easy to add further amounts of iron, carbon, or other elements until the steel is the required mixture.

Recycling will become more important in the future as technology improves for separating different kinds of waste from rubbish. Modern methods can separate different metals from a complicated mixture in scrap. Most foundries now collect even the grinding dust and slag which they produce, and these are reprocessed so that all but 5% of the metal content can be extracted. However, there are problems. Tin is a metal in short supply. Unfortunately, 99% of a 'tin can' is steel, so recycling cans to obtain pure tin is difficult.

EXAMPLES OF RECYCLED MATERIALS

1 'FERROUS' METALS, i.e. IRON AND STEELS

The word **ferrous** is often used in industry for any metal which is 'based' on iron. It usually means a steel alloy. All other kinds of metal or alloy are called **non-ferrous.**

Sources: scrap cars, ships, tin cans, etc.

Problems: it is easy to separate ferrous materials because they are magnetic, but they are often coated with other metals (e.g. tin in a can) and it is difficult to separate such substances from the steel.

Advantages: Large saving on energy and resources. One tonne of scrap steel produces the same amount of new steel as would be made by using 1.5 tonnes of iron ore, 1.0 tonne of coke, and 0.5 tonne of limestone, and uses less energy. There is also less waste to dispose of, and there are savings in mining the ore and importing it.

Other points: Large quantities now recycled; material added to a steel furnace may include up to 70% scrap.

2 ALUMINIUM

Sources: milk bottle tops, 'silver' paper, saucepans, aluminium cans, and lots of other aluminium alloys.

Advantages: Large saving on energy (much electricity needed to make pure aluminium from bauxite, p118, but electrolysis not needed when melting scrap). Saving on resources (the ore) and on mining and transport.

Other points: Most substances made of 'aluminium' are actually alloys, so the scrap contains other elements. When melted it is easy to add correct amounts of pure metal or other elements to produce the required alloy.

3 OTHER METALS

Many copper alloys are recycled, to produce new alloys. A large proportion of lead is recycled.

4 PLASTICS

Sources: Household waste (packaging, toys, etc.)

Problems: Only thermosoftening plastics (p339) can be completely recycled by softening and remoulding. Difficult to separate this type of plastics from other types. Even when thermosoftening plastics are separated, they will be a mixture of lots of different plastics and other materials, and so they cannot be recycled into a 'pure' type of plastic. Proper sorting can be done only by hand or by expensive machinery.

Advantages: Any recycled plastics save on resources, e.g. the fossil fuels used to produce the monomers (p339). Also helps to avoid piles of waste which do not rot. Not essential to recycle into pure plastics – a recycled *mixture* can be used to make shoe soles, bicycle saddles, toys, plant pots, etc.

5 GLASS AND PAPER

The recycling of these familiar substances is more obvious in daily life, and you may have discussed the advantages/difficulties in considerable detail. The recycling of these substances also helps to avoid pollution.

A SUMMARY OF THE MAIN ADVANTAGES OF RECYCLING WASTE

1 A saving of resources: trees, metal ores, fuels.
2 Improvement of the environment – fewer waste tips, less use of valuable land.
3 Saving money – smaller bills for the taxpayer.

CHECK YOUR UNDERSTANDING (Answers on p411)

1 Gold can be found as the metal, mixed with rock. Iron is found as iron ore, also mixed with rock. Why is it more difficult to obtain iron metal than to obtain gold metal?

2 The following chart shows some of the steps which take place when a resource is to be used. Study the steps and then answer the questions.

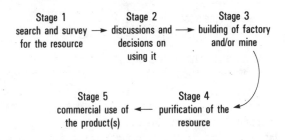

Fig 6.6 Steps to be taken when a resource is to be used

(a) Which stage could cost large sums of money and yet produce no commercial profit?
(b) Suppose that research in Stage 1 shows that an ore is mixed with large amounts of
    (i) a useless clay-like substance, and
    (ii) sulphur. In which ways could stage 4 cause environmental problems?
(c) If the resource is a metal oxide, what kind of chemical process must take place in order to obtain the pure metal?
(d) How will the position of the metal in the Activity Series influence the chemical process needed to obtain the pure metal?
(e) List some of the points which would be considered in deciding where to build a factory to obtain the pure metal.
(f) In most extraction processes, the most expensive running costs are the cost of the raw materials and one other factor. What is this second factor?

3 Most of the metal parts of a car are made of alloys. Which pure metals would you expect to find in a car, and where would you find them?

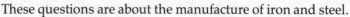

4 These questions are about the manufacture of iron and steel.

(*a*)   A large blast furnace can use up to 4000 tonnes of air in a single day. Which gas from the air is used in the furnace?

(*b*)   What does this gas do? (There is more than one answer.)

(*c*)   Why is limestone added in the furnace?

(*d*)   The pig iron formed by the furnace is very brittle because it is impure. What is the main impurity which causes it to be brittle?

(*e*)   What changes take place when pig iron is changed into steel?

(*f*)   Decide whether each of the following statements is true or false.

(i) Iron is changed into steel because iron rusts very quickly, but steel does not rust.

(ii) When small amounts of any other element are added to iron, it becomes brittle.

(iii) The properties of steel can be changed by heating it and then cooling it quickly.

(*g*)   In the manufacture of iron and steel, what problems have to be solved in order to protect the environment?

5 The first commercial process for making sodium metal was the Castner process. In this, sodium hydroxide was melted and electrolysed. The reactions taking place were:

At the anode, $4OH^- - 4e^- \rightarrow 2H_2O + O_2$
At the cathode, $4Na^+ + 4e^- \rightarrow 4Na$

This process has been replaced by the Downs' process (p116), in which sodium chloride is the electrolyte. Sodium chloride melts at 801°C, and sodium hydroxide at 322°C. The Downs' process has replaced the earlier process because it has several advantages. (The earlier process also has one advantage over the Downs' process, but this is partly overcome by modifying the electrolyte.)

(*a*)   Suggest reasons why the Downs' process replaced the Castner process.

(*b*)   What advantage did the Castner process have compared to the Downs' process?

(*c*)   How is this disadvantage in the Downs' process 'partly overcome by modifying the electrolyte'?

6.4 CORROSION

When a *metal* reacts with the *atmosphere* the reaction is called **corrosion**. The metal **corrodes**. Corrosion can be a serious problem if it causes the metal to become weaker. The reactions which cause corrosion might be between the metal and oxygen, or carbon dioxide, or water. Corrosion is also caused by acidic substances in the air, such as pollutant gases (e.g. sulphur dioxide) and acid rain. Corrosion can also involve more than one of these substances, e.g. rusting involves both oxygen and water.

If a metal is low in the activity series, corrosion is unlikely to be a problem. For example, copper metal reacts with both oxygen and carbon dioxide in the air and is eventually covered in a green coating. You may have seen this on bronze statues and copper lightning conductors. This reaction is not a serious form of corrosion. The green powder (which is a kind of carbonate) forms a thin layer only. It is quite attractive. More important, the metal underneath is as strong as before.

Iron, which is higher in the activity series, corrodes more rapidly and with a more serious effect. Corrosion in iron or steel *continues* right *through* the metal. It does not stop on the surface. In time, the strength of the metal is greatly reduced as the metal slowly crumbles to a red-brown powder. The corrosion of iron and steel is given a special name: **rusting.** This word should not be used for corrosion in any other metal.

When iron or steel meets *both* oxygen and moisture it rusts. This is one of the biggest disadvantages of iron and most forms of steel (but not stainless steel, etc). Steel is still used on a large scale in spite of this, because it is relatively cheap to produce, it is strong, easy to work with, and different kinds can be made for different uses. Even so, the cost of fighting corrosion costs millions of pounds each year in Britain alone.

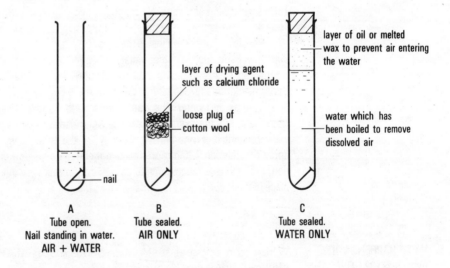

Fig 6.7 An experiment to show what causes iron to rust

You should be able to describe an experiment which shows that *both* air and water are needed to make iron rust. A typical example is shown in Fig 6.7. This is a good example of how a scientist designs an experiment to test *one* thing at a time. In each of tubes A and B, only *one* reagent (either air or water) can reach the iron nail. In C, *both* can do so. The results show that rusting can only take place if *both* air and water are present. You may also have done experiments to show that sodium chloride (common salt) makes rusting take place at a faster rate than normal. This is why cars should be washed very well if they have been driven on roads which have been salted in winter, or if they have been exposed to salt spray from the sea.

You may have taken an investigation into rusting a stage further. A typical experiment is shown in Fig 6.8. Typical results from such an experiment are as follows.

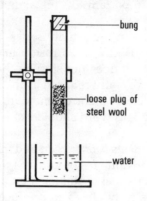

bung

loose plug of steel wool

water

5 tubes are set up as shown

tube 1 : steel wool is first degreased, soaked in water, drained

tube 2 : steel wool degreased, soaked in sodium chloride solution, drained

tube 3 : steel wool soaked in oil, drained

tube 4 : steel wool degreased, moistened with water, clean piece of magnesium ribbon pushed through ball of wool

tube 5 : as for tube 4, but using copper or tin instead of magnesium

Fig 6.8 A more detailed investigation into rusting

Tube 1.   Obvious signs of rusting. Water rises up inside the tube.
Tube 2.   Rusting very obvious; faster than in Tube 1. Water rises.
Tube 3.   No sign of rusting. No change in level of water inside tube.
Tube 4.   No rusting in the area where the magnesium touches the steel wool. Water level goes down inside the tube.
Tube 5.   Rapid rusting. Other metal unchanged. Water level rises inside the tube.

Rusting occurs in 1 and 2 because both air and water can reach the steel wool. Sodium chloride makes rusting take place more quickly. In 3, the oil protected the metal from both air and water. The water level rose in 1 and 2 because rusting needs oxygen from the air. As the oxygen is used up, water rises to take its place. In theory, the water will rise until it is one-fifth of the way up the tube (oxygen is one-fifth of the air, approximately). In 4, the more reactive metal (magnesium) protects the iron from rusting. In 5, the less reactive metal causes iron to rust very quickly. The reactions taking place in these two tubes are explained on p145.

WHAT HAPPENS WHEN IRON RUSTS? HOW CAN RUSTING BE PREVENTED?

When iron or steel rusts, it is being **oxidised.** The reaction is complicated, but it can be summarised:

$$\text{iron} \xrightarrow{+O_2} \text{iron oxide} \xrightarrow{+H_2O} \text{hydrated iron oxide,}$$
$$\text{or iron hydroxide, (rust)}$$

Rust, the brown powder, is therefore a hydrated oxide of iron. It gradually 'eats' away the metal until it has no structural strength.

We can prevent rusting by stopping *both* air and water from reaching the iron or steel. Common methods include painting, tin-plating, chrome-plating, coating with zinc (**galvanising**), coating with grease or oil, and covering with plastic. Another method which you may have studied is described below.

SACRIFICING A DIFFERENT METAL IN ORDER TO PROTECT IRON OR STEEL

In rusting, iron first forms iron (II) ions, Fe^{2+}. These are then oxidised to iron(III) ions, Fe^{3+}, by losing one electron each. They then form hydrated iron(III) oxide, which is rust.

The sacrificing of one metal in order to 'save' iron works on the same principle as the simple cell (p99), in which electrons can flow from one metal to another under certain circumstances. To make this happen we need:

(i) two *different* metals (or a metal and carbon), joined to each other, *and*

(ii) an electrolyte which 'bathes' the two metals. Atoms of the more reactive metal then lose electrons and become ions. The electrons move to the less reactive metal. The ions dissolve in the electrolyte.

The main effect of these changes is that the more reactive metal gradually dissolves as ions. Suppose that we bolt a block of magnesium metal to the steel hull of a ship, below the water line. We have the conditions to form a 'simple cell', but on a much larger scale of course. The conditions are:

(i) two different metals (magnesium and steel) joined to each other and

(ii) an electrolyte (sea water) which bathes the two metals. The more reactive metal (magnesium) gradually dissolves as its atoms each lose two electrons and form ions. The electrons move into the steel. The steel (mainly iron) cannot lose electrons by changing its atoms into Fe^{2+} ions, and so rusting cannot start. We describe this process as using one metal as a sacrifice to protect another, or **sacrificial protection**. Zinc can be used instead of magnesium.

This is important because it is extremely expensive (in time and money) to take a ship into dry dock and treat a rusting hull. However, it is relatively easy to keep bolting on a new piece of more reactive metal when necessary. The sacrifice of the more reactive metal is not a problem because it is not part of the structure of the ship. The system does not work perfectly, of course, but it greatly reduces corrosion. If you did an experiment like the one summarised in Fig 6.8, you should understand why the steel wool which was touching the magnesium ribbon showed less rust than the others, even though both air and water were present. You should also understand why the use of a metal *less* reactive than iron (tube 5) *increases* the rate at which iron rusts. This time, *iron* is the more reactive metal. It dissolves as Fe^{2+} ions, which therefore starts the rusting process.

GALVANISED IRON OR STEEL

A similar principle to the one just described provides extra protection when iron is *galvanised* (covered with a layer of zinc). The iron is protected from air and water by the zinc, and so does not rust. If the surface is damaged, however, there is still a 'second line of defence' which protects the iron. Suppose a crack appears in the zinc coating. This exposes some iron underneath. The crack may fill with rain water. This is an electrolyte because it contains ions, e.g. formed when carbon dioxide from the air dissolves in it. We have the conditions for a simple cell. Zinc, being more reactive than iron, 'dissolves' just as the magnesium did in the previous example. The iron does not rust; the zinc is sacrificed to protect the iron.

You might imagine that eventually the zinc would be used up and that the iron would then rust. This does not usually happen because there is also a third line of defence. The zinc ions formed as the metal dissolves react with other ions from the electrolyte to form a precipitate of zinc hydroxide which seals up the crack in the surface. The formation of zinc hydroxide is similar to the formation of iron(III) hydroxide, rust, but rust allows air and water to pass through it so that the process continues. Zinc hydroxide does not allow air and water to penetrate through it.

CHECK YOUR UNDERSTANDING (Answers on p412)

1 Two students were discussing experiments on rusting. One said that if a clean iron nail was placed in a test tube, and the tube was then completely *filled* with water and sealed with plastic film, the nail would not rust because the water would stop air from reaching the nail. The other student said that the nail would still go rusty. Who was right, and why?

2 Explain why car bodies often corrode more rapidly in winter than in summer. There should be more than one reason.

3 Suppose you were to leave a clean iron nail in each room in your house.
   (*a*)   In which room or rooms would the nail rust very quickly?
   (*b*)   In which kind of room would it rust most slowly?

4 How is rusting prevented in each of the following?
   (*a*)   an iron dustbin,
   (*b*)   the blades of a lawn mower which is being stored for the winter,
   (*c*)   the spokes in a bicycle wheel,
   (*d*)   an iron road bridge.

5 If a car body is made of stainless steel, it does not corrode. Suggest reasons why this is not done on a commercial scale.

6 Explain
   (*a*)   how a food can (mainly steel) is prevented from rusting, and
   (*b*)   why a food can corrodes *rapidly* once it has been damaged.

7 If a steel screw in a wall is painted over with gloss paint it helps to prevent rusting, but if it is painted over with emulsion paint, it rusts rapidly. Why?

CHECK LIST ▶   REMEMBER THAT SOME OF THESE POINTS MAY NOT BE RELEVANT FOR THE PAR-TICULAR SYLLABUS YOU ARE FOLLOWING.
YOU SHOULD UNDERSTAND THE FOLLOWING POINTS.

1 ▶ Oxidation and reduction. How to tell, from a word or symbolic equation, which substances are being oxidised or reduced.

2 ▶ Oxidising agent and reducing agent; some common examples.

3 ▶ Electron transfer in redox reactions (usually only for higher grades); applications in electrode reactions in electrolysis and ionic equations in displacement, etc.

4 ▶ Ore (mineral), raw materials. Main general steps in extracting a metal from an ore. Problems caused by industrial processes and how these can be reduced. You should be able to make sensible comments about industrial processes, if given appropriate information.

5 ▶ The manufacture of iron and steel, some of the energy and environmental factors.

6 ▶ Alloys; their usefulness and some common examples.

7 ♦ The main resources; finite and renewable resources.

8 ♦ Recycling and its advantages.

9 ♦ Corrosion. The special case of rusting; methods of prevention.

SPECIMEN EXAMINATION QUESTIONS

SEE GENERAL NOTE BEFORE QUESTIONS ON pp49 and 50
REMEMBER THAT YOU MAY BE ALLOWED TO USE A DATA
BOOK IN THE EXAMINATION.

1 The substances A to E are all natural sources of chemicals. Which of them is essentially a single compound?

    A Air   B Coal   C Limestone   D Petroleum

E Sea water   *[LEA spec (B), 1]*

2 Which one of the following will *never* rust?

    A Aluminium   B Galvanised iron   C Steel

D Well oiled iron   *[SEG spec (Alt) 1]*

3 Which *one* of the following gases is often used industrially for the reduction of a metal ore to the metal?

    A oxygen   B carbon monoxide   C methane   D nitrogen

E chlorine   *[NISEC spec 1]*

4 (*a*)   What two substances must be present with iron for it to rust?

    (*b*)   How does a layer of tin prevent iron from rusting?

    (*c*)   Zinc blocks are attached to the steel hulls of ships, as shown in Fig 6.9.

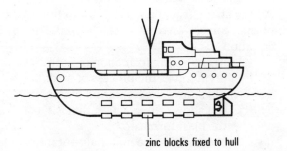

Fig 6.9 Diagram for question 4(c)

zinc blocks fixed to hull

    (i) How does the zinc protect the hull from rusting?

    (ii) What would be the effect of using copper blocks instead of zinc?

    (*d*)   (i) What is an alloy?

    (ii) Give *one* example of an alloy and state what it is made of.

    (iii) Explain why the alloy you have named above is useful.

                                      [SEG spec 1]

5 The following is a list of the typical contents of a dustbin for a family of four in one week.

    Aluminium 0.55 kg   Polythene/plastic 0.25 kg

Waste food 4.50 kg   Iron 1.30 kg   Glass 1.75 kg

Paper 4.15 kg.

Much of the waste in this dustbin can be changed back into useful metal, plastic, glass or paper products if it is processed correctly. First, some of the parts of the rubbish must be separated from the rest.

(a) (i) Give *one* method which could be used to separate objects made of iron from domestic rubbish.

(ii) Most scrap iron is converted into steel. What must be added to pure iron to change it into steel?

(iii) Give one important use of steel and state a property of steel which makes it particularly suitable for this purpose.

(b) (i) Waste glass can be remelted and used again. Give one problem which might be found when using empty bottles in this way.

(ii) Outline one *other* way in which the waste of glass containers can be avoided.

(c) (i) What percentage of the family's total waste is plastic?

(ii) Give *one* reason why plastic causes a serious pollution problem.

(iii) Plastic waste can be disposed of by burning it. Give one advantage and one drawback of this method.

(d) Explain why so many manufacturers use plastic packaging in spite of the pollution problems. [*SEG* spec (Alt) 2]

6 (a) A $C + O_2 \rightarrow CO_2$

B $CO_2 + C \rightarrow 2CO$

C $Fe_2O_2 + 3CO \rightarrow 2Fe + 3CO_2$

D $CaCO_3 \rightarrow CaO + CO_2$

E $CaO + SiO_2 \rightarrow CaSiO_3$

All the above reactions take place in the blast furnace. Write the letter of the correct answer to each of the following equations. Which equation

(i) shows the formation of iron?

(ii) involves the process of oxidation?

(iii) shows the formation of slag?

(iv) shows the reaction that is most likely to take place **first** in the blast furnace?

(b) Name the **three** materials put into the top of the blast furnace.

(c) Name **one** gas given out in the blast furnace.

(d) The corrosion of iron was investigated by giving six identical nails different treatments. One other nail was left untreated. All seven nails were then left for several weeks exposed to the atmosphere in a **small country town.** The results are given below.

Nail	Treatment	Cost of treatment	Mass of nail and coating BEFORE exposure to the atmosphere	Mass of nail and coating AFTER exposure to the atmosphere
A	Waxed	Low	5.0g	5.3g
B	Oiled	Low	5.0g	4.1g
C	Chromium plated	High	5.0g	5.0g
D	Painted	Low	5.0g	5.4g
E	Untreated		4.9g	6.1g
F	Galvanised	Fairly high	5.0g	5.1g
G	Dipped in salt solution	Low	5.0g	6.7g

Which nail

(i) was **best protected** against corrosion?

(ii) received a treatment which made corrosion worse than it would have been had it been left untreated?

(iii) received a treatment which is usually used on iron railings?

(e) (i) In which case was there an obvious mistake in the weighing of the nail and the coating after the experiment?

(ii) Give **one** reason for your answer.

(f) Give **one** reason why the rate of corrosion of iron is greater in a heavily industrialised area.

Use your copy of the Periodic Table of the elements to answer parts (g) and (h).

(g) How many of each of the following are there in one atom of iron?

(i) electrons

(ii) protons

(iii) neutrons

(h) Write the formula for each of the following compounds.

(i) iron(III) oxide

(ii) iron(III) fluoride   [MEG spec 2]

+7 Titanium is the eighth most abundant element in the earth's crust. It is more abundant than copper. It occurs in titanium(IV) oxide which is present to the extent of 0.01% in much sea-shore sand. The metal is extracted by first converting the titanium(IV) oxide to titanium(IV) chloride. The titanium(IV) chloride is then heated with sodium. Titanium has a lower density than iron, is stronger than steel and is also resistant to corrosion. Information about the abundance (in parts per million) and cost of titanium and copper are given in the table below.

	Titanium	Copper
Abundance (ppm)	4400	55
Cost (£/tonne)	3700	800

(*a*)   Write the formula of the naturally occurring oxide of titanium.

(*b*)   (i) What reagent might be used to convert titanium(IV) oxide to titanium(IV) chloride?
(ii) Complete the symbol equation for the reaction between titanium(IV) chloride and sodium: $TiCl_4 + 4Na \rightarrow$

(*c*)   Suggest *two* reasons why titanium metal is more expensive than copper.

(*d*)   Describe how simple cells could be set up and used to place titanium in the reactivity series of metals.
(i) Description of experiment
(ii) Possible results
(iii) Conclusion from results above

(*e*)   Give *two* reasons why titanium is particularly suitable for replacement hip joints.   *[NEA 2]*

†8   Titanium is the seventh most abundant element in the earth's crust. One form in which it occurs is rutile, TiO_2.

In extracting titanium from its ore, rutile is first converted into titanium(IV) chloride, $TiCl_4$, and this is then reduced to the metal by heating it with sodium or magnesium in an atmosphere of argon. Titanium(IV) chloride is a simple, molecular covalent substance.

(*a*)   Given that the titanium atom has four outer electrons used for bonding, draw a diagram to show the bonding in titanium(IV) chloride (only the outer electrons of the chlorine atoms should be shown).

(*b*)   Write a balanced equation for the reaction of titanium(IV) chloride with sodium.

(*c*)   (i) In which physical state would you expect to find titanium(IV) chloride at room temperature?
(ii) Explain why the physical state of titanium(IV) chloride differs from that of sodium chloride at room temperature.

(*d*)   Suggest a reason why it is necessary to carry out the reaction of titanium(IV) chloride with sodium in an atmosphere of argon.

(*e*)   Titanium is expensive in spite of the fact that it is relatively abundant in the earth's crust. Suggest a reason for this.

(*f*)   Titanium is used in the structures of supersonic aircraft and space vehicles. Suggest **two** properties it might have that make it more suitable than other metals for this purpose.

[LEA spec (A), 3]

†9 The table below summarises the results obtained when small pieces of various metals are added to aqueous solutions containing metal ions.

Solution	Metal added				
	copper	iron	manganese	tin	zinc
copper(II) sulphate	–	copper displaced	copper displaced	copper displaced	copper displaced
iron(III) sulphate	no change	–	iron displaced	no change	iron displaced
manganese(II) sulphate	no change	no change	–	no change	no change
tin(II) chloride	no change	tin displaced	tin displaced	–	tin displaced
zinc sulphate	no change	no change	zinc displaced	no change	–

Manganese is the most reactive metal in the table.

(*a*) (i) Place the other metals in the order of their chemical reactivity.

(ii) From the results given, how can it be decided that manganese is the most reactive metal?

(*b*) (ii) Describe what you would see if excess powdered iron were added to aqueous copper(II) sulphate.

(ii) Write the ionic equation for the reaction between iron and aqueous copper(II) sulphate.

(*c*) The experiments shown in Fig 6.10 were set up to investigate the rusting of iron.

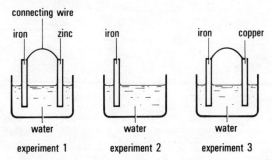

Fig 6.10 Diagram for question 9(c)

The iron in experiment 3 rusted the most, the iron in experiment 1 rusted the least. Explain these results.

(*d*) Suggest why strips of magnesium are attached to the steel hulls of ships.

(*e*) Polythene containers and tin-coated steel cans are products of modern industrial society. The disposal of them causes a pollution problem. Which of these causes the greater problem? Explain your answer.   [MEG spec 3]

GENERAL PROPERTIES OF METALS AND THEIR COMPOUNDS. TESTS FOR UNKNOWN SUBSTANCES

CONTENTS

The important general properties of metals are summarised in Table 3.1 (p68). See also bonding in metals (p68), the Activity Series (p89) and salt preparations (p182), all of which involve important reactions of metals. Many of the reactions of the metals are mentioned in other parts of the book. In these cases, cross references only are given in this chapter.

7.1 PROPERTIES AND USES OF INDIVIDUAL METALS AND THEIR COMPOUNDS

1 SODIUM AND POTASSIUM

(i) Very reactive (e.g. at the top of the Activity Series, p92). They are reactive because their atoms need to lose only one electron in order to have a fully filled outer energy level. These atoms can lose their electrons comparatively easily (see changes in Group 1 of the Periodic Table, p256).

(ii) Very soft, and have a very low density (float on water).

(iii) React with oxygen and other gases in the air, so stored under oil. When heated in air, they melt (low melting points) and burn with coloured flames (sodium yellow, potassium lilac) to form their oxides.

A typical series of reactions when left in the air is shown in Fig 7.1.

Fig 7.1 Reactions of sodium and potassium when left in air

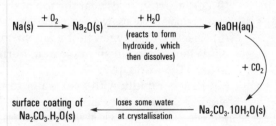

(iv) Other reactions: With *cold* water (p95); with chlorine (p320).

COMPOUNDS OF SODIUM AND POTASSIUM

(i) *All* sodium and potassium compounds are soluble in water.

If you need to have a *solution* containing some sulphate, carbonate or chloride ions (for example), you can safely choose the sodium or potassium compound because it will always dissolve. This is particularly useful when you are making precipitates, such as insoluble salts (p185).

(ii) These compounds are ionically bonded.

(iii) All sodium and potassium compounds are white unless they also contain a transition element.

The only common coloured compounds of sodium and potassium are their orange dichromate(VI) compounds and the purple manganate(VII).

SOME USES OF SODIUM AND ITS COMPOUNDS

The metal: in 'orange' street lamps, where its vapour causes the colour; the molten metal as a coolant in nuclear reactors (it has a low melting point and is a good conductor of heat).

Sodium hydroxide: the most common alkali in the world; used in manufacture of paper, artificial silk, soap and grease removers (e.g. oven cleaners).

Sodium carbonate: glass and paper making.

Sodium chloride: food industry (as common salt) e.g. for food flavouring and preservation; also in glazing pottery and the manufacture of sodium, chlorine (p119) and sodium hydroxide (p119).

Sodium hydrogencarbonate: as an 'antacid' (neutraliser) in the stomach, to neutralise acid spillages, and in baking powder (p179).

---

2 CALCIUM, MAGNESIUM, ZINC AND THEIR COMPOUNDS

CALCIUM METAL

(i) Very reactive (e.g. near the top of the Activity Series, p92). This is because its atoms easily lose two electrons to form calcium ions, Ca^{2+}.

(ii) Reacts with oxygen in the air, so sometimes stored under oil. When heated in air or oxygen, burns with brick-red flame to form the oxide, p93.

(iii) Reacts rapidly with cold water to form hydrogen and an alkaline solution of calcium hydroxide (lime water). Calcium hydroxide is not very soluble in water, so some is formed as a precipitate and the water goes cloudy.

MAGNESIUM AND ZINC METALS

(i) These fairly reactive metals form their oxides when heated in air or oxygen. Magnesium burns with a dazzling white flame, and is more reactive than zinc (p93).

(ii) Other reactions: with steam (p95), with dilute acids to form a salt of the metal and hydrogen (p94). (The magnesium reaction is more vigorous.)

(iii) Being reasonably high in the Activity Series, they will displace less reactive metals from solutions of their salts (p96).

(iv) The main ore of zinc is called zinc blende.

THE COMPOUNDS OF CALCIUM, MAGNESIUM AND ZINC

All three parent elements have the same valency (combining power), which is 2. If you learn the formulas of magnesium compounds, you automatically know the formulas of the calcium and zinc compounds; just swap Ca or Zn for Mg. All the common compounds of these elements are white, and ionically bonded.

SOME USES OF MAGNESIUM, CALCIUM, ZINC AND THEIR COMPOUNDS

Magnesium metal: useful in a wide variety of low-density alloys, particularly with aluminium. Zinc metal:

(*a*) in a variety of alloys such as brass (p137);

(*b*) to protect iron/steel from corrosion by covering with a thin layer of zinc (galvanising, p145);

(*c*) in dry cells (e.g. torch batteries, p99) because it is the most convenient fairly reactive metal in the activity series.

Magnesium compounds: sometimes used in medicines, e.g. a suspension of the hydroxide is the active ingredient of 'milk of magnesia' (to neutralise acidity in the stomach), and the sulphate is a laxative (Epsom salts).

Calcium carbonate (limestone): in the blast furnace (p134); to prepare the oxide and hydroxide (see next substance); as marble in building.

Calcium hydroxide: in the manufacture of mortar and cement; as a cheap industrial base; for neutralising acid soils; for softening hard water.

Calcium sulphate: to prepare plaster of paris, plaster and plasterboard, as 'blackboard chalk'.

Zinc compounds: in paints; in ointments, such as calamine lotion (which contains the carbonate).

3 ALUMINIUM AND ITS COMPOUNDS

ALUMINIUM METAL

(i) The metal does not normally show its reactive nature because it is protected by a thick but tough film of oxide.

(ii) The protective layer of oxide makes the metal unreactive in cold water or steam, it does not burn in air, and it does not react rapidly with acids (see Activity Series, p94).

(iii) See **anodising**, p.120

(iv) Aluminium is one of the few metals which react with *alkalis*. This is why aluminium pans react with alkaline cleaning fluids, (and they also react with fruit juices, which are acidic, although not rapidly because of the oxide coating).

ALUMINIUM COMPOUNDS

All the common ones are white.

SOME USES OF ALUMINIUM AND ITS COMPOUNDS

The metal can be worked or shaped by almost every metal-working process, so it is used in a wide variety of ways. In addition, it has a low density and yet, when alloyed, can be as strong as steel. It resists corrosion (because of its oxide layer), is a good conductor of heat and electricity, and is non-toxic. When anodised (p120) it can be dyed attractively. 30% of aluminium used in Europe is recycled.

You should be able to suggest which of the above advantages make aluminium very useful for the following: saucepans; storage tanks; milk churns; packaging foil; in alloys for aircraft bodies, 'aluminium'-framed greenhouses, and long-distance power cables.

Aluminium oxide is used in the treatment of water and paper, in glass-making, pottery, and as a catalyst in industry.

4 IRON AND ITS COMPOUNDS

IRON METAL

(i) It is magnetic.

(ii) Its reaction with cold water is rusting (p143). It also reacts slightly when heated in steam (p95).

(iii) It does not burn when heated in air, and it reacts only slowly with dilute acids unless heated, (see Activity Series, p94).

(iv) It reacts when heated in chlorine (p320) and when heated with sulphur (p309).

IRON COMPOUNDS

(i) All common iron compounds are coloured.

(ii) Remember that there are iron(II) compounds (in which iron has a combining power or valency of 2) and also iron(III) compounds (valency 3). Most of the *common* compounds of iron are iron(II) compounds.

(iii) Iron(II) compounds are easily oxidised to iron(III) compounds. Oxygen in the air and many other oxidising agents will do this, e.g. hydrogen peroxide, concentrated sulphuric acid and chlorine.

USES OF IRON AND ITS COMPOUNDS

Most of the iron produced is changed immediately into steel (p137). Small quantities are used as cast iron (brittle, but can be useful) and wrought iron (a purer form of iron which is softer and can be *worked*, e.g. into chains and ornamental gates). (Although it is not really a *use*, you should understand that small amounts of iron compounds are needed by the body, to produce red blood cells.)

5 LEAD, COPPER AND THEIR COMPOUNDS

LEAD METAL

(i) Unreactive with acids, water and air (low in the Activity Series).

(ii) Very dense but also very soft.

LEAD COMPOUNDS

The only common soluble lead salt is lead(II) nitrate, $Pb(NO_3)_2$. All lead compounds are toxic.

COPPER METAL

(i) Unreactive with acids, water and air (low in the Activity Series).

(ii) Attractively coloured metal, fairly easy to work.

COPPER COMPOUNDS

(i) The metal forms copper(I) and copper(II) compounds. The common ones are all copper(II) compounds.

(ii) All copper(II) compounds are coloured.

(iii) All copper compounds are toxic.

SOME USES OF LEAD AND ITS COMPOUNDS

About 50% of the lead produced is used in storage batteries such as those used in cars. Nearly half of the lead used comes from recycled metal. Smaller quantities are used in making coloured pigments, pipes, cable sheathing and solder.

SOME USES OF COPPER AND ITS COMPOUNDS

(*a*)   The metal is a good conductor of heat and electricity, resists corrosion and is easy to work. For these reasons, over half of the copper made is used in electrical wiring and motors.

(*b*)   Its resistance to corrosion (particularly its lack of reaction with water or steam) and its ease of working means that about 20% of the metal made is used in plumbing (pipes and boilers).

(*c*)   Common alloys containing copper include the bronzes (copper and tin), the brasses (copper and zinc) and the 'coinage' alloys (copper+tin+zinc for pennies, etc. and copper+nickel for 'silver' coins).

(*d*)   The attractive appearance of the pure metal is used in decorative and ornamental work.

(*e*)   Copper(I) oxide, which is a red colour, is used in making red glass, and copper(II) sulphate is used in garden fungicides and in electroplating.

7.2 GENERAL PROPERTIES OF COMPOUNDS OF METALS

When you need to remember something about a particular compound of a metal, try to think about it like this:

1   Ask yourself what *type* of compound it is. For example, suppose that you are asked for some information about calcium carbonate. What type of compound is this? It is a *carbonate*. Try to remember the *general* properties of carbonates of metals. Most of these will then apply to calcium carbonate. It is much easier to do this than to try to learn information about each *separate* carbonate.

2   Then look at the problem from 'the other way round'. Calcium carbonate is also a compound of *calcium* as well as being a carbonate. If you remember the *general* properties of calcium compounds (p156) you will be able to add further information. For example, as all calcium compounds are white and ionic, then calcium carbonate must be white and ionic.

3   Finally, try to remember anything special about the substance.

If you do not think of *types* of chemicals in this way, there is a real danger that you could fail to answer a question which is in fact quite easy. Suppose that you are asked how to prepare a sample of zinc sulphate. Many students would rack their brains trying to remember how they have made this particular substance in the laboratory. This may be the wrong approach. It is quite possible that they may never have prepared this particular chemical. They are making the mistake of thinking of zinc sulphate as a particular, individual chemical, rather than as a general type. If we ask ourselves what *type* of chemical zinc sulphate is, the problem becomes one of how to prepare a sulphate of a metal. Sulphates of metals are salts (p181). As zinc sulphate is a soluble salt (see p182) we can use any of the typical methods (p182). The possible reactions are

(*a*)   sulphuric acid+zinc oxide (acid+base);

(*b*)   sulphuric acid+zinc hydroxide (acid+base);

(*c*)   sulphuric acid+zinc carbonate (acid+carbonate);

(*d*)   sulphuric acid+zinc metal (acid+metal, though this is not the best choice as the reaction is slow). The *details* of the method we choose will be the same as when we used the method in the laboratory, but perhaps with different chemicals.

1 OXIDES OF METALS

An oxide of a metal is a *compound*. It contains two elements only; a metal and oxygen.

WHAT REACTIONS HAVE I SEEN IN WHICH OXIDES OF METALS ARE FORMED?

(i) See Table 4.2, p93.
(ii) See the **thermal decompositions** of carbonates and nitrates (p97).

IMPORTANT GENERAL PROPERTIES OF OXIDES OF METALS

(i) Most oxides of metals are **bases.** They will neutralise an acid to form a salt and water only. (See salt preparations, (p183).)
(ii) Some are **amphoteric** (see classification of oxides, p218), e.g. ZnO, Al_2O_3.
(iii) See Table 7.1.

Table 7.1: Some common oxides of metals

Formula	Name	Colour	Any special points
Na_2O	sodium monoxide	white	reacts with water to form sodium hydroxide
Na_2O_2	sodium peroxide	pale yellow	
CaO	calcium oxide	white	common name 'lime' or 'quicklime'. Reacts with water to form calcium hydroxide
MgO	magnesium oxide	white	
ZnO	zinc oxide	white	yellow when hot Amphoteric
Al_2O_3	aluminium oxide	white	Amphoteric
Fe_2O_3	Iron(III) oxide	red	Main component of most common 'iron ore'
PbO	lead(II) oxide	yellow	Amphoteric
CuO	copper(II) oxide	black	

Notes   (i) The reaction between calcium oxide and water is exothermic, producing an alkaline solution:

$$CaO(s) + H_2O(l) \rightarrow Ca(OH)_2(aq)$$

(ii) If you have studied the **reduction** of any of these oxides, revise the details, e.g.
CuO by C or H_2
PbO by C
ZnO by CO, etc.

2 HYDROXIDES OF METALS

A hydroxide of a metal is a compound. It contains a metal joined to the *hydroxide* radical, OH.

WHAT REACTIONS HAVE I SEEN IN WHICH A HYDROXIDE OF A METAL IS FORMED?

Hydroxides of metals (except those of sodium and potassium) are **insoluble** in water. They are formed as **precipitates** when two solutions are mixed. One solution must contain *metal* ions and the other solution must be an *alkali*. All solutions of alkalis contain *hydroxide* ions. For example, suppose that we want to make copper hydroxide. We can mix a *solution* of a copper salt (the sulphate, nitrate or chloride) with any alkali (e.g. sodium hydroxide solution or ammonia solution). The first solution contains metal ions (copper ions in this case). The second solution contains hydroxide ions, because it is an alkali. The two solutions react to form a precipitate of copper hydroxide.

Fig 7.2 Precipitating the hydroxide of a metal

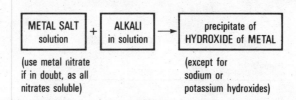

These hydroxides are sometimes coloured. They are used to test for different metals in solution (p167). Some of them *do dissolve* if excess alkali is used (Table 7.2). These special points are different for each hydroxide, and they are used in the tests for metals. The formation of these insoluble hydroxides is best shown by ionic equations such as

$$Cu^{2+}(aq) + 2OH^-(aq) \rightarrow Cu(OH)_2(s).$$

Table 7.2 Some common hydroxides of metals

Formula	Name	Colour	Does it dissolve in water?	Does it dissolve in excess NaOh soln?	Does it dissolve in excess NH_3 soln?
NaOH	sodium hydroxide	white	yes	–	–
KOH	potassium hydroxide	white	yes	–	–
$Ca(OH)_2$	calcium hydroxide	white	slightly	no	–
$Mg(OH)_2$	magnesium hydroxide	white	very slightly	no	no
$Fe(OH)_2$	iron(II) hydroxide	dirty green	no	no	no
$Fe(OH)_3$	iron(III) hydroxide	brown	no	no	no
$Al(OH)_3$	aluminium hydroxide	white	no	yes – amphoteric	no
$Cu(OH)_2$	copper(II) hydroxide	blue	no	no	yes – forms a complex salt
$Zn(OH)_2$	zinc hydroxide	white	no	yes – amphoteric	yes – forms a complex salt

Note Any hydroxides which are insoluble in water can be precipitated as described on above. However, if too much alkali is used in the reaction, the precipitates which are formed may then dissolve again)see last two columns of table). The WJEC Syllabus also includes the hydroxide of lead.

IMPORTANT GENERAL PROPERTIES OF HYDROXIDES OF METALS

(i) Hydroxides of metals are **bases.** They neutralise acids to form a salt and water only (see salt preparations, p183).
(ii) Some metal hydroxides dissolve in sodium hydroxide solution (or potassium hydroxide) because they are amphoteric (Table 7.2 and p218).

(iii) Some hydroxides of metals dissolve in ammonia solution, because they form complex salts with ammonia (Table 7.2).

3 CARBONATES OF METALS

A carbonate of a metal is a compound. It contains a *metal* joined to the *carbonate radical*, CO_3.

WHAT REACTIONS HAVE I SEEN IN WHICH CARBONATES OF METALS ARE FORMED?

Carbonates of metals (except those of sodium and potassium) are **insoluble** in water. (See the note about hydroxides on p162. Hydroxides and carbonates are very similar in this way.) Like hydroxides of metals, they are formed as **precipitates** when two solutions are mixed. One solution must contain *metal* ions, and the other solution must contain *carbonate* ions. The only two *solutions* which can contain carbonate ions are sodium carbonate and potassium carbonate; all other carbonates are insoluble.

Fig 7.3 Precipitating the carbonate of a metal

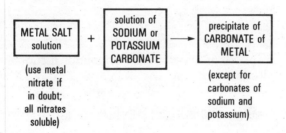

The formation of insoluble carbonates is best shown by ionic equations, e.g.:

$$Mg^{2+}(aq) + CO_3^{2-}(aq) \rightarrow MgCO_3(s)$$

IMPORTANT GENERAL PROPERTIES OF THE CARBONATES OF METALS

(i) Carbonates of metals fizz (**effervesce**) when mixed with dilute acids. The reaction forms a salt of the metal, carbon dioxide gas (which causes the fizzing) and water. This reaction is used to make salts (p182), to prepare carbon dioxide gas (p306), and as a test for carbonates (p168).

(ii) See thermal decomposition, (p97).

(iii) See Table 7.3.

Table 7.3 Some common carbonates of metals

Formula	Name	Does it dissolve in water?	Appearance	Other points
Na_2CO_3	sodium carbonate	yes	colourless crystals or white powder	
$CaCO_3$	calcium carbonate	no	white powder	Occurs in nature as chalk, limestone, marble
$MgCO_3$	magnesium carbonate	no	white powder	
$ZnCO_3$	zinc carbonate	no	white powder	
–	aluminium carbonate	–	–	Does not exist
$FeCO_3$	iron(II) carbonate	no	green powder	
–	iron(III) carbonate	–	–	Does not exist
$CuCO_3$	copper(II) carbonate	no	green powder	

Notes   (i) sodium hydrogencarbonate, $NaHCO_3$, is like the carbonate in its reaction with dilute acids, but the two compounds behave differently when heated. Sodium carbonate does not decompose when heated (apart from giving off water of crystallisation) but the hydrogencarbonate decomposes, giving off carbon dioxide:

$$2NaHCO_3(s) \rightarrow Na_2CO_3(s) + H_2O(g) + CO_2(g)$$

(ii) a solution of sodium carbonate in water is slightly *alkaline*.

4 NITRATES OF METALS

A nitrate of a metal is a compound. It contains a metal joined to the nitrate radical, NO_3.

WHAT REACTIONS HAVE I SEEN IN WHICH NITRATES OF METALS ARE FORMED?

Nitrates of metals are **salts.** You may have prepared a nitrate by any of the salt preparations which use an *acid* (p182). The acid used to make nitrates is nitric acid.

     metal oxide   + nitric acid → metal nitrate + water
     (base)   (a salt)
     metal hydroxide   + nitric acid → metal nitrate + water
     (a base)
     metal carbonate   + nitric acid → metal nitrate + water
                                       + carbon dioxide

SOME IMPORTANT GENERAL REACTIONS OF NITRATES

None. Remember that *all* nitrates are soluble.

5 SULPHATES OF METALS

A sulphate of a metal is a compound. It contains a metal joined to the *sulphate radical*, SO_4.

WHAT REACTIONS HAVE I SEEN IN WHICH SULPHATES OF METALS ARE FORMED?

Sulphates of metals are **salts.** Most of them are soluble, and so they can be made by any of the salt preparations which use an acid (p182). The acid used to make sulphates is sulphuric acid, H_2SO_4, e.g.:

> fairly reactive + sulphuric acid → metal sulphate + hydrogen metal

See above for other reactions, and replace nitric acid by sulphuric acid.

Note also that calcium sulphate, lead(II) sulphate and barium sulphate are *insoluble* in water. They cannot be made by the methods described above. Instead, they are precipitated by mixing a solution containing sulphate ions with a solution containing the metal ions. The precipitation of barium sulphate in this way is used as a test for a soluble sulphate (p168).

GENERAL REACTIONS OF SULPHATES

None (but see Table 7.4).

Table 7.4 Some common sulphates of metals

Formula	Name	Soluble in water?	Usual appearance	Other points
Na_2SO_4	sodium sulphate	yes	white crystals	
$CaSO_4$	calcium sulphate	*very* slightly	white powder	found naturally as gypsum and anhydrite
$MgSO_4$	magnesium sulphate	yes	colourless crystals	common name Epsom salts
$ZnSO_4$	zinc sulphate	yes	white crystals	
$FeSO_4$	iron(II) sulphate	yes	green crystals (white if anhydrous)	
$CuSO_4$	copper(II) sulphate	yes	blue crystals (white if anhydrous)	anhydrous form used to prove if water is present
$BaSO_4$	barium sulphate	no	white powder	normally only seen as the precipitate in a positive sulphate test

Notes When gypsum is heated, it loses *some* of its water of crystallisation to form plaster of Paris.

$$2(CaSO_4.2H_2O)(s) \rightarrow \begin{matrix} CaSO_4 \\ CaSO_4 \end{matrix} \!\!> H_2O(s) + 3H_2O(g)$$

6 CHLORIDES OF METALS   Chlorides of metals are compounds. They contain a metal joined to chlorine.

WHICH REACTIONS HAVE I SEEN IN WHICH CHLORIDES OF METALS ARE FORMED?

(*a*)   All chlorides of metals are **salts.** Most of them are soluble, and so they can be made by any of the salt preparations which use an acid (p182). The acid used to make chlorides is hydrochloric acid, HCl. (See p164 for examples of reactions, and simply replace nitric acid by hydrochloric acid.)

(*b*)   Many of the reactive or fairly reactive metals *burn* when heated in chlorine gas to form the metal chloride. You may have seen sodium or magnesium metals used in this way (Fig 7.4).

e.g. $\quad 2Na(s) + Cl_2(g) \rightarrow 2NaCl(s)$

$\quad\quad Mg(s) + Cl_2(g) \rightarrow MgCl_2(s)$

Fig 7.4 Formation of chlorides of metals

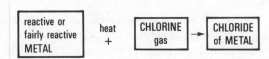

(c) Only two fairly common chlorides of metals are insoluble in water. These are lead(II) chloride, $PbCl_2$, and silver chloride, AgCl. They cannot be made by the methods in (a). Instead, they are precipitated by mixing a solution containing chloride ions with a solution containing the metal ions. The precipitation of silver chloride in this way is used as a test for a soluble chloride (p167).

(d) The chloride, bromide and iodide of silver are affected by light; you may have done an experiment to show this. These compounds are used to make photographic film and papers.

GENERAL REACTIONS OF CHLORIDES

None.

7.3 HOW TO TEST FOR COMMON COMPOUNDS OF METALS. TESTS FOR SOME COMMON GASES

1 TESTS FOR COMPOUNDS OF METALS

A compound of a metal is usually ionically bonded. It contains two types of ions – a **metal** ion and an ion of a **non-metal.** (The non-metal ion is often a **radical** (p23) such as the sulphate radical, SO_4, rather than a simple non-metal such as chlorine.)

For example, copper(II) sulphate ($CuSO_4$) contains two 'parts':

$$\text{COPPER(II) IONS} + \text{SULPHATE IONS}$$
$$Cu^{2+} \quad\quad\quad SO_4^{2-}$$

We can therefore test an 'unknown' compound of a metal for two different parts – a metal part and 'the rest'.

(a) TESTS FOR SOME COMMON IONS OF METALS

(i) Flame tests

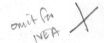
omit for NEA

Test	Result if positive
Clean a nichrome or platinum wire by dipping in hydrochloric acid and then a roaring Bunsen flame. Repeat until no colour given to flame. Moisten wire with the acid and pick up a small sample of the test substance on it. Hold wire and sample in roaring flame.	Deep golden yellow: sodium ions present Na^+ Apple green: barium ions present, Ba^{2+} Green-blue: copper ions present, Cu^{2+} Brick red: calcium ions present, Ca^{2+} Lilac: potassium ions present, K^+ Scarlet: lithium ions present, Li^+

(ii) Tests for metal (and ammonium) ions by using alkalis

When an alkali (e.g. sodium hydroxide solution, or ammonia solution) is added to a solution containing metal ions, the metal hydroxide is often precipitated. The *colours* of the precipitates, and whether or not they *dissolve in excess alkali* are used to decide which metal ions are present in the solution.

Notes (i) For an explanation of the reactions involved in these tests see Table 7.2 and p162).

(ii) The ammonium ion, NH_4^+, is included in the tests. It is not a metal ion, but it does sometimes 'take the place of' a metal in a compound, e.g. ammonium chloride, NH_4Cl.

Ion	Test	Result if positive
Aluminium	Take two samples. Do same tests as for calcium, but make sure excess ammonia used in (ii)	Sample (i): white precipitate which dissolves in excess. In (ii) white precipitate which does not dissolve in excess
Ammonium	Add dilute sodium hydroxide solution, then warm	Ammonia gas produced Test for gas (p168)
Calcium	Take two samples. To (i) add sodium hydroxide solution. Then add excess and stir. To (ii) add dilute ammonia solution	Sample (i): white precipitate which does not dissolve in excess. Sample (ii): no precipitate
Copper(II)	Add dilute ammonia solution, drop by drop, stirring constantly	Pale blue precipitate formed at first, which then dissolves to form a deep blue solution
Iron(II)	Add dilute sodium hydroxide solution or ammonia solution	Dirty-green precipitate
Iron(III)	As for iron(II)	Red-brown precipitate
Magnesium	Take two samples. Add dilute sodium hydroxide to (i) and dilute ammonia to (ii). Add excess in each case	White precipitate produced in each case. (May be only faint with ammonia). Neither precipitate dissolves in excess
Zinc	Take two samples. Carry out tests as for magnesium	In *both* tests a white precipitate forms which dissolves in excess

2 TESTS FOR SOME COMMON NON-METAL IONS

Remember, the 'metal' part is only part of a compound. The tests in this section are for the 'other' part of a compound.

Ion	Test	Results of test if positive
Soluble chloride	Add dilute *nitric* acid until solution is acidic. Then add silver *nitrate* solution	White precipitate formed

The precipitate is silver chloride. See p186 for chemistry of test. Ionic equation:

$$Ag^+(aq) + Cl^-(aq) \rightarrow AgCl(s)$$

Ion	Test	Results of test if positive
Soluble sulphate	Add dilute hydro*chloric* acid until solution acidic. Then add barium *chloride* solution	White precipitate formed
	The precipitate is barium sulphate. See p186 for chemistry of test. Ionic equation: $Ba^{2+}(aq)+SO_4^{2-}(aq) \rightarrow BaSO_4(s)$	
Carbonates	Add a little dilute hydrochloric acid	Mixture fizzes (effervesces). Carbon dioxide gas given off. Test for gas as below
Nitrates	Add dilute sodium hydroxide until solution alkaline. Add a little Devarda's alloy or aluminium and warm	Ammonia gas formed. Test for the gas as below

Note In the first two tests, the chemicals used are in 'matching pairs'. To help you remember the correct pairs, the key hints *are in italics*.

3 TESTS FOR SOME COMMON GASES

As some of the tests for non-metal ions (above) produce *gases*, you must also know how to tell which gas is being formed.

Gas	Test	Result of test if positive
Ammonia	1 Expose gas to damp red litmus paper, **or**	Paper goes blue
	2 Expose gas to fumes of hydrogen chloride (e.g. from a bottle of concentrated hydrochloric acid)	Thick white cloud of ammonium chloride 'smoke' formed
Carbon dioxide	Pass gas into calcium hydroxide solution (lime water), e.g. by collecting small amount in teat pipette and squeezing it out into a small volume of calcium hydroxide solution in a test tube	Calcium hydroxide solution goes 'milky'. (This is because a fine precipitate of calcium carbonate, or chalk, is formed)
Chlorine	Expose gas to *damp* blue litmus paper	Paper goes pink and is then bleached
Hydrogen	Trap gas in a test tube. Put *lighted* taper quickly to mouth of test tube	Squeaky pop
Oxygen	Put *glowing* taper to sample in test tube	Taper relights
Hydrogen chloride	Expose gas to ammonia fumes (e.g. from bottle of concentrated ammonia solution)	Thick white cloud of ammonium chloride 'smoke'
Nitrogen	Try all other gas tests	If none positive, gas probably nitrogen
Sulphur dioxide	Expose gas to filter paper soaked in acidified potassium dichromate(VI)	Paper changes from orange to green

CHECK YOUR UNDERSTANDING (Answers on p412)

Note You do not need to learn *all* of the facts used in these questions. If necessary, look up information from the chapter.

1   Name each of the following gases.

(*a*)   This gas turns damp blue litmus paper pink, and then bleaches it.

(*b*)   This gas relights a glowing taper.

(*c*)   This gas reacts with calcium hydroxide solution and makes it go cloudy.

2   Name each metal described below.

(*a*)   Metal A reacts rapidly with dilute acids, but not with cold water. It is more reactive than zinc.

(*b*)   Metal B is stored in oil and burns, when heated in air, with a lilac coloured flame.

(*c*)   Metal C has an attractive appearance when pure. It will not react with dilute sulphuric or hydrochloric acid, but it does form a black oxide when heated in air.

(*d*)   Metal D reacts violently with cold water and burns when heated with a yellow coloured flame.

(*e*)   Metal E is used to galvanise steel.

(*f*)   Metal F is protected naturally by a thin layer of its oxide. It can be anodised.

(*g*)   When metal G is made, most of it is immediately changed into steel.

(*h*)   Metal H is dense but soft. It is used to make car batteries.

3   Name each of the following *compounds* of metals from the clues provided.

(*a*)   This substance is a base. It is a compound of copper. It contains two elements only.

(*b*)   This substance is a base. It is a compound of magnesium. It contains three elements.

(*c*)   This substance neutralises acids to form a salt and water only. It contains two elements. One is a metal which has a combining power (valency) of 2 in the compound, but it can also have a combining power of 3.

(*d*)   This substance reacts with acids to form carbon dioxide gas. It is a compound of a metal which burns with a brick red flame.

(*e*)   This substance is white but goes blue when water is added.

(*f*)   This substance gives a brick-red flame test, and forms a white precipitate when mixed with silver nitrate solution.

(*g*)   This gives a blue-green flame test, and also forms a white precipitate when mixed with barium chloride solution.

(*h*)   This substance is the most important and the most common strong alkali.

4   Name the following compounds.

(a) CuO (b) Na_2CO_3 (c) $Al_2(SO_4)_3$ (d) $Cu(OH)_2$
(e) $FeCl_2$ (f) $FeCl_3$ (g) $Mg(NO_3)_2$

5   Name the acid you would use to make each of the following salts.
    (*a*)   magnesium nitrate
    (*b*)   iron(II) chloride
    (*c*)   copper(II) sulphate.

6   Salts are usually chlorides, nitrates, sulphates or carbonates of metals. Look up information about the solubility of the following compounds and answer the questions.
    (*a*)   Which salts of calcium can be made by precipitation?
    (*b*)   Which metals form compounds, all of which are soluble?
    (*c*)   Which kind of salt is always soluble, no matter which metal it contains?
    (*d*)   Which salts of sodium could be made by precipitation?
    (*e*)   Which carbonates can be made by precipitation?

7   The members of each of the following groups have something in common. Decide what it is in each case.
    (*a*)   Limestone, marble, chalk.
    (*b*)   Brass, solder, duralumin.

8   Decide whether each of the following is true or false.
    (*a*)   Sodium chloride is often made by adding sodium metal to dilute hydrochloric acid.
    (*b*)   Nitrates can be prepared by reacting a metal oxide with dilute nitric acid.
    (*c*)   Sulphates can be made by reacting a metal carbonate with any kind of dilute acid.

9   Name the metal present in each of the following.
    (*a*)   A solution of this substance gives a red-brown precipitate when mixed with sodium hydroxide solution.
    (*b*)   A solution of this substance forms a blue precipitate when an alkali is added.

10 A student has suggested that a salt can be made by each of the following reactions. In actual fact, there is something wrong with each of the suggestions. For each salt, explain why the suggested reaction would not work and suggest one which would. You will need to look up information.
    (*a*)   To make aluminium sulphate, react aluminium carbonate with dilute sulphuric acid.
    (*b*)   To make copper(II) sulphate, mix a solution containing copper(II) ions with a solution containing sulphate ions and filter off the precipitate of copper(II) sulphate.
    (*c*)   To make zinc sulphate, mix solutions of zinc chloride and dilute sulphuric acid and crystallise the salt formed in the usual way.
    (*d*)   To prepare calcium sulphate, mix solutions of sodium sulphate and calcium carbonate.
    (*e*)   To prepare copper(II) chloride, react copper metal with dilute hydrochloric acid.

CHECK LIST ▶ SYLLABUSES VARY CONSIDERABLY IN DEALING WITH THE COMPOUNDS OF METALS. YOU SHOULD CHECK CAREFULLY THAT YOU REVISE ONLY THE INFORMATION WHICH IS RELEVANT TO YOUR SYLLABUS. THE GUIDE ON P.13 SHOULD HELP. REMEMBER THAT *SOME* FACTS MUST BE LEARNED, BUT NOT *ALL* OF THE FACTS IN THIS CHAPTER. IT IS MORE IMPORTANT THAT YOU SHOULD UNDERSTAND HOW TO *USE* INFORMATION WHICH IS GIVEN TO YOU.

SPECIMEN EXAMINATION QUESTIONS

See general note before questions on pp49 and 50.

Remember that you may be allowed to use a data book in the examination.

1 What tests could you do to tell the difference between the following substances? In each case, say what you would do and what you would expect to happen.

(*a*)   Copper(II) oxide and carbon,

(*b*)   magnesium and iron.   [*SEG* spec I]

2 The element which is less dense than water, melts at 98°C and conducts electricity is

A copper   B hydrogen   C iodine   D sodium
E sulphur

3 A substance has the following properties.

Its solution in water conducts electricity. It becomes white when heated but gives a coloured solution in water. There is no evolution of gas when it is added to aqueous sodium carbonate.

The substance could be a

A metallic element   B non-metallic element   C solid acid
D non-electrolyte   E hydrated salt   [*LEA* spec (B), 1]

4 Which one of these substances decreases in mass when heated in air?

A Copper(II) oxide   B Magnesium   C Sodium chloride
D Zinc carbonate

5–7 The table below gives the results of tests on four gases A,B,C and D. All four gases are colourless.

Gas	Colour seen when tested with damp indicator paper	Effect of lighted splint
A	Blue	Splint extinguished
B	No change	Gas ignites
C	No change	Splint burns more brightly
D	Red	Splint extinguished

Which one of the above gases, A,B,C or D, is

5 Hydrogen?   6 Oxygen?   7 Hydrogen chloride?

[*SEG* spec (Alt) 1]

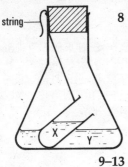

string

Fig 7.5 Diagram
for question 8

8 In Fig 7.5 X is aqueous silver nitrate and Y is aqueous sodium chloride.

When the apparatus is inverted to mix them

A   the total mass increases

B   the total mass decreases

C   a white precipitate is formed

D   a gas is given off

E   there is no apparent change in the mixture

[*LEA* spec (A), 1]

9–13 In questions 9–13 choose from the following list the letter representing the gas described by the statement in the question. Each letter may be used once, more than once, or not at all.

A ammonia   B chlorine   C hydrogen   D nitrogen

E sulphur dioxide

9 A gas which is coloured. **10** A gas which is produced commercially by the fractional distillation of liquid air. **11** A gas which forms white fumes in contact with hydrogen chloride. **12** A gas which is a by-product of the burning of fossil fuels. **13** A gas which bleaches damp blue litmus paper.

[*NISEC* spec 1]

†14 Aqueous sodium hydroxide can be used to distinguish between members of each of the following pairs of substances. Describe how you would carry out these tests, giving the observations and results of each test and stating how you would identify any gas evolved. Write an equation for each reaction occurring.

(*a*)   ammonium chloride and potassium chloride

(*b*)   magnesium and aluminium

(*c*)   aqueous iron(II) sulphate and aqueous iron(III) sulphate.

(*NISEC* spec 3)

†15 The labels have become unreadable on three bottles which were known to contain ammonium chloride, calcium carbonate and iron(II) sulphate. What *chemical* tests would you carry out to enable you to relabel the bottles correctly? Your answers must include at least one *positive chemical test* for each substance that would **not** be given by any of the others.

[*LEA* spec (A), 3]

ACIDS, BASES AND SALTS. pH AND NEUTRALISATION

CONTENTS

8.1 ACIDS AND BASES

ACIDS

There are many acids, but only three are commonly used in the laboratory. These are shown in Fig 8.1.

Fig 8.1 The three acids commonly used in the laboratory

SULPHURIC ACID H_2SO_4	HYDROCHLORIC ACID HCl	NITRIC ACID HNO_3

Another common acid is the organic acid, ethanoic acid, CH_3COOH. This is sometimes called acetic acid.

Acids are sometimes **dilute** (mixed with lots of water). They can

Fig 8.2 Hazard symbols

also be **concentrated.** Remember that an acid sometimes has very different properties when it is concentrated. Always put (aq) after the formula of an acid if it is dilute, e.g. HCl(aq). Be particularly careful with the formula HCl. This formula also refers to the *gas* hydrogen chloride. If we mean the gas, we should write the formula as HCl(g). Most dilute acids are not particularly dangerous, but many acids are transported in the concentrated form, when they can be very dangerous unless used carefully. **Hazchem** signs (Fig 8.2) have been developed to warn people about using different acids, and to advise what to do in emergency (e.g. if a road tanker is involved in an accident).

IMPORTANT REACTIONS OF DILUTE ACIDS

Common acidic solutions include: vinegar, fruit juices, battery acid, fizzy drinks and acid rain.

1 Action on indicators

Solutions of acids change the colour of an indicator. These colour changes are listed, and compared with those given by alkalis, on p177.

2 Acids react with carbonates and hydrogencarbonates

All dilute acids react with *any* carbonate or hydrogencarbonate, to form a salt, carbon dioxide and water.

Note   (i) It is useful to practise writing balanced equations for the reactions between the common acids and a variety of carbonates.
(ii) If you understand ionic equations, remember that just one ionic equation applies to *any* acid+carbonate reaction:

$$CO_3^{2-}(aq \text{ or } s) + 2H^+(aq) \rightarrow CO_2(g) + H_2O(l)$$

The other ions which are present (from the carbonate and acid) remain 'free' in solution as **spectator ions.**

3 Some acids react with some metals

There is no *general* way in which an acid reacts with a metal. What happens depends upon each metal and each acid. An understanding of the Activity Series is very helpful for these reactions (see p92 and Table 4.3 on p94).

BASES

A base is a kind of 'chemical opposite' to an acid. There are many different bases. The most useful thing to remember is that **any oxide or hydroxide of a metal is a base.** It is much better to remember this simple fact, than to try to remember whether each chemical you come across is a base.

The large family of bases is divided into a small subgroup called the **alkalis.** An alkali is simply a base which can dissolve in water. An alkali has the same properties as all bases, but in addition it can dissolve in water. There is no point in learning the name of each base, because there are so many of them, but it is useful to remember the common alkalis. There are only three:

Fig 8.3 The three common alkalis

SODIUM HYDROXIDE NaOH	POTASSIUM HYDROXIDE KOH	AMMONIA SOLUTION $NH_3(aq)$

Calcium hydroxide, (lime water, $Ca(OH)_2$) is also an alkali, but it is rarely considered to be so.

The alkalis can be more dangerous than some of the dilute acids. Sodium and potassium hydroxides, even when very dilute, can damage the surface of the eye. They also react with skin, and must be treated with great care. Note that a substance which 'dissolves' flesh is called **caustic.** Sodium and potassium hydroxides are caustic.

IMPORTANT REACTIONS OF BASES AND ALKALIS

1 Alkalis change the colour of indicators

Only *solutions* of bases (alkalis) can affect indicators. All acids and alkalis give the following colour changes with common indicators.

Indicator	Colour in acid	Colour in alkali
litmus solution	red	blue
red litmus paper	stays red	blue
blue litmus paper	red	stays blue
universal	red, orange or yellow (p179)	blue or purple

2 Bases will neutralise acids

The reaction between a base (or an alkali) and an acid is very important. In general, *any* acid and *any* base react like this:

$$ACID + BASE \rightarrow A\ SALT + WATER$$

The two substances **neutralise** each other (cancel each other out) if they are mixed in equal proportions. This reaction is used to make salts (p.183) and to neutralise any spillage of acid or alkali. If you can work out full chemical equations, it is useful to do so for some typical reactions of this type.

Examples of this type of reaction include:

copper(II) oxide + hydrochloric acid $\rightarrow$ copper(II) chloride + water

(a salt)

(a base because it is an oxide of a metal)

calcium hydroxide + nitric acid $\rightarrow$ calcium nitrate + water

(a salt)

(a base because it is a hydroxide of a metal)

Alkalis are suppliers of hydroxide ions

Solutions of the alkalis (but not the insoluble bases) contain free hydroxide ions, OH^-. The solutions are used to precipitate hydroxides of other metals (p162). These reactions are also used to test for metal compounds in solution (p167).

4 Bases and alkalis react with ammonium compounds

When any base or alkali is warmed with an ammonium compound, the gas ammonia is formed. This can be detected by the test described on p168. We can make use of this reaction in two ways:

(*a*)   It is used to prepare ammonia gas in the laboratory; and

(*b*)   it can be used to discover whether an 'unknown' substance is an ammonium compound (p167), e.g.

calcium   + ammonium → ammonia + calcium + water
hydroxide   chloride   chloride
$$Ca(OH)_2(s) + 2NH_4Cl(s) \rightarrow 2NH_3(g) + CaCl_2(s) + 2H_2O(l)$$
(a base)

5 Special reactions given by two particular alkalis

Sodium and potassium hydroxides (and no other base or alkali) will react with oxides of metals if they are **amphoteric** (p218). The only common amphoteric oxides are aluminium oxide, Al_2O_3, and zinc oxide, ZnO. The reaction in each case produces a salt (e.g. sodium aluminate or potassium zincate) and water. Similarly, the *hydroxides* of these same two metals also react with these two alkalis, to produce similar salts. See Table 7.2, p162, and the tests on p167.

In a similar way, aluminium and zinc *metals* will also react with these two alkalis. No other common metals react with alkalis. Aluminium and zinc are unusual in reacting with *both* acids and alkalis to form a salt+hydrogen. Their oxides and hydroxides are equally unusual in reacting with *both* acids and alkalis to form a salt and water.

WHAT MAKES AN ACID AN ACID (AND A BASE A BASE)?

All acidic *solutions* have the reactions of acids, because they all have two things in common. Firstly, all acids need to be *dissolved* in a solvent (usually water) before they can behave as acids. Secondly, the acid *reacts* with the water to give up $H^+(aq)$ ions. It is the presence of $H^+(aq)$ ions which makes a solution acidic. A substance can only act as an acid if it can give up H^+ ions. Usually, it needs water to do this.

You have probably seen experiments in which *solid* acids such as citric or tartaric acid are dissolved in a *dry* organic (molecular) liquid such as methylbenzene. Such solutions do not show any of the normal reactions of acids. They do not change the colour of indicators, react with metals, react with carbonates, and so on, as long as the substances are *dry*. As soon as water is added, however, the substances give the usual properties of acidic solutions.

It can also be shown that *pure* liquid acids, such as concentrated sulphuric acid, are not electrolytes. As soon as water is added, such liquids become both acidic *and* electrolytes. The addition of water forms ions. The ions mean that the substance becomes an electrolyte. As some of the ions are $H^+(aq)$, the solution also becomes acidic.

$$\text{ACID} + \text{WATER} \rightarrow H^+(aq) + \text{SOME OTHER ION}$$
$$\text{e.g. } HCl(g) + \text{water} \rightarrow H^+(aq) + Cl^-(aq)$$

As the H^+ ion is really a proton, an acid is sometimes defined as a substance which is capable of producing a proton.

You should understand why a mixture of sodium hydrogencarbonate and a solid acid such as tartaric acid does not react until water is added. Baking powder is made of such a mixture. It only reacts and produces carbon dioxide when water is added. Health salts work in a similar way.

Bases, of course, are the 'opposites' of acids. They are substances which can *receive* a H^+ ion. Only substances which can do this can be called a base. The oxide ion in metal oxides (O^{2-}) and the hydroxide ion in metal hydroxides (OH^-) are both able to combine with a H^+ ion. That is why these substances are bases. Ammonia is a base for the same reason; it can combine with a H^+ ion to form the NH_4^+ (ammonium) ion. If you understand ionic equations, you will see that all these reactions are similar:

$$O^{2-}(s) + 2H^+(aq) \rightarrow H_2O(l)$$
$$OH^-(aq) + H^+(aq) \rightarrow H_2O(l)$$

8.2 pH AND NEUTRALISATION. SALTS

THE pH SCALE

All solutions of acids contain $H^+(aq)$ ions. A solution which is very acidic contains a high concentration of $H^+(aq)$ ions. Acid solutions can therefore vary a great deal; some have high concentrations of $H^+(aq)$ ions, and others have only low concentrations. In order to measure the concentration of $H^+(aq)$ ions, and to compare the acidity of substances, we use a scale of numbers called the pH scale. The scale normally runs from pH 0 to pH 14. A solution of pH 1 has a very high concentration of $H^+(aq)$ ions: it is very acidic. Acidity gradually decreases up the scale until at pH 7 acidity 'vanishes' and the substance is **neutral**. Above pH 7, a substance is alkaline. pH 8 is a weakly alkaline solution, but a solution of pH 14 is very alkaline.

The easiest way of finding the pH of a solution is to add a few drops of *universal indicator*. (This is sometimes called full-range

Fig 8.4 The pH scale

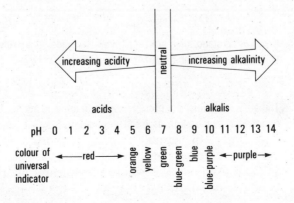

indicator.) This is a mixture of indicators and can change to several different colours, according to the pH (Fig 8.4).

There are many 'everyday' examples of the importance of pH values. For example, farmers and gardeners need to know the pH of soil before certain crops or plants can be grown at their best.

NEUTRALISATION

Acids and bases are chemical opposites. When an acid is mixed with a base, they 'destroy' (**neutralise**) each other. A neutral solution is neither acidic nor alkaline, and has a pH of 7.

Suppose that we have a solution of an acid in a beaker. The pH of the solution will be fairly low (somewhere between 1 and 7). Suppose that we then start to add a solution of an alkali to the acid. As the alkali is added it starts to neutralise the acid. The pH of the liquid in the beaker starts to rise. (In other words, the solution in the beaker becomes less acidic.) Eventually, when just the right amount of alkali has been added, the acid will be neutralised and the pH of the solution will be 7. (The reaction between the two chemicals will have produced a salt and water; none of the original acid or alkali will be left.)

If alkali is added *after* the neutralisation point has been reached, the solution will become alkaline. The pH of the solution will continue to rise, past the 7 mark. The opposite process occurs if an acid is added to an alkali. However, there is one special case which is worth remembering. If an *insoluble base* is added to an acid, it starts to neutralise the acid, exactly as an alkali does. In this special case, however, we can add 'too much' insoluble base without changing the pH. Once the acid has been neutralised, an excess of the insoluble base cannot dissolve and therefore it cannot affect the pH. This idea is very useful in making salts (p183). We do not need to measure an exact amount of the insoluble base. All we need to do is make sure that we use *an excess* (more than we need just to neutralise the acid). It is then a simple matter to remove the excess by filtering. On the other hand, when we make a salt by using an *alkali* and an acid, it is important that we do not use an excess of the alkali (p183).

Remember:

$$\text{ACID} + \text{BASE} \rightarrow \text{A SALT} + \text{WATER}$$

If you understand ionic equations, you will understand why the reaction between *any* acid and *any* alkali can be shown as:

$$H^+(aq) + OH^-(aq) \rightarrow H_2O(l).$$

The other ions which are present (spectator ions) do not join together unless the water is removed by evaporation, as in salt preparations.

Examples of neutralisation are important in everyday situations. There may be a need for a farmer or gardener to neutralise an acid soil, for example. We would use calcium hydroxide or calcium carbonate to do so. An excess of acid in the stomach can cause pain. One way of dealing with this is to neutralise the excess acidity by swallowing a **safe** weak base, e.g. 'milk of magnesia' or sodium hydrogencarbonate. Similarly, spillages of acid in a laboratory or after an accident can be neutralised by adding a substance such as sodium hydrogencarbonate. All of these 'anti-acids' or neutralisers are chosen because they are safe to use, and an excess of them cannot cause harm.

SALTS

Many students do not realise just how many common substances are salts. Because salts are so common, we need to know how to make them.

You may find it useful to think of a salt as being formed from 'two parents'. One of the 'parents' will almost certainly be an acid. The other will be a compound containing a metal or the ammonium ion. We can think of an acid as consisting of two parts. There is the *hydrogen part* (which is given up as H^+ ions when it reacts) and the 'rest' which forms a salt.

Fig 8.5 Formation of salts

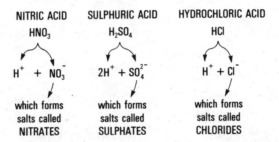

To make a salt, therefore, we need to choose the proper 'parent' chemicals; usually a metal compound (or an ammonium compound) and an acid. We must choose the proper acid, too; hydrochloric acid for a **chloride**, and so on.

Remember: The most common salts are

ANY METAL
(or the AMMONIUM RADICAL, NH_4) } joined to {
CHLORINE (a chloride)
or
SULPHATE
or
NITRATE
or
CARBONATE

METHODS OF MAKING SALTS

It is easy to decide which 'parent acid' to use in order to make a particular salt. It is more difficult to choose the 'other parent', because sometimes there are several possibilities. It is important that you *understand* the ideas used in this section. There is no point in just *learning* one or two examples you have used in the laboratory. Instead, you must be able to work out for yourself how to prepare a particular salt, even if you have not made it before. By simply changing the names of the chemicals, hundreds of different salts can be made.

The first thing you need to know is: **is the salt I need to make soluble in water?** You do not have to *learn* all solubilities! You will usually be given information, or allowed to look up information in a book of data. You may find it useful, however, to remember that:

> ALL NITRATES ARE SOLUBLE
> ALL SODIUM SALTS ARE SOLUBLE
> ALL POTASSIUM SALTS ARE SOLUBLE

If the salt is soluble, you can choose between methods 1–4. If the salt is insoluble, you **must** choose method 5, and precipitate it.

Remember also, that if the salt is soluble, it is likely that there will be *more than one way of making it*. In most cases you can decide which method you are most confident about, and describe it.

1 MAKING A SALT BY NEUTRALISING AN ACID WITH A CARBONATE

This is one of the most useful ways of making a salt. Almost any carbonate and any acid react as follows:

ACID+CARBONATE → A SALT+CARBON DIOXIDE+WATER

For example, if you wish to make the salt copper(II) sulphate, you could start with **copper(II) carbonate** and dilute **sulphuric acid**. You should be able to work out which carbonate and acid to use to make a variety of different salts.

Carbonates of metals are insoluble except for those of sodium and

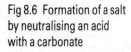
Fig 8.6 Formation of a salt by neutralising an acid with a carbonate

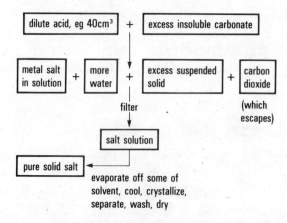

potassium. The general method is to add the solid carbonate to the acid in a beaker until the **carbonate is in excess.** It is easy to tell when enough has been added, because when the acid has been neutralised the 'fizzing' stops and the carbonate no longer dissolves. The carbonate is then in excess. It can then be filtered off, to leave a salt dissolved in water. The salt is then crystallised in the usual way (p74) The method can be summarised as shown in Fig 8.6.

Note If sodium or potassium carbonates are used, only *just* enough to neutralise the acid should be added. The carbonate is added in *small* quantities with stirring until addition no longer causes effervescence. Any excess, being soluble, would dissolve in the solution and contaminate the salt.

2 MAKING A SALT BY NEUTRALISING AN ACID WITH *AN INSOLUBLE BASE*

This method, and the previous one, are the most useful ways of making salts. All insoluble bases react with acids as follows:

$$\text{ACID} + \text{BASE} \rightarrow \text{A SALT} + \text{WATER}$$

Remember that any **oxide** or **hydroxide** of a **metal** is a base, and most bases are insoluble (see alkalis, p176). If you wish to make copper(II) sulphate, you could use *either* **copper(II) oxide** or **copper(II) hydroxide** (as the base) and dilute **sulphuric acid.** Note that this is just as good as using the carbonate, as in the previous example.

The general method is the same as in the previous example. An excess of the insoluble base is added to the acid in a beaker. It is easy to see when this point has been reached, because the base will 'dissolve' slowly as long as there is some acidity in the solution. Once the acid has been neutralised, the excess base is filtered off, to leave a solution of the salt. The salt is then crystallised in the usua way. **Note** The reaction is sometimes slow, and it is useful to warm the acid before adding the base. See Fig 8.7.

Fig 8.7 Formation of a salt by neutralising an acid with an insoluble base

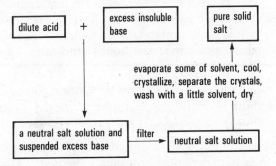

3 MAKING A SALT BY NEUTRALISING AN ACID WITH A SOLUBLE BASE (ALKALI)

As all alkalis are bases, this is exactly the same chemical *reaction* as in the previous example. However, there are two important practical differences.

(i) It is not a very useful method, as there are only *two* common alkalis (sodium and potassium hydroxides). As a contrast, there are *many* insoluble bases.

(ii) As alkalis are soluble, it is important not to add excess. Any excess would dissolve in the salt solution, and contaminate the salt. It is therefore important to mix *exactly the correct* amounts of acid and alkali so that the acid is *just* neutralised. The method therefore requires more care, and is less convenient.

The method involves the following steps.

(i) A *fixed* volume of the alkali is placed in a conical flask (e.g. 25cm^3 are used, accurately measured by a **pipette**).

(ii) A few drops of an **indicator** are added (e.g. methyl orange).

(iii) A **burette** is filled with the acid, and the volume of liquid in the burette is noted.

(iv) Acid from the burrette is added slowly to the alkali in the beaker. The mixture is gently swirled to mix the liquids. This is continued until the indicator *just* changes colour.

(v) The volume of acid which has been taken from the burette is noted. This is a **rough** guide for the volume of acid needed to neutralise the alkali.

(vi) Steps (i) to (iv) are repeated, but this time the acid is added rapidly until about 1.5cm^3 less than the rough volume has been added. The acid is then added *one drop* at a time, swirling after each one, until the indicator just changes colour. This volume of acid, which is an **accurate** reading, is noted.

(vii) The steps are repeated for a third time, but this time *no indicator* is added, and a volume of acid is used which is exactly equal to the accurate reading. The solution formed should be a salt solution, containing neither acid nor alkali, which have been neutralised. The solution is crystallised in the usual way to obtain the salt. (Note that if an indicator is used in this final stage, it will contaminate the salt.)

If you have prepared a salt by this method, make sure that you understand why each step is taken. Many students do not understand why it is important to take a rough reading, and many forget that the final attempt is made without an indicator. Typical salts which can be made by this method are:

sodium hydroxide(aq)+hydrochloric acid(aq) → sodium chloride
sodium hydroxide(aq)+sulphuric acid(aq) → sodium sulphate
sodium hydroxide(aq)+nitric acid(aq) → sodium nitrate

(The sodium hydroxide can be replaced by potassium hydroxide, in order to make potassium salts.) The method can be summarised as in Fig 8.8.

4 MAKING A SALT BY NEUTRALISING AN ACID WITH METAL

Like the previous method, this is not particularly useful. The problem

Fig 8.8 Formation of a salt
by neutralising an acid
with a soluble base

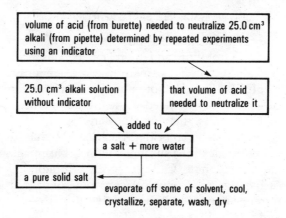

with this method is that some metals are too reactive to add to acids, and some do not react with acids at all (p94). Do not use this method unless you are quite clear about this point. For example, can you see that it would not be possible to make copper(II) sulphate by this method? Or sodium chloride?

If you are sure that a particular combination of metal and acid will react to produce a salt, the experimental steps are easy. They are very similar to those in methods (1) and (2). The acid is placed in a beaker. Sometimes it is useful to warm it, especially if the metal is not very reactive. An *excess* of the metal is then added, to make sure that the acid has been neutralised. (When an excess has been added, the fizzing stops, and the metal no longer dissolves.) The excess metal is then filtered off, to leave a salt solution. The solution is then crystallised in the usual way to produce the salt (Fig 8.9).

The following summary is typical:

ACID+METAL → A SALT+HYDROGEN

Fig 8.9 Formation of a salt
by neutralising an acid
with a metal

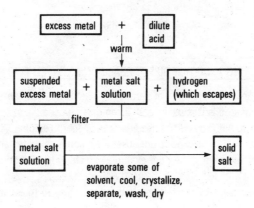

Suitable metals to use (with any of the common acids) are zinc, magnesium and iron.

5 MAKING AN INSOLUBLE SALT BY PRECIPITATION

The first four methods have been for making *soluble* salts, which are made in solution and then obtained as solids by evaporation and crystallisation. This method is used **only** for salts which are **insoluble.** See the note about solubilities earlier in this section, on p182. If you do need to learn the names of the more common insoluble salts, then here they are:

chlorides: silver chloride, $AgCl$; lead(II) chloride, $PbCl_2$

sulphates: lead (II) sulphate, $PbSO_4$; barium sulphate, $BaSO_4$; calcium sulphate, $CaSO_4$ (slightly soluble)

carbonates: all insoluble except those of sodium and potassium

nitrates: **none** (all nitrates soluble)

iodides: lead(II) iodide, PbI_2

If you need to precipitate an insoluble salt, the method is as follows.

Step (i) Mix a **solution** containing the required 'metal part' with a **solution** containing the required 'non-metal part'. For example, suppose we need to make the insoluble salt, silver chloride. We need to mix a **solution** containing '**silver** something' (the metal part) with a **solution** containing 'something **chloride**' (the non-metal part). Note that the two substances to be mixed must dissolve in water. As all nitrates are soluble, we can safely choose **silver nitrate** as our first solution. As all sodium and potassium compounds are soluble, we can safely choose **sodium chloride** for our second solution. (Compare this with the precipitation of hydroxides, p162, and carbonates, p163.)

Step(ii) is to filter off the precipitate (or use a centrifuge).

Step (iii) is to wash the precipitate with pure water, and then dry it.

If you understand ionic equations, all precipitation reactions are best shown in this way. The ionic equation shows only the ions which combine. All other ions are spectator ions, e.g.

$$Ag^+(aq) + Cl^-)aq) \rightarrow AgCl(s)$$
$$Ba^{2+} + SO_4^{2-}(aq) \rightarrow BaSO_4(s)$$

6 MAKING A SALT BY DIRECT REACTION BETWEEN TWO ELEMENTS

Methods 3,4 and 5 are not particularly useful, as each can be used for only a few salts. This method is less useful still. It can only be used if a salt contains *two* elements only. For example, it cannot be used to make copper(II) sulphate, $CuSO_4$, which contains three elements. The method is only useful for some chlorides and some sulphides. It is not very convenient, either. For example, if a chloride is being prepared, chlorine has to be made and then it needs to be used with great care.

If you have used this method, for example to make sodium chloride (by burning sodium in chlorine) or to make iron(II) sulphide (by heating iron with sulphur), then you should revise the details, e.g.:

$$2Na(l) + Cl_2(g) \rightarrow 2NaCl(g)$$
$$Fe(s) + S(s) \rightarrow FeS(s)$$

8.3 STRONG AND WEAK ACIDS AND BASES

Many students think that a **concentrated acid** is the same as a **strong acid**. This is not so. A concentrated acid is one which is mixed with very little water, if any at all. A strong acid means something completely different.

'Acidity' is caused by an acid 'splitting up' to release $H^+(aq)$ ions (p.178). Some acids are better at doing this than others. If an acid *easily* 'splits up' when it is added to water, so that most of the hydrogen atoms in it are given up as $H^+(aq)$ ions, it is described as a **strong acid**. The three common laboratory acids, hydrochloric, sulphuric, and nitric, are all strong acids. Organic acids such as ethanoic acid are usually **weak acids**. When they are dissolved in water, only a small proportion of the hydrogen atoms they contain are given up as $H^+(aq)$ ions.

To make this easier to understand, consider what might happen if a hundred 'molecules' of (i) a strong acid, and (ii) a weak acid, are each dissolved in the same volume of water. HA is the formula of the acid.

(i) Strong acid

	water+HA →	$H^+(aq)$ +	$A^-(aq)$
number of units initially	100	0	0
number of units after adding to water	1	99	99

(ii) Weak acid

	water+HA →	$H^+(aq)$ +	$A^-(aq)$
number of units initially	100	0	0
number of units after adding to water	99	1	1

In this example, the acid in (i) is 99 times as strong as the acid in (ii). This is because 99 times as many acid units, $H^+(aq)$, are produced from the same number of molecules.

Similarly, sodium hydroxide is a **strong alkali** because it splits up almost completely when added to water to produce a high concentration of $OH^-(aq)$ ions. Ammonia solution is only a weak alkali. When ammonia gas dissolves in water, only a low concentration of $OH^-(aq)$ ions is produced.

CHECK YOUR UNDERSTANDING (Answers on p414)

1. Which of these statements is true?
   (a)   All bases are alkalis, **or**
   (b)   All alkalis are bases.
2. Which of the following are bases? Copper(II) oxide; potassium hydroxide; sulphur oxide; magnesium oxide; chlorine oxide; hydrogen oxide; calcium chloride; sugar; magnesium nitrate; calcium hydroxide.
3. Which of the following will **not** change the colour of an indicator?
   (a)   an acid
   (b)   an insoluble base
   (c)   an alkali

4   Complete the following word equations:
  (a)   Acid+base →   +
  (b)   Acid+   → a salt+carbon dioxide+
  (c)   copper(II) oxide+hydrochloric acid →   +
  (d)   sodium carbonate+sulphuric acid →   +   +
  (e)   magnesium oxide+   → magnesium chloride+water

5   Describe what you would expect to see happen to the pH of the solution in the beaker, in each of the following experiments.
  (a)   Some dilute acid is placed in a beaker. Some insoluble base is added slowly to the acid until an excess of the base has been added.
  (b)   Some dilute acid is placed in a beaker. A solution of an alkali is added slowly until an excess of the alkali has been added.

6   Which of the following are salts? copper(II) sulphate; copper(II) chloride; sulphur chloride; calcium oxide; sodium nitrate; sodium hydroxide; carbon oxide; copper(II) oxide.

7   Zinc sulphate is a salt which is soluble in water. Its formula is $ZnSO_4$. Which of the following methods could **not** be used to make this salt?
  (a)   acid+base
  (b)   acid+alkali
  (c)   acid+metal
  (d)   precipitation
  (e)   acid+carbonate
  (f)   heating together a mix of zinc, oxygen and sulphur.

8   Name the chemicals which you would need to make the soluble salt sodium nitrate by each of the following methods.
  (a)   acid+carbonate
  (b)   acid+alkali

9   All nitrates are soluble. All sodium and potassium compounds are soluble. Name the starting chemicals you would use to make each of the following **insoluble** salts.
  (a)   calcium carbonate
  (b)   silver chloride
  (c)   barium sulphate
  (d)   copper (II) carbonate

10   Choose from the list of pH values, the value most likely to be found in each of the substances.
  pH values: 1, 5, 7, 8
  Substances: hydrochloric acid; sodium chloride solution; lemon juice; calcium hydroxide solution (lime water)

11   Decide whether each of the following is true or false.
  (a)   Hydrochloric acid, HCl, will give a chloride test,
  (b)   Sulphuric acid, H_2SO_4, will give a sulphate test.

12   The table below shows the results of an experiment in which one solution (A) was mixed with another solution (B). The last column is a prediction about whether there should be a precipitate when the two are mixed. The first entry in the table has been completed as an example.
     Read the information about solubilites given on pp182 and 186, and then complete the missing information in the table.

Solution A	Ions present	Solution B	Ions present	Precipitate or not? If yes, give formula of precipitate
sodium chloride	Na^+ Cl^-	silver nitrate	Ag^+ NO_3^-	Yes; AgCl
sodium carbonate	Na^+ CO_3^{2-}	copper(II) sulphate	Cu^{2+} SO_4^{2-}	?
sodium carbonate	Na^+ CO_3^{2-}	potassium chloride	?	?
lead(II) nitrate	?	zinc chloride	?	?
copper(II) chloride	?	zinc sulphate	?	?
copper(II) chloride	?	silver nitrate	?	?
sulphuric acid	?	calcium chloride	?	?
?	K^+ CO_3^{2-}	?	Pb^{2+} NO_3^-	?
sodium iodide	?	lead(II) nitrate	?	?

13 Why does baking powder 'fizz' when water is added?

14 Try to write balanced equations (using symbols, not words) for the following reactions.

(a)   copper(II) oxide+hydrochloric acid

(b)   copper(II) hydroxide+sulphuric acid

(c)   calcium carbonate+hydrochloric acid

(d)   magnesium+hydrochloric acid

(e)   sodium carbonate+nitric acid

CHECK LIST ▶

REMEMBER THAT SOME OF THESE POINTS MAY NOT BE RELEVANT FOR THE PARTICULAR SYLLABUS YOU ARE FOLLOWING.
YOU SHOULD UNDERSTAND THE FOLLOWING POINTS.

1▶ The names and formulas of the common acids.

2▶ Hazard signs.

3▶ The properties of acids, bases and alkalis.

4▶ Word equations for the common reactions, and also symbolic and ionic equations if you understand them.

5▶ Note carefully which acids and metals will react together.

6▶ What bases and alkalis are. How to decide whether a substance is a base. Names of the common alkalis.

7▶ Acids and bases as proton donors/acceptors; why acids do not show 'acidity' until water is added.

8▶ The pH scale; colours given by universal (full range) indicator.

9▶ Neutralisation.

10▶ What salts are. The methods of salt preparation you have studied. Word equations for the reactions, symbolic equations if possible. You *must* be able to suggest how to prepare a salt which you may never have made before, if you are given information about it.

11▶ Strong and weak acids and bases.

SEE GENERAL NOTE BEFORE QUESTIONS ON pp49 AND 50.
REMEMBER THAT YOU MAY BE ALLOWED TO USE A DATA
BOOK IN THE EXAMINATION.

1 The table below contains information about five compounds, A, B, C,
D and E.

Compound	A	B	C	D	E
melting point in °C	319	801	−115	−78	−117
boiling point in °C	1390	1413	−85	−33	78
pH of solution in water	14	7	1	11	7

From the compounds A to E select
(a) a liquid
(b) a salt
(c) an alkaline gas
(d) a compound which could be formed by adding sodium to
water
(e) two compounds which would react together.

2 Complete the table below, which describes the preparation of some
salts.

Reactants			Products
magnesium oxide +		→	magnesium sulphate +
+		→	zinc chloride+hydrogen
+ sodium sulphate		→	lead sulphate +

[*SEG* spec 1]

3 Complete the following word equations.
(a)   magnesium+oxygen →
(b)   sodium hydroxide+hydrochloric acid →
(c)   aluminium+copper oxide →

4 Complete the following symbol equations.
(a) $Fe(s)+S(s) →$
(b) $MgO(s)+2HCl(aq) →$ +
(c) $CaCO_3(s)+2HNO_3(aq) →$ +   +
(d) $H^+(aq) + (aq) → H_2O(l)$

5 Dilute sulphuric acid reacts with
A   calcium carbonate to form calcium sulphate and oxygen
B   copper to form copper(II) sulphate and hydrogen
C   iron to form iron(II) sulphate and water
D   magnesium hydroxide to form magnesium sulphate and
water   [*NEA* spec (A), 1]

6 The table gives the pH of 6 solutions (a) to (f).

Solution	(a)	(b)	(c)	(d)	(e)	(f)
pH	2	3	4	6	8	10

The two solutions which could produce a solution of pH 7 when mixed are

A (a)+(d)   B (e)+(f)   C (a)+(b)   D (a)+(f)   E (c)+(d)

7 Scientists in Canada are finding that acid rain is polluting their lakes and killing the fish. The most likely substance that they might add to the water to counter this is

A ammonia   B chlorine   C limestone   D salt   E sugar

[LEA spec (B), 1]

8 Which one of the substances listed below could produce a solution of pH 7 if it was added, in the correct proportions, to a strongly alkaline solution?

A Distilled water   B Hydrochloric acid   C Limewater
D Sodium hydroxide solution.

9 When excess magnesium is added to hydrochloric acid the following reaction occurs.

$$Mg(s)+2HCl(aq) \rightarrow MgCl_2(aq)+H_2(g)$$

The first process needed after the reaction to obtain pure crystals of magnesium chloride is

A distillation   B evaporation   C filtration
D neutralisation.

10 Which one of these equations represents a neutralisation reaction?

A $Mg(OH)_2+H_2SO_4 \rightarrow MgSO_4+2H_2O$
B $2H_2+O_2 \rightarrow 2H_2O$
C $CuO+H_2 \rightarrow Cu+H_2O$
D $MgCO_3 \rightarrow MgO+CO_2$ *[SEG* spec (Alt) 1]

11 The following table shows the solubility of a number of substances.

Substance	Solubility in water
Barium sulphate	Insoluble
Calcium sulphate	Slightly soluble
Lead(II) nitrate	Soluble
Lead(II) oxide	Insoluble
Lead(II) sulphate	Insoluble
Sodium sulphate	Soluble

Which of the following pairs of substances would be most suitable for preparing lead(II) sulphate for use as a white pigment in paint?

A   Lead(II) oxide and sodium sulphate;
B   Lead(II) nitrate and sodium sulphate;
C   Lead(II) oxide and barium sulphate;

D   Lead(II) nitrate and barium sulphate;
E   Lead(II) nitrate and calcium sulphate.

12   Salts **always**
A   form coloured solutions
B   dissolve in water
C   conduct electricity in the solid state
D   can be made by dissolving a metal in an acid
E   contain both positive and negative ions.

13   When some acid which has been spilled is neutralised by adding an alkaline solution, which of the following is **always** true?
A   The pH of the acidic solution decreases
B   A salt is produced
C   The solution ceases to conduct electricity
D   The volume of alkaline solution added must be the same as the volume of the acidic solution
E   A colourless gas is given off.

14   A pupil found that a certain aqueous solution has a pH of exactly 7.0. From this information alone, she was able to deduce correctly that the solution
A   could only be pure water
B   contained a salt
C   was neutral
D   was safe to drink
E   boiled at 100°C.   [*LEA* spec (A), 1]

15   When answering this question, use the names of the compounds given here:

carbon dioxide   sodium chloride   silver nitrate
copper(II) carbonate   potassium hydroxide   silver chloride
zinc oxide   zinc sulphate

(*a*)   (i) Which one of the compounds will give off a gas when dilute hydrochloric acid is added to it?
(ii) Give the name or formula of the gas formed.

(*b*)   (i) Which one of the compounds will dissolve in water forming a solution which will neutralise nitric acid?
(ii) Write a word equation for the reaction which occurs.

(*c*)   (i) Name two compounds which, when dissolved in water and the solutions are mixed, will form a white precipitate of an insoluble salt.
(ii) Give the name or formula of the salt formed.

(*d*)   (i) Name a compound which is a white solid, is insoluble in water and neutralises dilute sulphuric acid forming a soluble salt.
(ii) Give the name or formula of the salt formed.
                                                    [*NEA* spec (A), 1]

16   Many acidic substances are found in nature or in the home. These substances can be detected by the use of indicators.
(*a*) .   (i) Name a suitable indicator to detect acids.

(ii) What is observed when this indicator is placed in an acidic solution?

(b)   The pH scale is used to indicate how acid or alkaline a substance is.

(i) Give the name of a household substance that might have a pH of 5.

(ii) A colourless liquid has a pH of 7. What does this indicate about the solution?

(c)   The battery in a car contains fairly concentrated sulphuric acid. Explain why it is important not to spill any of the acid, and how it could be neutralised using ordinary household substances.

[LEA spec (A),2]

†17   Aspirin is an acid which may be represented by the formula H^+A^-, where A^- is a complicated organic ion. Aspirin itself is not very soluble, but its sodium salt, known as 'soluble aspirin', dissolves easily in cold water. Addition of dilute hydrochloric acid to a solution of soluble aspirin causes aspirin to appear as a precipitate.

(a)   Describe carefully how you would prepare a sample of pure dry aspirin from a solution of soluble aspirin, explaining why your method is appropriate.

(b)   Theoretically you would expect to obtain 178 g of aspirin from 200 g of soluble aspirin. Explain carefully why you would actually get less than this amount.   [LEA spec (A), 3]

WORKING WITH GASES. THE AIR. OXYGEN AND HYDROGEN

CONTENTS

9.1 WORKING WITH GASES

You will have prepared several gases during your chemistry course. It is unlikely that you will need to remember details of how to prepare each gas. However, it is important that you *understand* how to use various pieces of apparatus. You could be given some facts about a particular gas, and then be asked to suggest a suitable apparatus for its preparation and collection.

There are usually two stages in preparing a gas. These two stages are combined together by using the correct apparatus.

1 The gas is *made* in a suitable 'generator' by a chemical reaction.
2 The gas is then *collected* by a suitable method.

APPARATUS USED TO MAKE A GAS

Three common methods are shown in Fig 9.1.

Fig 9.1 Gas generators

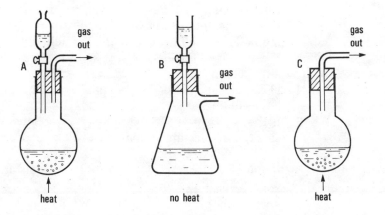

Notes

1 If the generator needs to be *heated*, a **round-bottomed flask** should be used (A or C in Fig 9.1). This reduces the risk of cracking.
2 If the chemical reaction inside the generator is between two liquids, or between a liquid and a solid, A or B can be used. The **tap funnel** allows us to add a liquid when we are ready to do so, even during the reaction, without taking the apparatus to pieces and without allowing the gas to escape through the 'wrong' tube.
3 C is used when the reaction is between two or more *solids*.

APPARATUS USED TO COLLECT A GAS

Five common methods are shown in Fig 9.2, labelled D–H. If *small* volumes of gas are being collected, the gas jar in E, F and G is replaced by a boiling tube.

Fig 9.2 Apparatus used to collect a gas

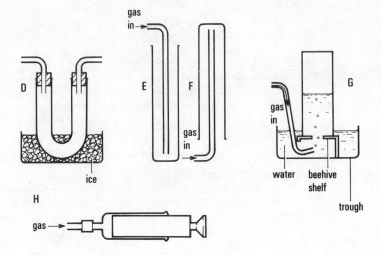

Notes

1   If a gas is **more dense than air**, E can be used. This method of collection is sometimes called **downward delivery**.

2   If a gas is **less dense than air**, F can be used for collection. This method is sometimes called **upward delivery**.

3   If a gas does *not dissolve very much in water*, and *does not react with water*, G can be used.

4   H can be used for *any* type of gas, but is not convenient for collecting large volumes.

5   If the gas being collected is **toxic** (poisonous) or has an unpleasant smell, the collecting system must be placed in a **fume cupboard**.

6   Method G makes the gas 'wet'. Do not use this method if a *dry* gas is required. More important, do not dry a gas and then collect it over water! This is a common mistake.

7   Never collect the first sample of gas which comes through the delivery tube. The generator and tubes are full of air to start with, and the first sample of gas to come out will be mainly air.

8   Sometimes a third stage is included, between the generator and the collecting system. This middle stage is to purify the gas or to dry it before collecting it. Most gases you will prepare are pure enough or dry enough to use in the laboratory and do not need this extra stage. If you have purified any gases before collecting them, make sure that you revise the details.

9   Collectors E and F will almost certainly mix some air with the gas. Also, unless the gas is coloured, it is difficult to decide when the gas jar is full. These are disadvantages of these methods of collection. Note the length of the delivery tubes in each case; shorter tubes would cause even more mixing with air.

10 Advantages of G include:

    (i) we can see when the gas jar is full, and

    (ii) there should be no air mixed with the gas.

For disadvantages, see note 6.

11 Advantages of collecting a gas in a syringe (H) include:

    (i) the collected sample is easy to carry around;

    (ii) known volumes can be collected or 'pushed out';

    (iii) air is unlikely to mix with the gas provided that the first sample of gas is not collected (see note 7); and

    (iv) we can easily decide when the syringe is full.

Disadvantages include:

    (i) syringes are expensive (if glass) and easily broken;

    (ii) inconvenient to change if more than one syringe of gas is required; and

    (iii) if a gas is produced rapidly, the syringe is filled quickly and the collection is difficult to control.

12 D is used only if the gas can be changed easily into a liquid by cooling. Very few gases can be collected in this way in a simple laboratory.

13 If you have discussed how to prepare a *solution* of a *very* soluble gas, (e.g. HCl, or NH_3) make sure that you understand the technique.

WAYS OF DRYING GASES   Three common ways are shown in Fig 9.3

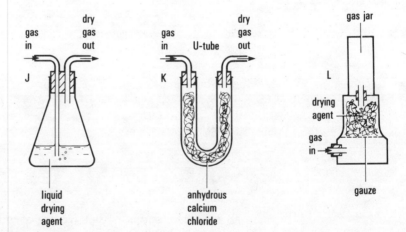

Fig 9.3 Drying or purifying systems

Notes

1 See note 6 above.

2 When a delivery tube passes gas *into* a liquid, the tube must dip *below* the surface of the liquid. Tubes which take a gas away after it has bubbled through a liquid *must not enter* the liquid (see J in Fig 9.3).

3 A common liquid drying agent is *concentrated* sulphuric acid. This would be used in J.

4 There are several solid drying agents in common use. They include *anhydrous* calcium chloride and silica gel. They would be used in K.

5 L is a drying tower. It contains a solid drying agent. If the gas being dried is less dense than air, it can be collected by placing a gas jar on top of the tower, as in Fig 9.3. Ammonia gas is often dried and collected like this.

WORKING OUT WHICH APPARATUS TO USE FOR A PARTICULAR GAS

Table 9.1 gives some information about gases. You do not need to learn the information in the table. Some of the gases mentioned in the table may be unfamiliar to you. This is not important. What is important is that you should be able to use the information in the table, together with information about the reaction which is used to make each gas, in order to plan how you would make and collect the gas. If you understand the points made in this section, you should be able to answer the questions on p201.

Table 9.1 Physical properties of some common gases

Name and formula	Odour	Toxic?	Colour
air	—	no	—
carbon monoxide, CO	—	very	—
carbon dioxide, CO_2	faint	only at high concentrations	—
chlorine, Cl_2	choking, powerful	very	green-yellow
hydrogen, H_2	—	no	—
hydrogen chloride, HCl	sharp	yes	—
nitrogen, N_2	—	no	—
ammonia, NH_3	choking, powerful	yes	—
oxygen, O_2	—	no	—
sulphur dioxide, SO_2	sharp	yes	—
sulphur trioxide, SO_3	sharp	yes	—
hydrogen sulphide, H_2S	rotten eggs	very	—
nitrogen dioxide, NO_2	sharp	very	brown

As an example, suppose that we are asked to suggest how we could prepare and collect some oxygen gas. We might be given the following information: If a solution of hydrogen peroxide is added to the solid catalyst copper(II) oxide, a reaction takes place in which oxygen gas is formed. No heating is needed. Oxygen has approximately the same density as air. It does not react with water, it is not toxic, and it dissolves only slightly in water.

A suitable system would be to use B and G (Figs 9.1 and 9.2). The solid catalyst would be placed in the conical flask. The solution of hydrogen peroxide would be in the tap funnel. A would not be necessary as heating is not needed. C would not be convenient, because the catalyst and liquid would have to be mixed before the rest of the apparatus was connected together, and the gas would be escaping.

D cannot be used to collect it, as oxygen boils at −183°C and so cannot be cooled sufficiently in a simple laboratory to change it into a liquid. E and F are unsuitable because oxygen has about the same density as air. Revise your notes carefully for each gas you have prepared and collected, and make sure that you understand why the apparatus was used in each case.

Density compared to air	Solubility in water (cm³ in 100 cm³ at room temperature and pressure)	Melting point (C°)	Boiling point (°C)
—	2.0	—	—
slightly less	2.5	−207	−190
more dense	100	sublimes at −78	—
much more dense	263	−101	−34
much less dense	2.1	−259	−253
slightly more dense	46 100	−114	−85
same	1.6	−210	−196
less dense	80 670	−78	−33
same	3.4	−219	−183
much more dense	4 730	−73	−10
solid at room temperature	reacts violently	17	44
slightly more dense	260	−86	−60
more dense	soluble, reacts with water	−11	21

CHECK YOUR UNDERSTANDING (Answers on p414).

Use Table 9.1 to help with these questions.

1   Which gases could you collect over water in an open laboratory?
2   Which gases could you collect over water in a fume cupboard?
3   Which gases could you collect by upward delivery in an open laboratory?
4   Which gases could you collect by downward delivery in an open laboratory?
5   Which gases could you collect by upward delivery in a fume cupboard?

6 Which gases could you collect by downward delivery in a fume cupboard?

7 Which gases could you collect easily as solids?

8 Which gases could you collect easily as liquids?

9 Study Fig 9.4. It shows a young student's plan for an experiment to obtain fairly pure nitrogen gas from the air. The idea is to remove oxygen, carbon dioxide and water vapour from a sample of air so as to leave nearly pure nitrogen. Hot copper removes oxygen by combining with it to form copper(II) oxide. A concentrated solution of a strong alkali such as sodium hydroxide removes carbon dioxide (which is acidic).

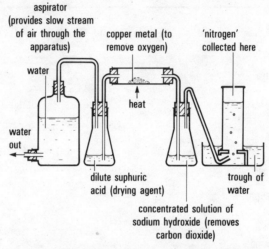

Fig 9.4 An incorrect way of removing nitrogen from air

aspirator (provides slow stream of air through the apparatus)

copper metal (to remove oxygen)

'nitrogen' collected here

water

heat

water out

dilute suphuric acid (drying agent)

trough of water

concentrated solution of sodium hydroxide (removes carbon dioxide)

THIS DIAGRAM INCLUDES SEVERAL DELIBERATE MISTAKES

(*a*)   The plan contains six important mistakes. What are they?

(*b*)   Only one student obtained full marks for designing the experiment, because not only was the apparatus chosen correctly and in the correct order, but the student was the only one to state that it was important not to collect the gas immediately. Why?

(*c*)   The nitrogen obtained in such an experiment is not pure. What other substances are likely to be present?

10 Study Fig 9.5. The diagram shows a student's plan to prove that when copper metal is heated *without air* it will not go black. Can you suggest how the apparatus could be used, and how it works?

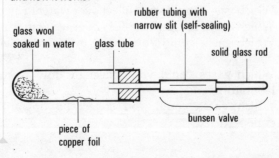

Fig 9.5 A bunsen valve

glass wool soaked in water

rubber tubing with narrow slit (self-sealing)

glass tube

solid glass rod

bunsen valve

piece of copper foil

11 A Kipp's generator (Fig 9.6) is useful in the laboratory for preparing gases which are needed fairly frequently and in reasonable quantities. Can you suggest how it works, and why it is so useful?

Fig 9.6 The Kipp's generator

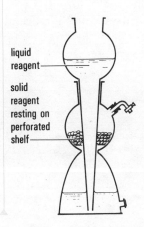

liquid reagent

solid reagent resting on perforated shelf

9.2 THE AIR

The air is a **mixture**. This means that the different things which are mixed together can be separated from each other. The proportions of the various substances are not fixed. Air varies from place to place (e.g. the air above a city is different from the air above a country village). It also varies in the same place from time to time (e.g. the air above a city at midday is different from the air above the same city in the rush hour).

The table below shows what a typical sample of *dry* air might be like. Ordinary air always contains water vapour (not included in the table as it varies a great deal). The air also contains very small traces of many other gases, and solids such as soot, bacteria and pollen. The gases may include **pollutant** gases such as sulphur oxides (especially near industrial cities) and carbon monoxide (particularly in large towns). You do not need to learn the *details* in the table. It is important to remember that the air is *mainly* nitrogen (about 80%), that most of what is left is oxygen, and the names of other substances likely to be present.

Component	Composition by volume (%)
nitrogen	78.08
oxygen	20.95
argon	0.93
carbon dioxide	0.03
neon	0.002
other noble gases	0.0006

SOME TYPICAL EXPERIMENTS WITH AIR

1 TO SHOW THAT AIR CONTAINS APPROXIMATELY 20% (ONE-FIFTH) OXYGEN

You may have seen an experiment with two glass syringes (Fig 9.7). If so, check your notes and make sure that you understand the experiment. This experiment uses some important scientific ideas. Make sure that you can answer the following questions.

Fig 9.7

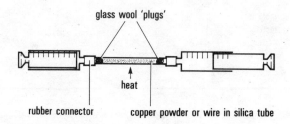

glass wool 'plugs'

heat

rubber connector   *copper powder or wire in silica tube*

(a)   Why is the tube *filled* with copper?
(b)   Why is the tube not made of ordinary glass?
(c)   Why are 'plugs' used, e.g. of glass wool?
(d)   Why is the tube *cooled down* (e.g. with a damp cloth) *before* the volume of gas in the syringes is noted?
(e)   Why does the copper change colour?
(f)   Why is the heating and cooling repeated several times?
(g)   Why will a lighted taper not continue to burn in the gas which is left at the end of the experiment?

2 TO SHOW THAT AIR CONTAINS WATER VAPOUR AND CARBON DIOXIDE

There are several experiments which can be used to show this. Revise the one or ones you have used. One typical experiment is shown in Fig 9.8. To understand what it shows you need to know:

Fig 9.8 Two further components of air

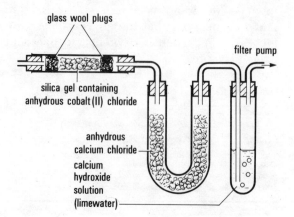

glass wool plugs

filter pump

silica gel containing anhydrous cobalt (II) chloride

anhydrous calcium chloride

calcium hydroxide solution (limewater)

(*a*)   Silica gel is a good **drying agent**. It absorbs any water vapour which is around it.

(*b*)   Anhydrous cobalt(II) chloride is *blue*. When water is present the compound becomes hydrated, and the colour changes to pink. (You could use anhydrous copper(II) sulphate instead. It changes from white to blue when it becomes hydrated.)

(*c*)   Anhydrous calcium chloride is a drying agent. Silica gel could be used instead in the U-tube.

(*d*)   Calcium hydroxide solution (lime water) is used to test for carbon dioxide (p168).

Make sure that you can work out answers to the following questions.

(*a*)   Why are the glass wool plugs used?

(*b*)   What would you expect to see in the 'silica gel' tube?

(*c*)   What does the observation in (*b*) tell you?

(*d*)   What would you expect to see in the tube containing the calcium hydroxide solution?

(*e*)   What does the observation in (*d*) tell you?

(*f*)   Why is it necessary to use the U-tube containing the drying agent?

WAYS OF SEPARATING THE MIXTURE OF GASES CALLED AIR

Most of the mixtures we separate in laboratories or industry are either mixtures of *liquids* or *solids*. For example, we need to be able to separate mixtures of liquids such as petroleum into various 'parts' to produce petrol, etc.

Similarly, we need to be able to separate mixtures of solids such as rock salt into pure salt. Air is a mixture of *gases*. Air is our most important source of oxygen, and it is the only source of the noble gases such as argon. It is important, therefore, to understand how air can be separated into some of the gases it contains.

1 MAKING OXYGEN FROM LIQUID AIR

The easiest way of obtaining *large* quantities of pure oxygen is first to change air into liquid air. The air then becomes a liquid mixture. It can be separated in a similar way to separating petroleum into fractions, i.e. by *fractional distillation*. The main difference between the two examples is that liquid air is at a very low temperature. Liquid petroleum is separated at a much higher temperature.

The sequence of operations is:

(*a*)   Water vapour and carbon dioxide are removed from the air. If left in, these would freeze *solid* when the air is cooled. The solids would block pipes, etc.

(*b*)   The air is cooled and compressed (repeatedly) until it changes into a liquid. Air changes into a liquid at about −215°C.

(*c*)   The liquid 'air' (mainly a mixture of liquid nitrogen, liquid oxygen, and liquid noble gases) is allowed to 'warm up' slightly in a large evaporating column until the temperature reaches the boiling point of *one* of the gases in the mixture. For example, liquid nitrogen boils at −195°C. When all of the nitrogen has boiled off, the temperature can rise to −183°C, at which point liquid oxygen boils. (Note that −183°C is 'hotter' than −195°C!) Compare this with what happens inside a fractionating column at an oil refinery. You should understand that the basic idea is the same. In this way, very pure supplies of oxygen, nitrogen and the individual noble gases are obtained from air.

2 OBTAINING NITROGEN FROM THE AIR IN THE LABORATORY

See p202. You should find the problem provides useful revision of the ideas in this chapter. Note that a large bottle (Fig 9.4) is a simple and useful way of forcing a slow stream of air through some apparatus. If water flows *into* the bottle, air is forced *out*. If water is allowed to flow *out* of the bottle, air is pushed *in*.

REACTIONS WHICH USE UP OXYGEN FROM THE AIR

We take large amounts of oxygen from the air, mainly for making steel (p137). In addition, three processes which occur naturally also remove oxygen from the air.

1 RESPIRATION

Living things obtain their energy from food substances by **respiration**. Foods are **oxidised** inside living things. Oxygen is normally needed for this. The oxidation of food produces energy, to keep the animal or plant alive. In addition, **waste products** are formed. Many living things need to *breathe* in order to get enough oxygen inside the cells to oxidise food. They also remove waste products such as carbon dioxide when they breathe out.

Sugars such as glucose are common foods used by both plants and animals. Glucose contains three elements: carbon, hydrogen and oxygen. When it is oxidised by oxygen, the carbon changes into carbon dioxide. The hydrogen changes into water vapour. These two substances (carbon dioxide and water) are waste products. They are removed from the animal or plant (often by being breathed out).

$$\text{GLUCOSE} + \text{OXYGEN} \xrightarrow{\text{respiration}} \text{CARBON DIOXIDE} + \text{WATER} + \text{ENERGY}$$

(a food)   (from the air)   waste products

Glucose has the formula $C_6H_{12}O_6$. The full equation for respiration using glucose is:

$$C_6H_{12}O_6 + 6O_2 \rightarrow 6CO_2 + 6H_2O + \text{energy}$$

Note that respiration is not the same as breathing. Do you know the difference?

Air which is breathed out (**exhaled air**) is different from the air which is breathed in (**inhaled air**).

(*a*)   It is warmer,

(*b*)   it contains less oxygen (because some has been used for respiration), and

(*c*)   it contains more carbon dioxide and water vapour (waste products from respiration).

2 RUSTING (p143)

3 BURNING (COMBUSTION)

Fig 9.9 The fire triangle

Most substances will not burn unless (a) they are heated and (b) oxygen is present. This is shown by the **fire triangle** (Fig 9.9).

Combustion (burning) can only take place when *all three* sides of the triangle are complete. We must have a substance which can burn (a **fuel**), it must be heated, and oxygen must be present. (One of the most important principles in fire fighting is to remove one or more of these three factors. If you have studied fire fighting, and different kinds of fire extinguishers, revise your notes.) When a substance burns, it uses up oxygen and forms oxides. Energy (usually heat and light) is also given out. Respiration is a kind of 'safe burning of food' to release energy slowly.

$$\text{substance} + \text{oxygen} \xrightarrow[\text{(or burning)}]{\text{combustion}} \text{oxide (or oxides)} + \text{energy}$$

When a substance burns, its mass increases because it *combines* with oxygen. Many combustions are very important. For example, we burn fuels to provide energy. The various elements in the fuel all become oxides, and energy is given out, e.g.:

METHANE + OXYGEN $\xrightarrow[\text{(or burning)}]{\text{combustion}}$ CARBON DIOXIDE +
(natural gas)

    WATER + ENERGY
(as steam)

$$CH_4(g) + 2O_2(g) \longrightarrow CO_2(g) + H_2O(g) + \text{energy}$$

Note that burning and respiration have two things in common:

(i) They both use up oxygen from the air.

(ii) They both produce energy.

They often have a third factor in common. Most of the fuels we burn contain **carbon** and **hydrogen** combined together, (e.g. petrol, natural gas, paraffin, which are **hydrocarbons**, p329). Most foods also contain carbon and hydrogen (e.g. fats and sugars). The waste products of both processes are therefore often **carbon dioxide** (from the carbon) and **water** or **steam** (from the hydrogen).

A REACTION WHICH PUTS OXYGEN BACK INTO THE AIR

If we only *removed* oxygen from the air (by the processes just described) we would reach the very serious situation of not having enough oxygen. Life as we know it could not then exist. Fortunately, there is also a process which puts oxygen back into the air to replace that which is removed. This process is called **photosynthesis**. It is one of the most important reactions in the world. It keeps the oxygen of the air 'in balance', and also provides nearly all of our food. Even most meat, for example, has been formed by animals which feed on grass, and the foods in the grass have been made by photosynthesis.

In photosynthesis, plants change carbon dioxide and water into sugars (foods) and oxygen. This is the 'opposite' of most combustion processes. The usual *products* of respiration (and of many combustions) are the *starting* substances for photosynthesis. This process can only take place in plants which have the green-coloured **chlorophyll** in their leaves, and in sunlight. Respiration or combustion gives energy *out*, but photosynthesis takes energy *in* (from sunlight).

$$\text{ENERGY} + \text{CARBON} + \text{WATER} \xrightarrow{\text{chlorophyll}} \text{GLUCOSE} + \text{OXYGEN}$$
   (from   DIOXIDE   (a sugar)
sunlight)

$$\text{Energy} + 6CO_2 + 6H_2O \longrightarrow C_6H_{12}O_6 + 6O_2$$

THE BALANCE OF CARBON DIOXIDE AND OXYGEN IN THE AIR

Air usually contains about 20% oxygen, and a much smaller proportion of carbon dioxide. As explained, some processes take oxygen *out* of the air (and usually replace it with carbon dioxide). Also, photosynthesis removes carbon dioxide and replaces it with oxygen. For millions of years photosynthesis and the processes which remove oxygen from the air have roughly balanced out, so that the proportions of oxygen and carbon dioxide in the air hardly changed (see the carbon cycle, p308). Modern civilisation has upset this balance in two main ways:

(i) We now need and use more energy than ever before. This is needed to make electricity, to run cars and other forms of transport, for heating, etc. To provide this energy, enormous quantities of fossil fuels are burned. These large scale combustions all produce carbon dioxide (in addition to water and energy). More carbon dioxide is being made than at any previous stage in history. This enters the air at a faster rate than it is being removed by photosynthesis. Make sure that you understand this point. Fuels have always been burned to provide energy, and so carbon dioxide has always been produced in the process. The difference is that in the past this was only done on a small scale compared with what happens today. Our way of living, particularly in the developed countries, uses energy and power on a very large scale.

(ii) It is difficult for the green plants to change this 'extra' carbon dioxide into food and oxygen by photosynthesis. We have made this even more difficult by cutting down large areas of tropical rain forests, for example, to provide timber, to allow industrial development, and the construction of roads and towns, etc. Processes like this have reduced the number of trees, and therefore the amount of photosynthesis.

Nature's balance between oxygen and carbon dioxide has been disturbed. As there is a comparatively *large* proportion of oxygen in the air, there appears to be very little change in the oxygen concentration. The proportion of carbon dioxide in the air is very small, however, and an increase in its concentration is more obvious.

WHAT CAN WE DO TO HELP RESTORE THE CARBON DIOXIDE/OXYGEN BALANCE?

1   Stop cutting down trees (especially tropical rain forest) at a faster rate than we are planting new trees.
2   Reduce our use of energy (which is often wasteful), and so cause less fossil fuel to be burned.
3   Develop other ways of producing energy which do not use fossil fuels, and which do not form carbon dioxide, (e.g. nuclear power, p46).

A PROBLEM CAUSED BY AN INCREASE IN THE CARBON DIOXIDE CONCENTRATION: THE 'GREENHOUSE EFFECT'

Carbon dioxide is not toxic at the low concentrations which occur in air. An increase in its concentration does have another effect, however.

The glass walls of a greenhouse allow sunlight to enter. The ultra violet part of sunlight warms up the air and the contents inside the greenhouse. The hot contents then radiate heat energy, mainly as infra red rays (low energy) rather than ultra violet rays (high energy). Glass does not allow infra red rays to pass through it very easily. Heat is therefore trapped inside the greenhouse. It remains hot because heat energy escapes only slowly, e.g. by conduction through the glass (a poor conductor) or by convection through open windows.

In a similar way, the surface of the earth is warmed by the ultra violet rays in sunlight. Much of this heat energy is then lost as the surface cools by giving out infra red rays. These rays take energy away from the surface and into the air. Carbon dioxide in the air acts like the glass walls of a greenhouse. It allows ultra violet rays from the sun to pass through so that the surface of the earth can warm up. However, again like glass, it does not easily allow infra red energy to escape. Carbon dioxide in the air therefore helps to prevent heat energy escaping from the surface, and therefore it helps to stop the surface from cooling down during the night. As the concentration of carbon dioxide in the air increases, less heat energy is lost from the surface of the earth and the average temperature of the surface gradually increases (Fig 9.10).

It has been calculated that doubling the concentration of carbon dioxide in the air will increase the average surface temperature by between 2 and 3°C. This may appear to be insignificant, but even slight changes in surface temperature can cause great changes to

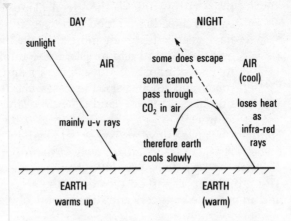

Fig 9.10 The Greenhouse effect.

wind patterns and other weather factors. Some people believe that if the concentration of carbon dioxide continues to rise over the next 100 years or so there will be perhaps catastrophic effects on our climate.

9.3 AIR POLLUTION

The air is one of our most important natural resources. It is important that we keep it clean and reasonably pure. Various substances can cause pollution. These **pollutants** can cause diseases of the chest and lungs, they can help to start certain kinds of cancer, cause fog to form, cause corrosion in metals and buildings, blacken paint, affect soil pH and crop production, and affect the health of animals.

Atmospheric pollution is caused by smoke and gases which enter the air from volcanic activity, from chimneys of factories and houses, and from exhaust gases of cars, etc. We live in an age when energy is needed more than ever before, and much of this energy is made by the burning of fossil fuels. When raw fuels are burned, pollutants are *always* formed. Pollution controls are expensive, but we must be prepared to pay the price.

The main pollutants are considered below. You may also have discussed the problem of unburned hydrocarbons.

1 CARBON MONOXIDE

Most fuels are fossil fuels, and all fossil fuels contain carbon. When the fuel burns, the carbon in it is usually changed to carbon dioxide. Unfortunately, **carbon monoxide** (CO) is sometimes formed instead of carbon dioxide (CO_2). This happens when there is not enough oxygen for the fuel to burn *completely*. (You may have used the expressions **complete combustion** and **incomplete combustion**.) When the oxygen supply is not enough for complete combustion, the carbon is oxidised to CO instead of CO_2. Incomplete combustion takes place where there is poor ventilation, or blocked jets and pipes, or when the controls (e.g. on a boiler) are not set correctly. In fact, most fuels burn so rapidly that it is very difficult to get enough oxygen to them, and so *some* incomplete combustion nearly always takes place when a fossil fuel burns. It even happens inside a car engine when petrol is burned, and this is why exhaust gases from cars contain carbon monoxide.

Carbon monoxide is a dangerous pollutant. It is invisible, and has no taste or smell. It is very toxic (poisonous). It stops the red blood cells carrying oxygen round our bodies to where it is needed. The total amount of carbon monoxide in the air is not increasing, because natural processes gradually change it into carbon dioxide. However, it is an important **local pollutant**. This means that its concentration can rise in a particular area, and cause problems in that area. For example, concentrations of carbon monoxide have built up to dangerous proportions in some cities during the rush hour.

Fig 9.11 Formation of carbon monoxide

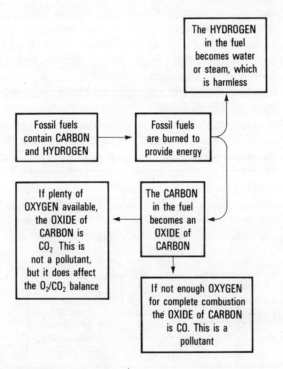

WAYS OF REDUCING CARBON MONOXIDE POLLUTION

(*a*)   Burn less fossil fuel; find alternative fuels which do not form carbon monoxide when they are used.

(*b*)   Improve the *ways* in which fossil fuels are burned, e.g. car engines are now much more efficient than they used to be. Most of the petrol is now burned completely.

(*c*)   Change any carbon monoxide which is formed into carbon dioxide *before* it enters the air. This is now done in special 'catalyst chambers' used in a car exhaust system, for example.

2 OXIDES OF SULPHUR. ACID RAIN

Sulphur is present in all living things, mainly in proteins. Fossil fuels are formed by the 'rotting down' of dead animals or plants, and usually contain sulphur. The proportion of sulphur varies according to the type of fuel, and where it has come from. When fossil fuels are burned, the sulphur in them is changed into an oxide of sulphur, usually **sulphur dioxide**, SO_2. This is a gas, and so it escapes into the air. Sulphur dioxide is an important pollutant. Most of the sulphur dioxide which enters the air comes from coal. Very large amounts of coal are burned in power stations to make electricity.

Sulphur dioxide is a poisonous gas. It can cause 'breathing' problems and diseases of the chest and lungs. It is also an acid gas, and dissolves in water to form an acid solution. This can happen with water vapour in the air, so that the water can fall to earth as **acid rain**. Acid rain is not a *major* problem in Britain, although it is getting worse. The prevailing winds in Britain blow away most of the sulphur dioxide produced by our power stations before it can dissolve in water and fall over Britain as acid rain. Much of it is blown towards the rest of Europe, and in particular towards Norway, Denmark and Sweden. So although Britain does not suffer as much as some other countries from the effects of acid rain, we are responsible for causing some of the problem.

Acid rain corrodes metals, the stonework of buildings, and even the mortar which holds bricks and stones together. It attacks even fairly unreactive metals such as copper, so that heating systems and plumbing are affected. It causes some metal ions which are normally 'locked' safely into soil particles to be 'freed'. These can then escape and be washed into rivers or lakes, and cause all sorts of problems for fish and plants. Acid rain also changes the pH of the water in rivers and lakes, with serious effects on living things.

Fig 9.12 Pollution caused by oxides of sulphur

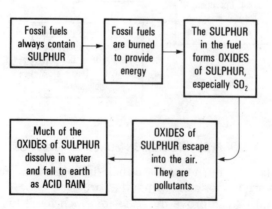

WAYS OF REDUCING POLLUTION CAUSED BY OXIDES OF SULPHUR

(*a*)   Remove the sulphur from the fossil fuel before it is burned (**desulphurise** the fuel). This is done with *liquid* fuels, such as petrol, and with fuels which are *gases*, such as natural gas. Unfortunately, it is very difficult and expensive to remove sulphur from a *solid* fuel such as coal. The burning of coal continues to be a major problem, particularly because such large amounts of it are burned at power stations.

Note that the removal of sulphur from fossil fuels is one of the most important ways of obtaining this important non-metal.

(*b*)   Waste gases which contain oxides of sulphur can be passed through filters and chemicals to remove the pollutants before they enter the air. (In industry the 'cleaning' of a waste gas before it enters the air is called scrubbing.)

(*c*)   Tall chimneys are used to pass waste gases into the air. Any pollutants which do escape are then diluted in the air before they can reach ground level. This method does not prevent the problem. It just dilutes it.

3 OXIDES OF NITROGEN

Like sulphur, the non-metal nitrogen also forms several oxides which are gases. These oxides of nitrogen are often shown as NO_x, in which x can vary. Most of the air (about 80%) is nitrogen. Usually, nitrogen is almost completely unreactive. This is fortunate, because it means that whenever things burn in air, they only react with the oxygen in the air and not with the nitrogen. However, at *very high temperatures* nitrogen will combine with the oxygen in the air to form oxides of nitrogen. The burning of petrol or diesel in an engine produces very high temperatures, and therefore oxides of nitrogen are formed in car engines, etc. These oxides leave the vehicle in the exhaust gases, and enter the air.

Oxides of nitrogen are toxic, and they also help to cause breathing problems and diseases of the chest and lungs. They also dissolve in water to form acids, so they help to cause acid rain. The problems caused by oxides of sulphur and oxides of nitrogen are very similar. However, the problem caused by oxides of nitrogen is comparatively small.

Fig 9.13 Pollution caused by oxides of nitrogen.

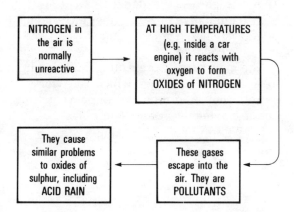

4 POLLUTION CAUSED BY SOLID PARTICLES IN THE AIR

Smoke is mainly small particles of solid carbon 'floating' (**suspended**) in the air. In the past, very large quantities of smoke were produced by the burning of coal in homes, and by coal-fired steam engines, etc. Many industrial processes also produce large quantities of smoke. This smoke may contain metal particles, tars and salts as well as carbon.

Any form of smoke (including tobacco smoke) is a pollutant. It may contain substances which help to cause cancer. The solid particles in the smoke are often very small. They can enter the lungs and stay there. Smoke therefore helps to cause breathing problems and diseases of the chest and lungs, including cancer and bronchitis. Smoke also produces a dirty environment.

WAYS OF PREVENTING POLLUTION FROM SMOKE

(*a*)   This particular form of pollution has been much improved by the **Clean Air Act** which was introduced in Britain in 1956. This allowed local councils to introduce **smokeless zones**. In a smokeless zone, solid fuels can be used only if they are **smokeless**. Industry also had to follow strict regulations about smoke control from factories.

(*b*)   Very efficient smoke and dust filters are now used in industry to remove solid particles from waste gases before they are allowed to enter the air.

5 POLLUTION CAUSED BY LEAD COMPOUNDS IN THE AIR

Special **compounds of lead** are added to petrol before it is used as a fuel. This is to make sure that the petrol burns efficiently in the engine. Lead compounds are therefore found in the exhaust gases from cars whenever 'leaded petrol' is used. The lead compounds escape into the air, especially where there is busy road traffic. The lead compounds can then be breathed in, or they can settle on vegetables and fruit and be eaten.

Compounds of 'heavy' metals such as lead and mercury are **toxic**. They are particularly dangerous because they build up inside the body (**cumulative poisons**); they are excreted only slowly. Lead compounds are nerve poisons. In particular, they can cause brain damage in young children.

The main way of preventing pollution from compounds of lead is to develop car engines which can work efficiently with **lead-free petrol**. The amount of lead in petrol is being reduced. It should be possible to remove it completely.

1   Which two gases are found in normal air but not in liquid air?

2   Methane (CH_4) is a *hydrocarbon* but a sugar such as glucose ($C_6H_{12}O_6$) is not. Why not?

3   (*a*)   Which two elements are found in all fossil fuels in large proportions?
(*b*)   Name one other element usually found in fossil fuels, which can cause a pollutant gas to be formed.
(*c*)   When a fossil fuel burns, what substance does it use up?
(*d*)   For each of the elements named in (*a*) and (*b*), name the substances formed when a fuel is burned completely.
(*e*)   Which of these elements can form a different product under certain circumstances?
(*f*)   What is this other product, and when is it formed?

4   Which gas could you obtain from the air and use for the following processes? (The same gas may be used more than once if necessary.)
(*a*)   making fire extinguishers,
(*b*)   filling the plastic bags which contain potato crisps before the bags are sealed,
(*c*)   filling ordinary electric light bulbs,
(*d*)   filling a weather balloon.

5   The following table shows the concentrations of lead found in different parts of the air. The figures are in microgrammes of lead per cubic metre of air.

Area	Concentration of lead
large city in Britain	0.1 to 2.0
busy road tunnels	up to 200
rural areas of Britain	0.01 to 1.0
Los Angeles, USA city centre	up to 7.6
South Pole	0.004
small town in Britain	0.1 to 0.5
Fleet Street, London	up to 5.4
motorways in Los Angeles	20 to 70

(*a*)   Where is the highest concentration of lead found, from the examples in the table?
(*b*)   Where is the lowest concentration of lead found, from the examples in the table?
(*c*)   Use your calculator to answer this part. By how many times is the highest value in the table greater than the lowest value in the table? Is it
A   8 times
B   20 times
C   80 times
D   20 000 times or
E   50 000 times?

(*d*) Why is the concentration of lead in the air over a large city greater than over a small town?

6 Can you suggest why there is more likely to be a severe ground frost in winter on a clear night rather than on a cloudy night?

7 Air dissolves in water. The dissolved air can be removed and collected by boiling a sample of water using suitable apparatus. When this is done, the proportion of oxygen in the air can be found by doing an experiment like the one described on p204. It is found that the proportion of oxygen in air which has been dissolved in water is about 30%. Can you suggest an explanation?

9.4 OXYGEN. TYPES OF OXIDE

OXYGEN

Oxygen is the most abundant element on earth. Nearly 50% by mass of the earth's crust and oceans consists of *combined* oxygen, (oxygen in compounds). Its most common compounds include carbonates (e.g. limestone, $CaCO_3$), oxides such as sand (mainly silicon oxide), silicates and water. In addition, *free* oxygen makes up about 21% by volume of the air. The element consists of molecules, O_2.

PHYSICAL PROPERTIES OF OXYGEN

State at room temperature	Solubility in water	Colour	Odour	Density relative to air	Toxic?	Temperature at which turns into liquid at ordinary pressure (b p) in °C
gas	slight	none	none	about same	no	−183

Note Only slightly soluble in water, but enough to enable fish to 'breathe' dissolved oxygen from the water, and for plants to live in the sea.

PREPARATION OF OXYGEN

You may have produced oxygen in electrolysis experiments (e.g. p113). It is usually prepared as follows.

Solid reagent: manganese (IV) oxide. (This black powder acts as a catalyst.)

Liquid reagent: dilute hydrogen peroxide solution, H_2O_2. No heating needed.

$$\text{Hydrogen peroxide} \xrightarrow[\text{catalyst}]{\text{manganese (IV) oxide}} \text{oxygen}$$

$$2H_2O_2(aq) \xrightarrow[\text{catalyst}]{MnO_2} 2H_2O(l) + O_2(g)$$

You should be able to suggest a suitable generator and a suitable system for collecting the gas from those on p198.

MANUFACTURE OF OXYGEN FROM LIQUID AIR (p205)

CHEMICAL PROPERTIES OF OXYGEN

1 Reactions between oxygen and other elements to form oxides

Most **elements** react with oxygen when heated either in the gas or in the air. The reaction forms a compound of oxygen called an **oxide**. Some reactive elements **burn** when heated in oxygen, e.g. magnesium. Other less reactive elements do not burn, but instead they form a **surface coat** of the oxide, e.g. copper.

magnesium+oxygen → magnesium oxide
copper+oxygen → copper(II) oxide
$2Mg(s)+O_2(g) \rightarrow 2MgO(s)$
$2Cu(s)+O_2(g) \rightarrow 2CuO(s)$
(see p92 for more details.)

The following table shows how some common *non-metals* react with oxygen. Many *compounds* also burn when heated in air or oxygen. Many of these compounds are used as fuels.

Element	Reaction details
hydrogen	The colourless gas burns with a blue flame if it is burned at a jet. A *mixture* of hydrogen and oxygen will *explode* if a flame or spark is applied. Steam is the only product. $2H_2(g)+O_2(g) \rightarrow 2H_2O(g)$
sulphur	The pale yellow solid melts when heated (amber liquid) and then burns with a bright blue flame to form invisible oxides of sulphur. These oxides have a sharp, choking smell. The oxides are acidic, and turn damp blue litmus paper red. $S(l)+O_2(g) \rightarrow SO_2(g)$
carbon	The black solid only reacts when red hot. It smoulders or perhaps burns with a white flame producing an invisible gas. $C(s)+O_2(g) \rightarrow CO_2(g)$

2 Oxygen as an oxidising agent

All reactions of oxygen are **oxidations** (p129).

USES OF OXYGEN

1   Over 50% of the oxygen which is made from liquid air is used in making steel (p137).
2   Smaller amounts are used to aid breathing (e.g. in hospitals, aircraft, diving), to make rocket fuels and explosives, and in high temperature metal cutting.

TYPES OF OXIDE

An oxide is a compound. It contains two elements, one of which is oxygen. The other element can be a metal or a non-metal. Oxides can be divided into four main types.

1 OXIDES OF METALS (BASIC OXIDES)

All oxides of the common metals are **solids** at room temperature.

All oxides of the common metals are **bases** (see p176). See also Table 7.1 (p161) and Table 4.2 (p93).

The oxides of the more reactive metals form *solutions* in water. These solutions are alkalis (p176).

2 OXIDES OF NON-METALS WHICH ARE ACIDIC OXIDES

Common oxides of non-metals are either *gases or liquids* at room temperature (compare with metal oxides, previous section).

Most oxides of non-metals are **acidic**. (Those which are not are neutral, but never basic. Most oxides of non-metals are therefore 'opposite' to oxides of metals.)

Note that if an acidic oxide dissolves in water it forms an acid solution. An obvious example of this is the way in which sulphur dioxide (an oxide of a non-metal) dissolves in rain water to form acid rain.

3 OXIDES OF NON-METALS WHICH ARE NEUTRAL OXIDES

A few oxides of non-metals are not acidic. These few exceptions are **neutral** oxides. They do not react with either acids or alkalis, and they do not change the colour of indicators. The two most common examples are pure water, H_2O (which is really hydrogen oxide) and carbon *monoxide*, CO (Fig 9.14).

Fig 9.14 Main types of oxide

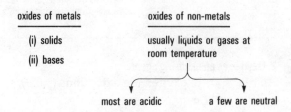

4 AMPHOTERIC OXIDES

All oxides of metals can act as bases, but a *few* of them also have an extra property. These exceptions can behave as an acidic oxide, as well as a basic oxide. These 'two-in-one' oxides are called **amphoteric oxides**. The most common examples are aluminium oxide, Al_2O_3, and zinc oxide, ZnO. The hydroxides of aluminium and zinc are also amphoteric (see p162).

aluminium oxide+an acid →a salt+water

e.g.

aluminium oxide + hydrochloric acid →aluminium chloride + water
(in this example the oxide is acting as a base).

aluminium oxide + an alkali→ a salt (called an aluminate)
(in this example, the oxide is acting as an acid).

9.5 HYDROGEN

Hydrogen is one of the most common elements on earth. It is always found *combined* in compounds, never as the free element. Water is a common compound of hydrogen, and all fossil fuels contain hydrogen combined with carbon.

PHYSICAL PROPERTIES OF HYDROGEN

State at room temp	Solubility in water	Colour	Odour	Density relative to air	Toxic?	Temperature at which turns into liquid at ordinary pressure in °C (ie bp)
gas	slight	none	none	much less dense	no	−253

PREPARATION OF HYDROGEN

Although hydrogen is not toxic, great care must be taken when it is prepared. When the gas is *mixed* with air or oxygen, it forms an **explosive mixture**. There must not be a flame near any apparatus in which the gas is being made or collected. Large volumes of the gas should not be collected if a flame is to be applied to it.

You will have seen several reactions which produce hydrogen:

1 Some metals react with cold water or steam to produce the gas (p195).
2 It is sometimes formed at the negative electrode (cathode) in electrolysis reactions, e.g. the electrolysis of acids or 'acidified water' p113.
3 Some metals react with dilute acids to form hydrogen, (p94).

Reaction (3) is normally the most convenient way of preparing a sample of hydrogen in the laboratory.

Typical solid reagent: zinc metal (as granules)
Typical liquid reagent: dilute hydrochloric acid. No heating required.

zinc + hydrochloric acid → zinc chloride + hydrogen
$$Zn(s) + \quad 2HCl(aq) \quad \rightarrow \quad ZnCl_2(aq) \quad + \quad H_2(g)$$

You should be able to suggest a suitable generator and collecting system from those on pp197–200.

THE MANUFACTURE OF HYDROGEN

Large quantities of the gas are used in industry. It is produced by reacting natural gas (mainly methane, CH_4) with steam:

natural gas + steam →   hydrogen   + oxides of carbon
(methane)   (mainly CO_2)

e.g. $CH_4(g) \quad + 2H_2O(g) \rightarrow \quad 3H_2(g) \quad + \quad CO_2(g)$

CHEMICAL PROPERTIES OF HYDROGEN

1 COMBUSTION (THE BURNING) OF HYDROGEN

There are two ways in which hydrogen can 'burn'. If it is *mixed* with air or oxygen, and a flame is applied, the mixture **explodes**. On a small scale, (test tube), a miniature 'explosion' or 'pop' is used as a test for the gas.

However, if pure hydrogen is burned in air or oxygen, it burns quietly with a blue flame. Steam is the *only* product (apart from heat energy) in either of these reactions. The steam can be condensed to a liquid and proved to be pure water.

hydrogen + oxygen → steam
$2H_2(g) \quad + \quad O_2(g) \quad \rightarrow 2H_2O(g)$

2 HYDROGEN IS A REDUCING AGENT

See p129. Hydrogen is a reducing agent because it will **remove oxygen** from compounds such as oxides. The hydrogen combines with the oxygen in the compound and changes into steam. For example, if copper(II) oxide is heated in a stream of hydrogen gas, it is **reduced** to copper metal. The black solid changes to pink-brown copper metal.

copper(II) oxide + hydrogen →   copper + steam
$CuO(s) \quad + \quad H_2(g) \quad \rightarrow \quad Cu(s) \quad + H_2O(g)$

USES OF HYDROGEN

1 THE MANUFACTURE OF AMMONIA BY THE HABER PROCESS

About 40% of the hydrogen which is manufactured is used for this important purpose (p314).

2 THE MANUFACTURE OF ORGANIC CHEMICALS

A variety of organic chemicals are made by using hydrogen at some stage in their manufacture, for example nylon, and the alcohol methanol.

3 HYDROGEN AS A FUEL

Only small quantities are used in this way at the moment, (e.g. for rockets, space travel). However, the use of hydrogen as a fuel is in theory very attractive. Its advantages include:

1 If a *cheap* way of making it from water can be discovered, it will be easy to make.
2 It gives out a great deal of heat energy when it burns.
3 Water or steam is the *only* product of the reaction.
This is not a pollutant. (Compare this with what happens when a fossil fuel is burned.)

    The main problems are:

1 Not easy to transport the gas *safely* in a convenient way.
2 Any leaks are potentially very dangerous, because when it is mixed with air, it is explosive.

4 THE MANUFACTURE OF COOKING FATS AND MARGARINE

Most *plant* fats are *liquids* at room temperature (e.g. maize oil, sunflower seed oil). If these oils are heated with hydrogen and a catalyst they change into *solid* fats. Other substances are added (e.g. colour, vitamins) and they are then used as margarine or cooking fat.

    Most animal fats are solids at room temperature, whereas most plant fats are liquids. This difference can be explained by the chemical structure of the two types of fat. All fats, whether from animals or plants, contain large organic molecules. These molecules usually include long chains of carbon atoms. The fats from plants include a considerable number of carbon-carbon **double covalent bonds** (p34). They are **unsaturated** (p334). Animal fats, on the other hand, are **saturated** or nearly saturated. This is why they are solids at room temperature. When the unsaturated plant oils are heated with hydrogen and a nickel catalyst, the hydrogen **adds** (p334) to the double bonds. The plant fats or oils then become saturated and solids at room temperature.

CHECK YOUR UNDERSTANDING (Answers on p416)

Fig 9.15 The reduction of copper(II) oxide by hydrogen

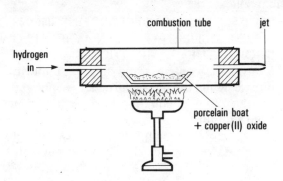

1 An experiment was being demonstrated as shown in Fig 9.15. Hydrogen was being used to reduce heated copper(II) oxide. The hydrogen leaving the combustion tube was burned, forming a jet of flame at the end of the short glass tube. However, before the jet of hydrogen was ignited, samples of gas were taken in test tubes, and each of these was tested for hydrogen. Eventually the demonstrator was satisfied that it was safe to light the jet of hydrogen, and did so.

(a) What might have happened if a light was placed near to where the hydrogen was leaving the tube, *before* samples were collected and tested?

(b) Why might this have happened?

(c) How did the demonstrator know that it was safe to light the jet of gas?

2 When a metal oxide is reduced to the metal as shown in Fig 9.15, it is usual to allow the metal which is formed to cool down in a stream of hydrogen before the combustion tube is opened. Why?

3 Name two metal oxides which could not be reduced to the metal by the method shown in Fig. 9.15

CHECK LIST ▶ REMEMBER THAT SOME OF THESE POINTS MAY NOT BE RELEVANT FOR THE PARTICULAR SYLLABUS YOU ARE FOLLOWING.

YOU SHOULD UNDERSTAND THE FOLLOWING POINTS.

1 ▶ General principles for preparing and collecting gases.
2 ▶ Composition of the air. How to show that the air contains about 20% oxygen, and also carbon dioxide and water.
3 ▶ Making oxygen (and other gases) from liquid air.
4 ▶ Processes which use up/produce oxygen.
5 ▶ The 'greenhouse effect'. The carbon dioxide/oxygen balance in the air.
6 ▶ Air pollution.
7 ▶ Preparation, properties, uses, test for oxygen.
8 ▶ Types of oxide.
9 ▶ Preparation, properties, uses, test for hydrogen.

SPECIMEN EXAMINATION QUESTIONS

SEE GENERAL NOTE BEFORE QUESTIONS ON pp49 and 50.
REMEMBER THAT YOU MAY BE ALLOWED TO USE A DATA BOOK IN THE EXAMINATION.

1 Many fuels contain some sulphur impurity, which forms sulphur dioxide when the fuel is burned.

(a) Write an equation to show the formation of sulphur dioxide from sulphur.

(b) How does sulphur dioxide cause rainwater to become acidic?

(c) Give *two* reasons why acidic rainwater is a nuisance.

[*SEG* spec 1]

2 Which one of the following elements burns in oxygen forming an acidic oxide?

A hydrogen   B iron   C sodium   D sulphur

3 Which set of apparatus shown in the diagrams would be used to collect ammonia?   [*NEA* spec (A), 1]

Fig 9.16 Diagram for question 3

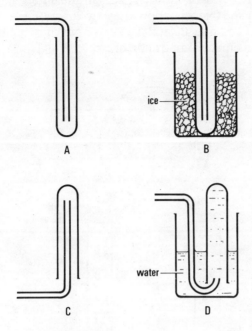

4–8 Questions 4 to 8 concern the following gases:

A Argon   B Carbon dioxide   C Nitrogen   D Oxygen
E Sulphur dioxide

Select, from A to E, the gas which

4 does not occur naturally in the air

5 is the third most abundant gas in air

6 can be made by burning methane

7 is not composed of molecules containing more than one atom

8 is a by-product of the thermal decomposition of limestone

           [*LEA* spec (B), 1]

9 When air reacts with hot copper, which gas is removed from the air?

A Carbon dioxide   B Nitrogen   C Oxygen
D Water vapour

10 A pan of burning cooking oil can be extinguished by putting a wet cloth over the pan. The reason for doing this is to

A cool down the pan   B prevent carbon monoxide escaping
C prevent oil from spitting   D prevent oxygen from reaching the flames   [*SEG* spec (Alt), 1]

11 The amount of carbon dioxide in the air is decreased by

A respiration   B photosynthesis   C the burning of fuel oil
D the manufacture of calcium oxide from limestone
E the extraction of iron

12 When air is bubbled through water in a fish tank the pH gradually changes from 7 to 6. The gas in air which could be responsible for this change is

A argon   B carbon dioxide   C hydrogen   D nitrogen
E oxygen   [*LEA* spec (A), 1]

13 The two most abundant gases in the air are nitrogen (approximately 80%) and oxygen (approximately 20%).

(*a*)   Shade in and label the pie-chart in Fig 9.17 to show this approximate composition of air.

Fig 9.17 Diagrams for question 13(*a*) and (*e*)

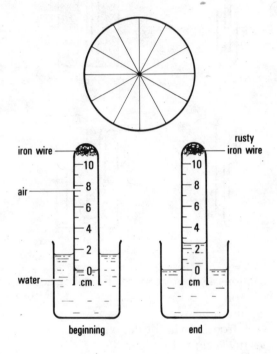

(*b*)   To separate nitrogen from oxygen, the air is first liquefied. Use the Data Book to find out which of these elements is easier to liquefy. Explain your answer.

(*c*)   How is nitrogen separated from liquid air?

(*d*)   Give two large scale uses of nitrogen.

(*e*)   A pupil designed an experiment to measure the amount of oxygen in a sample of air. The second diagram in Fig 9.17 shows the apparatus at the beginning and end of the investigation.

(i) Explain as fully as you can why the water rose up the test tube.

(ii) The water level rose by 2.5 cm and so the pupil calculated that 25% of the air in the sample was oxygen. Explain why the apparatus did not give the known value for the percentage of oxygen of 20%.   [*NEA* spec (A), 1]

14 Petrol today contains small quantities of lead compounds to enable more petrol to be made from a given amount of petroleum. When the

petrol burns in the car engine, lead compounds escape into the atmosphere. The bar chart in Fig 9.18 shows the average concentrations of lead in soil samples at different distances from the edge of a road.

Fig. 9.18 Diagram for question 14

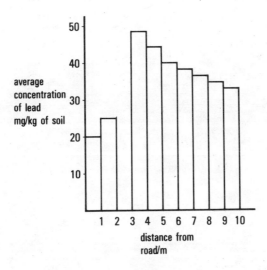

(*a*)   What is the average concentration of lead in the soil 7 metres from the edge of the road?

(*b*)   At a distance of 3 metres from the road the average concentration of lead is 33 mg/kg of soil. Complete the bar chart by putting in this result.

(*c*)   At what distance from the road is the average concentration of lead in soil greatest?

(*d*)   Why is it wise to carry out experiments with several samples at each distance?

(*e*)   Why is it unwise to grow vegetable in an allotment by the side of a busy road?

(*f*)   Give one disadvantage of selling 'lead free' petrol in place of 'leaded' petrol.   (*LEA* spec (B), 2]

WATER. SOLUTIONS. WATER POLLUTION

CONTENTS

10.1 WATER

THE IMPORTANCE OF WATER

Water is by far the most important *compound* found on earth. In spite of the apparently large supply of water, in Britain we are sometimes faced with a shortage of *drinking water* in the summer. Some parts of the world are desperately short of usable water. The problem is that most of the water on earth is either unusable for most purposes because it is not pure (e.g. sea water and river water), or it is not found in areas where it is desperately needed.

We need very large volumes of water both in industry and in our homes as part of our way of life. In industry water is needed for cooling some reactions, for generating electricity at power stations (where, as steam, it drives turbines), for cleaning, for transporting things, and as a liquid in which important chemical reactions take place. We need water to grow our food crops: drought is a serious problem in some parts of the world. We need water to wash away the waste from inside our bodies, and to wash waste from our homes and factories. We need water to clean our bodies, clothes and many other things. Many of the reactions you have studied in chemistry can only happen if the chemicals are dissolved in water.

In addition, water is used as a *raw material*, as a substance which can take part in chemical reactions just as any other chemical can. The importance of water can be summarised in the fact that we can live for something like five weeks without food, but for only seven days or so without water.

THE WATER CYCLE

Most of the water in, on or around the earth has been here since the earth began. We keep using this same water over and over again. Only a small proportion of the total amount of water is 'pure' at any moment. The rest, mainly in rivers or seas, contains dissolved substances. You will have done experiments in which you have evaporated water to see if any solids were left behind when all the water has been evaporated. For example, you may have used apparatus such as that shown in Fig 10.1. You will have found that most *natural* water (sea water, river water, etc.) contains dissolved solids. These are left behind when the water has evaporated. When sea water is evaporated, the solid left behind is mainly common salt, sodium chloride.

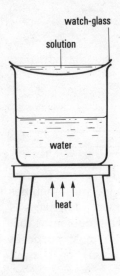

watch-glass

solution

water

heat

Fig 10.1 A simple
evaporation technique

Whenever water is heated, only *pure* water evaporates from the
surface of the liquid, no matter how impure the water is to start with.
This type of 'heating and evaporation' takes place in nature. The heat
from the sun evaporates pure water from the seas, rivers and lakes.
This water forms clouds and then condenses, falls as rain, and eventually flows back into the rivers, lakes and seas. This natural process is
very similar to what happens when we distil a solution containing
water in order to obtain pure water.

Your Water Authority traps *some* of this water on its way back to
the sea, treats it as described in the next section, and sends it as
drinking water to your home. The water which evaporates from the
seas, etc. is *pure* water, but by the time it has reached reservoirs, etc. it
has dissolved some carbon dioxide from the air, picked up bacteria,
and dissolved substances from rocks and the soil, and so it must be
treated before it is safe to drink.

Your Water Authority also treats *used* water from homes and
industry so that it is safe to put back into the rivers without causing
pollution. The treatment of used water usually takes place at a
sewage works. (You may have studied the treatment of sewage in
more detail – if so, revise your notes.) These various processes are
summarised in Fig 10.2.

Fig 10.2 The water cycle
(*modified from material
supplied by Severn Trent
Water Authority*)

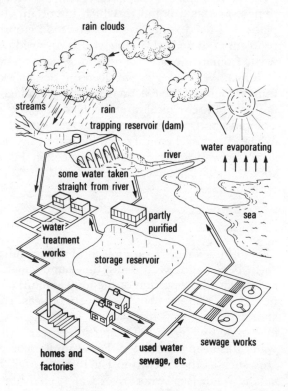

OBTAINING WATER FIT FOR DRINKING (SOMETIMES CALLED POTABLE WATER)

The methods used to make natural water fit for drinking vary. They depend upon the impurities which the water contains. For example, water which has flowed over moorland peat will be acidic. Such water may be partly or completely neutralised at the treatment works. Water which has flowed over limestone will contain dissolved chemicals which make it **hard** (p234). Such water may be softened at the treatment works. If the water has a lot of suspended solid in it, chemicals may be added to make these solids join together to form larger pieces which settle out in large settling tanks. Some authorities add fluorine (in the form of a fluoride) to help prevent tooth decay.

However, certain stages always occur at a water treatment works, no matter what the water may contain.

1 FILTRATION

Large floating objects such as pieces of wood are removed by wire mesh screens. Smaller solid particles are then filtered out in **filter beds**. These contain layers of sand and gravel. As water trickles through the beds, most of the solid particles are trapped on the sand and gravel. The filter beds are cleaned when necessary by forcing water through in the opposite direction.

2 TREATING THE WATER WITH CHLORINE (CHLORINATION)

Chlorine gas is very poisonous. In *very small* quantities, it is harmless to us, especially if dissolved in water. Even very small quantities, however, are still poisonous to smaller forms of life such as the bacteria which cause disease. Water which is to be used for drinking is therefore **chlorinated** at the treatment works. This process kills bacteria in the water. By the time that the water reaches our homes, the smell and taste of the gas have almost disappeared. Sometimes the taste is still obvious if the water has been heavily chlorinated, e.g. if there is a higher risk of bacteria being present. Water in swimming pools is also chlorinated, but slightly higher concentrations of chlorine are used because the water is not for drinking and because there is likely to be a higher concentration of bacteria in the water.

OBTAINING PURE WATER

Tap water is safe to drink, but it is not *pure* water. It contains dissolved air, dissolved chlorine, and dissolved substances which have joined it during its journey over rocks, etc. Note that the treatment described in the previous section does not remove these *dissolved* substances. Drinking water is tested to make sure that the dissolved substances it still contains are harmless to health. Indeed, some of the dissolved substances are very *useful*. For example, fluoride ions help to prevent tooth decay, calcium ions (which cause hardness, p234) help bone and teeth formation and help to prevent heart disease, and small amounts of iodine that the body needs are normally supplied in water.

However, when water is used for medical purposes and for some industrial reactions, *any* dissolved substances could cause problems, and then we need really pure water.

OBTAINING PURE WATER BY DISTILLATION

If water is boiled, and the water vapour which evaporates off is condensed *separately* from the original solution (e.g. in a Liebig condenser), then we have obtained **distilled water**. This will be pure water; any dissolved solids will be left behind, and any dissolved gases will be boiled off.

Distillation is rarely used for the purification of water because a considerable amount of fuel is needed to produce even a small amount of distilled water. The so-called 'distilled water' supplied by garages, for car batteries, is more likely to be **deionised water**.

DEIONISED WATER: ANOTHER WAY OF OBTAINING PURE WATER

This process uses an **ion exchange resin**. This is usually an unreactive, covalent 'backbone' of atoms, e.g. a polymer such as polystyrene. On this 'backbone' ionic groups are weakly attached. To produce pure water, these ions must be a mixture of both H^+ ions and OH^- ions.

When tap water passes through the resin, any positively charged ions in the water are exchanged for H^+ ions on the resin. Any negatively charged ions are exchanged for OH^- ions on the resin. The H^+ and OH^- ions then join together to make more water molecules, H_2O. The water which trickles out at the bottom of the resin is pure; all the ions which were in it have been removed and replaced with H^+ and OH^- ions, which form more water molecules. The water has been **deionised**. Modern deionisers are quicker, cheaper to run, easier to use and far more portable than any form of distillation apparatus. (A special kind of ion exchange column is used to soften water, as described on p237.)

PROPERTIES OF PURE WATER

2 PHYSICAL PROPERTIES

(*a*)　Pure water freezes at 0°C and boils at 100°C at a pressure of 1 atmosphere.

(*b*)　Pure water is colourless and has no taste.

(*c*)　Water is a very good **solvent**. Most substances dissolve in it, even if only slightly.

2 TESTS FOR WATER

(*a*)　The simplest way of proving that a liquid is *pure* water is to find its freezing point. If the liquid is not water, or if it is water with something dissolved in it, it will have a freezing point other than 0°C (see effect of impurities on freezing point, p84).

(*b*)　There are several tests to show that a liquid *contains* water. (These do not prove that a liquid is *pure* water.) The common ones are:

Blue, anhydrous COBALT(II) CHLORIDE (paper or crystals) becomes pink if water is present;
White, anhydrous COPPER(II) SULPHATE goes blue if water is present.

3 CHEMICAL PROPERTIES OF WATER

(a) Reaction of water with other substances

Water can *react* with many substances. Some examples include: Water or steam reacts with some metals (p95). Water and oxygen react with iron or steel to cause rusting (p143). Steam is used in industry to manufacture hydrogen (p220). Water combines with **anhydrous salts** to form **hydrated salts**. You may also have discussed the way in which atmospheric moisture is absorbed by/reacts with other substances (e.g. sodium metal, sodium hydroxide), and you may have used the word **hydrolysis** to describe some reactions.

(b) Hydrated and anhydrous compounds

When a substance **combines** with water, it usually becomes **hydrated.** This combined water is called **water of crystallisation**. A hydrated solid may be perfectly dry, even though it contains water, because the combined water is 'locked up' inside the solid. It can be removed by heating, when the solid becomes **anhydrous**. The removal of combined water from a substance is called **dehydration**. Dehydration is not the same as drying. Drying is the removal of 'loose' water which has not been combined, but which has simply made the substance wet. You may need to understand how to find the per cent water of crystallisation in a substance.

Note that hydration and dehydration are **reversible** processes. They can be made to go 'either way'; an anhydrous solid can be hydrated, and a hydrated solid can be dehydrated.

Many metal salts contain water of crystallisation. It is useful to remember that the anhydrous and hydrated forms of the same salt are often quite different in appearance. For example, hydrated copper(II) sulphate consists of blue crystals, but the anhydrous salt is a white powder.

Note that when a reaction is reversed, everything is reversed, even energy changes:

$$\begin{array}{c} \text{HYDRATED COPPER(II)} \\ \text{SULPHATE} \\ (CuSO_4.5H_2O) \end{array} \underset{\text{heat energy given out}}{\overset{\text{heat energy needed}}{\rightleftharpoons}} \begin{array}{c} \text{ANHYDROUS + WATER} \\ \text{COPPER(II)} \\ \text{SULPHATE} \\ (CuSO_4) \end{array}$$

We use the symbol $\rightleftharpoons$ to show that a reaction is reversible.

(c) Confirming that water is made up of hydrogen and oxygen

It can be shown that when hydrogen is burned in oxygen, water is the **only** product.

$$2H_2(g) + O_2(g) \rightarrow 2H_2O(g)$$

It can also be shown that when we split water up, only hydrogen and oxygen are formed, e.g. the electrolysis of 'acidified water', p113. If a Hofmann voltameter is used, the volume of hydrogen produced at the negative electrode is twice the volume of oxygen formed at the positive electrode. This shows that water is formed by combining two volumes of hydrogen with one volume of oxygen (see equation).

10.2 HARD WATER

WHAT IS HARD WATER?

Drinking water, although safe to drink, still contains *dissolved* substances. If the dissolved substances include **calcium** or **magnesium** compounds, these cause problems of a special kind. Water which contains dissolved calcium or magnesium compounds is called **hard** water.

HOW DOES WATER BECOME HARD?

In Britain, calcium compounds are mainly responsible for hardness of water. There are two main ways in which they become dissolved in natural water.

1 HARD WATER FORMED BY THE SIMPLE DISSOLVING OF CALCIUM SULPHATE

Calcium sulphate occurs naturally in Britain. Sometimes it is found as **gypsum** ($CaSO_4.2H_2O$), and in some areas as **anhydrite** ($CaSO_4$). Calcium sulphate is only *slightly* soluble in water, but enough to make the water hard. If water flows over rocks containing calcium sulphate, very small quantities dissolve. This kind of hardness is sometimes called **permanent**.

2 HARD WATER FORMED BY A REACTION BETWEEN LIMESTONE AND RAIN WATER

Calcium carbonate occurs naturally in Britain, usually as the mineral limestone. Calcium carbonate is **insoluble** in water, and so it cannot simply dissolve in water as calcium sulphate does. However, it *reacts* with water which contains dissolved carbon dioxide, and changes into a calcium compound which *is* soluble. This compound, (calcium hydrogencarbonate) then dissolves in the water and makes it hard. Note that all rain water picks up carbon dioxide from the air, and so this process is common. The carbon dioxide makes the water acidic, and it may help to think that it is this weak acid solution which attacks and dissolves the limestone. This kind of hardness is sometimes called **temporary**. Note that only **dissolved** calcium or magnesium compounds can cause water to be hard.

The chemical reaction which takes place is:

$$CaCO_3(s) + H_2O(l) + CO_2(aq) \rightleftharpoons Ca(HCO_3)_2(aq)$$

This slow 'dissolving' of limestone has produced the many caves, caverns and tunnels which are found in limestone areas. Note that although the process is often described as the 'dissolving' of limestone, this is only the *apparent* reaction. Limestone is really insoluble, and it only appears to dissolve because it reacts and then changes into a substance which is soluble.

Note also that the reaction is reversible. If water evaporates off from a solution of calcium hydrogencarbonate, the reaction goes 'the other way', and insoluble calcium carbonate is formed again. This reverse reaction takes place when a drop of the solution slowly evaporates when suspended from a cave roof. The formation of the solid calcium carbonate from the drops is responsible for the stalactites and stalagmites which are found in limestone caves. The reverse reaction also takes place when this kind of hard water is boiled. This is why kettles used in hard water areas become covered with a layer of solid. The solid is calcium carbonate.

HOW CAN WE TELL WHEN WATER IS HARD?

Only a small amount of soap is needed to make ordinary water form a good **lather**. It takes much more soap to form a lather with hard water. To try this test, we need to take equal volumes of the water to be tested and deionised water, e.g. $10 \, cm^3$ of each. Each sample is place in a clean conical flask. Soap solution is then added to one of the samples, one drop at a time. After each drop, the mixture is given a good shake. The drops are counted. This is continued until a lather is formed, which lasts for half a minute after shaking has stopped. The same thing is then done with the other sample, and the results are compared.

WHY IS HARD WATER INCONVENIENT?

There are three main reasons for **softening** water.

1 The calcium or magnesium compounds in hard water react with soap to form an insoluble solid. This is seen as a dirty coloured precipitate. It sticks to the sides of sinks, baths, etc. and is often called a 'scum'.

2 Soap cannot 'clean' things while it is reacting with hard water. It can only 'do its job' as a cleaning agent after all the magnesium and calcium compounds have been used up. The soap used up in this reaction is wasted. (If you have studied this reaction in more detail, e.g. with sodium stearate as an example of a soap, and calcium stearate as the scum, revise your notes carefully.)

3 When hard water is boiled (or even simply heated) the calcium and magnesium compounds dissolved in it change into insoluble compounds, which precipitate out of solution. Layers of these solids build up inside kettles as 'kettle fur' in hard water areas. The problem is worse on an industrial scale, where millions of litres of water may be used for heating. Pipes and boilers which contain hot, hard water become coated with layers of calcium carbonate and other solids. The system no longer works efficiently, and if pipes become blocked, the danger of a serious accident increases.

METHODS USED FOR SOFTENING WATER

Note Some syllabuses divide the methods into those used for (*a*) permanently hard water, and (*b*) temporarily hard water, and you may need to revise this. You may also need to revise one or more of: (i) **soapless (synthetic) detergents** and their advantages with hard water, (ii) the manufacture of soap, (iii) the use of calgon in softening water.

As only *dissolved* calcium or magnesium compounds cause water to be hard, hard water can be softened by any method which either

       (i) removes the calcium or magnesium ions from the water, or

       (ii) changes the dissolved compounds into insoluble ones.

Note that it is the magnesium or calcium **ions** which cause hardness. The other ion in the compounds (e.g. sulphate or hydrogen-carbonate) is only a 'spectator ion' so far as hardness is concerned.

1 SOFTENING WATER BY USING EXCESS SOAP

This is only done in homes, when water is to be used for washing, bathing, etc. The first amount of soap which is used is 'wasted' in reacting with the calcium or magnesium compounds in the water. After that, the soap cleans normally. Obviously, this can only be used on a small scale, and if the water is to be used for bathing, etc. The soapy water, in which a scum is formed, would be of little use for anything else!

2 SOFTENING WATER BY DISTILLATION

Any kind of water can be purified by distillation. Any dissolved substances, such as calcium compounds, are left behind. This is an expensive way to soften water, and it is rarely used today, except where heating can be done cheaply.

3 SOFTENING WATER BY ADDING SODIUM CARBONATE (WASHING SODA)

Hydrated sodium carbonate crystals ($Na_2CO_3 . 10H_2O$) are commonly called 'washing soda' because they can be added to hard water to make it soft enough to wash in, without wasting soap.

The sodium carbonate *reacts* with the dissolved calcium or magnesium compounds in the hard water. The soluble compounds are changed into *insoluble* calcium or magnesium carbonate. These precipitate out. As the water no longer contains *dissolved* calcium or magnesium compounds, it has been softened.

SODIUM CARBONATE + DISSOLVED CALCIUM COMPOUND → INSOLUBLE CALCIUM CARBONATE + DISSOLVED SODIUM SALT

If you understand ionic equations you will realise that the sodium ions from the sodium carbonate are SPECTATOR IONS. So are the other ions of the calcium or magnesium compounds. The only ions which *react* are the Ca^{2+} or Mg^{2+} ions (from the hard water) and the CO_3^{2-} ions from the sodium carbonate, e.g.:

$$Ca^{2+}(aq) + CO_3^{2-}(aq) \rightarrow CaCO_3(s)$$

4 ION EXCHANGE

Read the description of how water can be purified by ion exchange on p232. It is not necessary to *purify* water (i.e. remove all the ions) in order to *soften* it. To soften it, we need to remove only the Ca^{2+} or Mg^{2+} ions. We can do this by exchanging them with some other positively charged ions, which do not cause hardness, from an ion exchange resin.

Usually, sodium ions are present on the resin and exchange with the Ca^{2+} or Mg^{2+} ions. (Positively charged ions are sometimes called **cations**, p107. An ion exchange resin which exchanges positively charged ions only is therefore called a **cation exchange resin**.) Small ion exchangers of this type can be fitted to household taps in hard water areas (Fig 10.3).

Fig 10.3 Method of softening water.

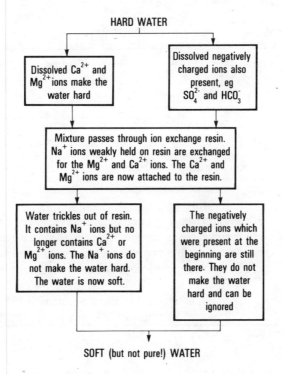

HOW SOAP WORKS

If you have considered soap as having a **covalent tail (backbone)** and an **ionic head**, and how this structure helps to remove dirt and grease, revise your notes.

CHECK YOUR UNDERSTANDING (Answers on p416)

1 A student tested a colourless liquid with some anhydrous copper(II) sulphate. The solid changed from white to blue. The student concluded that the liquid was water. Do you agree with the conclusion? If not, say why not.

2 A student decided to compare two different samples of river water, to find out how hard they were. The student poured some of each type of water into separate conical flasks. Some distilled water was placed in a third flask, for comparison. Soap solution was added, one cm^3 at a time, to each flask. The mixture was shaken after each addition. This was done until a lather was formed which lasted for half a minute or so. From this information, we cannot be sure that a fair comparison was made between the different types of water. Why not?

3 $20cm^3$ of each of three water samples were tested with soap solution. Sample A needed 25 drops of soap solution to form a lather, B needed 5 drops, and C 15 drops.
   (a)   Which of the samples could be distilled water?
   (b)   What can you conclude about the other two samples?

4 Why is it better to use soap in a fixed volume of hard water (e.g. in a sink or bowl) rather than in running hard water?

5 What is the main difference between an ion exchange resin used to soften water, and one which is used to purify water?

6 Water is softened by either
             (i) removing certain ions completely from the water, or
             (ii) changing some dissolved substances into insoluble ones.
   Which of these methods ((i) or (ii)) is used in each of the following?
   (a)   distillation
   (b)   adding washing soda
   (c)   ion exchange.

7 After a period of time, an ion exchange resin used to soften water becomes 'discharged'. In other words, it can no longer soften water. Such a resin can be 'regenerated' and used again. Which of the following methods could be used to regenerate it?
   (a)   Pass pure water through it for several hours.
   (b)   Pass a solution of calcium nitrate through it.
   (c)   Pass a concentrated solution of common salt, sodium chloride, through it.
   (d)   Pass hard water through the resin in the opposite direction to that which is normally used.

10.3 SOLUTIONS. SOLUBILITY

Water has been described as the 'universal solvent' because it dissolves most substances, even if only slightly. This can be a very useful property. It can also be a problem, when water dissolves substances which cause pollution.

Water is a particularly good solvent for substances which are held together by **ionic bonding**. However, there are many exceptions to this general rule. All of the insoluble salts mentioned on p186 are ionically bonded substances, but they do not dissolve in water. However, water does dissolve *most* ionically bonded substances.

Similarly, water is not a good solvent for *most* **covalently** bonded substances. This is particularly true if a covalently bonded substance forms simple molecules (p265). Common examples are petrol, oil, paraffin and many other organic liquids. This simple guide also has many exceptions, e.g. sugar (which is covalent and molecular).

Make sure that you understand the words **solvent** and **solute**, (p74). Another important term is **saturated solution**. When a soluble solid is added in small quantities, with stirring , to a fixed volume of solvent, a point is eventually reached when no more solid will dissolve. The solid which is being added then forms a layer on the bottom of the container and no longer dissolves, no matter how much we stir it. The solution at this point is **saturated**. It cannot hold any more dissolved solid (unless we change the conditions, such as temperature.)

The amount of solid which can be dissolved in a solvent to make it saturated is called the **solubility** of the solid. The solubility depends upon four things:

1 the solvent which is being used,
2 the solid which is being added,
3 the volume of solvent which is used, and
4 the temperature of the solvent.

In order that we can compare the solubilities of different substances, we need to fix some of these conditions. We therefore measure the solubility of a solid as follows: *The solubility of a solid in water is the mass of solid (in g) which will dissolve in 100g of water at a known temperature to form a saturated solution.* You do not need to learn these exact words, but you must remember the important points: the number of g in 100g water at a stated temperature. The same idea is used for other solvents. To make sure that a solution is saturated, measurements are usually taken when there is *excess, undissolved* solid in the solvent.

HOW TO WORK OUT THE SOLUBILITY OF A SOLID FROM SOME EXPERIMENTAL RESULTS

There are several ways of finding the solubility of a solid by experiment. The following results are from one such experiment. Make sure that you understand how the experiment is done. Revise the details of any experiment you have done.

Temperature of solution: 25°C
Mass of empty evaporating basin: 25.0 g
Mass of evaporating basin and solid after careful evaporation of the solvent: 26.2 g
Volume of water = 20.0 cm³
1 cm³ of water weighs 1.0 g, ∴ 20.0 cm³ of water has a mass of 20.0 g.

CALCULATION

Mass of solid dissolved in 20 cm³ of water at 25°C = 26.2 g −
$$\frac{25.0\,g}{1.2\,g}$$

1.2 g of solid dissolve in 20 cm³ of water at 25°C.
(5×1.2 g) of solid dissolve in 100 cm³ water at 25°C = 6.0 g.
The solubility of the solid in water at 25°C is 6.0 g.

Note that an important part of the calculation, and one which many students forget, is the scaling up of the results to show how much solid will dissolve in *100* g of water.

The above is the *easiest* kind of solubility calculation. You may have done a more accurate one in which you find the volume of water in the sample of saturated solution by *weighing*. For this, an extra measurement is needed. In the experiment used as the example, the extra measurement would be to weigh the evaporating basin when it contains the sample of saturated solution. Suppose that:

Mass of evaporating basin containing unknown volume of saturated solution = 46.2 g
We can then calculate: (using the earlier figures)
Mass of saturated solution = 46.2 g −
$$\frac{25.0\,g}{21.2\,g}$$
As the mass of dissolved solid is 1.2 g (see earlier),
therefore mass of solvent = 21.2 g −
$$\frac{1.2\,g}{20.0\,g}$$
The rest of the calculation, and the answer, are the same as before.

This is more accurate then measuring the *volume* of the water, as in the first example. For example, you may measure 20.0 cm³ of *solution* very accurately, but this is not the same as the volume of *water* (the solid takes up some volume too!). The weighing method finds the mass of water alone.

Another point many students forget is the need to mention the *temperature* when you write the solubility of a solid.

SOLUBILITY CURVES

The solubility of a solid depends upon the temperature. For most solids, the *solubility increases* as the *temperature increases*. In other words, for most substances, a hot solvent will dissolve more solid than a cold solvent. We usually show how the solubility of a solid

Fig 10.4 The solubility curves for potassium nitrate and potassium chloride in water.

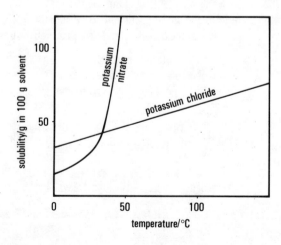

changes with temperature by plotting a graph. One axis of the graph is the solubility of the solid (in the usual units of g per 100 g of water). The other axis is the temperature. A graph of this kind is called a **solubility curve**. It is possible to plot solubilities of more than one substance on the same graph. A typical solubility curve is shown in Fig 10.4. You could be asked to use some data to plot a solubility curve. Make sure that you know how to do this. In particular, make sure that you can choose sensible scales for your axes on the graph.

SOME USES OF SOLUBILITY CURVES AND SOLUBILITY INFORMATION

1 An experiment may measure solubility at only five different temperatures, but a solubility curve allows you to work out solubilities at other temperatures. Make sure that you know how to do this.

2 It is possible to work out the mass of solid which would come out of solution if a saturated solution is cooled, from one temperature to another. Suppose that we have worked out the following solubilities from a solubility curve:

> solubility of X is 23 g per 100 g water at 100°C
> solubility of X is 12 g per 100 g water at 50°C.

From this we can work out that if 100 g of water saturated with X at 100°C were cooled to 50°C, then (23–12) g of X would come out of solution, i.e. 11 g of X.

Remember that solubilities are normally measured in g per 100 g of water. So if 50 g of solution were cooled (rather than 100 g), only 5.5 g of X would crystallise out in the example.

3 If the solubilities of two solids, A and B, in a mixture are quite different, it is possible to separate B from A by a process called **fractional crystallisation**. If you have used this technique, make sure that you understand it.

THE SOLUBILITY OF GASES IN WATER

Some gases are extremely soluble in water, even at ordinary pressures, e.g. ammonia, hydrogen chloride and sulphur dioxide.

Most gases are only slightly, or moderately, soluble in water. Such gases include oxygen, the air, carbon dioxide and chlorine. Although oxygen is only slightly soluble, enough dissolves from the air to allow fish and other forms of life to live in water. The slight amount of air which dissolves in water also gives the water a 'taste'. Boiled water, which does not contain dissolved air, tastes quite different from ordinary water.

The solubility of a *solid* in water depends only on the temperature under ordinary conditions. The solubility of a *gas*, however, depends upon *two* things: the pressure and the temperature. The solubility of any gas is *increased* if the pressure is *increased*. Carbon dioxide is only moderately soluble in water at ordinary pressures, but is much more soluble if the pressure is increased. Most fizzy drinks (lemonade, beer, etc.) contain carbon dioxide dissolved under pressure. If you look at a fizzy drink inside an unopened bottle, you will not see any gas bubbles. All of the carbon dioxide is dissolved in the liquid, under pressure. When the bottle is opened, the pressure is released, and some of the carbon dioxide can no longer remain dissolved. It then starts to bubble out, and makes the drink fizzy.

Most students find it easy to remember that a gas dissolves more easily if the pressure is increased. However, they often make a mistake about the effect of temperature on the solubility of a gas. The effect is the opposite to what happens with a solid. As the temperature is *increased*, the solubility of a gas *decreases*. This is why the pressure builds up inside a bottle of a fizzy drink on a hot day. The temperature of the liquid rises, and the carbon dioxide becomes less soluble in the warm liquid. Some of it bubbles out of the liquid, collects above the top of the liquid, and raises the pressure inside the bottle.

This effect also explains why bubbles of gas form in a jug of water if it is left on a table in a warm room. The water contains some dissolved air. This air becomes *less* soluble as the temperature of the water rises. Bubbles of air come out of the water as the water can no longer dissolve all of the air it originally contained.

SUMMARY OF FACTORS WHICH AFFECT THE SOLUBILITY OF A GAS OR SOLID IN A LIQUID

State at room temperature	Temperature increase	Pressure increase
solids	usually become more soluble	rarely used with solids
gases	always become less soluble	always become more soluble

CHECK YOUR UNDERSTANDING (Answers on p416)

1 What is incorrect or missing in each of the following statements?
  (*a*) The solubility of substance X is 12.3 g in 100 g of water.
  (*b*) The solubilities of most gases and solids increase as the temperature increases.

2 Use Fig 10.4 (p240) to work out:
  (*a*) the approximate solubility of potassium chloride at 75°C,
  (*b*) the approximate solubility of potassium nitrate at 25°C,
  (*c*) the approximate temperature at which the two solids have the same solubility,
  (*d*) the approximate temperature at which 100 g of potassium nitrate would dissolve in 100 g of water,
  (*e*) the approximate mass of potassium chloride which would dissolve in 50 g of water at 100°C.

3 Calculate the solubilities of each of the following substances, in the usual units of g per 100 g of water.
  (*a*) substance A, of which 8 g dissolve in 25 g of water at 40°C,
  (*b*) substance B, of which 4 g dissolve in 40 g of water at 25°C,

(c)   substance C if 6 g dissolve in 20 g of water at 30°C.

4 Use the following results from an experiment to calculate the solubility of the solid.

(a)   Substance D, in experiment 1 (as used on p239)

mass of empty evaporating basin: 25.0 g

mass of evaporating basin+solid, after evaporation: 27.5 g

mass of water in which solid was dissolved: 25.0 g

(b)   Substance E, in experiment 2 (as used on p240)

mass of empty evaporating basin: 30.0 g

mass of evaporating basin+sample of saturated solution: 58.5 g

mass of evaporating basin+solid after evaporation: 33.5 g.

5 A pupil poured some water into a beaker until it was approximately half full. The pupil then added weighed amounts of a solid to the water, a little at a time, with stirring. This was continued until no more solid would dissolve, and there was excess undissolved solid at the bottom of the beaker. The mass of solid used at this point was 28 g. The student concluded that the solubility of the solid in water was 28 g.

A friend said that the solubility of the solid was not 28 g, and said that three mistakes had been made in the experiment. What were they?

6 If a gas which is moderately soluble in water is being collected over water, why is *warm* water sometimes used in the trough?

7 If a saturated solution of potassium chloride in 100 g water is cooled from 100°C to 50°C, approximately how much solid would crystallise out from solution? (Use Fig 10.4, p240, to answer the question.)

10.4 WATER POLLUTION

Water has always seemed cheap and plentiful. To wash waste into rivers and seas seemed both simple and convenient. It became someone else's problem! Now we are learning to keep dangers to an absolute minimum. We are very concerned to protect the environment, and Water Authorities are very experienced in looking for a wide range of possible pollutants. The main types of water pollution are described under the following headings.

1 THE IMPORTANCE OF DISSOLVED OXYGEN IN WATER

Water which has a relatively high level of dissolved oxygen allows many forms of life to live within it, even very active forms such as fish, which use up a lot of oxygen. Water which contains very little dissolved oxygen can only support the life of leeches, worms, and certain kinds of bacteria which do not need oxygen. Unfortunately, these particular types of bacteria are often those which cause disease. If there is only a small amount of dissolved oxygen in a river, therefore, several things happen. Various forms of life, especially active forms such as fish, can no longer live in it. The river becomes 'dead'.

Also, it becomes a breeding ground for dangerous, disease-carrying bacteria. Unfortunately, some kinds of pollution cause dissolved oxygen to be used up, and so these things then start to happen.

WAYS IN WHICH DISSOLVED OXYGEN CAN BE REMOVED FROM WATER

(a) USING UP DISSOLVED OXYGEN TO OXIDISE WASTE SUBSTANCES

River water normally has a *natural* way of destroying many of the toxic (poisonous) substances which enter it. In normal river water there are very large numbers of relatively harmless bacteria. These use dissolved oxygen to **oxidise** many of the harmful substances into harmless waste. We use this kind of process at a sewage works, where bacteria oxidise the waste from our bodies before it is allowed to enter rivers, etc. If there are *large* amounts of toxic and waste substances in the river (e.g. if the river is polluted) the bacteria soon use up most of the dissolved oxygen in the water as they oxidise the waste. The water then becomes 'dead' and the effects described earlier begin to happen. If animal waste (e.g. sewage) enters river water before it has been partly oxidised at a sewage works, it will also cause this effect.

Note that the bacteria which need oxygen to live are called **aerobic bacteria**. Bacteria which do not need oxygen to live are called **anaerobic bacteria**. Many aerobic bacteria are relatively harmless, but many anaerobic bacteria cause disease.

(b) USING UP DISSOLVED OXYGEN TO DECOMPOSE DEAD PLANTS

The amount of plant material which can grow in a river is normally kept under control by natural processes. This normal balance can be upset if extra plant foods enter the water. The plants then grow very rapidly. The most likely kind of pollutant which can act as plant food is excess fertilisers draining off farm land after heavy rain. Another possible cause is excess detergents. Detergents contain phosphates, which are also plant foods.

If the plant life in a river grows more rapidly than normal, two things can happen.

(i) The river can become 'choked' with weeds, which is an unpleasant sight.

(ii) A lot of plant growth also means that there is a great deal of dead plant material when it dies. This dead material is normally oxidised by bacteria as it decomposes (rots). This decay uses up dissolved oxygen, and the effects described earlier then occur in the river.

2 A DIFFERENT KIND OF POLLUTION. POLLUTION CAUSED BY TOXIC (POISONOUS) SUBSTANCES

(a) IN RIVERS AND SEAS

Some substances which enter rivers and seas are poisonous to fish and other living things. Obvious examples include 'heavy metal' ions such as lead, copper and mercury ions. Excess pesticides (substances used to kill pests on food crops) and herbicides (weed killers) are other examples. Sometimes fish have been killed directly by such substances. There is another danger, however. Fish, shellfish, etc. take large volumes of water into their bodies every day. If this water is polluted, the fish may trap some of the pollutants in their bodies. Some pollutants can be *concentrated* inside the bodies of fish, even though they may be present in only very small concentrations in sea water. If we then eat the fish, we also eat the toxic material. Radioactivity can also be transferred in this way. Very strict controls are now used to check the level of toxic substances in food, and to control the output of toxic waste.

(b) IN DRINKING WATER

Rain, when first formed, is usually pure. If pollutants do enter drinking water, they must do so between the formation of rain and its arrival as tap water in our homes.

Most drinking water is obtained from reservoirs, which are often built in areas well away from industry. There is little risk of pollution in such cases. However, so much purified water is now needed in Britain, that some of the larger rivers are used as sources of drinking water. Obviously, water is only taken from rivers which are reasonably 'clean'. It is important to remember that when water is treated (p231) *dissolved* substances are not usually removed. Any river water which is to be treated for drinking is therefore carefully checked for dissolved, toxic substances.

The only important problem so far in Britain has been dissolved nitrates. These can enter the water from farmland on which fertilisers have been used. More important sources of nitrates are treated sewage and some industrial waste. Nitrates are serious pollutants for two reasons.

(i) They act as plant foods and so cause the problems described in 1(*b*) on p244.

(ii) They can be changed into nitrite ions in the body. (Nitrate ions are NO_3^-, and nitrite ions are NO_2^-.) Nitrite ions are toxic, especially for young children. They start to block the transport of oxygen round the body by blood. Babies suffering from this problem have been known to go 'blue'.

SUMMARY

Dissolved oxygen is needed in water

(i) for respiration of animals and plants,

(ii) so that bacteria can 'rot down', by oxidation, dead plants, industrial waste and human waste.

Dissolved oxygen is used up quickly if

(i) there are very large amounts of waste to rot down,

(ii) excess plants foods cause excess plant growth, which then has to be oxidised when it dies.

If water is very low in dissolved oxygen:

(i) active living things such as fish can no longer survive, and

(ii) the water becomes stagnant; disease-carrying bacteria live in it.

Water pollution is also caused by toxic substances entering the water, e.g. ions of metals, spillages of oil, pesticides, fertilisers, etc.

CHECK LIST ▶

REMEMBER THAT SOME OF THESE POINTS MAY NOT BE RELEVANT FOR THE PARTICULAR SYLLABUS YOU ARE FOLLOWING.

YOU SHOULD UNDERSTAND THE FOLLOWING POINTS.

1 ▶ The water cycle; water treatment.
2 ▶ How to purify water.
3 ▶ Properties of water; suitable tests.
4 ▶ Hard water, methods of softening.
5 ▶ The solvent properties of water.
6 ▶ Water pollution.

SPECIMEN EXAMINATION QUESTIONS

SEE GENERAL NOTE BEFORE QUESTIONS ON pp49 AND 50.
REMEMBER THAT YOU MAY BE ALLOWED TO USE A DATA BOOK IN THE EXAMINATION.

1 Drinking water which is good for the growth of healthy teeth and bones contains ions of the element . . .   [*NEA* spec (A), 1]

2 Which one of the following is best for removing grease marks from clothes?

A Bleach   B milk   C water   D white spirit.
[*SEG* spec (Alt), 1]

3 A solid suitable for purification by crystallisation from water is likely to

A   dissolve in cold water but not in hot water

B   be insoluble in hot and cold water

C   be very soluble in cold water

D   react with water to form a precipitate

E   be more soluble in hot water than in cold water.
[*LEA* spec (A), 1]

4   River water was found to contain large quantities of nitrogen containing fertilisers, and phosphates from domestic detergents. The river became choked with weeds and the amount of dissolved oxygen was greatly decreased.

(*a*)   Give the chemical name of a fertiliser which contains nitrogen.

(*b*)   How do you think the
(i) fertilisers got into the river?
(ii) phosphates got into the river?

(*c*)   What is the most likely cause of the rapid growth of weeds in the river?

(*d*)   What would be the effect of lowering the amount of dissolved oxygen in the river?   [*MEG* spec 2]

5   (*a*)   (i) Name *one* compound that is a common cause of hardness in water.
(ii) How does this compound react with soap (sodium stearate)?
(iii) How does sodium carbonate remove hardness from water?
(iv) State *one* disadvantage of adding sodium carbonate as a method for softening water and name an alternative method which avoids this problem.

(*b*)   A sodium salt was strongly heated using the apparatus shown in Fig 10.5.

Fig 10.5 Diagram for question 5.

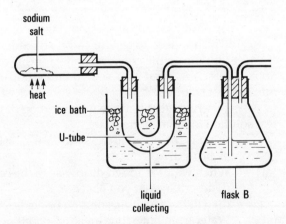

The reaction was: sodium salt→white solid+water+carbon dioxide. After heating, the water formed collected in the U-tube.

(i) How would you show that the liquid which collected in the U-tube contained water?
(ii) What liquid would you put in flask B to show that the gas bubbling through was carbon dioxide?
(iii) Describe a test you could use to show that the white solid contained sodium ions.
(iv) The result of the experiment shows that the salt contains hydrogen, oxygen and carbon.

Your test in (iii) would prove that the salt contains sodium. Explain why these results alone are not enough to prove that the salt contains *only* sodium, hydrogen, oxygen and carbon.   [*SEG* spec 1]

6   Magnesium sulphate crystals ($MgSO_4.7H_2O$) can be made by adding excess magnesium oxide (MgO), which is insoluble in water, to dilute sulphuric acid.

(*a*)   Why is the magnesium oxide added in excess?

(*b*)   The apparatus shown in Fig 10.6 could be used to separate the excess magnesium oxide from the solution. Label the diagram by putting the correct words for A, B, C and D.

(*c*)   Given the relative atomic masses: H = 1, Mg = 24, O = 16, S = 32, calculate the relative formula mass of

         (i) magnesium oxide, MgO, and

         (ii) magnesium sulphate crystals, $MgSO_4.7H_2O$.

(*d*)   Use your answers in (*c*) to calculate the maximum mass of magnesium sulphate crystals that could be obtained from 2.0 g of magnesium oxide.

(*e*)   Describe how you would obtain pure, dry crystals of magnesium sulphate from magnesium sulphate solution.

                                       [*LEA* spec (A), 2]

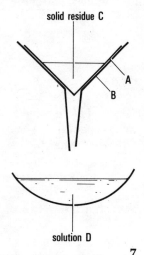

solid residue C

A

B

solution D

Fig 10.6 Diagram for question 6

7   The substance calcium carbonate occurs in nature as marble.

(*a*)   Name *two* other forms of calcium carbonate which occur in nature.

(*b*)   Write down the chemical formula of calcium carbonate.

(*c*)   Carbon dioxide can be detected by using a solution of another calcium compound.

         (i) Write down the common name of the calcium compound which is used to test for carbon dioxide.

         (ii) What is the chemical name for this compound?

(*d*)   Describe what you see when carbon dioxide is first passed into the test solution.

(*e*)   Describe what you see when carbon dioxide is passed into the test solution for some time.

(*f*)   What is the name of the solid formed when calcium carbonate is strongly heated?

(*g*)   When water is added dropwise to the cold solid from (*f*),

         (i) describe what you observe,

         (ii) will the resulting solution be acidic or alkaline?

(*h*)   Water from limestone areas is sometimes called hard water.

         (i) Describe how the reaction between rain water and limestone forms temporarily hard water.

(*j*)   Write a word equation for the reaction.

(*k*)   Write a symbol equation for this reaction.

(*l*)   Name one substance which would give rise to permanent hardness in water.

(*m*)   State a method for removing temporary hardness from water,

(*n*)   You are given three bottles of water labelled **A**, **B** and **C**. You are told that the bottles contain separately, distilled water, temporary hard water and permanently hard water. Describe how you would test the liquids so as to label the bottles correctly, i.e. distilled water; temporary hard water; permanent hard water. [*NISEC* spec 2]

8 (a)   (i) How is filtration of reservoir water carried out?

         (ii) What is the purpose of this filtration?

(b)   (i) How may a sample of pure water be obtained from sea water?

         (ii) Explain the process of evaporation in terms of movement of molecules.

         (iii) Why does the salt in seawater not circulate through the atmosphere in the way the water does?

(c)   (i) Name one pollutant of river water other than an agricultural fertiliser.

         (ii) State the source of this pollutant and describe its effect.

(d)   (i) Why is chlorine added to water supplies?

         (ii) Tap water usually contains chloride ions rather than chlorine itself. Describe chemical tests that would show (I) that tap water does not contain chlorine, (II) that tap water does contain chloride ions. (In each case you should name the substances you would use and describe what you would observe.)

         (iii) Explain in terms of electron transfer what happens when chlorine is converted into chloride ions. [*SEG* spec 3]

9 Fizzy drinks can be made by dissolving carbon dioxide gas, under pressure, into water. The drink is kept in a tightly stoppered bottle until needed. When the stopper is removed bubbles of carbon dioxide form making the drink fizzy.

    The carbon dioxide first dissolves in the water and some of the dissolved gas may react with water to form carbonic acid.

$$CO_2(g) + aq \rightleftharpoons CO_2(aq) \qquad\qquad \text{Equation 1}$$
$$CO_2(aq) + H_2O(l) \rightleftharpoons H_2CO_3(aq) \qquad\qquad \text{Equation 2}$$

(a)   Use equation 1 to explain the appearance of bubbles of carbon dioxide when the stopper of a fizzy drinks bottle is loosened.

(b)   Unless the bottles are tightly stoppered, these drinks tend to lose their fizziness quickly on warm days. Use equation 1 to explain why this happens.

(c)   What advantage may be gained by keeping bottles of water in the fridge before making fizzy drinks?

(d)   Write an equation to show how H_2CO_3 can behave as an acid in water. When carbon dioxide is bubbled into lime water a white precipitate of calcium carbonate forms. An equation for the reaction may be written as follows.

$$H_2CO_3(aq) + Ca(OH)_2(aq) \rightleftharpoons CaCO_3(s) + 2H_2O(l) \qquad \text{Equation 3}$$

If more carbon dioxide is bubbled into the mixture, the cloudiness disappears and a solution of calcium hydrogencarbonate is formed as shown below.

$$H_2CO_3(aq) + CaCO_3(s) \rightleftharpoons Ca(HCO_3)_2(aq) \qquad\qquad \text{Equation 4}$$

(*e*)   Write two separate ionic equations to summarise the reactions indicated by equation 3.

(*f*)   Use equation 4 to explain how domestic water supplies in many places contain calcium ions (Ca^{2+}).

(*g*)   How do the equations given earlier explain the formation of white deposits (such as kettle fur) in vessels used to boil tap water in hard water districts?

(*h*)   Sodium stearate ($C_{17}H_{35}COONa$) is a typical soap. Why is its use as a soapy detergent limited by the calcium ions which are often present in water?   [*SEG* spec (Alt), 4]

THE PERIODIC TABLE. STRUCTURE

CONTENTS

11.1 THE PERIODIC TABLE

Fortunately, we do not have to learn the properties of all of the elements and compounds which have been discovered. Chemists have arranged the elements into 'family groups'. All of the elements in a group are very similar to each other. If we study in detail just one member of a group, we can then predict what any other members of the group will be like. You will almost certainly be asked to make predictions of this kind, perhaps about elements you have not even seen. This is not difficult if you understand the main ideas which come from the **Periodic Table**.

The Periodic Table is one of the most important classification systems used in chemistry. Some syllabuses require a simple understanding of the history of the Table – revise your notes if necessary. The Table contains all of the elements. They are arranged in a special way, by placing them in the same order as their **atomic numbers** (p24). To put this another way, the elements are arranged in order according to how many electrons their atoms have in their outer energy levels. For example, the table starts with hydrogen, because this has atomic number 1. Beryllium (atomic number 4) is placed after lithium (atomic number 3). To put it the other way, beryllium is placed after lithium because atoms of beryllium have two electrons in their outer energy levels, but atoms of lithium have only one.

Fig 11.1 The electron structure of the first 20 elements in the Periodic Table

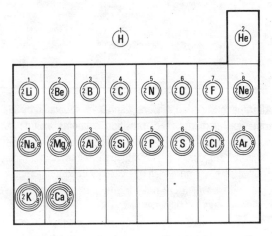

It is helpful to think of the first part of the Table as in Fig 11.1. This shows the first 20 elements, and this is the part of the table you are

likely to use the most. The figure also shows the electron arrangement of each of the first 20 atoms. You will see that each of the early rows of the table ends with an element which has atoms containing a full outer energy level of electrons. Note that the first row contains only two elements. One of these, helium, belongs in a vertical group (Group 0 or 8). The other element of this first pair, hydrogen, *does not belong to any of the vertical groups*. It is unique: it is placed on its own. (Many students forget this point.) A full Periodic Table is shown on p.424. You may be allowed to have a copy of the Periodic Table in the examination. *yes .*

SOME COMMON TERMS USED TO DESCRIBE PARTS OF THE PERIODIC TABLE

1   Vertical columns of elements in the table are called **groups**.
2   Each group is given a number. The first group, starting from the left, is Group 1. (The group number is also the same as the number of electrons in the outer energy levels of the atoms in the group. This is a very important point. For example, sodium is in Group 1. Atoms of sodium have one electron in their outer energy level.)
3   Some groups also have a common name, as well as a number.
    Group 1 is often called the **alkali metals.**
    Group 2 is sometimes called the **alkaline earth** metals.
    Group 7 is often called the **halogens**.
    Group 0 (sometimes called Group 8) is often called the **noble gases** (or, sometimes, the **inert gases**).
4   Horizontal rows in the table are called **periods**. These points are summarised in Fig 11.2

Fig 11.2 Regions of the Periodic Table

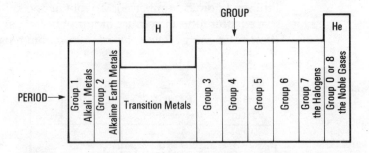

After the third period, Groups 2 and 3 are separated by a large block of metals called the **transition elements**. The transition elements include such common metals as iron, copper, cobalt and nickel. These metals have several properties in common.

1   They are hard, dense metals with high melting points and boiling points.
2   They often have more than one valency or combining power, e.g. iron has valencies of 2 or 3. Metals which are not transition elements only have one valency. For example, sodium always has the valency 1.
3   Their compounds are often coloured. For example, many copper compounds are blue or green, but all of the compounds of sodium are white. The only exceptions to the last point are the compounds of sodium which contain a transition element, e.g. sodium dichromate(VI). This contains the transition element chromium, and is coloured.

4   The elements, and their compounds, are often good catalysts. They are used in some important industrial processes, e.g. the Contact Process (p310) and the Haber Process (p314).

USING THE PERIODIC TABLE. SOME GENERAL POINTS

1 THE ELEMENTS IN ANY ONE GROUP HAVE SIMILAR PROPERTIES

The *chemical* properties of a substance depend upon the number of electrons in the outer energy level of its atoms. All those atoms which have the same number of outer electrons have very similar chemical properties. All of the elements in a particular group in the Table have the same number of electrons in the outer energy levels of their atoms. (Study Fig 11.1 carefully and make sure that you understand it.) This means that all of the members of a group have similar chemical properties. You must be able to give examples to show this, e.g. by using Groups 1, 2, 7 and 0. For example, the elements of Group 1 have the properties given on p.258, and these properties are not given by most other metals.

2 THE ELEMENTS IN ANY ONE GROUP ALL HAVE THE SAME COMBINING POWER (VALENCY)

The elements of Group 1 all need to lose one electron from their atoms to form stable structures. (It is very important that you understand this. Look again at ionic bonding, p.30, and the electron structures of the atoms of Group 1 shown in Fig 11.1.) The elements have a valency of 1 because of this. Similarly, elements of Group 2 have a valency of 2, because their atoms need to lose two electrons (Fig 11.1). Elements of Group 3 have a valency of 3, and those in Group 4 have a valency of 4. However, this pattern does not continue. The elements of Group 5 do not usually have a valency of 5! This point is often confused by students.

The elements of Group 5 usually have a valency of 3 (8−5). Their atoms could become stable electron structures *either* by losing five electrons, *or* by gaining three electrons. It is easier to gain three than to lose five. These atoms therefore have a valency of 3. You should understand why the elements of Group 6 usually have a valency of 2 (**not** 6), the elements of Group 7 have a valency of 1 (**not** 7), and the elements of Group 0 have no valency at all. Use the electron structures in Fig 11.1 to help you understand this point.

Group number	1	2	3	4	5	6	7	0
Usual valency of elements	1	2	3	4	3	2	1	0

This information is sometimes helpful in working out the formula of a compound. For example, suppose that we are asked to write the formula of the oxide of the Group 2 element strontium, symbol Sr. You may never have heard of strontium oxide. However, if you know the formula of any *other* oxide of a Group 2 element, all you have to do is change the symbol of the other element for Sr. Magnesium is another element in Group 2. The formula of magnesium oxide is MgO. Therefore the formula of strontium oxide is SrO, (**not** Sr_2O, or SrO_2, or any other formula). If you really understand how to use the Periodic Table, you can improve your chemistry very quickly!

Many students 'give up' or make a wild guess when they are asked a question about a chemical they have never heard of. It is usually possible to work out an answer. You can only begin to do this if you understand important ideas such as those used in this unit. You must practise questions such as those found on pp.261–64.

3 WHERE ARE THE NON-METALS FOUND IN THE PERIODIC TABLE?

Atoms of non-metals usually have 5, 6, 7 or 8 electrons in their outer energy levels. Non-metals are therefore found on the **right-hand side** of the Table. (Again, study the electron structures shown in Fig 11.1.) Group 4, in the middle of the Table, contains both metals and non-metals, but the only two non-metals, carbon and silicon, are at the top.

You will remember (p68) that atoms of non-metals can form either ionic or covalent bonds. If they form ionic bonds they do so by *gaining* electrons. The ions of atoms in Group 5 have a charge of 3^-, those in Group 6 have a charge of 2^-, and those in Group 7 have a charge of 1^-.

All the other elements are metals. There are far more metals than non-metals. All of the elements on the **left-hand side** of the Table are metals. In addition, most of the elements in the centre part of the Table are metals.

Metals only take part in ionic bonding, never covalent bonding. (Compare with non-metals.) Atoms of metals have 1, 2 or 3 electrons in their outer energy levels. They need to lose electrons in order to form stable electron structures. They therefore form ions which are positively charged. The ions of elements in Group 1 have a charge of 1^+, those of Group 2 a charge of 2^+, and those of Group 3 a charge of 3^+.

4 HOW CHEMICAL REACTIVITY CHANGES IN A GROUP OF METALS

The members of any one group all have similar chemical properties, but some members are more reactive than others. In other words, some members do the same thing as other members, but do so more quickly or more easily. In groups of metals (Groups 1, 2 and 3) the reactivity **increases** as the atomic number of the elements **increases**. Putting this another way, **reactivity increases down any group on the left-hand side** of the Table. For example, in Group 1 both sodium and potassium have similar reactions with water, but potassium reacts more rapidly than sodium.

Atoms of metals need to lose electrons. To remove an electron requires energy. The further away the electron is from the nucleus, the less energy is required to remove it.

Look again at the electron structures of lithium, sodium and potassium (Fig 11.1, p.253). It is much easier for an atom of potassium to lose its outer electron than it is for an atom of lithium to do so, because the outer electron is further away from the nucleus in an atom of potassium. Potassium is therefore more reactive than sodium, which is more reactive than lithium.

5 HOW CHEMICAL REACTIVITY CHANGES IN A GROUP OF NON-METALS

In groups of non-metal (Groups 5, 6 and 7) the pattern of reactivity is the *opposite* to that which occurs in a group of metals. In groups of non-metals (groups on the **right-hand side** of the Table) **reactivity decreases** as the atomic number of the elements increases. In other words, **reactivity decreases going down a group on the right-hand side** of the Table. For example, in Group 7 chlorine and bromine have similar chemical properties, but chlorine is more reactive than bromine. (Compare their positions in Group 7.)

The reactivity trend in a group of non-metals is opposite to that in a group of metals, because atoms of non-metals need to **gain** electrons in forming ions, whereas atoms of metals need to **lose** electrons. Fluorine is more reactive than chlorine (Group 7) because the outer shell of fluorine atoms is fairly close to the nucleus. The attraction between nucleus and electrons helps to 'pull in' the extra electron the atom needs in order to have a fully filled outer energy level. The outer shell of iodine, on the other hand, is a long way from the nucleus and it is more difficult for iodine to gain an electron. Iodine is much less reactive than fluorine.

6 HOW CHEMICAL REACTIVITY CHANGES ACROSS A PERIOD

A Group 1 element needs to lose one electron from each atom when it reacts, but atoms of a Group 2 element need to lose two electrons. It is easier to lose one electron than to lose two. A Group 1 element is therefore more reactive than a Group 2 element in the same period. This trend continues across the period as far as Group 4. Chemical reactivity is always high at the beginning of a period, and falls to a low point in Group 4 (Fig 11.3).

After Group 4, elements need to *gain* electrons in order to form ions. The opposite therefore starts to happen. As it is easier to gain two electrons (Group 6 elements) than to gain three (Group 5 elements), reactivity *increases* again and reaches another peak at Group 7. Group 0 elements have little or no reactivity (Fig 11.3) and so reactivity falls away again at the end of a period.

Fig 11.3 Reactivity trends across a period

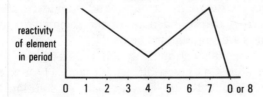

reactivity
of element
in period

0　1　2　3　4　5　6　7　0 or 8

7 HOW THE TYPE OF OXIDE VARIES ACROSS A PERIOD

There is a gradual change from metals to non-metals in going across a period from left to right. As oxides of metals are **bases** (p218), oxides of elements on the left-hand side are usually basic. As oxides of non-metals are usually acidic or neutral (p218), the oxides of elements on the right-hand side of a period tend to be acidic or neutral. Sometimes this gradual change from left to right across a period produces an 'intermediate' oxide which is **amphoteric** (p218), e.g. aluminium oxide (aluminium is in Group 3).

8 HOW ATOMIC SIZES VARY DOWN A GROUP

As the atomic number increases down any group, the size (radius) of the atoms also increases. **Atoms become larger down any group in the Table**. For example, an atom of sodium (atomic number 11, in Group 1) is larger than an atom of lithium (atomic number 3, also in Group 1), because it contains an extra shell of electrons. Note that this pattern is true for *any* group in the Table, unlike the reactivity trends, which depend upon whether the group is on the left-hand side or the right-hand side of the Table.

9 HOW IONIC SIZES VARY DOWN A GROUP

Be careful with this point, because metals and non-metals show different patterns. A **metal ion** is always **smaller** than the 'parent' atom from which it came. This happens because a metal atom *loses* one or more electrons when it forms an ion. It loses these electrons from its outer energy level, to leave this level empty. The ion formed therefore has one electron shell less than the 'parent' atom and it is smaller.

A **non-metal ion** is always **larger** than the 'parent' atom from which it is formed. A non-metal atom always *gains* one or more electrons when it forms an ion.

TRENDS IN GROUP 1 OF THE PERIODIC TABLE

(Some of these points have been mentioned earlier in the chapter, but they are repeated here so that all points about Group 1 are together for revision purposes.)

1 All the elements in Group 1 have atoms which contain one electron in their outer energy levels.
2 All the elements have a combining power (valency) of 1.
3 All the elements are metals.
4 The elements are unusually soft, for metals. They can be cut easily with a knife.
5 The metals are stored under oil because they react with air and water.
6 The metals have very low densities – they float on water.
7 The metals have very similar chemical properties, but they get more reactive 'down the group'. You should be able to describe this by referring to the reactions of the metals with cold water. The main points are summarised below:
Metal floats on surface. Violent reaction. Metal darts about on surface of water. Gas given off – hydrogen. Hydroxide of the metal is the other product – this is an alkali, so solution becomes alkaline. As metals become more reactive, the hydrogen can catch fire, e.g. with potassium, the hydrogen burns with a lilac flame. Typical equation:

sodium + water → sodium hydroxide + hydrogen
$$2Na(s) + 2H_2O(l) \rightarrow \quad 2NaOH(aq) \quad + \quad H_2(g)$$

8 The radii of the atoms increases 'down the group'.

9 The radii of the ions increase down the group, but each ion is smaller than the 'parent' atom.

TRENDS IN GROUP 2 OF THE PERIODIC TABLE

1 All the elements have atoms with two electrons in their outer energy levels.

2 All the elements have a combining power of 2.

3 All the elements are metals.

4 The metals have a fairly low density, but are more dense than the metals of Group 1.

5 The metals are less reactive than those of Group 1, because the Group 2 metals have atoms which need to lose two electrons to form stable structures, but those of Group 1 need lose only one electron.

6 The metals have very similar properties, but they get 'more reactive down the group'. You should be able to describe this by referring to the following reactions:

(a) REACTIONS WITH COLD WATER

For details see under Activity Series, p.95. Calcium is more reactive than magnesium; it reacts rapidly with *cold* water, e.g.

magnesium + steam → magnesium oxide + hydrogen
$$Mg(s) \quad + H_2O(g) \rightarrow \quad MgO(s) \quad + \quad H_2(g)$$
calcium + water → calcium hydroxide + hydrogen
$$Ca(s) \quad + 2H_2O(l) \rightarrow \quad Ca(OH)_2(aq) \quad + \quad H_2(g)$$

Note that hydrogen gas is formed in each case.

(b) REACTIONS WITH DILUTE ACIDS

You may have compared the way in which magnesium and calcium react with dilute acids. (For details, see under Activity Series, p.94) Again, the important thing is that the two metals react in the same kind of way, but calcium does so much more rapidly than magnesium.

7 The radii of the atoms increase 'down the group'.

8 The radii of the ions increase 'down the group', but each ion is smaller than the 'parent' atom.

TRENDS IN GROUP 7 OF THE PERIODIC TABLE (THE HALOGENS)

1 All the elements have atoms with seven electrons in their outer energy levels.

2 All the elements have a combining power of 1.

3 All the elements are non-metals.

4 The elements show a change of state 'going down the group'. The first member, fluorine, is a *gas* at room temperature. So is the next member, chlorine. Bromine, the next member, is a *liquid* at room temperature. Iodine is a *solid* at room temperature. This happens because the melting points and boiling points increase 'down the group'. For example, fluorine has such a low melting point and boiling point that it has 'already melted' and 'already boiled' at room temperature, and so is a gas. Bromine has a much higher boiling point. It is a liquid at room temperature, but has not yet boiled. The melting points increase 'going down' other groups, too, but in groups of metals the elements are nearly always solids at room temperature. In Group 7, the melting point differences show up more obviously, and the elements have different states at room temperature.

5 All of the elements can form coloured gases, with a typical sharp smell. The gases have the following colours: fluorine, yellow; chlorine, pale green; bromine, red-brown; iodine, purple.

6 The elements all exist as molecules containing two atoms, e.g. Cl_2, Br_2 and I_2.

7 The elements have very similar chemical properties, but they become **less reactive** 'down the group'.

You should be able to describe this by referring to the *displacement* reactions of the halogens. You may find it useful to compare these reactions with displacement reactions of metals in the Activity Series (p96). The idea is the same; a more reactive element will displace a less reactive element from one of its compounds. We can use this to produce a 'reactivity series' of halogens, just as we produced a reactivity series of metals.

You may have seen experiments in which chlorine (as the gas, or as its solution in water) is added to solutions of a bromide, and iodide, and a chloride. Similarly, bromine (as its solution in water) and iodine (as crystals) are added to solutions of a bromide, iodide and chloride. (Note that a halogen element ends in *-ine* (as in chlorine) but its compound ends in *-ide* (as in sodium chloride)).

You will have seen that chlorine is the most reactive of the three elements. It causes the most displacement reactions. Chlorine will displace bromine from a bromide, and iodine from an iodide.

$$Cl_2(aq) + 2NaBr(aq) \rightarrow Br_2(aq) + 2NaCl(aq)$$
$$\text{colourless} \quad \text{brown} \quad \text{colourless}$$

or, using an ionic equation,

$$Cl_2(aq) + 2Br^-(aq) \rightarrow Br_2(aq) + 2Cl^-(aq)$$

$$Cl_2(aq) + 2NaI(aq) \rightarrow I_2(aq) + 2NaCl(aq)$$

or, $$Cl_2(aq) + 2I^-(aq) \rightarrow I_2(aq) + 2Cl^-(aq)$$
$$\text{colourless} \quad \text{dark brown}$$

(F)

Cl

Br

I

increasing reactivity

Fig 11.4 Order of reactivity in the halogen group

Bromine will not displace chlorine from a chloride, but it will displace iodine from an iodide. It is therefore less reactive than chlorine.

$$Br_2(aq) + 2NaI(aq) \rightarrow 2NaBr(aq) + I_2(aq)$$
$$Br_2(aq) + 2I^-(aq) \rightarrow 2Br^-(aq) + I_2(aq)$$

Iodine will displace neither chlorine from a chloride, nor bromine from a bromide. The order of reactivity in the halogen group is shown in Fig 11.4.

Fluorine is *very* reactive but it is too dangerous to use in simple laboratory work. It would react even with some water in a test tube.

8 The radii of the atoms increase 'down the group'.

9 The radii of the ions increase 'down the group'. Each ion is *larger* than the 'parent' atom.

10 You may also have compared the way the halogens react with iron.

TRENDS IN GROUP 0 (OR GROUP 8 OF THE PERIODIC TABLE (THE NOBLE GASES)

1 All the elements have atoms with filled outer energy levels.

2 All the elements are very *unreactive*, because their atoms have *fully filled electron shells*. They do not combine with other substances under ordinary circumstances, and do not have a combining power.

3 All the elements are non-metals.

4 All the elements exist as single atoms. They are the only elements which do not contain groups of atoms, such as molecules.

5 All the elements are colourless, non-toxic gases at room temperature and pressure.

6 When electricity is passed through the gases under special conditions, coloured light is produced. This is used in 'neon' signs, etc. for display lights for shops, cinemas and so on.

7 The 'inertness' of these gases is used in electric light bulbs, weather balloons (helium) and where, for safety reasons, gas reactions need 'diluting'. Argon is used in welding (to prevent oxidation), and helium is used mixed with oxygen as a 'breathing mixture' for divers.

8 The radii of the atoms increase 'down the group'. The atoms do not form normal ions, so there is no trend in ionic radii.

OTHER RELATIONSHIPS

Some syllabuses require a simple understanding of the relationships in Group 4, by comparing, e.g. carbon and silicon. Revise your notes if necessary. You may also have considered the use of silicon in microelectronics, its abundance in the earth's crust, and the simple properties of silicates.

CHECK YOUR UNDERSTANDING (Answers on p417)

1 Part of the Periodic Table is shown below. The numbers are the atomic numbers of the elements. The letters stand for elements, but they are not the normal symbols.

Ask

3 A	4 B	5 C	6 D	7 E	8 F	9 G	10 H 2.8

11 I	12 J	13 K	14 L	15 M	16 N	17 O	18 N 2.8.8

(a) Which of the elements are noble gases?
(b) Which of the elements are in Group 1?
(c) Which of the elements have three electrons in their outer energy levels?
(d) Which will be the most reactive metal?
(e) Which will be the most reactive non-metal?

2 Use the Periodic Table on p.424 to answer the following questions.
(a) Is astatine (At) likely to be a solid, a liquid, or a gas at room temperature?
(b) Is rubidium (Rb) a metal or a non-metal?
(c) Is oxygen in the same period as sulphur?
(d) Is beryllium (Be) likely to be more reactive than magnesium?
(e) Is beryllium likely to be more reactive than boron (B)?

3 The following elements all belong to the same horizontal row in the Periodic Table but their positions have become mixed up.

$$^{12}_{6}A \qquad ^{16}_{8}B \qquad ^{7}_{3}C \qquad ^{20}_{10}D \qquad ^{9}_{4}E \qquad ^{11}_{5}F \qquad ^{14}_{7}G \qquad ^{19}_{9}H$$

Place the elements in the correct order.

4 In which group of the Periodic Table would you place each of the following elements?
(a) Element W, which has five electrons in its outer energy level.
(b) Element X, which has a total of seven electrons in each atom.
(c) Element Y, which has the symbol $^{24}_{12}Y$.

5 Arrange each of the following groups of elements into two pairs, so that the members of each pair have very similar chemical properties.
(a) W, X, Y and Z, which have the atomic structures shown in Fig 11.5.

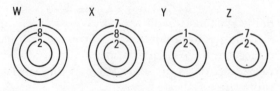

Fig 11.5 Diagram for question 5(a)

(b) $^{16}_{8}A \qquad ^{30}_{16}B \qquad ^{12}_{5}C \qquad ^{31}_{13}D$

6 F and G are elements in the same group. If the formula of the chloride of F is FCl_3, what will be the formula of the chloride of G?

7 Element A is in Group 2, element B is in Group 7, element C has a total of thirteen electrons in each atom, and element D has a total of seventeen electrons per atom. For each of these elements, say whether it is a metal or a non-metal.

8   Elements H, J and K are in the same group. Their atomic numbers are $_{12}H$, $_4J$ and $_{20}K$.

    (a)   Which group of the Periodic Table would these elements be in?

    (b)   Place the three elements in order of reactivity, placing the most reactive first.

9   Elements M, N and O are in the same group of the Periodic Table. Their atomic numbers are $_{15}M$, $_{23}N$ and $_7O$.

    (a)   Which group would they be in?

    (b)   Place them in order of reactivity, placing the most reactive first.

10   Elements A, B, C and D are in Group 7. A is a solid at room temperature, B is a gas, C is a liquid and D is a gas. D is more reactive than B. Place the elements in the order they would be in the group, placing the one with the lowest atomic number first.

11   The element with atomic number 10 is likely to have similar chemical properties to the element with atomic number:

        A 9   B 11   C 16   D 18   E 28.

12   Refer to the information given in question 3 and then answer the following

    (a)   Which two elements are likely to be least reactive?

    (b)   Which two elements are likely to be the most reactive?

13   Use the Periodic Table to suggest how the element astatine (symbol At) is likely to react with a solution of sodium iodide. The predict how iodine might react with a solution of potassium astatide.

14   The following are ionic and atomic radii (in nm) of members of the same group in the Periodic Table.

	Atomic radius	Ionic radius
A	0.133	0.078
B	0.157	0.098
C	0.203	0.133
D	0.216	0.149
E	0.235	0.165

    (a)   Is this a group of metals or a group of non-metals?

    (b)   Which of the elements would have the lowest atomic number?

15   The following data applies to five elements in the Periodic Table.

    Element A: valency 1, mp 97°C, atomic number 11.

    Element B: valency 4, mp 1410°C, electron structure 2,8,4.

    Element C: valency 1, mp −101°C.

    Element D: valency 1, electron structure 2,8,8,1.

    Element E: valency 0, electron structure 2,8.

    (a)   Which elements are in the same group?

    (b)   Which element is in the same group as carbon?

    (c)   Which two elements would react very vigorously together?

    (d)   Which element is most likely to form only covalent bonds?

    (e)   Which element would resemble helium?

(f)   Which element could most easily form a negative ion?

(g)   Give the symbols (with charges) of the ions which would be formed from atoms of (i) A, (ii) C.

(h)   Which of the elements are likely to react together to form a covalently bonded compound? Give the formula of the compound which would be formed.

16 Element Z has atomic number 11. It reacts with cold water to produce an alkaline solution. Element Z also reacts with chlorine to form a chloride which will dissolve in water and then conduct electricity.

2 8 1

(a)   What substance is formed which makes the solution alkaline?

(b)   What is the other product formed when Z reacts with water?

(c)   Write the electron structure for an ion of Z.   *2·8·*

2,

2·8,

(d)   If a concentrated solution of Z chloride was electrolysed, what would you expect to be formed at   *Na Cl.*

2·8·8·

        (i) the negative electrode, and

        (ii) the positive electrode?

11.2 STRUCTURE. ALLOTROPES

INTRODUCTION: WHAT DO WE MEAN BY 'STRUCTURE'?

All substances are made of atoms, molecules or ions. The way in which these particles are packed together and joined together is called the **structure** of the substance. The structure of a substance depends upon (i) how the particles are joined (bonded) together (ionic or covalent), and (ii) the relative size and number of the particles.

The particles of a gas are far apart and moving rapidly. Gases have no 'shape' because their particles have no fixed arrangement. Their particles are all free and moving. A gas, therefore, has no structure. To a large extent, this is also true of liquids, where the particles are also free to move about. In a solid, however, the particles may vibrate but they do not move about from place to place. The particles in a solid are 'locked together'. Solids, therefore, have a structure.

There are many different ways in which particles can be packed together, and so there are many kinds of structure. This partly explains why solids have such a variety of properties. For example, steel and rubber are both solids but they have very different properties. The differences are due partly to their different structures: the particles inside rubber are joined together and packed together in a very different way from those inside steel. The particles inside a particular solid are arranged in a *regular pattern*, and not in a random way. This is why crystals of a substance always have the same shape, no matter how big or small they are. The tiny particles inside the crystals are locked together into a fixed, regular pattern. If you have briefly discussed how X-rays can be used to investigate structure, revise your notes.

1 THE STRUCTURES OF SOME SOLID ELEMENTS

(a) THE STRUCTURES OF METALS

Elements have the easiest structures to understand because all of the particles inside an element are exactly the same. About 80% of all elements are metals. All metals have certain properties in common, e.g. they are good conductors of heat and electricity, because they all have similiar structures. In particular, they all have the same kind of bonding (p68). As the particles in any metal are always bonded in the same way, the only way in which the structure of a metal can be varied is by changing the *pattern of packing* of the particles. The different packing helps to explain why some metals are softer than others. For example, the particles in sodium metal are not packed so tightly as they are in iron, and this partly explains why sodium is much softer than iron. You may have studied the structures of metals in more detail, using terms such as **close packing**, and **co-ordination number** – revise if necessary.

The development of alloys depends on an understanding of structure. It is possible to 'improve' the basic properties of a metal by mixing it with particles of another substance (p136). The properties of an alloy depend to a large extent on the way the particles inside it are packed together. Similarly, the structure of a metal or alloy can be changed by **heat treatment**. Steel which has been cooled rapidly from being red hot by dipping in cold water or oil (this is called **quenching**) becomes much tougher. The difference is caused by a change in the way the particles pack together.

(b) SOME NON-METAL ELEMENTS WITH SIMPLE MOLECULAR STRUCTURES

Most of the non-metals have the kind of structure described here. The structure of the non-metal carbon is rather different, and this is described on p.267.

Most non-metals have a **simple molecular** structure. Common examples include iodine and sulphur. In this kind of structure small groups of atoms are joined together by covalent bonding to form molecules. In iodine each molecule has just two atoms, and has the formula I_2. In sulphur each molecule has eight atoms, and has the formula S_8. These molecules are separate from each other, but they 'hold hands' to form a structure. The bonds *inside* each molecule are strong, covalent bonds. The 'bonds' *between* the molecules (the 'holding of hands') are much weaker. When a solid with this kind of structure is heated, the forces between the molecules are broken, and the molecules separate from each other and are free to move about. The solid melts as this happens. Note that the bonds *inside* each molecule are not broken by heating. For example, when sulphur melts, the liquid still consists of S_8 molecules, because the atoms inside each S_8 molecule are held tightly together. The difference is that the S_8 molecules have separated from each other, and so there is no longer a structure. This very important point is often misunderstood. Using solid iodine as an example, Fig 11.6 shows which 'bonds' are broken when it melts.

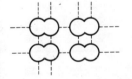

Fig 11.6 Simple representation of the structure in iodine, I_2. The dotted lines are the weaker forces *between* the molecules. These are broken on heating, and the I_2 molecules are then 'set free'

An important general property of molecular solids is that they have **low melting points and boiling points**, because the molecules easily separate from each other when heated. This is very different from a metal structure of the kinds of structure described on the next few pages, where *all* the bonds are *strong* and the structures have high melting and boiling points.

The bonds *inside* a molecule are sometimes called *intramolecular bonds*. The forces *between* molecules are sometimes called *intermolecular bonds*.

Iodine is the only common halogen element which is a solid at room temperature (p260). All the halogens consist of simple molecules, e.g. Cl_2, Br_2 and I_2. The forces between molecules of iodine are much stronger than those between the molecules of fluorine, bromine and chlorine. This means that, even at room temperature, the forces between molecules of fluorine, bromine and chlorine are *already broken*. The molecules (Cl_2, etc) are therefore already separated and the substances are gases. (In actual fact, bromine is *just* a liquid, but it is evaporating rapidly at room temperature.) At lower temperatures, fluorine, chlorine and and bromine can also become solids, just like iodine.

Two different kinds of sulphur

Solid sulphur has two **allotropes** (p267). Sulphur molecules are much larger than iodine molecules, because each molecule has eight atoms. The atoms in each molecule are held together by strong covalent bonds so that each molecule has the shape of a 'puckered ring' (Fig 11.7). The forces between the molecules are weak, and easily broken by heating. However, the S_8 molecules of sulphur can pack together in two different ways, to form two allotropes, or different solid structures. You may have done experiments to make the main allotropes of sulphur. One is **stable** (in other words it is quite 'happy' as it is) at temperatures below 96°C. This form is sometimes called **alpha sulphur** (α-sulphur) or rhombic sulphur. The other allotrope (**beta sulphur**, or β-sulphur) is only stable at higher temperatures, and is made by melting sulphur very carefully and allowing a thin solid crust to form on the surface. Crystals of this second allotrope grow down from the crust. This allotrope is sometimes called monoclinic sulphur. If you have made these allotropes of sulphur, revise the experiments carefully and make sure that you understand them.

Fig 11.7 Sulphur, S_8.
(*a*) The shape of one S_8 molecule
(*b*) How the molecules are held together in the solid by weak forces (dotted lines)

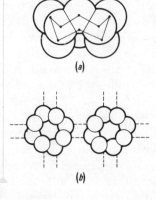

(*a*)

(*b*)

(c) STRUCTURES OF THE NON-METAL CARBON

Most elements which are non-metals have a structure which contains separate molecules, held together by weak forces between them. The structure of carbon is completely different, even though it, too, is a non-metal. The structure of carbon is a **giant molecule**. (Giant molecules are sometimes called **macromolecules**.) A giant molecule consists of a *large* number of atoms, all joined together by *strong* covalent bonds. There are no simple or separate units (like simple molecules) within it. The whole structure is a large, strong, network of atoms. Only a few *elements* have a structure of this kind, but many compounds are formed in this way (p269).

Some substances can have more than one structure. If there are two different structures in the same state (e.g. two different solid structures), each type is called an **allotrope**. Carbon is an example of this type. It has two solid allotropes, **diamond** and **graphite**. Diamond and graphite both consist *only* of carbon atoms, but their structures are quite different, even though they are both giant molecules.

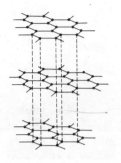

Fig 11.8 The structure of graphite. The dotted lines represent weak bonds between the layers

The structures of diamond and graphite

Graphite (Fig 11.8) consists of flat layers of carbon atoms. The atoms are joined six at a time to make hexagons. Each layer consists of many hexagons, but the hexagons are not separate units like molecules. For example, each atom is a member of more than one hexagon. The bonds between the atoms in the hexagons are all strong, covalent bonds. The layers are arranged one above the other to make a giant molecule. The bonds *between* the layers are different, however. These bonds are comparatively weak (but not as weak as those between molecules, e.g. in iodine). The packing of the atoms, and these weaker bonds between the layers, cause graphite to have very different properties from diamond, the other allotrope. Graphite is soft, slippery, and easily flakes off (this is why it is used in pencil leads). It can also conduct electricity (the only non-metal to do so), and its 'slipperiness' is used in lubricants, e.g. by mixing it in oil.

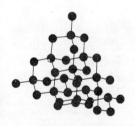

Fig 11.9 The structure of diamond. Each atom is bonded to those around it by four strong bonds

Diamond (Fig 11.9) also consists only of carbon atoms, but each atom in the structure is joined to four others by strong covalent bonds. There are no flat layers, or weaker bonds, as there are in graphite. The structure consists of a giant molecule (macromolecule) which is a strong, rigid mass of atoms. Unlike graphite, diamond will not conduct electricity. Diamond forms attractive, transparent crystals which are used in jewellery, but graphite is usually found as a black solid. Diamond is the hardest natural substance (compare this with the softness and slipperiness of graphite). Small diamonds can now be made synthetically (**artificial diamonds**). Synthetic diamonds are used in cutting instruments and drilling equipment. Remember that diamond and graphite do have some things in common. They both consist only of carbon atoms. They both have the structure of a giant molecule. They both have very high melting points and boiling points (as do any substances which have a giant structure).

Graphite	Diamond
1 Conducts electricity	Does not conduct electricity
2 Black solid	Transparent crystals
3 Soft and slippery	Very hard indeed
4 High mp and bp	High mp and bp

The different properties of diamond and graphite can be explained by different structures. In graphite, the horizontal layers can slide over each other because they are only weakly held to each other. This explains why graphite is soft, flaky and slippery. Diamond does not have any layers which can slide over each other. Instead, it has *strong* bonds in all directions, making a hard, rigid mass.

The atoms in graphite have more space between them than do the atoms in diamond. Diamond is therefore more dense than graphite: its atoms are packed more tightly. Another difference is the conduction of heat and electricity. The weak bonds between the layers in graphite allow electrons to move between the layers, and the mobile electrons conduct electricity and heat. The electrons which form the weaker bonds between layers are relatively 'free'. This is rather like the 'sea of electrons' in a metal structure (p68). Graphite is like a metal in this sense, and is used as electrodes. There are no relatively free electrons in diamond. (If you have discussed how the structure of graphite makes it useful for removing colour or odour from substances, revise your notes.)

2 THE STRUCTURES OF SOME SOLID COMPOUNDS

The previous examples of types of structure are all *elements*. In an element, all the particles are the same. In a *compound*, there are at least two different kinds of particle. The structures of compounds can therefore be more complicated than those of elements. However, the structures of compounds can be divided into three main types, and if you have understood the earlier examples with elements you should find these easy to understand.

(i) If the compound consists of a metal joined to one or more non-metals, it will have ionic bonding (p30). Its structure will be a **giant ionic structure**.

(ii) If the compound consists only of non-metals joined together, it will be covalently bonded. It may have a **simple molecular** structure, in which simple, separate molecules are joined together by weaker forces between them. (This is exactly the same idea as in the examples of I_2 and S_8 explained on pp265–6. The only difference is that the molecules of a compound contain atoms of different kinds, e.g. H_2O.)

(iii) Another type of structure may be formed if the substance is covalently bonded. In this type the structure is a **giant molecule** or macromolecule. (This is very similar to the way in which atoms are joined in diamond and graphite, except that once again there is more than one kind of atom present.)

(a) COMPOUNDS WHICH HAVE GIANT IONIC STRUCTURES

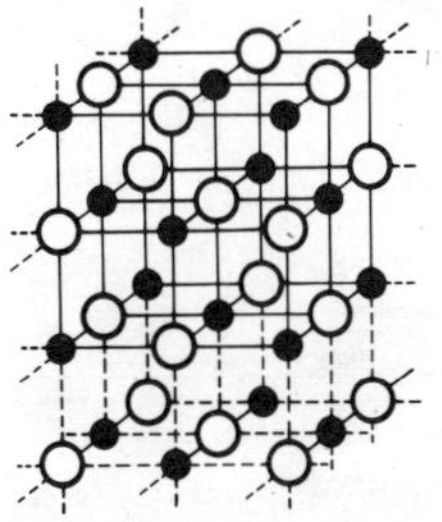

Sodium chloride is a common example. Its structure is shown in Fig 11.10. In all ionic structures, the ions are packed together so that they 'touch' each other in a regular pattern. Some ions in the structure will be positively charged. These will be the ions of metals (e.g. Na^+ in sodium chloride). Some other ions, which will be non-metal ions or radicals, will be negatively charged (e.g. Cl^- in sodium chloride). The structure is held together by the force of attraction between the oppositely charged ions.

Fig 11.10 The structure of sodium chloride, NaCl. The larger spheres represent the chloride ions. The solid lines indicate the unit cell

Ionic structures like this are *giant* structures because there are no simple, separate units within them (just as there are no separate units within the giant structures of diamond and graphite). The structure does not seem to end anywhere – it goes on in all directions, and *all* the forces between the particles are strong ones. As with all kinds of giant structure, no matter whether they contain atoms (like graphite) or ions (like sodium chloride), ionic structures have high melting points and boiling points. A great deal of heat energy is needed to separate the ions from each other. An ionic structure will, of course, have all the properties of ionically bonded substances described on p.33.

Note that many students make the mistake of thinking that sodium chloride contains separate NaCl units or molecules. They think in this way because we write the formula as NaCl. There are no such units inside the structure. Each sodium ion is joined to several chloride ions, and each chloride ion is joined to several sodium ions. We write the formula as NaCl simply to show that the ratio of sodium ions to chloride ions is 1:1. It just means that there are equal numbers of sodium and chloride ions. If you have used the term **empirical formula** (p292) you will understand that NaCl is an empirical formula. Similarly, the structure of solid magnesium chloride, $MgCl_2$, does not contain 'groups' or 'molecules' of formula $MgCl_2$, which are separate from each other. It does, however, contain twice as many chloride ions as magnesium ions.

(b) COVALENT COMPOUNDS WHICH ARE MADE OF SIMPLE MOLECULES

The solid form of water, ice, has a structure of simple molecules. Each molecule has the formula H_2O, it consists of two atoms of hydrogen and one atom of oxygen, joined together by very strong covalent bonds. The forces *between* the molecules of ice are weak. When ice is heated, the bonds between the molecules break. The H_2O molecules then separate from each other, and the ice melts (Fig 11.11). As with all simple molecular structures, ice has a low melting point because only a small amount of heat energy is needed to break the forces between the molecules. You may have used other examples instead of water (e.g. methane, carbon dioxide, or ethanol) but the principle is the same.

Fig 11.11 The structure of ice. The dotted lines represent weak forces between the molecules. The other bonds, represented by solid lines in the left-hand diagram, are strong covalent bonds

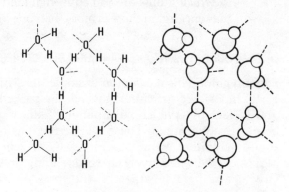

(c) COMPOUNDS WHICH ARE MADE OF GIANT MOLECULES

Typical examples include silicon oxide, (sand), SiO_2, and polymers such as polythene (p335); revise the ones you have used in your syllabus. There are no separate units or weak forces inside the structure. Instead, the atoms join together by strong bonds in all directions.

3 A GENERAL SUMMARY

The structures of elements and compounds have been described separately, but there are only two *main* kinds.

(a) SIMPLE MOLECULAR STRUCTURES

These can be elements (like iodine, I_2, or sulphur, S_8), or compounds such as water, H_2O. The structures contain *separate* units or molecules. The bonds *inside* each molecule are strong. The forces *between* the molecules are weak. The structures have low melting points and boiling points because little heat energy is needed to break the forces between the molecules, and cause the molecules to separate. Many molecular substances are already liquids or gases at room temperature because the weak forces between the molecules are already broken.

(b) GIANT STRUCTURES

There are three main types:
(i) metal structures,
(ii) giant molecules, which can be elements like carbon or compounds like silicon oxide, SiO_2 (sand), and
(iii) giant ionic structures, which can only be compounds and which are ionically bonded, such as sodium chloride. These three types all share an important property. There are no weak forces anywhere in the structure, and no separate units.

Because of this, they all have high melting points and boiling points. They are usually solids at room temperature.

1–5   These questions are about the following substances.

A   sulphur
B   hydrogen
C   diamond
D   sodium
E   graphite.

Choose from this list the substance which you think best fits each of the following descriptions.

1   At room temperature, most of the volume occupied by this substance is space.

2   This substance has a giant structure, but some bonds are weaker than others.

3   This substance has a molecular structure, each molecule containing eight atoms.

4   This substance has a giant structure, but it is unusual because it has a relatively low melting point and is soft.

5   This substance has a high melting point and does not conduct electricity.

6   Which kind of giant structure will conduct electricity when it is dissolved in water?

7   Say what kind of structure you think each of the following substances will have.

(a)   Solid A has a melting point of 1500°C and conducts electricity when in the solid state.

(b)   Solid B has a melting point of 27°C and does not conduct electricity even when molten.

(c)   Solid C has a melting point of 880°C and does not conduct electricity when in the solid state, but does so when molten.

(d)   Solid D has a very high melting point and conducts electricity when in the solid state, but it is not a metal.

8   The following list gives some of the forms in which elements and compounds can exist.

A   giant ionic structures
B   giant atomic structures
C   free ions
D   simple molecules
E   free atoms

For each of the following questions, choose the structure from the above list which best describes the substance.

(i) iodine;
(ii) sodium chloride crystals;
(iii) helium gas;
(iv) melted sodium chloride;

(v) graphite;

(vi) molten sulphur;

(vii) water;

(viii) carbon dioxide gas.

9 Sodium chloride and naphthalene are both solids at room temperature. Sodium chloride has no smell, but naphthalene has a fairly strong smell. One reason for this difference is the structures of the two solids.

(*a*)   What is the structure of sodium chloride?

(*b*)   What must happen before a substance can be 'smelled'?

(*c*)   Why do you think that sodium chloride has no smell?

(*d*)   What structure do you think napthalene might have?

(*e*)   How can this structure cause naphthalene to have a smell?

CHECK LIST ▶   REMEMBER THAT SOME OF THESE POINTS MAY NOT BE RELEVANT FOR THE PARTICULAR SYLLABUS YOU ARE FOLLOWING.

YOU SHOULD UNDERSTAND THE FOLLOWING POINTS.

1 ▶   How the Periodic Table is built up: groups, periods, and the main regions.

2 ▶   Some reactions of elements in groups (e.g. Groups 1, 2, 7 and 0) to show similarity of properties within a group.

3 ▶   Change in reactivity going down a group of metals, compared with a group of non-metals.

4 ▶   How to use the Table to predict the likely properties of an unfamiliar element or compound.

5 ▶   Changes across a period.

6 ▶   Types of structure, and their general properties. (You may need *details* of some, e.g. diamond, graphite, and the allotropes of sulphur.)

SPECIMEN EXAMINATION QUESTIONS

SEE GENERAL NOTES BEFORE QUESTIONS ON pp.49 AND 50. REMEMBER THAT YOU MAY BE ALLOWED TO USE A DATA BOOK (INCLUDING PERHAPS A PERIODIC TABLE) IN THE EXAMINATION.

Many of the *types* of examination questions on this unit have been included in the 'Check Your Understanding' sections. Here are a few more.

1–4   Use the Periodic Table in the Data Book to help you answer questions 1–4.

1   Which group of the Periodic Table contains elements which form ions with a single positive charge?

2   Name two gases which are present in the atmosphere and which are in the same *period* as lithium.

3   What is the family name of the elements in Group 0 of the Periodic Table?

4   Which two elements in Group IV of the Periodic Table are used to make a common alloy? (See page 11 of the Data Book.)

[NEA spec (A), 1]

5   The formula of a compound formed between barium (Group 2) and fluorine (Group 7) will be
A BaF   B BaF_2 C Ba_2F D Ba_2F_2

6   Chlorine is more reactive than bromine and bromine more reactive than iodine. To displace bromine from a solution of sodium bromide you could add
A   chlorine water
B   iodine solution
C   potassium chloride solution
D   sodium chloride solution

7   Which one of the following will *not* form a compound with chlorine?
A Argon   B Carbon   C Hydrogen   D Iron

[SEG spec (Alt), 1]

8   Use the Periodic Table in the Data Book for this question.
(*a*)   The element phosphorus is in Group 5 of the Periodic Table.
(i) What is the atomic number of phosphorus?
(ii) What is the electron arrangement in a phosphorus atom?
(iii) How many protons and neutrons are there in the nucleus of a phosphorus atom?
(iv) Write the molecular formula for a probable compound of phosphorus and hydrogen.
(v) Why would you expect the compound of phosphorus and hydrogen to be covalent?
(vi) If lumps of phosphorus are left in contact with the air they start to burn. Explain why this is unexpected in the light of your knowledge of the properties of nitrogen.
(*b*)   Phosphoric acid, H_3PO_4, is manufactured from phosphate rock. The reaction can be shown by the following equation.

$$Ca_3(PO_4)_2 + 3H_2SO_4 \rightarrow 2H_3PO_4 + 3CaSO_4$$

Relative atomic masses: H 1, O 16, P 31, Ca 40
(i) What is the formula mass of (a) calcium phosphate, $Ca_3(PO_4)_2$; (b) phosphoric acid, H_3PO_4?
(ii) What mass of phosphoric acid could be formed from (a) 310 kg of calcium phosphate; (b) 620 kg of calcium phosphate?
(iii) The calcium sulphate in this reaction forms as a precipitate and is filtered off. How could you test to see if any sulphate remains in the filtrate?   [SEG spec 1]

9   This question is about elements in the Periodic Table.
(*a*)   Using only the symbols shown in Fig 11.12, give the symbol for
(i) an element which is in Group III of the Periodic Table;
(ii) an element which forms an ion with a 2− charge;
(iii) a non-metal used in making computer hardware;
(iv) a metal that is used in making light alloys;

Fig 11.12 Diagram for question 9

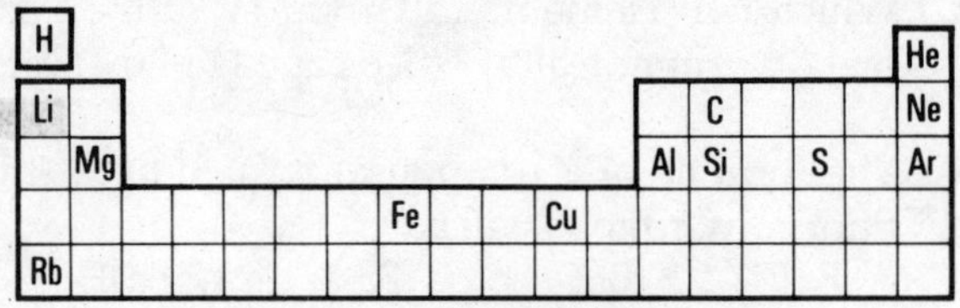

H																	He
Li														C			Ne
	Mg											Al	Si		S		Ar
					Fe			Cu									
Rb																	

(v) an element that is used in illuminated signs;

(vi) the element that reacts most violently with fluorine.

(b)   Place the symbol for each of the following elements in its correct place in the Periodic Table in Fig 11.12.

Element	Symbol	Atomic number
oxygen	O	8
calcium	Ca	20
bromine	Br	35

[*LEA* spec (B), 2]

10 (a)   State *three* differences in the properties of sodium chloride and tetrachloromethane (carbon tetrachloride).

(b)   Explain in terms of the electronic structures of the compounds why they have these differences in properties.

(c)   Use your knowledge of chemistry to explain the following facts as fully as you can.

(i) Aluminium wire carries electricity in power lines.

(ii) Graphite is used as a lubricant.   [*NEA* spec (A), 3]

11 The table below gives information about four elements, V, W, X and Y which are in the same group of the Periodic Table.

Element	Atomic number	Melting point/°C	Boiling point/°C
V	9	−220	−188
W	17	−101	−33
X	35	−7	58
Y	53	114	183

(a)   Use the melting and boiling points to give the letters of all the elements in the table which, at atmospheric pressure and at room temperature, are

(i) solids;

(ii) liquids;

(iii) gases.

(b)   Describe what happens to the particles of a solid when it melts to form a liquid.

(c)   The next element in this group after Y is Z.

(i) Would you expect Z to exist under room conditions as a solid, liquid or gas? State your reasons.

(ii) How many electrons will there be in the outer shell of a Z atom?

(iii) Using the symbol Z, write down the formula of the ion of Z.   [*LEA* spec (A), 3)

EQUATIONS. THE MOLE

CONTENTS

12.1 FORMULA MASSES. EQUATIONS

1 FORMULA MASS   Make sure that your understand what 'relative atomic mass' means (p29). The relative atomic mass of hydrogen is 1, of oxygen 16, and of chlorine 35.5. You do not need to learn these numbers – you will be given them when you need to use them. These atomic masses allow us to compare the masses of different atoms. For example, if the relative atomic mass of hydrogen is 1 and that of chlorine is 35.5, it tells us that an average atom of chlorine is 35.5 times as heavy as an average atom of hydrogen. (Relative atomic masses are sometimes given the symbol A_r.)

We can use relative atomic masses to compare the masses of bigger particles such as molecules. We call the mass of these larger particles the **formula mass**. (For a more detailed explanation of this term, see p.288.) Suppose that we need to know the formula mass of a hydrogen molecule (not a hydrogen atom). First we need to know the formula of a hydrogen molecule. It is H_2. Then we add together the separate relative atomic masses of each atom in the formula:
1 atom of hydrogen has relative atomic mass 1 (data on p.424).
There are two atoms of hydrogen in the formula H_2.
Therefore, formula mass = $1+1 = 2$
The formula mass of the hydrogen molecule, H_2, is 2.
This is like saying that a molecule of hydrogen is twice as heavy as an atom of hydrogen. (You may have used **relative molecular mass** instead of formula mass. It is almost the same thing. Relative molecular mass is sometimes given the symbol M_r.)

To take a more complicated example, let us work out the formula mass of sulphuric acid, using the data on p.424. The formula of sulphuric acid is H_2SO_4. This formula contains:

2 atoms of H, each having relative atomic mass 1.	$1+1 = 2$
1 atom of S, relative atomic mass 32	$= 32$
4 atoms of oxygen, relative atomic mass 16	$4\times16 = 64$
	Total $= 98$

The formula mass of sulphuric acid is 98. This is like saying that one molecule of sulphuric acid is 98 times as heavy as a hydrogen atom.

CHECK YOUR UNDERSTANDING (Answers on p418)

Calculate the formula masses of each of the following, using the data on p.424.

1　Sodium hydroxide, NaOH.
2　Ammonia, NH_3.
3　Potassium oxide, K_2O
4　Copper(II) hydroxide, $Cu(OH)_2$
5　Sodium chloride, NaCl
6　Nitric acid, HNO_3
7　Iron(III) oxide, Fe_2O_3
8　Water, H_2O.
9　Sodium carbonate (hydrated), $Na_2CO_3.10H_2O$

2 WRITING EQUATIONS

(a) WORD EQUATIONS

All chemical reactions can be summarised by an **equation**. An equation shows the chemicals we start with, on the left-hand side (the **reactants**), and the chemicals which are formed on the right-hand side (the **products**). You will sometimes have written equations in words. These are much easier than those with formulas, because word equations do not need to be *balanced* (next section).

You may be asked to write a word equation for a particular reaction. It is important that you understand the main *types* of chemical reaction. They are summarised below. You then have to recognise which *type* of reaction a particular example refers to, and you should then be able to work out the missing information. The *main* types are:

(a)　ACID+BASE → A SALT+WATER
(b)　ACID+FAIRLY REACTIVE METAL → A SALT+ HYDROGEN
(c)　ACID+CARBONATE → A SALT+CARBON DIOXIDE+WATER
(d)　METAL+OXYGEN → METAL OXIDE
(e)　OXIDE OF METAL LOW IN ACTIVITY SERIES+ HYDROGEN → METAL+WATER(STEAM)
(f)　Reactions where one metal **displaces** another (p96).
(g)　Reactions where one halogen **displaces** another (p.260).
(h)　REACTIVE METAL+OXIDE OF LESS REACTIVE METAL → OXIDE OF REACTIVE METAL+LESS REACTIVE METAL

Some other reactions do not fit into general types like those above, such as the precipitation of insoluble salts (p185).

Suppose that we are asked to complete the following word equation:

SODIUM HYDROXIDE+SULPHURIC ACID → ?+?

The first thing we have to do is to decide the *type* of reaction which is taking place. Sodium hydroxide is a base (p176) and sulphuric acid is an acid. The reaction is of the type ACID+BASE → A SALT +WATER. The salt in this case will be sodium sulphate (see p.183). The complete word equation is therefore:

SODIUM HYDROXIDE+SULPHURIC ACID → SODIUM SULPHATE+WATER

CHECK YOUR UNDERSTANDING (Answers on p418)

Write word equations for each of the following reactions. Remember – the first thing to do is to decide the type of reaction, and then work out the missing names.

1 Sodium carbonate+hydrochloric acid →
2 Zinc oxide+sulphuric acid →
3 Copper(II) oxide+nitric acid →
4 Zinc metal+copper(II) sulphate solution →
5 Chlorine+potassium bromide solution →
6 Calcium metal+oxygen →
7 Hydrochloric acid+calcium metal →
8 Copper(II) oxide+hydrogen →
9   +   → copper(II) sulphate+carbon dioxide+water
10   +   → zinc chloride+hydrogen
11 In which of the following would there **not** be a reaction?
   (a)   Copper+hydrochloric acid;
   (b)   aluminium oxide+copper;
   (c)   bromine+sodium chloride;
   (d)   copper+iron(II) sulphate.

(b) WRITING EQUATIONS USING FORMULAS. BALANCING EQUATIONS

You will have seen some equations written in chemical formulas. These are much more difficult than word equations because
(*a*)   each formula must be correct, and
(*b*)   the equation must be **balanced**.
If you intend to aim for a high grade, you will need to be able to write equations using formulas, for many of the main types of reaction you have studied.

You may be asked to write an equation from memory, or to change a word equation into formulas, or you may be given an incomplete equation with formulas and be asked to complete it. Any equation using formulas *must* be **balanced**. This means that the total number of atoms of each kind must not change during the reaction. All of the atoms which are shown to be there at the beginning (the left-hand side of the equation) must be there at the end (the right-hand side of the equation). Atoms can 'change partners', but we cannot end up with a different number of atoms than we started with. (You may have done an experiment to prove the **Law of Conservation of Mass**, which shows that the total mass of substances at the end of a reaction is equal to the total mass of the reactants.)

For example, magnesium metal reacts with dilute hydrochloric acid to form hydrogen gas and the salt magnesium chloride. (You could be *given* this information, and be asked to write an equation. The question could be made more difficult by just naming the reactants, and not the products. You then have to work out the *type* of reaction and the *names* of the products as on p.280 before you write the equation in formulas.) The word equation is:

MAGNESIUM+HYDROCHLORIC ACID $\rightarrow$ MAGNESIUM CHLORIDE+HYDROGEN

The *unbalanced* equation using formulas is:

$$Mg + HCl \rightarrow MgCl_2 + H_2$$

Note that the formula of each substance *must* be checked at this stage (p42). Note also that hydrogen gas must be shown as H_2. It consists of molecules of hydrogen, H_2, and not atoms of hydrogen. Many students forget that most gases exist as molecules, not atoms.

At the moment the equation shows:

Atom	Atoms on left-hand side of equation	Atoms on right-hand side of equation
Mg	1	1
H	1	2
Cl	1	2

The equation is not balanced for H and Cl atoms.

The balanced equation is:

$$Mg + 2HCl \rightarrow MgCl_2 + H_2$$

Check:

Atom	Atoms on left-hand side of equation	Atoms on right-hand side of equation
Mg	1	1
H	2	2
Cl	2	2

Strictly, we should now add state symbols to the equation (p58). The final equation is therefore:

$$Mg(s) + 2HCl(aq) \rightarrow MgCl_2(aq) + H_2(g).$$

Note that you might think that writing H_2Cl_2 on the left-hand side would have balanced the equation, instead of writing 2HCl. You must **never change the formula of a chemical while balancing an equation.** The correct formula of hydrochloric acid is HCl. We can have 2HCl, or 50HCl, or any number of HCl, but we cannot have

H_2Cl_2, or H_2Cl_3, etc. because no such substance exists. (You may need to understand how to work out a balanced equation from some experimental results.)

CHECK YOUR UNDERSTANDING

Set for homework

For each of the following equations, write a table as shown earlier: **Atom   Atoms on left-hand side of equation   Atoms on right-hand side of equation.** Use the table to decide which of the equations are not balanced. Then rewrite each unbalanced equation in a balanced form. The answers are given on p.284, where the same equations (correctly balanced) are used in some calculations. If you get any of them wrong, make sure that you understand your mistakes.

1. $H_2 + O_2 \rightarrow H_2O$
2. $Na + H_2O \rightarrow NaOH + H_2$
3. $2Mg + O_2 \rightarrow 2MgO$
4. $Na + O_2 \rightarrow Na_2O$
5. $Ca + 2HCl \rightarrow CaCl_2 + H_2$
6. $NaOH + HCl \rightarrow NaCl + H_2O$
7. $NaOH + H_2SO_4 \rightarrow Na_2SO_4 + H_2O$

The following equations are more difficult, but you may enjoy the challenge of balancing them!

8. $Na_2SO_4 + Ca(NO_3)_2 \rightarrow CaSO_4 + NaNO_3$
9. $NH_3 + H_2O + Na_2SO_4 \rightarrow (NH_4)_2SO_4 + NaOH$
10. $NaOH + Cl_2 \rightarrow NaCl + NaClO_3 + H_2O$
11. $X_2O_5 + H_2O \rightarrow H_3XO_4$
12. $H_2XO_4 + C \rightarrow H_2O + XO_2 + CO_2$

(If you have been successful with **8–12**, then balancing equations should hold no fears!)

---

3 USING A BALANCED EQUATION

A properly balanced equation gives us some very important information. It tells us the proportions in which chemicals react together. It also tells us the proportions of products which are formed.

Suppose that we are given the balanced equation used earlier:

$$Mg + 2HCl \rightarrow MgCl_2 + H_2.$$

This tells us that one *formula mass* of magnesium reacts with two *formula masses* of hydrochloric acid. It also tells us that one *formula mass* of magnesium chloride is formed, plus one *formula mass* of hydrogen. This is like saying 'one load of magnesium' reacts with 'two loads' of hydrochloric acid to produce 'one load of magnesium chloride' + 'one load of hydrogen'. We can work out the actual masses of these formula masses or 'loads' as shown earlier in the unit on p279. Therefore, we can work out how much of each chemical we need, and how much of each product will be formed.

For example, using the above equation:

$$\begin{array}{ccccc} Mg & + & 2HCl & \rightarrow & MgCl_2 & + & H_2 \end{array}$$

Mg	2HCl	MgCl$_2$	H$_2$
1 formula mass	2 formula masses	1 formula mass	1 formula mass
= 24	= 2×(1+35.5)	= 24+(2×35.5)	1+1
	= 2×36.5	= 24+71	= 2
	= 73	= 95	

We usually use formula masses in grams. We can therefore say that:

24g of magnesium will react with 73g of hydrochloric acid to form 95g of magnesium chloride and 2g of hydrogen.

It would be just as correct to say that 24 tonnes of magnesium will react with 73 tonnes of hydrochloric acid to form 95 tonnes of magnesium chloride and 2 tonnes of hydrogen. Calculations of this type are very important. They all depend upon a properly balanced equation. In industry, we can work out how much of a substance should be formed from known amounts of starting materials, and this kind of information is vital in planning a new factory.

CHECK YOUR UNDERSTANDING (Answers on p419)

If you get any of the following questions wrong, make sure that you understand your mistakes. For relative atomic masses, use p.424.

1. In the reaction $2H_2(g)+O_2(g) \rightarrow 2H_2O(g)$, how much water would be formed from 16g of oxygen, if all the oxygen is used up?

2. In the reaction $2Na(s)+2H_2O(l) \rightarrow 2NaOH(aq)+H_2(g)$, what mass of sodium hydroxide would be formed if 46g of sodium reacted completely with water?

3. In the reaction $2Mg(s)+O_2(g) \rightarrow 2MgO(s)$, what mass of oxygen would be needed to react with 12g of magnesium?

4. In the reaction $4Na(s)+O_2(g) \rightarrow 2Na_2O(s)$, what mass of sodium oxide could be formed from 46g of sodium?

5. In the reaction $Ca(s)+2HCl(aq) \rightarrow CaCl_2(aq)+H_2(g)$, how much calcium metal would be needed to react with 73g of hydrochloric acid?

6. In the reaction $NaOH(aq)+HCl(aq) \rightarrow NaCl(aq)+H_2O(l)$, 40g of hydrochloric acid were mixed with 40g of sodium hydroxide. One of these quantities is in excess (in other words, more of it used than is necessary). Which is in excess, and how much of it would be wasted?

7. The following equations are included here as answers to the problems on p.283.

$$Na_2SO_4(aq)+Ca(NO_3)_2(aq) \rightarrow CaSO_4(s)+2NaNO_3)(aq)$$

(Do not worry if you got some of the state symbols wrong!)

$$2NH_3(g)+2H_2O(l)+Na_2SO_4(aq) \rightarrow (NH_4)_2SO_4(aq)+2NaOH(aq)$$

$$6NaOH(aq)+3Cl_2(g) \rightarrow 5NaCl(aq)+NaClO_3(aq)+3H_2O(l)$$

$$X_2O_5 + 3H_2O(l) \rightarrow 2H_3XO_4$$
$$2H_2XO_4 + C(s) \rightarrow 2H_2O(l) + 2XO_2 + CO_2(g)$$

4 SOME MORE COMPLICATED EXAMPLES OF USING A BALANCED EQUATION

Sometimes we have to work in *fractions* of a formula mass. The earlier examples used whole formula masses. Suppose that we are asked how much magnesium oxide would be formed by burning 4.8g of magnesium in oxygen. The balanced equation is:

$$2Mg(s) + O_2(g) \rightarrow 2MgO(s).$$

We can set out the calculation like this:

$2Mg(s)$	$+$	$O_2(g)$	$\rightarrow$	$2MgO(s)$
2 formula masses		1 formula mass		2 formula masses
$2 \times 24 = 48$		$16 + 16 = 32$		$2 \times (24 + 16) = 80$

48g of magnesium would react with 32g of oxygen to form 80g of magnesium oxide.

4.8g of magnesium is $\frac{1}{10}$ (0.1) of 48g.

Therefore, 4.8g of magnesium would produce $\frac{1}{10} \times 80$g of magnesium oxide, or 0.1×80g of magnesium oxide = 8.0g.

CHECK YOUR UNDERSTANDING (Answers on p419)

1 When calcium carbonate is heated strongly, the following reaction takes place:

$$CaCO_3(s) \rightarrow CaO(s) + CO_2(g).$$

How much (i) calcium oxide, and (ii) carbon dioxide, would be formed from 25g of calcium carbonate?

2 A solution containing 8.0g of sodium hydroxide is neutralised by hydrochloric acid (equation on p.284). What mass of sodium chloride will be produced if the solution is evaporated to dryness?

3 When copper(II) sulphate crystals are heated, the water of crystallisation is driven off as steam. The reaction is:

$$CuSO_4.5H_2O(s) \rightarrow CuSO_4(s) + 5H_2O(g).$$

What mass of anhydrous copper(II) sulphate can be obtained by heating 25.0g of the hydrated salt?

---

5 IONIC EQUATIONS

Revise the chemical test for a chloride (p167). Suppose that a chloride test is done on

(a)   a solution of sodium chloride and
(b)   a solution of potassium chloride.

A white precipitate of silver chloride is formed in each case. The following equations could be used to summarise the results:

$$NaCl(aq) + AgNO_3(aq) \rightarrow AgCl(s) + NaNO_3(aq)$$
$$KCl(aq) + AgNO_3(aq) \rightarrow AgCl(s) + KNO_3(aq)$$

These are perfectly correct, properly balanced equations, but they are slightly misleading. They suggest that sodium nitrate and potassium nitrate have been *formed*. In fact they have not. The *solution* formed contains *separate* sodium and nitrate (or potassium and nitrate) ions. These ions have not combined to form sodium nitrate or potassium nitrate. Similarly, the starting solution did not contain 'sodium chloride' or 'potassium chloride' or 'silver nitrate'. The solution contained *separate* ions of sodium, chloride, silver and nitrate for example. Some of the ions in the mixture, therefore, were present as separate ions at the beginning and are still separate ions at the end. They have not changed or reacted at all. In the first example, $Na^+(aq)$ and $NO_3^-(aq)$ ions are unchanged. In the second example $K^+(aq)$ and $NO_3^-(aq)$ ions are unchanged. It would be better not to include these ions in the equation, as they have not changed. They are **spectator ions**. A better equation in cases like this is the **ionic equation** which shows only those ions which react or change:

$$Ag^+(aq) + Cl^-(aq) \rightarrow AgCl(s)$$

Ionic equations are very useful in chemistry. They are shorter than full equations. They give a more accurate idea of what has actually changed in a reaction. Often, *one* ionic equation can be used for many *apparently* different reactions. For example, the ionic equation above can be used for *any* test for a chloride in solution. It does not matter which chloride is being used; the other ions are always spectator ions. Similarly, the ionic equation $H^+(aq) + OH^-(aq) \rightarrow H_2O(l)$ can be used for *any* neutralisation between an alkali and an acid, no matter which acid or alkali is being used.

Ionic equations are not easy, however. You need to understand ionic bonding and other basic ideas before you can be confident about using them. It is important to realise that ionic equations cannot be used for every chemical reaction. They can be used only where *ions* react, usually in solution. Remember also that ionic equations must be balanced. This includes negative and positive charges on the ions. For example:

$$Fe(s) + Ag^+(aq) \rightarrow Fe^{2+}(aq) + Ag(s)$$

is not balanced, but

$$Fe(s) + 2Ag^+(aq) \rightarrow Fe^{2+}(aq) + 2Ag(s)$$

is balanced.

COMMON EXAMPLES OF IONIC EQUATIONS

(a) Displacement reactions in the Activity Series (p96)
A more reactive metal displaces a less reactive metal from one of its compounds. The spectator ion is 'the rest' of the metal compound. For example, magnesium displaces copper from copper(II) sulphate solution. The sulphate ion is the spectator ion. The only *change* is:

$$Mg(s) + Cu^{2+}(aq) \rightarrow Mg^{2+}(aq) + Cu(s)$$

(b) **Displacement reactions of the halogens (p260)**

E.g.

$$Cl_2(aq) + 2Br^-(aq) \rightarrow 2Cl^-(aq) + Br_2(aq)$$

(c) **The precipitation of insoluble salts (p185)**

E.g.

$$Ca^{2+}(aq) + SO_4^{2-}(aq) \rightarrow CaSO_4(s)$$

(d) **Neutralisation between an acid and an alkali**

$$H^+(aq) + OH^-(aq) \rightarrow H_2O(l)$$

(e) **The precipitation of insoluble hydroxides (p162)**

E.g.

$$Fe^{2+}(aq) + 2OH^-(aq) \rightarrow Fe(OH)_2(s)$$

(f) **The precipitation of insoluble carbonates (p163)**

E.g.

$$Cu^{2+}(aq) + CO_3^{2-}(aq) \rightarrow CuCO_3(s)$$

(f) Acid + metal

$$Mg + 2H^+ \rightarrow Mg^{2+} + H_2.$$

12.2 THE MOLE

1 THE MOLE AS A UNIT

Chemists do not usually compare the properties of two substances by taking an equal *mass* of each. For example, we would not compare 12g of magnesium with 12g of copper. This is because 12g of magnesium does not contain the same number of atoms as 12g of copper. Chemistry is all about the way in which atoms react, so comparing 12g of magnesium with 12g of copper would not be a fair comparison.

Chemists therefore need to be able to count the number of particles in a substance. This is not impossible, even though we cannot 'see' atoms. We use a 'standard pack' of atoms as our basic unit, just as six eggs may be the simplest standard pack of eggs. The amount of substance which contains the chemist's standard pack of particles is called **the mole.** The relative atomic mass of any element, in grams, is a mole of atoms.

For example, the relative atomic mass of hydrogen is 1. 1g of hydrogen is a mole of hydrogen atoms. The relative atomic mass of oxygen is 16. 16g of oxygen is a mole of oxygen atoms. 1g of hydrogen contains exactly the same number of atoms as 16g of oxygen. This number is the number of atoms in the basic pack (the mole). (We know what this number of particles is. There are 6.02×10^{23} particles in a mole. This very large number is called the **Avogadro constant,** in honour of the Italian, Avogadro. It is not necessary to learn this number – just think of it as 'a mole's worth of atoms' – the chemist's basic pack.) Note that if you have studied the **faraday constant** in electrolysis, you may also need to understand that the faraday is a mole of electrons.

Not for IVBA.

CHECK YOUR UNDERSTANDING (Answers on p419)

(For relative atomic masses, see p424.)

1   How many grams of each of the following would you need to weigh out in order to have a mole of atoms?

     (a)   copper
     (b)   zinc
     (c)   iron
     (d)   magnesium
     (e)   sulphur.

2   How much would you need to weigh out in order to have

     (a)   0.5 moles of sulphur atoms
     (b)   0.1 moles of iron atoms
     (c)   0.25 moles of magnesium atoms
     (d)   2.0 moles of oxygen atoms
     (e)   3.5 moles of nitrogen atoms?

3   In each of the following pairs, which mass contains the greater number of atoms?

     (a)   18g of carbon or 6.5g of zinc
     (b)   7g of oxygen or 7g of nitrogen
     (c)   16g of sulphur or 8g of oxygen.

---

2 MOLES OF FORMULA UNITS

Most substances do not consist of atoms. (In fact, only the noble gases exist as free atoms.) Instead, they may consist of molecules like H_2, or H_2SO_4. Ionically bonded substances such as sodium chloride contain a giant network of ions (p269) rather than either atoms or molecules. We cannot refer to 'moles of atoms' when using *most* substances, therefore. We have a general term which covers all examples which are not atoms. We use the **formula mass** as in the examples below and on p.279. The formula mass of a substance, in grammes, contains a **mole of formula units.**

Examples: The formula mass of a hydrogen molecule, H_2, is $1+1 = 2$. Therefore 2g of hydrogen contains a mole of H_2 formula units. 2g of hydrogen is the chemist's basic pack of H_2 units. (The number of H_2 units in a mole is exactly the same number of *atoms* as there are in a mole of hydrogen atoms.)

The formula mass of sulphuric acid, H_2SO_4, $= (1+1)+32+(4\times16) = 98$. Therefore, 98g of sulphuric acid is a mole of H_2SO_4 formula units. 98g of sulphuric acid is the chemist's basic pack of H_2SO_4 units.

The formula mass of sodium chloride, $NaCl$, $= 23+35.5 = 58.5$. Therefore, 58.5g of sodium chloride is a mole of NaCl formula units. 58.5g of sodium chloride is the chemist's basic pack of NaCl units. To put all three examples another way, the number of H_2 units in 2g of hydrogen is the same as the number of H_2SO_4 units in 98g of sulphuric acid, and also equal to the number of NaCl units in 58.5g of sodium chloride.

CHECK YOUR UNDERSTANDING (Answers on p419)

1   What mass would you need in order to have a mole of formula units of each of the following?

     (a)   hydrogen molecules H_2.

(b)   chlorine molecules
(c)   nitrogen molecules
(d)   ammonia molecules
(e)   nitric acid
(f)   calcium carbonate
(g)   magnesium fluoride, MgF_2
(h)   potassium oxide, K_2O.

2 What mass of substance is there in each of the following?
(a)   2.0 moles of potassium chloride formula units,
(b)   0.5 moles of sodium hydroxide formula units,
(c)   0.25 moles of copper(II) sulphate (anhydrous) formula units.

3 How many moles of formula units are in each of the following masses?
(a)   69g of potassium carbonate, K_2CO_3,
(b)   107g of ammonium chloride, NH_4Cl,
(c)   53.5g of iron(III) hydroxide.

3 MOLES IN CHEMICAL EQUATIONS

Revise the calculations done on equations on p.284. If you understand the idea of the mole, you should be able to think of these earlier calculations in terms of moles of substances rather than formula masses. The answers will be the same, of course. For example, in the reaction:

$$Mg(s) + 2HCl(aq) \rightarrow MgCl_2(aq) + H_2(g)$$

we can say that one mole of magnesium atoms reacts with two moles of hydrochloric acid formula units, to produce one mole of magnesium chloride formula units and one mole of hydrogen formula units. You will find statements like this very useful in later sections.

4 MOLES AND VOLUMES

Many chemical reactions involve gases. Gases are very difficult to weigh; they are mainly empty space. We can still work out *amounts* of gases, however, by measuring volumes rather than masses. Just as we can *weigh* out a mole's worth of a solid or a liquid, we can *measure out* (as a volume) a mole's worth of a gas.

The volume of a gas varies according to both temperature and pressure (p57). We therefore need to fix the temperature and the pressure each time we make comparisons of the volumes of gases. The conditions we use for comparison are **room temperature and pressure** (often abbreviated to rtp). These conditions are 25°C and 760mm mercury pressure (1 atmosphere).

If we weigh out a mole's worth of hydrogen formula units (2g) and measure its volume at rtp we find that it is **24 litres**. So a mole's worth of hydrogen formula units, H_2, measures 24 litres at rtp. This same volume is taken up by a mole's worth of *any* gas at rtp. Instead of weighing a mole's worth of a gas, it is much easier to measure out 24 litres of it instead. **A mole of any gas occupies a volume of 24 litres at room temperature and pressure** (25°C and 760mm mercury pressure). For example, 24 litres of oxygen at rtp is a mole's worth of oxygen formula units (molecules), O_2. (This also means that 24 litres of oxygen at rtp is the same as 32g of oxygen. It also means that 24 litres of oxygen at rtp contains 6.02×10^{23} formula units of oxygen – the chemist's basic pack of particles.)

CHECK YOUR UNDERSTANDING (Answer on p420)

1   What is the volume occupied at rtp by
    (a)   a mole of hydrogen molecules,
    (b)   two moles of chlorine molecules,
    (c)   0.5 moles of carbon dioxide,
    (d)   0.1 moles of hydrogen sulphide gas, H_2S?

2   What is the volume, at rtp of
    (a)   16g of oxygen, O_2
    (b)   71g of chlorine, Cl_2
    (c)   10g of hydrogen,
    (d)   4.4g of carbon dioxide, $CO_2 = 44$
    (e)   16g of sulphur dioxide?   64

3   What is the mass of
    (a)   24 litres of ammonia gas, $NH_3 = 17$
    (b)   6.0 litres of carbon monoxide, $Co = 28$
    (c) $240cm^3$ of nitrogen? $N_2 = 28g$

2400φ

---

5 EQUATIONS AND VOLUMES

If you understand how to calculate the masses of substances which would be used up or formed in reactions (p284), you should be able to do the same with *volumes* of gases. Remember, it is more convenient to measure a gas by its volume than by its mass.

For example, suppose that we are asked calculate the volume of carbon dioxide gas (measured at rtp) which would be given off when 10.0g of potassium hydrogencarbonate are completely decomposed by heating in the following reaction. (Note that if the equation is not provided for you, the first step in the calculation must be to produce a fully balanced equation for the reaction.)

$$2KHCO_3(s) \rightarrow K_2CO_3(s) + H_2O(g) + CO_2(g)$$
2 moles $KHCO_3 \rightarrow$ 1 mole CO_2
200g $KHCO_3 \rightarrow$ 1 mole CO_2
10g $KHCO_3 \rightarrow \dfrac{10}{200} \times$ 1 mole CO_2, $= \dfrac{1}{20}$ mole CO_2

1 mole of any gas occupies 24 litres at rtp

Therefore, $\dfrac{1}{20}$ mole of CO_2 at rtp occupies $\dfrac{1}{20} \times$ 24 litres, = 1.2 litres.

CHECK YOUR UNDERSTANDING (Answers on p420)

1   (a)   Write a fully balanced equation for the reaction between zinc metal and dilute hydrochloric acid.
    (b)   What volume of hydrogen, measured at rtp will be formed when 6.5g of zinc reacts completely with dilute hydrochloric acid?

2   Calcium carbonate reacts with dilute nitric acid as:

$$CaCO_3(s) + 2HNO_3(aq) \rightarrow Ca(NO_3)_2 + CO_2(g) + H_2O(l)$$

What volume of carbon dioxide, measured at rtp, would be formed if 2.5g of pure calcium carbonate reacted completely with dilute nitric acid?

12.3 USING MOLES TO FIND FORMULAS

**1 PERCENTAGE
COMPOSITION OF A
COMPOUND**

Experiments are often done to find the proportions of each element in a particular compound. Usually, this is calculated as a proportion by mass. Suppose that magnesium oxide is analysed in this way. The results of such an experiment might be given as

(a)   in every 40g of magnesium oxide there are 24g of magnesium and 16g of oxygen, or

(b)   magnesium oxide contains 60% magnesium by mass and 40% oxygen by mass. Usually, the composition is given as a percentage by mass.

It is sometimes useful to be able to calculate the percentage of each element by mass in a compound from the formula of the compound. If we know the formula, there is no need to do an experiment. For example, suppose that we are asked to calculate the percentage composition, by mass, of sulphuric acid, H_2SO_4.

(a)   Write down the formula of the compound: H_2SO_4.

(b)   Find the formula mass: $(1+2)+32+(4\times16) = 98$.

(c)   Calculate each atomic mass as a percentage of the formula mass. If more than one atom of a particular element is present in the formula, then the 'total mass' of these atoms must be used. In this example, two atoms of hydrogen are in the formula, so we use two as the mass of hydrogen, not one

$$\text{per cent hydrogen} = \frac{2}{98} \times 100\% = 2.05\%$$

$$\text{per cent sulphur} = \frac{32}{98} \times 100\% = 32.65\%$$

$$\text{per cent oxygen} = \frac{64}{98} \times 100\% = 65.30\%$$

(d)   Check that the percentages add up to 100. In this example, sulphuric acid contains 2.05% by mass of hydrogen, 32.65% by mass of sulphur, and 65.30% by mass of oxygen.

Note that if a hydrated compound is being considered, the percentage of water should be calculated as a complete separate unit, rather than considering the water as the individual elements hydrogen and oxygen. For example, in hydrated magnesium chloride, $MgCl_26H_2O$, formula mass 203, the percentage composition by mass is:

$$\text{per cent magnesium} = \frac{24}{203} \times 100\% = 11.82\%$$

$$\text{per cent chlorine} = \frac{71}{203} \times 100\% = 34.98\%$$

$$\text{per cent water} = \frac{108}{203} \times 100\% = 53.2\%$$

(The figure 108 for water arises because there are six formula units of water in the compound. Each formula unit of water has a relative mass of 18, and $6\times18 = 108$.)

CALCULATING THE PERCENTAGES OF ELEMENTS IN FERTILISERS

The three most important elements needed for plant growth are nitrogen, phosphorus and potassium (p318). Various chemicals are manufactured which contain these elements. The proportions of the elements are varied, because some crops need more nitrogen than others, and so on. Each type of fertiliser, therefore, has to be clearly marked so that the proportions of the elements within it can be understood. The proportions of the elements are normally given as percentages by mass in the fertiliser. This is one of the most important uses of this kind of calculation. The percentage composition of a fertiliser is often called the NPK value, after the symbols used for the three most important elements in plant foods.

CHECK YOUR UNDERSTANDING (Answers on p420)

1   Calculate the percentage composition by mass of each of the following compounds.
  (a)   calcium carbonate,
  (b)   anhydrous copper(II) sulphate,
  (c)   methane, CH_4,
  (d)   potassium hydrogencarbonate, $KHCO_3$.

2   Determine the percentage composition by mass of each of the following hydrated compounds.
  (a)   sodium carbonate-10-water, $Na_2CO_3.1OH_2O$;
  (b)   iron(II) sulphate-7-water, $FeSO_4.7H_2O$.

3   The percent composition by mass of nitrogen in a fertiliser is called the 'N value'. Calculate the N value in
  (a)   ammonium sulphate, $(NH_4)_2SO_4$;
  (b)   ammonium nitrate, NH_4NO_3.

4   Look again at your answers to question 3. Why is it more efficient to use a tonne of ammonium nitrate rather than a tonne of ammonium sulphate as a nitrogenous fertiliser?

---

2 FINDING A FORMULA FROM A PERCENTAGE COMPOSITION

Empirical Formulae

This is the reverse of what has been explained in the previous section. We could be given the result of an experiment, which shows the composition of a compound by mass. This information could be given directly, or it might have to be worked out from experimental results. The steps in the calculation are as follows.

(a)   Write a statement about the masses of the elements which combine together in the compound. E.g. 8.32g of lead combine with 1.28g of sulphur and 2.56g of oxygen. (If the information is given in percentages, it is used in the same way. For example, if a compound contains 40% Cu, 20% S, and 40% O, we would write: 40g of copper combine with 20g of sulphur and 40g of oxygen.)

(b)   Divide the mass of each element by the relative atomic mass of the element. This converts the masses into moles of atoms. $\frac{8.32}{207}$ moles of lead atoms combine with $\frac{1.28}{32}$ moles of sulphur atoms and $\frac{2.56}{16}$ moles of oxygen atoms. Therefore 0.04 moles Pb atoms combine with 0.04 moles S atoms and 0.16 moles 0 atoms.

(c)   Change these moles ratios into whole numbers by dividing each of them by the smallest (0.04 in this example). Therefore one mole of lead atoms combine with one mole of sulphur atoms and four moles of oxygen atoms. This ratio is the same as one atom Pb : one atom S : four atoms O. The formula of the compound is $PbSO_4$.

        Any formula calculated in this way is an **empirical formula**. This means that it is the simplest ratio which shows how the atoms are combined in the substance. The real formula is called the **molecular formula**. This shows the *exact* number of atoms in a molecule, if the substance is molecular. For example, suppose that the simplest (empirical) formula for a substance is HO. This might also be the same as the molecular formula. But the molecular formula might also be H_2O_2, or H_3O_3, etc. all of which still have the ratio of one hydrogen atom: one oxygen atom, i.e. an empirical formula of HO.

CHECK YOUR UNDERSTANDING (Answers on p421)

1   An experiment shows that 2.0g of calcium combine with 3.55g of chlorine to form a compound. What is the empirical formula of the compound?

2   Calculate the empirical formula for each of the following compounds, for which the composition by mass is given.
- (a)   magnesium 9.5g, chlorine 28.4g;
- (b)   copper 40%, sulphur 20%, oxygen 40%;
- (c)   nitrogen 1.40g, hydrogen 0.4g, carbon 0.6g, oxygen 2.4g;
- (d)   carbon 75%, hydrogen 25%.

---

3 USING AN EMPIRICAL FORMULA TO CALCULATE A MOLECULAR FORMULA

The previous section explained how to calculate an empirical formula. If the substance is ionic, the empirical formula is the only one which can be written, for ionic substances have giant structures in which there are no units such as molecules. (Revise, if necessary, how to work out the formula of an ionic compound from the charges on its ions.) If the substance is molecular, however, it is possible to take the calculation one step further and work out the **molecular formula**, i.e. the actual numbers of atoms in a molecule. For this extra step we need to know the molecular (or formula) mass of the compound. Note that sometimes the empirical formula is the same as the molecular formula.

Suppose that a substance has been shown to have an empirical formula of HO by a calculation like that in the previous section. The molecular mass of the substance is 34. The molecular formula is always a simple multiple of the empirical formula. In other words, the molecular formula is HO, or 2×HO (i.e. H_2O_2), or 3×HO (i.e. H_3O_3), etc. The 'mass of the formula unit' for the empirical formula is 17 (1+16). 2×17 = 34 (the formula mass of the molecule). Therefore the molecular formula is 2×HO = H_2O_2.

CHECK YOUR UNDERSTANDING (Answers on p421)

1   Calculate the molecular formula for each of the following compounds, for which the percentage composition by mass is given:
- (a)   carbon 80%, hydrogen 20%, relative molecular mass 30;
- (b)   hydrogen 5.9%, oxygen 94.1%, relative molecular mass 34,
- (c)   carbon 38.75%, hydrogen 16.1%, nitrogen 45.2%, relative molecular mass 31.

12.4 MOLES AND SOLUTIONS. VOLUMETRIC ANALYSIS

1 CONCENTRATIONS OF SOLUTIONS

The concentration of a solution is usually measured either in grams of dissolved substance per litre of solution (shown as g/l or g l^{-1}) or in **moles** of dissolved substance per litre (shown as moles/l or moles l^{-1}). Note that one mole of sodium chloride dissolved in 1 litre of *water* is not quite the same as one mole of sodium chloride dissolved in 1 litre of *solution*. We always use the volume of the *solution* in calculating concentrations.

SOME EXAMPLES OF CONCENTRATIONS USING MOLES

(a)　　　A solution which contains 1.0 moles of dissolved substance in 1 litre of solution has a concentration of 1.0 mole/l. This concentration is sometimes call a 1.0 molar solution, and is shown as I.0M. For example, one mole of formula units of sodium chloride, NaCl, is (23+35.5)g = 58.5g. If 58.5g of sodium chloride are dissolved in water, and the total volume of the solution is made up to 1.0 litre, the sodium chloride solution will have a concentration of 1.0 mole/l (I.0M)

(b)　　　If 5.85g of sodium chloride were dissolved as in (a), the sodium chloride solution would have a concentration of 0.1 mole/1 (0.1M).

(c)　　　Suppose that 5.85g of sodium chloride were dissolved in water, and the solution made up to a volume of 250cm³. The solution would contain 0.1 moles of sodium chloride in 250cm³: The standard unit of concentration is moles per litre, **not** moles per 250cm³. There would be (4×0.1) = 0.4 moles of sodium chloride in 1 litre of solution. The concentration of sodium chloride in the solution is therefore 0.4 moles/l (0.4M).

(d)　　　Suppose that we are asked to calculate the mass of sodium hydroxide which must be dissolved in 250cm³ of solution to produce a solution of concentration 0.1 moles/l.

1 mole of NaOH is 23+16+1 = 40g.

40g of NaOH dissolved in 1.0 litre of solution would have a concentration of 1.0 mole/l.

4.0g of sodium hydroxide dissolved in 1 litre of solution would have a concentration of 0.1 mole/l.

Therefore, 250cm³ of such a solution would need 1.0g NaOH.

(e)　　　How many moles of formula units of hydrochloric acid are contained in 25cm³ of a solution which has a concentration of 0.1 mole/l?

1.0 litre of the acid contains 0.1 moles of formula units.

1.0 cm³ of the acid contains $\frac{0.1}{1000}$ moles of formula units.

Therefore, 25.0 cm³ of the acid contain $25 \times \frac{0.1}{1000}$ moles of formula units = 0.0025 moles of formula units.

CHECK YOUR UNDERSTANDING (Answers on p421)

1　What is the concentration of a solution containing 2.0g of sodium hydroxide in 500cm³ of solution?

2　How many moles of anhydrous sodium carbonate are present in 200cm³ of a solution which has a concentration of 2.0 mole/l (2.0M)?

3 How many moles of sodium chloride are there in 500cm^3 of a solution which has a concentration of 0.1 mole/l (0.1M)?

4 What mass of sodium hydroxide would have to be dissolved in 100cm^3 of solution in order to produce a solution of concentration 0.5 moles/l?

VOLUMETRIC ANALYSIS

(a) PREPARING A STANDARD SOLUTION

A standard solution is one which has been made up *accurately* to a known concentration. In volumetric analysis, one of the solutions is a standard solution. If you have prepared a standard solution as part of your practical work, revise the method and make sure that you understand it.

(b) PERFORMING A TITRATION IN VOLUMETRIC ANALYSIS

In volumetric analysis, two solutions are reacted together. The concentration of *one* of the solutions is known. We calculate the concentration of the other solution by finding out how much of it reacts with a known volume of the first solution. A **pipette** is used to fix the volume of one solution. The other solution is placed in a **burette**. The volume of the liquid in the burette is noted. The liquid from the burette is then slowly reacted with the fixed volume of the other liquid until the reaction is complete. Usually an indicator is used to show when this point has been reached (the **end point**). The final volume of the liquid in the burette is noted, so that we can decide how much of it has been used for the reaction. The steps are then usually repeated several times, until we are satisfied that the result is accurate. The whole procedure is called a *titration*. If you have done a titration as part of your course, revise the details and make sure that you understand them.

Calculations using titration results

1 Ensure that you know the concentration of *one* of the two solutions involved. If this is not given directly, it will be necessary to work it out from the mass of solid dissolved in a certain volume of solution.

2 Suppose that 25.0cm^3 of a solution of hydrochloric acid of concentration 0.1 mol/l (0.1 M) react with 21.5cm^3 of a solution of sodium hydroxide, and we need to calculate the concentration of the sodium hydroxide solution.

3 Write down the balanced equation for the reaction:

$$HCl(aq) + NaOH(aq) \rightarrow NaCl(aq) + H_2O(l)$$

4 Calculate the number of moles used in the titration for the chemical the concentration of which is known, e.g.:

25.0cm^3 of hydrochloric acid used, of concentration 0.1 mole/l (0.1M).
1000cm^3 of the hydrochloric acid solution contain 0.1 moles.

∴ 1 cm^3 of the hydrochloric acid solution contains $\frac{1}{1000} \times 0.1$ moles.

∴ 25 cm^3 of the acid solution contains $25 \times \frac{1}{1000} \times 0.1$ moles.

5 From the equation, calculate how many moles of the *other* substance this has reacted

with. In this example, one mole of hydrochloric acid reacts with one mole of sodium hydroxide.

∴ If $\dfrac{25\times0.1}{1000}$ moles of acid are used, $\dfrac{25\times0.1}{1000}$ moles of alkali will react with it.

6   Calculate how many moles of this second substance would be contained in 1000cm^3 of its solution; this is the concentration required, e.g.:

$\dfrac{25\times0.1}{1000}$ moles of alkali are used. This was in 21.5 cm^3 of solution.

∴ 1 cm^3 of the alkali solution contains $\dfrac{25\times0.1}{1000\times21.5}$ moles.

∴ 1000 cm^3 of the alkali solution contains

$\dfrac{1000\times25\times0.1}{1000\times21.5}$ moles $= \dfrac{25\times0.1}{21.5}$ moles $= 0.11$ moles.

The alkali solution has a concentration of 0.11 mol/l (0.11M).

CHECK YOUR UNDERSTANDING Answers on p421)

1   Determine the concentrations (in mole/l) of the following solutions:
(a)   hydrochloric acid, 25.0cm^3 of which neutralise 20.0cm^3 of a sodium hydroxide solution of concentration 0.15 moles/l (0.15M),
(b)   sodium hydroxide, 10.0cm^3 of which neutralise 15.0cm^3 of hydrochloric acid of concentration 2.5 mole/l (2.5M).
(c)   sodium hydroxide, 10.0cm^3 of which neutralise 25.0cm^3 of hydrochloric acid of concentration 0.4 moles/l (0.4M).

CHECK LIST ▶

REMEMBER THAT SOME OF THESE POINTS MAY NOT BE RELEVANT FOR THE PARTICULAR SYLLABUS YOU ARE FOLLOWING.
YOU SHOULD UNDERSTAND THE FOLLOWING POINTS.

1 ▶   How to calculate formula masses (relative molecular masses).
2 ▶   Writing equations: in words, balanced ones with formulas, and if possible ionic equations.
3 ▶   Using a balanced equation to work out reacting masses.
4 ▶   The mole: how to calculate moles of atoms, and moles of formula units.
5 ▶   Calculations with volumes of gases formed in reactions.
6 ▶   How to calculate the % composition by mass of a compound.
7 ▶   How to find an empirical formula from experimental data, and how to work out a molecular formula from it.
8 ▶   How to work out the concentraion of a solution in mol l^{-l}
9 ▶   Calculations with titrations.

Homework

SEE GENERAL NOTE BEFORE QUESTIONS ON pp49 AND 50.
REMEMBER THAT YOU MAY BE ALLOWED TO USE A DATA
BOOK IN THE EXAMINATION.

1   (a)   Balance the equation

$$\ldots\ldots Fe + \ldots\ldots O_2 \rightarrow \ldots\ldots Fe_2O_3$$

(b)   Which one of the following statements about this reaction is true?

A   The mass ratios of iron to oxygen in iron(III) oxide is 2:3
B   Equal masses of iron and oxygen react together
C   The mass of the product is greater than the mass of the reactants.
D   . The mass ratio of iron to oxygen is the same in the reactants as in the product.   [*SEG* spec 1)

2   An oxide of sulphur contains 16g of sulphur and 16g of oxygen. (Relative atomic masses: S = 32, O = 16.)The formula of the oxide is
    A SO   B S_2O C SO_2 D SO_3 E S_3O

3   A metal M forms a hydroxide $M(OH)_3$. The mass of one mole of the hydroxide is 78g. What is the relative atomic mass of M? (Relative atomic masses: H = 1, O = 16.)
    A 27   B 30   C 59   D 61   E 78   [*LEA* spec (B), 1]

4   The reaction between magnesium and silver nitrate solution is represented by

$$Mg + 2AgNO_3 \rightarrow Mg(NO_3)_2 + 2Ag$$

What is the maximum mass of silver that could be obtained using 2.4g of magnesium? (Relative atomic masses: Mg 24, Ag 108.)
    A 10.8g   B 21.6g   C 108.0g   D 216.0g
                                                    [*SEG* spec (Alt), 1]

5   The relative molecular mass of an oxide MO is 223. What is the relative molecular mass of the oxide M_3O_4? (Relative atomic mass: O = 16.)
    A 685   B 700   C 707   D 717   E 885

6   What mass (in grams) of sodium hydroxide, NaOH, must be dissolved to make 1 dm^3 (l) of a solution of concentration 1.0 mole/dm^3 (l) (Relative atomic masses: H = 1, O = 16, Na = 23.)
    A 10g   B 20g   C 40g   D 80g   E 250g
                                                    [*NISEC* spec 2]

7   Which of the fertilisers below would supply the greatest amount of nitrogen for each kilogramme of compound used?

	Formula	Relative molecular mass
A Urea	$CO(NH_2)_2$	60
B Ammonium sulphate	$(NH_4)_2SO_4$	132
C Ammonium nitrate	NH_4NO_3	80
D Ammonium bromide	NH_4Br	98
E Potassium nitrate	KNO_3	101

[*LEA* spec (B), 1]

8   The apparatus shown in Fig 12.1 was used to form a chloride of iron by the reaction between iron and dry chlorine. Anhydrous calcium chloride was used to dry the chlorine gas.

Fig 12.1 Diagram for question 8

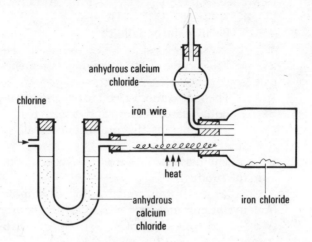

(*a*)   Why did the mass of the U-tube and its contents increase during the experiment?

(*b*)   What safety precaution should be taken with the gas leaving the apparatus?

(*c*)   The iron wire started to glow during the experiment and it continued to glow even after the heat was removed. What can be concluded about the reaction from this observation?

(*d*)   16.25g of iron chloride was produced from a 5.6g sample of iron wire.

(i) How many moles of iron atoms are there in 5.6g of iron wire? (Relative atomic mass: Fe = 56.)

(ii) What mass of chlorine combined with 5.6g of iron wire?

(iii) How many moles of chlorine atoms combined with 5.6g of iron wire? (Relative atomic mass: Cl = 35.5.)

(iv) How many moles of chlorine atoms would combine with 1 mole of iron atoms?

(v) What is the simplest formula of the iron chloride?

(*e*)   Another compound of iron, $FeCl_2$, is produced when hydrogen chloride, HCl, is passed over heated iron. Hydrogen gas, H_2, is also produced. Write a word and a balanced symbolic equation for this reaction.   [*LEA* spec (B), 2]

+9   An experiment was carried out to find the formula of a metal iodide by reacting a known mass of metal (M) with excess iodine. The excess iodine was removed by extracting with ethanol and the product completely dried.

(*a*)   From the results below calculate the formula of the iodide of the metal (Relative atomic masses: M = 65, I = 127.)

(*b*)   Discuss the reactivity series of the halogens in terms of the displacement of their ions from aqueous solution.

Mass of empty tube	4.75g
Mass of tube and metal	5.55g
Mass of tube and metal iodide	8.67g

†10 25.0cm³ of sodium hydroxide solution were neutralised by 37.5cm³ of 0.10 M hydrochloric acid.

(*a*)   Write the symbol equation for the reaction.

(*b*)   Calculate the molar concentration of the sodium hydroxide solution.

(*c*)   Calculate the concentration of the sodium hydroxide solution in grams/litre using the relative atomic masses given in the Data Book.

(*d*)   What would you use to find the end point of the titration and how would you know when the end point had been reached?

(*e*)   Describe how you would adapt the method to prepare pure crystals of the salt formed.   [*NEA* spec (A), 2]

†11 1cm³ of 3.0 M sodium hydroxide solution was added to 5cm³ of 1.0 M iron(III) chloride solution in a test tube. After shaking to mix, and allowing to stand for ten minutes, the height of the precipitate was measured. The experiment was repeated using different volumes of the 3.0 M sodium hydroxide solution. The results are shown below:

Volume of 3.0 M sodium hydroxide added/cm³	1	2	3	4	5	6	7
Height of the precipitate/mm	4	8	12	16	20	20	20

(*a*)   On the grid (see Fig 12.2) draw a graph of these results.

Fig 12.2 Example of grid provided for question 11

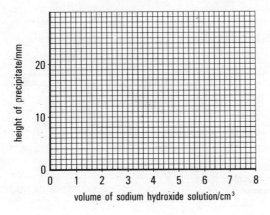

(*b*)   Explain why the height of the precipitate did not change from the 5th to the 7th cm³.

(c)   Calculate the number of moles sodium hydroxide in $5cm^3$ of 3.0 M sodium hydroxide solution.

(d)   The equation for the reaction is

$$3NaOH(aq)+FeCl_3(aq) \rightarrow Fe(OH)_3(s)+3NaCl(aq)$$

State the number of moles of iron(III) chloride required to react with exactly $5cm^3$ of 3.0 M sodium hydroxide solution.

(e)   Show how the answer to (d) compares with the results of the experiment.

(f)   Describe how you would attempt to obtain a pure dry sample of the precipitate formed in the experiment.   [LEA spec (B), 3]

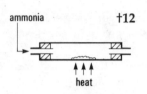

ammonia

heat

Fig 12.3 Diagram for question 12

†12   When metallic sodium is heated in a stream of ammonia, hydrogen and solid sodamide are produced. (See Fig 12.3.)

(a)   The gases coming out of the tube are hydrogen and some unreacted ammonia.

   (i) Describe a test to show that ammonia is present in the gas.

   (ii) Sketch on the diagram a piece of apparatus that could be used to collect hydrogen without any unreacted ammonia.

   (iii) Describe a test for hydrogen.

(b)   Sodamide reacts with water to produce sodium hydroxide solution and ammonia.

$$NaNH_2(s)+H_2O(l) \rightarrow NaOH(aq)+NH_3(g)$$

Calculate the maximum volume of ammonia that could be produced at room temperature and atmospheric pressure if 1.95g of sodamide, $NaNH_2$, reacted with excess water. (Relative atomic masses: $H = 1$, $N = 14$, $Na = 23$. One mole of gas molecules at room temperature and atmospheric pressure occupies $24\,000cm^3$.)

(c)   Both sodamide and ammonia could act as fertilisers. State why they could be used for this purpose.

(d)   Treatment of land with fertilisers can cause contamination of rivers. Explain how this could happen with the two substances mentioned in (c) and give one undesirable consequence of the contamination.

†13   The table below gives information about six different gases.

Formula of molecule	HF	N_2	O_2	Ar	CO_2	SO_2
Relative molecular mass	20	28	32	40	44	64
Volume in cm^3 occupied by 1g at room temperature and atmospheric pressure	1200	860	760	600	540	380

Plot a graph of volume (vertical axis) against relative molecular mass (horizontal axis), starting the vertical scale at 300cm^3. Use your graph to predict

(i) the volumes occupied by 1g of hydrogen chloride (HCl) and 1g of ethyne (C_2H_2) at room temperature and atmospheric pressure,

(ii) the formula of a gas which contains only nitrogen and oxygen and of which the volume of 1g is 520cm^3 at room temperature and atmospheric pressure. (Relative atomic masses: H = 1, C = 12, N = 14, O = 16, Cl = 35.5)

[*LEA* spec (A), 3]

MORE NON-METALS: CARBON, SULPHUR, NITROGEN AND CHLORINE

CONTENTS

13.1 CARBON AND ITS COMPOUNDS

1 CARBON – THE ELEMENT

Carbon occurs in nature as the free *element* in diamonds and in small quantities as graphite. The element is also found in many impure forms, such as soot, coke, coal and charcoal. Carbon *compounds* are very common. Many of them have been formed by living animals or plants, e.g. the fossil fuels such as petroleum and natural gas. The most familiar compound of carbon is carbon dioxide, which is found in the air. Many minerals contain carbon, especially carbonates such as calcium carbonate, found as chalk, etc.

PHYSICAL PROPERTIES OF THE ALLOTROPES OF CARBON (SEE p267)
CHEMICAL PROPERTIES OF CARBON

Atoms of carbon have four electrons in their outer shells. They need to lose four electrons, gain four, or share four in order to have a stable electron arrangement. This is very difficult, and so carbon is not very reactive.

1 When heated to a high temperature, in air or oxygen, it burns. Usually no flames are produced; it glows, or it may not show any sign of reaction. (You may have used charcoal bricks for a barbecue. If so, you will know that the reaction produces a lot of heat.) Carbon dioxide is formed:

$$CARBON + OXYGEN \rightarrow CARBON\ DIOXIDE$$
$$C(s) + O_2(g) \rightarrow CO_2(g)$$

2 It will reduce oxides of less reactive metals (p98).

USES OF CARBON

Diamonds: jewellery, cutting and drilling.

Graphite: electrodes, pencil leads, lubricant mixed with oil (explanation, p.267), moderator in nuclear reactors (p47), to purify things because of its ability to absorb gases and coloured impurities.

2 CARBON DIOXIDE, CO$_2$

PHYSICAL PROPERTIES OF CARBON DIOXIDE

State at room temp	Solubility in water	Colour	Odour	Density relative to air	Toxic?
gas	slight	none	none	more dense	only at high concentrations

LABORATORY PREPARATION OF CARBON DIOXIDE

The gas is usually prepared by adding a dilute acid to a carbonate of a metal.

Typical solid reagent: calcium carbonate, CaCO$_3$
Typical liquid reagent: dilute hydrochloric acid, HCl.
No heating needed.

CALCIUM CARBONATE+HYDROCHLORIC ACID →
CARBON DIOXIDE+CALCIUM CHLORIDE+WATER
$CaCO_3(s)+2HCl(aq) \rightarrow CO_2(g)+CaCl_2(aq)+H_2O(l)$

You should be able to suggest a suitable generator and a suitable collecting system from those shown on pp.197–99.

INDUSTRIAL MANUFACTURE OF CARBON DIOXIDE

In industry it is made as a by-product from fermentation reactions (p340) and from natural gas (p220).

CHEMICAL PROPERTIES OF CARBON DIOXIDE

(a) Its effect on burning substances

Carbon dioxide will not allow most substances to burn in it. For example, a burning taper or candle goes out (is **extinguished**) as soon as it is placed in the gas. Magnesium is an exception. Burning magnesium gives out so much heat energy that it continues to burn, even in carbon dioxide. A crackling sound is heard, and white magnesium oxide is formed as well as black specks of carbon.

MAGNESIUM+CARBON DIOXIDE →
MAGNESIUM OXIDE + CARBON
$2 Mg(s)+CO_2(g) \rightarrow 2MgO(s)+C(s)$

This ability to 'put out flames' is used in fire extinguishers. Carbon dioxide is more dense than air and forms a 'blanket' over a burning object. The layer of gas prevents oxygen reaching the flames, and so the fire goes out. (One side of the fire triangle is blocked.) It is very useful because it does not leave a mess after being used (unlike foam) and is harmless once it has diffused away.

Note that the fact that a lighted taper is extinguished by carbon dioxide is **not** a test for the gas. Other gases will also do this, e.g. nitrogen.

(b) Carbon dioxide is a weak acidic gas

As with many oxides of non-metals, carbon dioxide is acidic (p218). It dissolves in water to form a weak acid (carbonic acid, H_2CO_3) and the gas will turn *damp* blue litmus paper a wine-red colour.

(c) The reaction of carbon dioxide with calcium hydroxide solution (lime water): a test for the gas

The reaction between carbon dioxide and calcium hydroxide solution (lime water) is used as a test for the gas (p168):

CARBON DIOXIDE+CALCIUM HYDROXIDE → CALCIUM CARBONATE+WATER

$$CO_2(g) + Ca(OH)_2(aq) \rightarrow CaCO_3(s) + H_2O(l)$$

There is a second stage in this reaction. If carbon dioxide continues to bubble through the solution *after* the precipitate has formed, the cloudy solution goes clear again. The insoluble calcium carbonate formed in the first stage reacts with more carbon dioxide to form *soluble* calcium hydrogen carbonate, which dissolves. This occurs in nature when hard water is formed. See equation and details on p.234.

USES OF CARBON DIOXIDE

(*a*)   In fire extinguishers (p306). The gas is either kept under pressure in the extinguisher, or is made when needed by reacting a carbonate with a dilute acid inside the extinguisher.

(*b*)   When dissolved in water under pressure it makes fizzy drinks.

(*c*)   It is produced when baking powder or 'health salts' are used. Baking powder is a dry mixture of sodium hydrogencarbonate, and a *solid* acid such as tartaric acid. No reaction takes place until water is added. When water is added, the acid reacts with the hydrogen carbonate to form carbon dioxide. The gas helps to make baking mixtures light and spongy. Health salts fizz when water is added because a similar reaction then takes place.

(*d*)   It is used to transfer heat energy from certain kinds of nuclear reactors.

CARBON MONOXIDE, CO   This gas is colourless, has no smell, and is very toxic. It is toxic because it prevents the red blood cells from carrying oxygen round the body. You need to know that

(i) it is a pollutant (p210), and

(ii) it is used in the blast furnace to reduce iron ore to iron (p135). If you have studied any other reactions, revise your notes.

4 THE CARBON CYCLE

Carbon is found in all living things. Nearly all of the carbon atoms on earth have been present since the earth began. These carbon atoms can change partners, and they can be present in different animals and plants, but the same carbon atoms keep 'cycling' round in nature, just like water in the water cycle. It is possible that some of the carbon atoms in your body once formed part of a tree in a forest millions of years ago, then were part of a dinosaur, then part of the wood of a Viking ship, then part of Shakespeare's body, etc. Carbon dioxide is the main 'agent' for transferring atoms of carbon from one partner to another in this cycle. Most of the carbon atoms inside living things 'escape' in the form of carbon dioxide, either during respiration or when they decay after death. A simple carbon cycle is shown in Fig-13.1. (Note also how the carbon dioxide/oxygen balance is changing, p208.)

Fig 13.1 A carbon cycle

Note: It is unlikely that you need to LEARN this cycle, but you must UNDERSTAND it

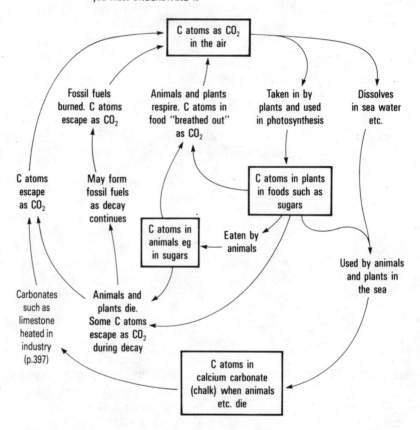

13.2 SULPHUR AND ITS COMPOUNDS

1 SULPHUR – THE ELEMENT

Sulphur occurs naturally as the free *element* in sulphur beds in various parts of the world. It is found in *compounds* in a wide variety of substances, particularly in fossil fuels (coal, oil, natural gas) and in minerals as sulphides or sulphates of metals.

PHYSICAL PROPERTIES OF SULPHUR

Sulphur is a yellow solid. It has a molecular structure and therefore a fairly low melting point (p265). It has allotropes (p266). It is insoluble in water but will dissolve in some organic solvents. It is a typical non-metal – a poor conductor of heat and electricity, and pieces of it are brittle.

INDUSTRIAL SOURCES OF SULPHUR

Some is mined directly as the element, (you may need to understand the **Frasch** process) but most is now obtained by **desulphurising** fossil fuels (p212).

not for IVEA

CHEMICAL PROPERTIES OF SULPHUR

(a) Burning sulphur in air or oxygen (see p.217)

$$SULPHUR + OXYGEN \rightarrow SULPHUR\ DIOXIDE$$
$$S(l) + O_2(g) \rightarrow SO_2(g)$$

(b) The reaction between sulphur and iron

If a mixture of iron and sulphur is heated, the two elements combine together to form a dark grey solid, iron(II) sulphide, FeS. Heat is given out as the two elements combine, and the mixture glows.

$$IRON + SULPHUR \rightarrow IRON(II)\ SULPHIDE$$
$$Fe(s) + S(s) \rightarrow FeS(s)$$

USES OF SULPHUR

1. About 90% of the sulphur which is produced is used for only one purpose – to make sulphuric acid (p310).
2. Smaller quantities are used for a variety of purposes, including making safety matches, vulcanising rubber (making rubber more hard-wearing, e.g. for car tyres), insecticides and fungicides.

2 SULPHUR DIOXIDE, SO_2

This colourless, toxic gas has a very sharp, choking smell. It is included in your syllabus for three main reasons. It is a pollutant (p212), and it is used to make sulphuric acid (p310). If you have also discussed its properties and uses in bleaching (e.g. wood pulp), sterilizing, and preserving food/drink, you should revise them.

3 SULPHURIC ACID, H₂SO₄

Sulphuric acid is one of the most important industrial chemicals. More than 130 million tonnes are made each year, because it has so many uses.

PHYSICAL PROPERTIES OF SULPHURIC ACID

The *dilute* acid looks like water, but the *concentrated* acid is a very dense, **viscous** (thick, difficult to pour), colourless liquid, which must be used with great care.

THE MANUFACTURE OF SULPHURIC ACID BY THE CONTACT PROCESS

Raw materials:
(*a*) sulphur dioxide (formed by burning sulphur);
(*b*) oxygen (obtained from liquid air)
These gases must be pure and dry.
The chemical reactions:

1 Sulphur dioxide reacts with oxygen to form sulphur trioxide, SO_3:

$$\text{SULPHUR DIOXIDE} + \text{OXYGEN} \xrightarrow[\text{catalyst}]{\text{temperature of 500°C}} \text{SULPHUR TRIOXIDE}$$

$$2SO_2(g) + O_2(g) \xrightarrow[\text{catalyst of vanadium oxide}]{\text{temperature 500°C}} 2SO_3(g)$$

[handwritten margin note: Leam Condition, 500°C, Catalyst V_2O_5.]

2 The sulphur trioxide reacts with water to form sulphuric acid. Sulphur trioxide reacts *violently* with pure water, so it is dissolved in the water in concentrated sulphuric acid. This reaction is less violent, and the acid changes into even more concentrated sulphuric acid as the water in it is 'used up'.

SULPHUR TRIOXIDE + WATER (in concentrated sulphuric acid)
→ VERY CONCENTRATED (ALMOST PURE) SULPHURIC ACID
$SO_3(g) + H_2O(l) \rightarrow H_2SO_4(aq)$

Other points:
(*a*) The reaction in 1 is reversible;
(*b*) Some of the concentrated acid formed in (2) is diluted and used again in 1;
(*c*) The high temperature and catalyst are needed to increase the speed of reaction.

ENERGY AND ENVIRONMENT FACTORS IN MAKING SULPHURIC ACID

(*a*)   The reactions are very efficient – very little sulphur dioxide is unused or escapes.

(*b*)   Very little waste of any other kind.

(*c*)   Very efficient in energy. All the reactions are **exothermic** (p357) once started, so there is no need for electricity or fuel for the process. More heat energy is produced than is needed, and so the extra energy is used to produce heating and electricity for other processes. This helps to keep the price of the acid comparatively low.

DANGERS IN USING CONCENTRATED SULPHURIC ACID

The concentrated acid is very **corrosive**, and attacks anything which contains water, including human skin. The acid can cause serious burns if not used with great care. It reacts violently with water, or with any liquid which contains water. For this reason, the concentrated acid must *never* be diluted by adding water to it. The reaction would be so 'energetic' that some of the water would be changed into steam instantly, which would 'spit out' with drops of the acid. It can be diluted by mixing the two liquids 'the other way round', by adding the acid to water. Even this is dangerous, however, and it should be done only by trained people or under supervision. Goggles and gloves should be worn automatically when the concentrated acid is being used.

Large quantities of the acid have to be transported by rail and in road tankers. It would be safer to transport it as the dilute acid, but this would be far too expensive: each load would be mainly water! The acid is transported in concentrated form, and you will have seen tankers carrying it. All display the sign for 'corrosive' (p175), as should bottles of the concentrated acid in the laboratory.

CHEMICAL REACTIONS OF SULPHURIC ACID

The concentrated acid behaves quite differently from the dilute acid. The concentrated acid is *not* a typical acid. Its main type of reaction is described below. In addition, it is a powerful oxidising agent. If you have studied any examples of its use as an oxidising agent, make sure that you revise them.

CONCENTRATED SULPHURIC ACID AS A DEHYDRATING AGENT

The concentrated acid will remove water which is *chemically combined* to another substance. For example, hydrated copper(II) sulphate crystals, $CuSO_4.5H_2O$, are not *wet* but they do contain water. The water is chemically joined to the copper(II) sulphate. If a few drops of concentrated sulphuric acid are added to some blue crystals of hydrated copper(II) sulphate, the acid removes the water. It **dehydrates** the crystals. White, powdered, anhydrous copper(II) sulphate is formed.

$$CuSO_4.5H_2O(s) - 5H_2O \text{ (to concentrated} \rightarrow CuSO_4(s)$$
$$\text{sulphuric acid)}$$

Similarly, if the concentrated acid is added to ordinary sugar (sucrose), it removes combined water in the crystals to leave a black solid, carbon.

$$C_6H_{12}O_6(s) - 6H_2O \text{ (to concentrated} \rightarrow 6C(s)$$
$$\text{(sugar)} \qquad \text{sulphuric acid)}$$

Do not confuse dehydration with drying (p233). Concentrated sulphuric acid can both dry things and dehydrate things. It is often used to dry gases (p199).

CHEMICAL PROPERTIES OF DILUTE SULPHURIC ACID

This is a typical dilute acid, and its reactions have been described in other sections, e.g. with indicators (p177), with metals (p92), with carbonates (p178), with bases (p177). Many of these reactions can be used to make salts (p182).

THE TEST FOR SULPHURIC ACID

Dilute sulphuric acid and dilute hydrochloric acid are difficult to tell apart. They are both typical dilute acids, and give the same reactions. Many students forget that sulphuric acid is, however, a *sulphate*, and so it will give the sulphate test (p168). Similarly, dilute hydrochloric acid is a *chloride* and will give the chloride test (p167).

USES OF SULPHURIC ACID

The acid is used in a *wide* variety of ways. The most important single use is the manufacture of fertilisers. It is also used to make rayon, dyes, plastics, drugs, explosives, and many organic chemicals, especially detergents. A more 'everyday' and obvious use is in car battery acid, but this use is very small indeed compared to the others.

13.3 NITROGEN AND ITS COMPOUNDS. FERTILISERS

1 NITROGEN – THE ELEMENT

Nitrogen occurs naturally as the *element* in the air, forming about 78% by volume. It is also present in a large number of *compounds*. For example, all living things contain proteins, and all proteins contain nitrogen. Some syllabuses require a more detailed study of proteins, using terms such as **amino acids**, and tests to show the presence of proteins (and of nitrogen within them); revise your notes if necessary.

PHYSICAL PROPERTIES OF NITROGEN

Nitrogen is a colourless, odourless, non-toxic gas which has about the same density as air and is slightly soluble in water.

MANUFACTURE OF NITROGEN

From liquid air (p205).

CHEMICAL PROPERTIES OF NITROGEN

Nitrogen is almost inert, or unreactive. There is no positive test for the gas. The only reaction you need to know is its use in the Haber Process (p314).

USES OF NITROGEN

1   Used to make ammonia by the Haber Process. The ammonia is then used to make fertilisers and nitric acid.
2   Liquid nitrogen (temperature approximately −200°C) is used to preserve biological materials (e.g. kidneys for transplants) and to 'freeze dry' foods such as vegetables.
3   Its inertness makes it useful for flushing out oil tanks and pipe lines (any other method might cause fire or explosion) and for storing foods in packages to prevent oxidation (e.g. packets of bacon).

2 AMMONIA, NH_3

PHYSICAL PROPERTIES OF AMMONIA

State at room temperature	Solubility in water	Colour	Odour	Density relative to air	Toxic?	Boiling point (°C)
gas	very high	none	sharp, choking	less dense	yes	−33

Notes

(i) Ammonia is easily changed into a liquid at room temperature by increasing the pressure.

(ii) It is a very unpleasant gas to work with – its sharp smell can make people gasp for breath, and it is likely to make the eyes 'run'.

(iii) The very high solubility of the gas in water is often shown by the *fountain experiment*.

The fountain experiment

A typical apparatus is shown in Fig 13.2. The experiment is done in a fume cupboard. The flask is *filled* with dry ammonia and then sealed, and placed with one tube in water as in the Figure. The clip on the

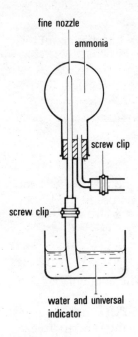

fine nozzle

ammonia

screw clip

screw clip

water and universal indicator

Fig 13.2 The fountain experiment

tube under the water is loosened. After a short delay, water rises rapidly up the tube. It forms a strong jet at the top, and sprays round like a fountain. Eventually water fills or nearly fills the flask. No ammonia can leave the flask and so obviously all the gas which was in the flask has dissolved in the water.

Ammonia gas is *very* soluble in water, and when the clip is opened some of the gas can dissolve in the water in the tube. This *immediately* reduces the pressure inside the flask, and so the atmospheric pressure is suddenly greater than that in the flask. The atmospheric pressure acting upon the surface of the water in the trough forces water up the tube, where more gas dissolves and the process continues. The water is thus forced rapidly up the tube and this continues until all of the gas has dissolved.

THE LABORATORY PREPARATION OF AMMONIA

If you have prepared this gas in the laboratory, make sure that you understand the preparation. In particular, make sure that you understand how the apparatus is linked with the physical properties of the gas, and how the drying agent is linked with the chemical properties of the gas.

THE INDUSTRIAL MANUFACTURE OF AMMONIA BY THE HABER PROCESS

Raw materials

(i) Pure nitrogen gas, obtained from air.
(ii) Pure hydrogen gas, usually obtained from natural gas (p220).

The chemical reaction

$$\text{NITROGEN} + \text{HYDROGEN} \xrightarrow[\text{450°C and catalyst}]{\text{200 atmospheres pressure}} \text{AMMONIA}$$

$$N_2(g) + 3H_2(g) \underset{\text{450°C and iron catalyst}}{\overset{\text{200 atmospheres pressure}}{\rightleftharpoons}} 2NH_3(g)$$

Learn conditions
200 atm.
450°C
Fe catalyst

Other points

1 The reaction is continuous and the ammonia is removed as soon as it is formed.
2 The reaction is reversible.
3 The gases must be pure. Impurities such as any sulphur (from natural gas) would poison the catalyst.
4 The high temperature and the catalyst are used to speed up the reaction. The high pressure also 'squeezes' the gas molecules closer together, making them react more quickly.

ENERGY AND ENVIRONMENT FACTORS

Four of the eight ammonia plants in Britain are at Billingham on the River Tees. They were built there because of good transport facilities (road, rail and sea) and because of the availability of raw materials. The hydrogen, for example, was at one time manufactured by reacting coke with steam. The coke was made from coal obtained from the nearby coal fields.

The process is fairly clean. Very little ammonia escapes into the air, or into the large quantities of water which are used for cooling. The only solid waste is the occasional 'used catalyst'. The main reaction, and the formation of hydrogen from natural gas, are *exothermic*. Once started, the process produces a great deal of energy as heat. Some of this heat is converted into electricity by producing steam to drive turbines. The process produces its own energy, therefore, for warming up the gases and to compress them to 200 atmospheres.

CHEMICAL PROPERTIES OF AMMONIA

(a) Ammonia is a base

Ammonia gas is a base. As it is soluble in water, it is also an **alkali**. It is the only common alkaline *gas*, and this property is used as a test for the gas, (p168). As it is a base, the gas will **neutralise** acids to form a salt. Salts of ammonia are called **ammonium salts**. Ammonium salts are important fertilisers.

Notes

(i) Although the formula of ammonia gas is NH_3, the **ammonium radical** is NH_4. (This forms the ion NH_4^-.) Some common ammonium salts are ammonium chloride, NH_4Cl, ammonium nitrate, NH_4NO_3, and ammonium sulphate, $(NH_4)_2SO_4$.

(ii) Ammonia gas is a base because it can combine with a proton from an acid (p179):

$$NH_3(g) + H^+(aq) \rightarrow NH_4^+(aq)$$

(b) Ammonia solution

When ammonia dissolves in water, *some* of it reacts with water to form ammonium hydroxide:

$$NH_3(g) + H_2O(l) \rightarrow NH_4OH(aq)$$

This solution is called **ammonia solution**. As the solution contains OH^- ions, it has all of the properties of an alkali, including the fact that it will precipitate insoluble hydroxides of metals (p162). The *concentrated* solution must be treated with great caution. When the stopper is released from the bottle, ammonia gas escapes, and a sudden reaction to this can cause an accident.

USES OF AMMONIA

The Haber Process which is used to make ammonia is one of the most important industrial processes. Most of the ammonia is used to make fertilisers, the importance of which is discussed on p.317. It is also used in smaller quantities in solution as a household cleaning agent to remove grease; in liquid form as a refrigerant; and to manufacture ammonium salts which have their own special uses. It is also used to make nylon and to manufacture nitric acid.

not for NEA.

3 NITRIC ACID, HNO₃

Nitric acid is manufactured from ammonia. (If your syllabus includes an outline of the manufacturing process, revise your notes.) The concentrated acid is a very reactive, corrosive liquid which must be used with great care. It is also a powerful oxidising agent.

The dilute acid has all the properties of dilute acids, except that it does not normally cause hydrogen to be formed when it reacts with metals, unlike most acids. When nitric acid reacts with metals, the brown gas nitrogen dioxide, NO_2, is formed. You may have used the dilute acid to make salts by reacting it with bases, alkalis or carbonates. The salts formed are nitrates.

4 THE NITROGEN CYCLE. THE WORLD FOOD PROBLEM

Nitrogen is vital to all living things. It is found in animals and plants in compounds called **proteins**. Animals cannot make proteins – they need to obtain them by eating other animals or plants. Plants _can_ make their own proteins. They take nitrogen compounds into their roots from the soil, and change these compounds into proteins. Nitrogen atoms are recycled in nature in a similar way to carbon atoms in the carbon cycle (p308). However, although nitrogen forms nearly 80% of the air by volume, it has very little direct part in the nitrogen cycle. Most animals and plants cannot use nitrogen as an element, in the air, because it is so unreactive. It has to be changed into _compounds_ of nitrogen before it can be used by most living things. This change, from the almost unreactive and 'useless' element into useful, soluble compounds is called **fixing nitrogen**.

It is useful to think of the nitrogen cycle starting with these soluble nitrogen compounds in the soil. The cycle is completed by returning nitrogen compounds to the soil. The main steps in the cycle are shown in Fig 13.3.

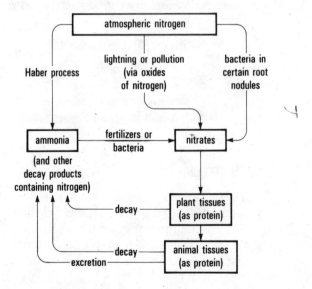

Fig 13.3 A simple nitrogen cycle

HOW NITROGEN COMPOUNDS ENTER THE SOIL

1   From animal waste, e.g. manure.
2   From fertilisers.
3   By the decay of dead animals and plants.
4   As very dilute nitric acid, formed when lightning causes some nitrogen in the air to form oxides of nitrogen. These oxides are also formed as on p213. The oxides dissolve in rain to form very dilute nitric acid.
5   From roots of certain plants such as peas, beans and clover. These plants are unusual. They *can* use nitrogen directly from the air, and change it into nitrogen compounds in their roots. (Actually, it is not the plants themselves which do this, but rather bacteria which live in their roots.)

WHAT HAPPENS TO NITROGEN COMPOUNDS IN THE SOIL

The various nitrogen compounds which enter the soil are all changed by bacteria into nitrates. Nitrates are soluble and can be absorbed easily by plant roots.

HOW THE NITROGEN CYCLE HAS BECOME UNBALANCED

The *natural* cycle was in balance for centuries. There was no need to add artificial fertilisers, made from ammonia. The branch in the cycle which involves the Haber Process used to make ammonia (Fig 13.3) is *not* part of the natural cycle. We have had to add it in order to keep the cycle in balance.

The world's population continues to grow at a rapid rate. We need to produce more and more food in order to keep people alive. Unfortunately, it is becoming more difficult to produce enough food. If fields are used to grow *as much as possible* in the *shortest possible time* the soil becomes low in nitrogen compounds. There is no time to let nature build up the nitrogen in the soil (through the nitrogen cycle) before the next crop must be sown or planted. We need, therefore, to 'fix' nitrogen atoms from the air, and add the soluble nitrogen compounds produced to the soil as **fertilisers**. We are giving nature a helping hand. The compounds used as fertilisers vary, but they are all made from ammonia if they contain nitrogen. Compounds used include ammonium salts, urea, nitrates or even ammonia itself.

In spite of the use of fertilisers, at least half of the people in the world are still suffering from some kind of food shortage. Scientists are tackling the food problem by:

(*a*)   developing improved strains of crops,
(*b*)   making better and safer pesticides, fungicides and herbicides (which allow plants to grow more efficiently but excess of which can cause pollution),
(*c*)   encouraging a fall in the birth rate, and

(*d*)   improving the amount of food which can be produced from a given area of land, e.g. by using fertilisers.

5 FERTILISERS AND SOIL pH

SOIL pH

If soil is left to nature, it usually becomes more acidic. This happens because calcium compounds (which are used to neutralise acidity) are gradually 'washed out' (**leached**), and because of acid rain. An acid soil is useful for growing some plants, but most vegetables and other farm crops give their best yields when grown in soils which are neutral or only slightly acidic. Calcium hydroxide (commonly called hydrated lime or slaked lime) or calcium carbonate (limestone) are added to soils to neutralise any extra acidity. The use of these compounds is also important in another way. Plants need calcium ions as part of their 'food', and these compounds therefore also act as a plant food.

WHICH ELEMENTS DO PLANTS NEED?

Plants produce their own sugar-type foods by photosynthesis (p208). In addition, plants need many other substances for growth and for chemical reactions which take place within them. These other substances are usually taken in in solution through the roots. All plants probably need traces of most of the elements, but the main ones they need are nitrogen, phosphorus, potassium (and calcium). The other elements, needed in small amounts, are called *trace elements*.

The 'big three' elements are often referred to by their chemical symbols, N,P and K. The main reasons why plants need these elements are given in Table 13.1.

Table 13.1 Why nitrogen, phosphorus and potassium are needed by plants

	Nitrogen (N)	Phosphorus (P)	Potassium (K)
Why plants need the mineral	Increases growth of stem and leaf. Helps build up chlorophyll	For root growth (∴ especially important for root crops). Accelerates ripening of the crop and also seed formation. Strengthens stems. Essential for seed germination	Not fully understood, but seems particularly important in the development of fruit and seeds, and in maintaining the general chemical reactions occurring in the plant. Promotes resistance to disease
Outward signs of deficiency	Undersized leaves, poor growth rate. Leaves pale green or often yellow	Poor root system. Stunted growth, small leaves. Leaves fall prematurely, less blossom than normal, low yield of grain or fruit. Dull, blue-green leaves	Edges of leaves turn yellow and eventually brown. Leaves may die early
Outward signs of excess	Growth too rapid – plant becomes too soft and is less resistant to disease and bad weather	Crop ripens too early, ∴ yields low	–

THE CHEMICALS USED AS FERTILISERS

Just as the nitrogen cycle no longer replaces the nitrogen which is taken out of the soil so quickly, phosphorus and potassium are also removed at faster rates than they can be replaced naturally. Animal manure and rotted vegetable waste (compost) are added to soils, and these contain all the main elements, and many of the others. However, the proportions of these elements in manure, etc. is very small, and they cannot replace the elements removed by most crops.

A fertiliser which is used to add nitrogen to the soil is often called a **nitrogenous** fertiliser. The main one is ammonium nitrate, NH_4NO_3. (You might like to calculate the percentage of nitrogen in this compound, as on p291. Note that the N symbol occurs twice in the formula.) Others include ammonium sulphate, $(NH_4)_2SO_4$, ammonia itself, and urea, $(NH_2)_2CO$.

The main fertilisers which supply phosphorus are phosphates such as calcium phosphate, $Ca_3(PO_4)_2$. The main fertiliser which supplies potassium is potassium chloride, KCl.

WHY ARE MANY DIFFERENT KINDS OF FERTILISER MADE? (see p291)

13.4 CHLORINE AND THE OTHER HALOGENS

1 CHLORINE – THE ELEMENT

Chlorine is not found naturally as the *element*, but it is widespread in *compounds* such as sodium chloride (in rock salt and in sea water).

PHYSICAL PROPERTIES OF CHLORINE

State at room temperature	Solubility in water	Colour	Odour	Density relative to air	Toxic?	Boiling point (°C)
gas	slightly soluble	pale green	sharp, choking	more dense	yes	−33

THE PREPARATION AND MANUFACTURE OF CHLORINE

If you have prepared chlorine in the laboratory, revise the method and apparatus used, and make sure that you understand why it is prepared and collected in this way.

Chlorine is a very important industrial chemical. It is manufactured by the electrolysis of sodium chloride solution (p114). It is also obtained by the electrolysis of molten sodium chloride (p116), but the main purpose of this last reaction is to produce sodium rather than chlorine. Chlorine is often transported in cylinders, for use in swimming pools, etc. The gas is very reactive and toxic. Each cylinder must be marked with signs for 'toxic' and 'oxidising agent' (p175). The gas must be used and transported with care.

CHEMICAL PROPERTIES OF CHLORINE

(a) Direct reaction with other elements to form chlorides

Chlorine is very reactive, and combines with many elements to form their chlorides. Two common examples are:

(i) Sodium If a small piece of sodium is made to burn on a combustion spoon and then placed in a gas jar of chlorine, the metal continues to burn with a yellow flame to form dense, white clouds of solid sodium chloride.

$$SODIUM + CHLORINE \rightarrow SODIUM\ CHLORIDE$$
$$2Na(l) + Cl_2(g) \rightarrow 2NaCl(s)$$

(ii) Magnesium If a piece of magnesium ribbon is made to burn on a combustion spoon and then placed in a gas jar of chlorine, it continues to burn with a white flame, forming dense white clouds of solid magnesium chloride.

$$MAGNESIUM + CHLORINE \rightarrow MAGNESIUM\ CHLORIDE$$
$$Mg(s) + Cl_2(g) \rightarrow MgCl_2(s)$$

You may have seen the reaction between chlorine and iron, or perhaps you have compared how the different halogens react with iron. If so, revise your notes carefully. Chlorine reacts rapidly with hot iron wool to form a black, shiny solid, iron(III) chloride. Bromine reacts less rapidly with iron wool, and a mixture of iron(II) bromide (yellow crystals) and iron(III) bromide (black crystals) is formed. When iodine vapour is passed over heated iron wool, there is little sign of a reaction, although some iron(II) iodide (a red solid) may be formed.

Note that as chlorine is a powerful oxidising agent, it removes three electrons from each iron atom when it reacts with iron wool, to form iron(III) chloride, not iron(II) chloride. (See definition of oxidation using electrons, p130.)

(b) Chlorine as a bleaching agent

In the presence of moisture, chlorine rapidly bleaches coloured flowers, litmus paper, inks, and indeed any substance coloured with a vegetable dye. The chlorine reacts with moisture to form an acid solution, which does the actual bleaching. Compounds of chlorine are safer to use than chlorine itself, and many of them are used as bleaches.

(c) The test for chlorine gas

This makes use of chlorine's ability to form an acid with water, which then acts as a bleach (p168).

(d) Chlorine as an oxidising agent

Chlorine is a powerful oxidising agent. Its bleaching action is really an oxidation – it oxidises dyes to colourless products. Common examples of its oxidising reactions are:

1 Displacement of other halogens from their salts (p260). The chlorine atoms *remove* electrons from the other substance and become chloride ions. (Definition, p130.)
2 If chlorine is bubbled through solutions of iron(II) salts, they are oxidised to iron(III) salts. Each Fe^{2+} ion loses an electron (to a chlorine atom) and becomes an Fe^{3+} ion, e.g.:

$$2FeCl_2(aq) + Cl_2(g) \rightarrow 2FeCl_3(aq) \text{ or, ionically,}$$
$$2Fe^{2+}(aq) + Cl_2(g) \rightarrow 2Fe^{3+}(aq) + 2Cl^-(aq)$$

See also its reaction with iron metal in (a).

(e) Reaction between chlorine and sodium hydroxide solution
(Included in NISEC syllabus; revise if necessary.)

USES OF CHLORINE

(a)   Preparation of bleaches (used in industry to bleach cotton, etc.). Safety note: There are several types of household bleaches. Different bleaches should never be mixed. Similarly, a bleach should not be mixed with any other type of cleaning agent such as ammonia solution. If a chlorine-based bleach is mixed with another substance, there is a possibility of a reaction. Chlorine gas, for example, may be formed.

(b)   To kill bacteria in drinking water (p231).

(c)   To kill bacteria in swimming pools.

(d)   In the manufacture of one of the most important plastics, poly(chloroethane), commonly called PVC.

(e)   The preparation of 'chlorinated solvents' used (for example) in dry cleaning, for degreasing metals and as thinners for liquid paper.

---

2 HYDROGEN CHLORIDE AND HYDROCHLORIC ACID

If you have studied some of the properties of the *gas* hydrogen chloride, revise your notes. The properties of its solution, hydrochloric acid, have been given as a typical dilute acid throughout the book.

---

3 THE HALOGENS: GROUP 7 OF THE PERIODIC TABLE

The general chemistry of chlorine, bromine and iodine as members of Group 7 of the Periodic Table is discussed on p260. Note also that the halogens all combine with hydrogen to form **hydrogen halides** such as hydrogen chloride, HCl, hydrogen bromide, HBr, and hydrogen iodide, HI.

1 Why do farmers and gardeners sometimes leave the *roots* of beans in the soil after the crop has been picked?

2 Fig 13.4 shows a 'jumbled-up' nitrogen cycle. Try to re-write it so that the steps are in a correct pattern, and compare your answer with the one shown on p316.

Fig 13.4 An incorrect nitrogen cycle

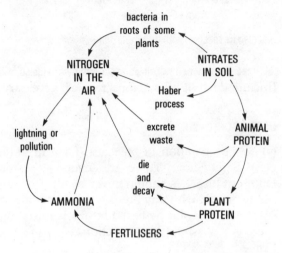

3 Why do you think that, of all the nitrogen-based fertilisers, urea, $(NH_2)_2CO$, is the most economical to transport over long distances?

4 Gardeners are always advised not to add calcium hydroxide to freshly-manured soil. Can you suggest why? You may find the following useful.
  (i) Calcium hydroxide has the typical properties of a hydroxide of a metal.
  (ii) Manure contains valuable ammonium compounds.

5 Use this book, and your notes, (not necessarily your memory!) to work out answers to this question. How, starting from sulphuric acid and one other compound in each case, could you make a sample of each of the following?
  (i) crystals of sodium sulphate -10-water,
  (ii) crystals of magnesium sulphate -7-water,
  (iii) barium sulphate,
  (iv) carbon.

6 Look up information in your notes and in this book to answer this question. A pale green solution forms a dirty-green precipitate when sodium hydroxide solution is added to it. Another sample of the same pale green solution changes to a brown colour when chlorine is bubbled through it. This brown solution then forms a red-brown solid when sodium hydroxide is added to it. Can you suggest an explanation for these facts?

| CHECK LIST ▶ | REMEMBER THAT SOME OF THESE POINTS MAY NOT BE RELEVANT FOR THE PARTICULAR SYLLABUS YOU ARE FOLLOWING. |

YOU SHOULD UNDERSTAND THE FOLLOWING POINTS.

1 ▶ Carbon, carbon dioxide, carbon monoxide – properties and uses according to your syllabus.
2 ▶ The carbon cycle.
3 ▶ Sulphur, and sulphur dioxide; properties and uses according to your syllabus.
4 ▶ The Contact Process for the manufacture of sulphuric acid.
5 ▶ Properties of concentrated sulphuric acid.
6 ▶ Properties of dilute sulphuric acid.
7 ▶ Nitrogen, ammonia, and dilute nitric acid; properties and uses according to your syllabus.
8 ▶ The Haber Process for the manufacture of ammonia.
9 ▶ The manufacture of nitric acid.
10 ▶ The nitrogen cycle; fertilisers.
11 ▶ Chlorine, hydrogen chloride, and dilute hydrochloric acid; properties and uses according to your syllabus.

SPECIMEN EXAMINATION QUESTIONS

SEE GENERAL NOTE BEFORE QUESTIONS ON pp49 AND 50. REMEMBER THAT YOU MAY BE ALLOWED TO USE A DATA BOOK IN THE EXAMINATION.

1–5 The answers to questions 1 to 5 should be chosen from the following list of gases. Each gas should be used only once. Ammonia, carbon dioxide, hydrogen, oxygen, sulphur dioxide:

1 is used in fire extinguishers
2 dissolves in water forming a solution which turns litmus blue
3 is added to food to preserve it
4 is used in the manufacture of margarine
5 is used to produce steel from impure iron.   [NEA spec (A), 1]
6 Which **one** of these substances is **not** a form of carbon?
   A diamond   B calcium   C coke   D charcoal   E graphite
7 When carbon burns completely in oxygen and the product of burning is dissolved in water, the pH of the solution would be approximately
   A 1   B 5   C 7   D 9   E 11
   Questions 8–11. In questions 8 to 11 choose from the following list the letter representing the chlorine-containing compounds described by the statement in the question.
   A ammonium chloride   B calcium chloride   C hydrogen chloride   D polyvinylchloride   E sodium chloride
   Select the compound which
8 is covalent and reacts with water to give chloride ions.
9 consists of covalent molecules of high molecular mass.
10 decomposes on gentle heating to give two compounds.

11 is produced commercially in an impure state when sea water is evaporated. [*NISEC* spec 1]

12 Use the diagram of the carbon cycle in the data booklet for this question.

(*a*)   What process provides plants with the carbon compounds they need?

(*b*)   What substance other than carbon dioxide is used up in this process?

(*c*)   Give one difference between the formation of coal and the formation of oil.

13 (*a*)   The flow diagram (Fig 13.5) shows the main stages in producing nitric acid from ammonia.

(i) Name the catalyst.

(ii) What is the substance I, formed in the catalyst chamber?

(iii) Why does the flow diagram not show the catalyst being added to the catalyst chamber?

(iv) Name the substance X, added to the absorber.

(*b*)   When a green powder is added to dilute nitric acid, carbon dioxide gas is given off and a blue solution forms:

green powder + nitric acid → carbon dioxide + blue solution

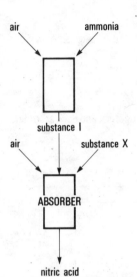

Fig 13.5
Diagram for
question 13

Name the green powder.

(*c*)   The nitrogen cycle in the data book may help you to answer this part of the question. Nitrates are used as fertilisers.

(i) What type of compound do plants make from nitrates?

(ii) Why cannot atmospheric nitrogen be used directly by most green plants?

(iii) Why does nitrate fertiliser often cause water pollution?

(iv) Give one effect of nitrate pollution of water.

(v) Plants absorb very little nitrogen in the form of ammonium compounds. How is ammonium sulphate therefore able to act as a fertiliser?

(vi) Which of the two compounds ammonium nitrate (NH_4NO_3) and ammonium sulphate [$(NH_4)_2SO_4$], contains the highest proportion by mass of nitrogen? Show how you arrive at your answer. (Relative atomic masses: N 14, H 1, S 32, O 16) [*SEG* spec 1]

14 Information about some common fertilisers is given in the following table.

Name	Formula	Solubility in water
Ammonium phosphate	$(NH_4)_3PO_4$	Readily soluble
	NH_4NO_3	Readily soluble
Potassium nitrate	KNO_3	Readily soluble
Urea	$CO(NH_2)_2$	Dissolves slowly

(*a*)   Name the compound whose formula is NH_4NO_3.

(b)   Calculate the mass of one mole of urea. (Relative atomic masses: H 1, C 12, N 14, O 16.)

(c)   Why is urea a slow-acting fertiliser?

(d)   How can good plant growth be maintained if chemical fertilisers like those in the table are *not* used?

(e)   Another substance which may be added to soil is hydrated lime, $Ca(OH)_2$.

(i) What is the chemical name for hydrated lime?

(ii) What is the main reason for adding hydrated lime to soil?

(iii) Why should hydrated lime and ammonium phosphate *not* be applied to the soil at the same time?

[*SEG* spec (Alt), 2]

15   Carbon dioxide can be prepared by adding hydrochloric acid to calcium carbonate.

(a)   (i) Name the salt produced by the reaction.

(ii) What else is produced by the reaction, besides the salt and carbon dioxide?

(b)   (i) When a gas jar containing carbon dioxide is upturned over a burning splint (Fig 13.6), the flame goes out.
What **two** properties of carbon dioxide does this illustrate?

(ii) What piece of equipment used widely in everyday life makes use of these properties?

(c)   If a piece of magnesium is burned in a gas jar of carbon dioxide, a white powder and particles of a black solid are formed.

(i) What is the black solid?

(ii) What is the white powder?

(iii) Write a word equation for the reaction in (c).

[*LEA* spec (A), 2]

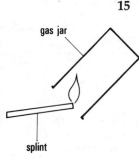

gas jar

splint

Fig 13.6 Diagram for question 15(b)

16   This question concerns sulphuric acid (H_2SO_4) and its manufacture by the contact process.

The starting materials used in the contact process are sulphur dioxide and oxygen. The sulphur dioxide is obtained from a variety of sources:

(i) by burning sulphur

$$S(s)+O_2(g) \rightarrow SO_2(g)$$

(ii) by burning ores which contain sulphur; iron pyrites (FeS_2) and zinc blende (ZnS) are commonly used

(iii) by burning the hydrogen sulphide which occurs in some natural gas

$$2H_2S(g)+3O_2(g) \rightarrow 2SO_2(g)+2H_2(g)$$

The sulphur dioxide is dried, purified and mixed with pure, dry air. The mixture is heated to about 450°C and then passed into a converter containing a catalyst (either vanadium(V) oxide or platinum). The sulphur dioxide is oxidised by the oxygen to sulphur trioxide

$$2SO_2(g)+O_2(g) \rightarrow 2SO_3(g)$$

Sulphur trioxide can be converted into sulphuric acid by adding it to water. However, direct dissolving of sulphur trioxide in water produces practical problems in industry.

(*a*)   Name two sources of sulphur dioxide

(*b*)   What is the chemical name for zinc blende?

(*c*)   Explain what is meant by 'The sulphur dioxide is oxidised'.

(*d*)   (i) In the equation

$$2SO_2(g) + O_2(g) \rightleftharpoons 2SO_3(g)$$

what does the symbol $\rightleftharpoons$ show?

(ii) Where does the oxygen come from in this reaction?

(*e*)   The catalyst in the converter is expensive and can be easily ruined.

(i) Why is the high cost worthwhile?

(ii) What precaution is taken to protect the catalyst?

(*f*)   Explain why the escape of sulphur dioxide from a factory producing sulphuric acid is unwise for

(i) economic and

(ii) environmental reasons.

(*g*)   Write word and balanced symbolic equations for the reaction that takes place when sulphur trioxide is added to water.

[*LEA* spec (B), 2]

ORGANIC CHEMISTRY. PLASTICS

CONTENTS

14.1 THE ALKANE FAMILY

1 WHAT ARE ORGANIC CHEMICALS?

Organic chemicals are compounds of *carbon*. (Carbon monoxide, carbon dioxide and the carbonates are also compounds of carbon, but they are not called organic chemicals, however.) Carbon can form millions of organic compounds because carbon atoms can join to *each other* by *strong* covalent bonds to form long chains of atoms. These chains can be of any length (e.g. two carbon atoms only, or several hundred carbon atoms) and can have any number of branches. Other elements cannot form long chains of atoms in this way. In spite of the complicated chains which are possible, most of the atoms in any organic chemical will be of carbon and hydrogen only.

2 THE ALKANES – A GROUP OF HYDROCARBONS

Compounds which contain *only* hydrogen and carbon are called **hydrocarbons**. There are many different hydrocarbons and so they are divided into smaller groups. The simplest of these groups is called the **alkanes**. The alkanes are a group of hydrocarbons in which all the bonds between the atoms are **single covalent** bonds (p34). (Revise the meaning of **homologous series** if you have used this expression.)

THE FIRST FEW MEMBERS OF THE ALKANE GROUP

All of the members have a name ending in -**ane**. The names and formulas of the first three members of the group are shown in Table 14.1. Each member has a different number of carbon atoms in its molecules. Note that when you draw a structural formula, each carbon atom must have four 'sticks' (four covalent bonds) and each hydrogen atom must have one 'stick'. Any other compound you might draw would not exist, and it certainly could not be an alkane. The structural formula

$$
\begin{array}{ccccccc}
 & H & & & & H & \\
 & | & & & & | & \\
H- & C & -H- & H- & C & -H \\
\end{array}
$$

adds up to C_2H_6 but it is *not* ethane! In fact, it could not possibly exist, because

(*a*)   each carbon atom has only three 'sticks', and

(*b*)   two of the hydrogen atoms have two 'sticks'.

Can you understand this? Compare it with the correct structure for ethane in Table 14.1.

Table 14.1 The first three alkanes

Name	Number of C atoms	Molecular formula	Structural formula
methane	1	CH_4	H $\mid$ H—C—H $\mid$ H
ethane	2	C_2H_6	H H $\mid$ $\mid$ H—C—C—H $\mid$ $\mid$ H H
propane	3	C_3H_8	H H H $\mid$ $\mid$ $\mid$ H—C—C—C—H $\mid$ $\mid$ $\mid$ H H H

The *first* part of each name in an organic substance tells us how many carbon atoms are present in a molecule of the substance. The ending of each name tells us which group the substance belongs to. For example, **meth** is the beginning which means one carbon atom, **eth** means two, and **prop** means three. Methane is therefore an alkane with one carbon atom per molecule, and ethane is an alkane with two carbon atoms per molecule. Ethane, ethene, ethyne, and ethanol are different organic chemicals, but they all begin with **eth**. This tells us that each of them has two carbon atoms per molecule. The ending tells us the group each belongs to. Ethane is an al**kane**, ethene is an al**kene**, ethyne is an al**kyne** and ethanol is an alcoh**ol**.

ISOMERISM

The fourth member of the alkanes is called **butane**. Butane has the molecular formula C_4H_{10}. Butane is different from the first three members. There are two different ways of arranging the atoms in a molecule of butane. We can show this only by drawing the structural formulas of the two 'varieties', because the molecular formula is exactly the same in each case, C_4H_{10}.

When two or more structures exist which have the same molecular formula but different structures, they are called **isomers**. The examples above are isomers of butane. They contain exactly the same number and kind of atoms, but they are arranged differently. Isomers are quite different from each other. They are different compounds.

The number of isomers per substance increases rapidly in the later members of the alkane group. You might like to try drawing the three isomers of pentane, C_5H_{12}, but you do not need to learn them. If you try this, do not confuse the structures:

They are in fact the same. Each contains five carbon atoms in a continuous chain. No matter how we twist or bend the chain, we cannot hide the fact that the structures are the same.

PHYSICAL PROPERTIES OF THE ALKANES

The first members of any organic group are often gases at room temperature and pressure. As the molecules get bigger down the group, the substances are liquids at room temperature and pressure, and later ones are solids. In other words, the melting and boiling points of the members of a group tend to increase as the molecules get bigger. The alkanes follow this pattern. The first four members are gases, although it is very easy to change the third one, propane, and the fourth one, butane, into liquids at room temperature by increasing the pressure. These are often sold as fuels in liquid form. The fifth one, pentane, is a liquid at room temperature. Later members are solids, such as candle fat, which is a mixture of alkanes.

Alkanes are formed naturally when vegetable or animal material rots. Some fossil fuels consist almost entirely of alkanes. Natural gas consists mainly of only one alkane, methane.

PHYSICAL PROPERTIES OF METHANE (A TYPICAL ALKANE)

State at room temperature	Solubility in water	Colour	Odour	Density relative to air	Toxic?
gas	insoluble	none	none	les dense	no

Note

(i) Liquid alkanes are less dense than water and, being immiscible with water, will float on its surface.

(ii) Pure methane has no smell, but natural gas has an odour because a substance is deliberately added to it to make any escape of gas obvious.

AN IMPORTANT CHEMICAL PROPERTY OF THE ALKANES: COMBUSTION

Alkanes contain only *single* covalent bonds. Such compounds are called **saturated**. Saturated compounds cannot 'add' anything on to their molecules because they are already 'full' – every bond in the molecule is fully used. An alkane can react only by breaking some bonds within its molecules. This happens when they burn in air or oxygen (Fig 14.1).

Fig 14.1 The breaking of bonds inside a methane molecule when it reacts

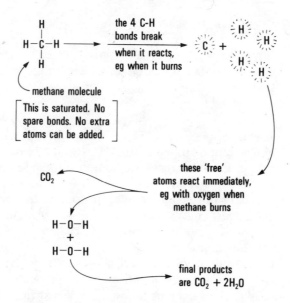

Many of the alkanes burn very easily, giving out a great deal of heat energy when they do so. For this reason, many of them are used as fuels. The products formed when they burn are always the same, no matter which alkane is being burned. The *carbon* atoms inside the molecules always form carbon dioxide, CO_2 (but see p210). The *hydrogen* atoms always form steam, which condenses to liquid water. E.g.:

$$\text{METHANE} + \text{OXYGEN} \rightarrow \text{CARBON DIOXIDE} + \text{STEAM}$$
$$CH_4(g) + 2O_2(g) \rightarrow CO_2(g) + 2H_2O(g)$$
$$\text{ETHANE} + \text{OXYGEN} \rightarrow \text{CARBON DIOXIDE} + \text{STEAM}$$
$$2C_2H_6(g) + 7O_2(g) \rightarrow 4CO_2(g) + 6H_2O(g)$$

(Revise any examples of **substitution** reactions of alkanes if you have studied them. The WJEC syllabus, for example, includes the reactions of alkanes with chlorine.)

USES OF METHANE AND OTHER ALKANES AS FUELS

1 Methane is a fuel, as natural gas.

2 Propane is kept as a liquid under pressure, e.g. in cylinders. When a tap is opened, pressure is released and some liquid changes into gas. Propane is used as a 'gas' fuel in this way, e.g. in large tanks as a household gas where there is no piped gas. On a smaller scale it is used in portable cylinders for fuel in caravans, etc.

3 Butane is also used as a fuel. Like propane, it is kept as a liquid under pressure. Butane is used as cigarette-lighter fuel, and for camping as 'camping gaz'.

4 Other alkanes are also used as fuels, e.g. petrol contains a mixture of liquid alkanes.

14.2 THE ALKENES – ANOTHER FAMILY OF HYDROCARBONS

The alkenes are another group of hydrocarbons because, like the alkanes, they contain carbon and hydrogen only. The difference between the two is the kind of covalent bonds within their molecules. In an alkene there is at least one **double covalent** bond between two carbon atoms, (p34). This is shown by placing a 'double stick' between the two carbon atoms. For example, the structural formula of ethene, the first member of the group, is:

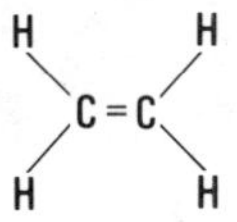

$$
\begin{array}{ccc}
H & & H \\
\diagdown & & \diagup \\
& C = C & \\
\diagup & & \diagdown \\
H & & H
\end{array}
$$

Compare this with ethane, the *alkane* which also has two carbon atoms inside its molecules:

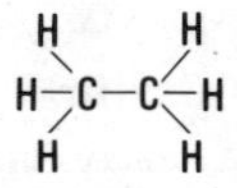

$$
\begin{array}{ccc}
H & & H \\
\diagdown & & \diagup \\
H - C & - & C - H \\
\diagup & & \diagdown \\
H & & H
\end{array}
$$

You will notice that in the alkene, each carbon atom which forms the double bond uses two of its four bonds in making the double bond. Each carbon atom which forms a double bond therefore has only two other bonds left. In an *alkane*, every carbon atom uses one bond to join to the next carbon atom (except in methane) and then has three bonds left to join to other atoms, e.g. to H or another C atom.

The first two members of the alkenes are called **ethene** and **propene**. Their structures are shown below. The first two members are gases at room temperature and pressure. ('Methene' does not exist.)

	Molecular formula	Structural formula
ethene	C_2H_4	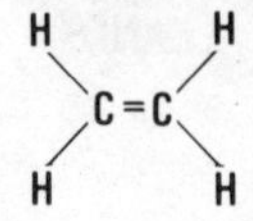
propene	C_3H_6	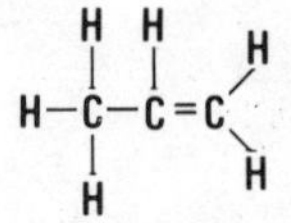

CHEMICAL PROPERTIES OF THE ALKENES

Alkenes are more reactive than alkanes. It is the C=C bond which makes them reactive. Compounds which contain one or more double covalent bonds are **unsaturated**. Such molecules can form 'spare bonds' without causing the molecule to break apart. For example, if the *double* bond in a molecule of ethene *breaks* and becomes a *single* bond, then:

(i) all of the atoms in the molecule are still held together, and
(ii) two 'spare bonds' are formed on the carbon atoms.

This kind of reaction happens quite easily. We describe the alkenes as unsaturated because their molecules are not yet 'filled'. If the double bond breaks as shown above, we can **add** two more atoms to the 'spare bonds' and make a bigger molecule, with more atoms in it than before. The bigger molecule is then saturated – we cannot add any more atoms to it. The alkanes are already saturated, and cannot add other atoms.

When an unsaturated molecule reacts like this we call the reaction an **addition reaction**. We have added two molecules together to make *one*, new, larger, saturated molecule. E.g.:

HYDROGEN+ETHENE → ETHANE (an alkane)
$H_2(g)+C_2H_4(g) \rightarrow C_2H_6(g)$

or,

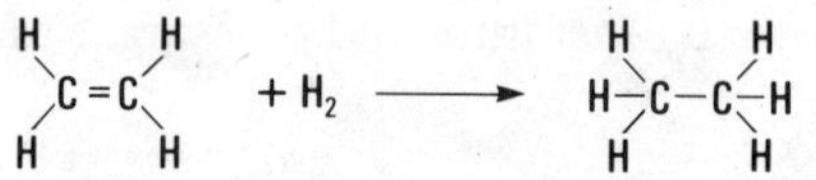

Summary of this section: alkenes are unsaturated hydrocarbons. They are very reactive. They take part in addition reactions.

EXAMPLES OF ADDITION REACTIONS OF THE ALKENES

1 How alkenes make plastics and other polymers

Many common plastics are made from alkenes, or from other unsaturated molecules. These plastics are made by *adding* a large number of unsaturated molecules together, to form a large, saturated molecule. Plastics or other polymers made like this are called **addition polymers**. This is described in more detail in the next section. To use a simple example, large numbers of ethene molecules can be added together to form the plastic poly(ethene), commonly called poly-thene. It is an addition reaction because two or more molecules react together to become one. The following equation shows how two molecules of ethene can add together.

$$
\begin{array}{ccc}
\overset{H}{\underset{H}{}}C=C\overset{H}{\underset{H}{}} & + & \overset{H}{\underset{H}{}}C=C\overset{H}{\underset{H}{}}
\end{array}
\longrightarrow
\quad
\text{SPARE}-\overset{H}{\underset{H}{C}}-\overset{H}{\underset{H}{C}}-\overset{H}{\underset{H}{C}}-\overset{H}{\underset{H}{C}}-\text{SPARE}
$$

The process can then continue. When poly(ethene) is being made, hundreds of molecules of ethene join together like this to form a long chain. We can show this 'whole reaction' like this (n means a very large number):

$$
n\left[\begin{array}{c}\overset{H}{\underset{H}{}}C=C\overset{H}{\underset{H}{}}\end{array}\right] \longrightarrow \left[\begin{array}{c}\overset{H}{\underset{H}{}}C-C\overset{H}{\underset{H}{}}\end{array}\right]_n
$$

2 The test for an alkene – its reaction with bromine-water

Bromine-water is a solution of bromine in water. It is a pale yellow-orange colour. Any sample of an alkene will react *rapidly* when shaken with bromine water, causing the colour to disappear. Alkanes do not give this reaction. It is used as a simple test, to tell the difference between an alkane and an alkene.

This is another example of an addition reaction. Two molecules react together to become one. Bromine molecules add to the double bond in the alkene, to form a colourless product. As the coloured bromine molecules are removed, the colour of the solution disappears.

$$
\begin{array}{ccccc}
C_2H_4 & + & Br_2 & \rightarrow & C_2H_4Br_2 \\
\text{ethene} & \text{bromine in solution} & & \text{1,2-dibromoethane (colourless)}
\end{array}
$$

$$
\overset{H}{\underset{H}{}}C=C\overset{H}{\underset{H}{}} \quad + Br_2 \longrightarrow \quad Br-\overset{H}{\underset{H}{C}}-\overset{H}{\underset{H}{C}}-Br
$$

(You may also have used the reaction with acidified potassium manganate(VII) as a test for alkenes.)

3 Reactions of unsaturated molecules with hydrogen

Many natural plant oils are unsaturated, because they contain C=C bonds, e.g. olive oil. Hydrogen can react with these oils to form *solid* fats which are used to make margarine (p221). This is another example of addition. The hydrogen adds to the double bonds:

$$\left(\begin{array}{c}\text{rest of}\\\text{molecule}\end{array}\right) - \overset{\overset{\displaystyle H}{|}}{C} = \overset{\overset{\displaystyle H}{|}}{C} - \left(\begin{array}{c}\text{rest of}\\\text{molecule}\end{array}\right) + H_2 \longrightarrow \left(\begin{array}{c}\text{rest of}\\\text{molecule}\end{array}\right) - \overset{\overset{\displaystyle H}{|}}{\underset{\underset{\displaystyle H}{|}}{C}} - \overset{\overset{\displaystyle H}{|}}{\underset{\underset{\displaystyle H}{|}}{C}} - \left(\begin{array}{c}\text{rest of}\\\text{molecule}\end{array}\right)$$

Unsaturated fats are liquids but they become solids after hydrogen has been added. They are still not completely saturated, however, and such fats are described as being rich in 'polyunsaturates'. It is thought that too much animal fat, which is often saturated or nearly so, could be a cause of heart disease.

OTHER CHEMICAL REACTIONS OF THE ALKENES

Like the alkanes, the alkenes will also burn in air or oxygen. Again like the alkanes, the main products are carbon dioxide (from the carbon atoms) and steam (from the hydrogen atoms). However, alkenes are much more likely to show **incomplete combustion** (p210) than the alkanes. Some of the carbon becomes carbon monoxide or even carbon the element. The flame, when an alkene burns, is always smoky and yellow because of this. In theory, alkenes could be used as fuels, but it would be pointless to use them in this way. They are much too valuable. Unlike alkanes, they are chemically reactive, and in particular can be built up by addition reactions into larger molecules such as plastics. Alkanes cannot be used in this way because they are saturated.

USES OF ALKENES

The most important use is in the manufacture of plastics and other polymers. They are also used to make alcohols, anti-freeze solutions and detergents.

THE MANUFACTURE OF ALKENES

Alkenes are not found naturally in large quantities, but large quantities are needed. They have to be made from alkanes which are found naturally in petroleum (crude oil). The alkanes with large molecules cannot be used easily as fuels so they are **cracked** (p366) to produce smaller molecules, including alkenes.

14.3 PLASTICS AND OTHER POLYMERS (LARGE MOLECULES)

Polymers are giant molecules (macromolecules) (p267). They are built up by linking together a large number of smaller units called **monomers**.

n(monomers) → a polymer, (where n is a large number)

The polymer may have long, 'straight' chains, or it may have branches and more complicated structures.

Some polymers occur in nature. These are called **natural polymers**. Examples include starch (a polymer of sugar molecules), silk, wool and cotton. Polymers which do not occur in nature and are manufactured are called **synthetic polymers**. These include all the plastics, and synthetic fibres such as nylon, terylene and artificial silk. The rest of this section discusses one group of synthetic polymers, the plastics, in more detail.

Some syllabuses include the breakdown of large molecules (carbohydrates, proteins, plastics) into smaller units, and then the separation and identification of these units. For example, you may have broken down starch (a carbohydrate which is a polymer of glucose) into simple sugars (its monomers) and then identified the sugar by paper chromatography. You may also have mentioned other large molecules such as fats, and considered how these substances are broken down in digestion. Revise these points if necessary.

PLASTICS

Plastics can be divided into several types (Fig 14.2).

Fig 14.2 Types of polymer

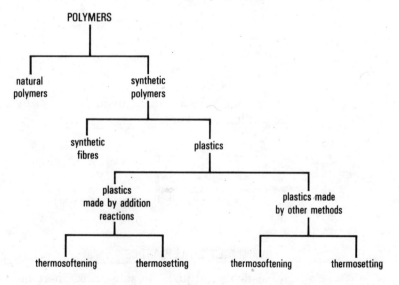

This section deals only with those made by addition reactions.

Many of these have a monomer which always has the same type of structure:

where X varies. The simplest monomer of this type is ethene, where X is a hydrogen atom:

$$\begin{matrix} H & & H \\ & \diagdown \; C = C \; \diagup \\ H & & H \end{matrix}$$

If X is a chlorine atom, the monomer is the one used to make poly(vinylchloride) (pvc). If X is a ring of six carbon atoms (a benzene ring) the monomer is used to make poly-(styrene), and so on. These monomers all react to build up a polymer in exactly the same way. Read the description of the addition of ethene molecules (p335). A similar reaction happens to any of these monomers when they add together to form a polymer. (These plastics are all **addition polymers**. If you have also studied a **condensation polymer** such as nylon, revise your notes.)

POLY(ETHENE), OR POLYTHENE

See p335. A special catalyst is used to make the monomers combine.

POLY(VINYLCHLORIDE), OR PVC

The monomer of this is very similar to ethene, but one of the hydro-gen atoms is replaced by a chlorine atom:

$$\begin{matrix} H & & Cl \\ & \diagdown \; C = C \; \diagup \\ H & & H \end{matrix}$$

The monomers are made to add together by using a special catalyst and a high pressure:

$$n\left(\begin{matrix} H & Cl \\ | & | \\ C = C \\ | & | \\ H & H \end{matrix}\right) \longrightarrow \left[\begin{matrix} H & Cl \\ | & | \\ C - C \\ | & | \\ H & H \end{matrix}\right]_n$$

ADVANTAGES OF ALL PLASTICS

'Plastic' is not just one substance. There are many kinds of plastic, each with its own special advantages. However, all plastics have some properties in common. These properties are *very* useful. It is unusual to find so many useful properties in just one kind of sub-stance.

1 Good heat insulators.
2 Strong but flexible.
3 Easily moulded into shape.
4 Rot-proof and corrosion-proof.
5 Light (low densities)
6 Easily coloured.

7 Water-proof.
8 Good electrical insulators.
9 Many can be made into 'yarn' for clothing.
   In addition, plastics can be divided into two other types:

THERMOSOFTENING (THERMOPLASTIC) PLASTICS

These plastics soften and eventually melt when heated, but without changing their structure. They can then be remoulded and used again. This cycle can be repeated many times.

Examples of this type are poly(ethene), pvc, poly(styrene), nylon and terylene. These plastics are flexible, and can be used when some bending or stretching is necessary (e.g. in clothing). They are not heat-resistant, however, and cannot be used for kitchen worktops, etc.

THERMOSETTING PLASTICS

These can only be heated, melted and moulded *once*. When they 'set' they form a rigid structure, with lots of side chains all locked together. This is a 'permanent' structure – these plastics cannot be softened, melted and remoulded.

Examples of this type include Bakelite (used for making light fittings), and melamine (used for kitchen worktops). These plastics are hard, rigid, and more heat-resistant than the thermosoftening ones. They cannot be used where bending or stretching is necessary (e.g. in clothing).

SOME PROBLEMS WITH PLASTICS

1 The monomers are nearly all made from petroleum. The world's supply of petroleum will not last for ever. We may eventually have to use coal, another fossil fuel, to make the monomers. The technology for this on a large scale does not yet exist – the price of plastics could rise.
2 There are dangers when plastics catch fire. Many of them have low ignition temperatures (they will burst into flames without strong heating). Some of them then give off toxic, choking fumes. For example, pvc forms the toxic, acid gas hydrogen chloride when it burns. Many burning plastics also melt, dropping hot liquid on to any person nearby. Plastics are used on a large scale in the home, e.g. for ceiling tiles and for stuffing furniture. Fires which involve plastics are therefore not uncommon.
3 The fact that plastics resist corrosion or rotting is a very useful property. Unfortunately, after the plastic has been finished with, this property can become a disadvantage. We cannot dispose of the plastic easily! We cannot leave it to rot down, as we do with much of our rubbish. In theory, if we could separate the *thermosoftening* plastic waste from the rest, we could re-use (recycle) it. At the moment this

cannot be done on a large scale. (An ordinary member of the public cannot tell the difference between the different kinds of plastic.) However, technology has improved this situation. Plastics have been developed which are **biodegradable**. This means that bacteria *can* break them down (they do rot) after they have been used.

14.4 ALCOHOLS, SUCH AS ETHANOL

Alcohols form another group of organic chemicals. Unlike the alkanes and alkenes, the alcohols are not hydrocarbons. They do contain atoms of carbon and hydrogen, but they also contain atoms of oxygen. We can think of the alcohols as having a 'skeleton' of carbon and hydrogen atoms (like an alkane), which also contains an OH group. It is this OH group which makes the alcohol different from other substances. The most common example is ethanol, C_2H_5OH, which has the structural formula:

```
     H  H
     |  |
 H—C—C—OH
     |  |
     H  H
```

PHYSICAL PROPERTIES OF ETHANOL

Ethanol is a colourless liquid with a characteristic odour. It evaporates rapidly, even at room temperature.

THE LABORATORY PREPARATION OF ETHANOL

STAGE 1: THE FERMENTATION

This can be summarised as shown in Fig 14.3.

Fig 14.3 First stage in preparation of ethanol: fermentation

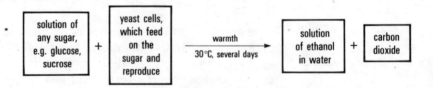

Yeast is a living organism, although when dried it appears to be dead. As soon as it receives food (sugar), water and warmth, it 'comes alive'. The yeast cells contain **enzymes** (biological catalysts). These break down the sugar into carbon dioxide and ethanol. Energy is also produced in the process, which the yeast needs to grow and reproduce. This breakdown of foods such as sugars by yeast is called **fermentation**. The mixture bubbles as it ferments.

The fermentation stops if any one of these things happens:
(a)   The solution becomes too cold for the enzymes to work.

(*b*)   The yeast uses up all the food (sugar).

(*c*)   The concentration of the ethanol in the solution becomes too great for the yeast cells.

Note: This process is a kind of respiration, but yeast does not need oxygen. Respiration without air or oxygen is called **anaerobic respiration**. This is less efficient than **aerobic respiration**, because the sugar is not completely broken down into carbon dioxide and water (p206). Instead, some of it is converted into ethanol. Note also that enzymes are very sensitive catalysts. They are destroyed by heating, so fermentation solutions should be kept warm but not hot.

STAGE 2: FRACTIONAL DISTILLATION

After the fermentation has taken place for several days, the flask will contain a dilute solution of ethanol in water. There will also be yeast in it, and probably some unused sugar. The solution is therefore a *mixture*. A fairly pure sample of ethanol can be removed from it by distillation (Fig 3.7, p77), although fractional distillation (Fig 3.9, p80) is better.

When the mixture is boiled any yeast cells stay in the solution and are killed. Sugar molecules also stay in the solution. Ethanol molecules evaporate, however, as ethanol boils at 78°C, well before water reaches its own boiling point. The vapour coming off from the mixture is therefore mainly ethanol vapour. This is condensed separately and collects as a colourless liquid. The sample will not be *pure* ethanol: it will always contain some water. The distillate can be shown to be 'rich' in ethanol by the fact that it will burn. The mixture in the flask before distillation will not burn.

THE INDUSTRIAL MANUFACTURE OF ETHANOL

1   Some is made on a large scale by the fermentation of sugars, although other 'foods' can be used, e.g. potatoes, rice, sugar cane, and even wood pulp. Excess, cheap wines are also distilled to form fairly pure ethanol.

2   Large quantities of ethanol are now made from ethene, which is obtained by the cracking of petroleum (p366). Steam *adds* (p334) to the ethene in the presence of a catalyst to form ethanol.

$$C_2H_4(g) + H_2O(g) \xrightarrow{\text{catalyst}} C_2H_5OH$$

ALCOHOLIC DRINKS

Many drinks contain some ethanol. Common examples are beer, lager, cider, wines and spirits (e.g. whisky, gin and vodka). The terms 'alcoholic drink' is unfortunate, because some people think that there is only one kind of alcohol. For example, some people have drunk certain kinds of anti-freeze thinking that the alcohol it contains is the same as the alcohol in beer or wine. This is not so. The different types of drink vary in flavour and in the % of ethanol present. Some examples are given in Table 14.2.

Table 14.2 Some alcoholic drinks

(a) The % of ethanol in different drinks

Water	Beer cider	Table wines	Fortified wines (eg sherry)	Spirits (eg whisky)	Pure ethanol
0	3 5	8 15	21	40 50	100

(b) How different drinks are made

Type of drink	Made from
Beer	Fermenting an extract from barley (malt). Hops added, as a preservative and to give bitter flavour
Table wine	Fermenting the sugars in grape juice. Other ingredients in the juice, or storing in wood, gives each wine its special flavour
Home-made wines	Flavour comes from fruit or vegetables which are usually boiled with water. Sugar is then added, for fermentation. Can have a higher alcohol concentration than commercial wines
Fortified wines	Wines are made in normal way (grape juice), matured, and extra ethanol added
Spirits	By distilling the liquid formed by a special fermentation, e.g. whisky from fermentation of malt extract

HOME BREWING

It is estimated that over 1 million people in Britain make some wine. Home brewing of beer is even more popular. The following precautions must be understood:

(*a*)   All equipment must be clean and sterilised. Certain kinds of bacteria, which collect in unclean equipment, will change any ethanol into ethanoic acid. The wine or beer then tastes like vinegar.

(*b*)   Air should be kept out of the container during fermentation. Air will contain the same bacteria mentioned in (*a*). However, the container must not be *sealed*, because carbon dioxide gas must be allowed to escape. Wine makers often use an *air lock* (Fig 14.4), which allows carbon dioxide to bubble through (under pressure) and escape, but does not allow air to enter.

(*c*)   When bottling beer, only the *recommended amount* of sugar should be added to each bottle. The sugar starts the fermentation process again, inside the bottle. The carbon dioxide which is produced is trapped inside the beer and gives the liquid its 'fizz'. If too

Fig 14.4 An air lock

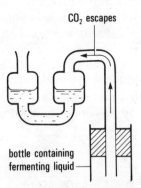

CO₂ escapes

bottle containing
fermenting liquid

much sugar is added, fermentation will go on for too long, the pressure of carbon dioxide will build up, and the bottle is likely to 'explode'.

(d)   Wine and beer must never be bottled while still fermenting, or the bottles will almost certainly 'explode'.

(e)   No attempt must ever be made to increase the ethanol concentration of home-made drinks. For one thing, this is illegal. It is also for your own protection. Any attempt to concentrate the ethanol will almost certainly also concentrate some other alcohols, which will be present in small amounts. These could be dangerous in larger concentrations. For example, the alcohol methanol is likely to be present. Methanol can damage permanently the optic nerve in the eye, causing blindness. Methylated spirit contains methanol; alcoholics have been known to drink it, with serious consequences.

Note that cheap wines, or any alcoholic drink with a *low* concentration of ethanol, will go sour after a few days if left exposed to the air. The bacteria mentioned in (*a*) and (*b*) change the ethanol into ethanoic acid. The only exception is if the drink contains a preservative, e.g. the hops in beer. Drinks with a *high* ethanol concentration will not go sour in this way, e.g. a bottle of whisky will keep for years after being opened. The high alcohol concentration kills the bacteria. This is why nurses and doctors use 'pure ethanol' to disinfect an area of skin before making an injection.

ALCOHOL ADDICTION

An occasional drink does not cause any harm. It can be pleasant to have a leisurely drink with friends. Drinking wine with a meal can add to the enjoyment of the meal, and help to digest it. (The ethanol helps to dissolve fatty substances which do not dissolve in water.) However, the dangers connected with irresponsible use of alcoholic drinks have rightly received the same amount of publicity as those involved with smoking. No doubt you will have discussed:

(i) ethanol can become addictive;

(ii) drinking larger than average amounts over a long period can cause permanent liver damage;

(iii) excess is connected with other medical problems, such as high blood pressure, heart disease, and being overweight;

(iv) excess slows down reactions (danger of driving after drinking), causes aggressive behaviour (people do things they would not normally do, especially argue and fight), and general lack of judgment;

(v) some so-called advantages are really imagined, e.g. it does not 'warm you up' in winter, and it does not reduce stress.

REACTIONS AND USES OF ETHANOL

1 ETHANOL CAN BE OXIDISED TO ETHANOIC ACID

As described above, certain bacteria can change ethanol into an acid, ethanoic acid. This acid is commonly called acetic acid. It causes the sour flavour in vinegar. The reaction is an oxidation. (It can also be caused by a chemical oxidising agent such as hot, acidified potassium dichromate(VI), which changes colour from orange to green as it oxidises the alcohol.)

$$C_2H_5OH + 2[O] \rightarrow CH_3COOH + H_2O$$

This oxidation is used on a large scale to manufacture ethanoic acid for industrial use. It is also used to make vinegar. Wine vinegar, for example, is made by trickling cheap wine over wooden pieces which are full of bacteria. The ethanol changes into ethanoic acid. Other types of vinegar are made in a similar way, but different flavourings are used, e.g. malt vinegar.

2 ETHANOL IS A GOOD SOLVENT

Ethanol is used on a large scale as a solvent, e.g. for paints and dyes. Many organic substances will not dissolve in water, but they will dissolve in ethanol.

3 ETHANOL WILL BURN. IT IS USED AS A FUEL

Ethanol burns with a clean blue flame to form carbon dioxide, water vapour and heat energy.

$$2\,C_2H_5OH + 7O_2 \rightarrow 4CO_2 + 6H_2O + energy$$

Ethanol is potentially a very good fuel. Much heat is produced when it burns, and no pollutants are formed. It is a clean fuel. It is used as a fuel, on a fairly small scale, in an 'impure' form called **methylated spirits**. This is a convenient liquid fuel for camping stoves, etc. Ethanol could find a more widespread use in the future as a liquid fuel, e.g. to replace petrol, if it can be made cheaply and quickly on a large scale.

ETHANOIC ACID. ESTERS   A few syllabuses also include some simple properties of ethanoic acid, CH_3COOH, which is formed by oxidising ethanol, as described earlier. You may also have considered some other organic acids with larger molecules, such as stearic acid, the sodium salt of which is used as soap. The NISEC syllabus also includes a simple understanding of esters. Revise these points if appropriate.

CHECK YOUR UNDERSTANDING (Answers on p421)

In each of these questions, read all of the parts carefully. You should be able to decide that all of the parts in a question are correct statements except for one (the odd one out) **or** all of the parts may be incorrect except for one (the odd one out). Decide which statement is the odd one out for each question.

1   A   Crude oil contains sulphur compounds.
    B   Crude oil is a mixture of many substances, mainly hydrocarbons.
    C   The simpler molecules obtained by the fractional distillation of crude oil have high boiling points.
    D   The heavier fractions from crude oil are not required in the same quantities as are the simpler fractions.
    E   Cracking produces more of the simpler molecules, including unsaturated molecules.

2   A   Coal, oil and natural gas are all fossil fuels.
    B   Peat is an early stage in the formation of coal.
    C   Coal is of mainly vegetable origin.
    D   Crude oil is of mainly animal origin.
    E   Coal is normally treated to remove sulphur compounds before being used directly as a fuel.

3   A   Natural gas is mainly methane.
    B   Coal contains hydrocarbons.
    C   Most of the coal mined in Britain is used at power stations.
    D   Coal can be destructively distilled by burning it in a distillation unit.

4   A   The alcohols all contain the group OH.
    B   In general, as molecular mass increases, the boiling points and melting points of the members of an organic family increase.
    C   Yeast is used in brewing to give beer its flavour.
    D   Liquid ethanol will burn to form carbon dioxide and steam.
    E   The alcohol in alcoholic drinks is ethanol.

5   A   Ethanol can be obtained from either sugar or starch by fermentation.
    B   The rate of fermentation is increased if high temperatures are used.
    C   During fermentation, yeast cells feed on the sugar or starch.
    D   Carbon dioxide is another product of fermentation.
    E   During fermentation, yeast does not need to 'breathe' oxygen.

6   A   Polymers are macro (giant) molecules.

    B   Polymers consist of a large number of monomer molecules.

    C   Polymers are always synthetic.

    D   Addition polymerisation is the linking together of simple monomers to form a single, large molecule.

7   A   Carbohydrates contain carbon and hydrogen only.

    B   Starch is a carbohydrate.

    C   Glucose is a carbohydrate.

    D   Glucose is a monomer of starch.

    E   Starch is depolymerised in digestion.

CHECK LIST ▶

REMEMBER THAT SOME OF THESE POINTS MAY NOT BE RELEVANT FOR THE PARTICULAR SYLLABUS YOU ARE FOLLOWING.

YOU SHOULD UNDERSTAND THE FOLLOWING POINTS.

1 ▶ The alkanes: properties, names and formulas of the first members.

2 ▶ The alkenes: properties, names and formulas of first two.

3 ▶ Isomerism.

4 ▶ Saturated, unsaturated, addition, substitution.

5 ▶ Plastics and other polymers: examples, monomers, advantages and disadvantages, thermosetting and thermosoftening types.

6 ▶ Alcohols such as ethanol: formula, properties, fermentation.

7 ▶ Alcoholic drinks: types, home-brewing, dangers.

8 ▶ Ethanoic acid, formula and properties.

SPECIMEN EXAMINATION QUESTIONS

SEE GENERAL NOTE BEFORE QUESTIONS ON p49 AND 50. REMEMBER THAT YOU MAY BE ALLOWED TO USE A DATA BOOK IN THE EXAMINATION.

1   Which **one** of the structures in Fig 14.5 is the structural formula of an alkane?

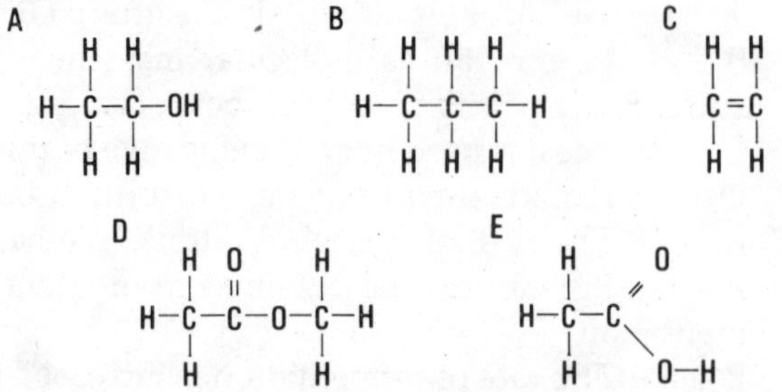

Fig 14.5 Diagram for question 1

[*NISEC* spec 1]

2   Which one of the following is the formula of an organic compound?

A CH_4 B $NaCl$ C NH_3 D SO_2

3   Which one of the gases listed below burns in oxygen to form carbon dioxide and water vapour and also decolourises bromine water?

A Carbon monoxide (CO)   B Ethane (C_2H_6)   C Ethene (C_2O_4)
D Methane (CH_4)

4   Which one of the following is the chief reason that plastics are a pollution problem?

    A   Plastics are organic compounds.
    B   Plastics are resistant to bacterial action.
    C   Plastics do not react easily with acid.
    D   Plastics usually burn easily.

5   When methane gas burns in excess oxygen the balanced equation for the reaction which occurs is

    A $CH_4 + O_2 \rightarrow CO_2 + 2H_2O$
    B $CH_4 + 2O_2 \rightarrow CO_2 + 2H_2O$
    C $2CH_4 + O_2 \rightarrow 2CO_2 + 2H_2O$
    D $2CH_4 + 3O_2 \rightarrow 2CO + 4H_2O$

6   Some pieces of Perspex are carefully heated in a boiling tube connected to a cooled test tube (Fig 14.6).

Fig 14.6 Diagram for question 6

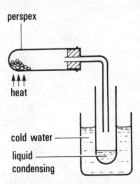

The liquid condensing in the cooled tube is
A liquid Perspex   B Perspex monomer   C Perspex polymer
D water

Questions 7–9. The flow diagram in Fig 14.7 gives some reactions which can take place starting with glucose.

Fig 14.7 Diagram for questions 7–9

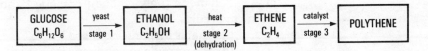

The process taking place in stage 3 is
A combustion   B cracking   C polymerisation
D reduction

8   The other product, besides ethene, formed in stage 2 is
A carbon dioxide   B hydrogen   C oxygen   D water

9   The formula for polythene can be written as
    A $(C_2H_4)n$
    B $(C_6H_{10}O_5)n$
    C $n(C_2H_4)$
    D $n(C_6H_{10}O_5)$ [*SEG* spec (Alt), 1]

10

Compound	Formula	Boiling point °C
A	CH_4	−162
B	C_2H_6	− 89
C	C_3H_6	− 48
D	C_3H_8	− 42
E	C_4H_{10}	
F	C_5H_{12}	+ 25

(a)   Five of the six hydrocarbons listed above belong to the homologous series called alkanes.

(i) Which hydrocarbon listed does *not* belong to the alkanes?

(ii) Is compound F a solid, liquid or a gas at 35°C?

(iii) By studying the table predict the boiling point of compound E.

(iv) Which *one* of the hydrocarbons is the main compound in natural gas?

(b)   Hydrocarbon B is said to be saturated and has the structural formula.

$$
\begin{array}{c}
\text{H} \quad \text{H} \\
| \quad\; | \\
\text{H}-\text{C}-\text{C}-\text{H} \\
| \quad\; | \\
\text{H} \quad \text{H}
\end{array}
$$

State what would happen if this compound were bubbled into bromine.   [MEG spec 2]

11   (a)   Name and give the formula of the main compound in natural gas.

(b)   A compound found in the oil fraction kerosene is decane, $C_{10}H_{22}$.

(i) Complete the word equation for burning decane completely in air.

(ii) What conditions might cause a poisonous gas to be formed when burning decane?

(iii) Name the poisonous gas referred to in (ii).

(c)   Polythene [poly(ethene)] is made by joining together many ethene molecules.

(i) What is this process called?

(ii) The formula of polythene is

$$
\left(
\begin{array}{c}
\text{H} \quad \text{H} \\
| \quad\; | \\
-\text{C}-\text{C}- \\
| \quad\; | \\
\text{H} \quad \text{H}
\end{array}
\right)_n
$$

What does the 'n' mean?

(iii) Draw the structure (structural formula) of ethene.

(iv) What feature of the ethene molecule allows it to be changed into polythene?   [*SEG* spec 2]

†12   The general formula for the alkene series of hydrocarbons is C_nH_{2n}. Ethene, C_2H_4, is the first member.

(*a*)   (i) Work out the molecular formula of the fifth member, hexene.

(ii) Ethene may be prepared by passing ethanol vapour over a heated aluminium oxide catalyst. Sketch an apparatus which you might use to carry out this reaction, showing how you would collect the ethene.

(iii) What would you do when using the apparatus shown in your answer to part (ii) to make sure that the ethene was reasonably free of air?

(iv) Write an equation for the reaction in (ii).

(*b*)   An organic compound X undergoes the following reactions.

(i) It burns completely in oxygen forming carbon dioxide and water only.

(ii) It rapidly decolourises bromine water.

(iii) It dissolves in sodium carbonate solution with fizzing. State as fully as possible what you can deduce about the structure of compound X from each reaction.

(*c*)   Propene has the structural formula shown below:

```
  H H   H
  | |   |
H-C-C=C
  |     \
  H      H
```

Write down the structural formulae for the products of the following reactions of propene:

(i) hydrogenation;

(ii) hydration;

(iii) polymerisation.

(*d*)   (i) State one environmental disadvantage of a polymer such as poly(propene).

(ii) Explain why poly(propene) is much less reactive than propene.   [*SEG* spec 3]

13   Read through the following account and study the map (Fig 14.8) carefully. Then answer the questions.

THE INVERGROG RESERVOIR PROJECT

A. L. McHol and Co are investigating the possibility of building a new whisky distillery on the Invergrog Industrial Estate. The proposed site is to the north-east of the town (See map). Their big problem is where to get pure water from to make the whisky.

There are many streams flowing from the hills to the west of Invergrog. At first the company thought there were five possible places to build a small reservoir. These are shown and numbered on the map (1, 2, 3, 4 and 5). When samples of water taken from two of

Fig 14.8 Diagram for
question 13

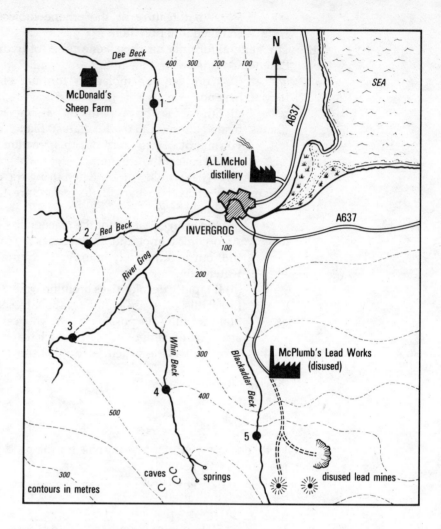

these locations were examined, they were found to contain too high a
level of pollution. An analysis of water from a third possible site
showed that it contained too many dissolved mineral salts.

Analysis of the mineral water from the third site (mg/litre)

hydrogencarbonate	180.60	calcium	44.80
sulphate	10.00	magnesium	20.00
chloride	15.60	fluoride	0.06
nitrate	0.20	sodium	12.50

To help them choose between the two remaining sites the company
carried out chemical tests to find the hardness of the water.

(*a*)   Explain as fully as you can why the water at two of the sites
was polluted.

(b)   What is the molarity of the mineral water with respect to sodium ions?

(c)   Which of the ions present in this spring water are associated with hardness in water?

(d)   Describe a simple method you could use to compare the hardness of the water from the two remaining sites. Your account should include the list of apparatus and chemicals you would use and details of how it is possible to make a fair comparison.

(e)   If the distillery needed to use very soft water, it could be treated by using an ion-exchange column. Explain briefly how this process works.

14   The table in Fig 14.9 includes the structural formulae of some monomers and the polymers that can be made from them.

Fig 14.9 Table for question 14

Monomer	Polymer
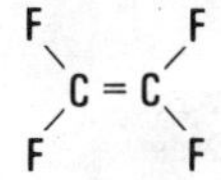 F F C = C F F tetrafluoroethene	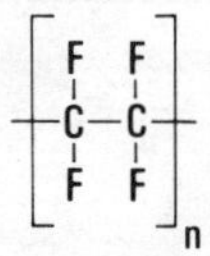 ┌ F F ┐ C—C └ F F ┘$_n$ polytetrafluoroethene
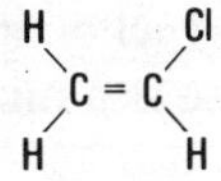 H Cl C = C H H chloroethene	polychloroethene
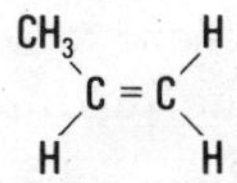 CH$_3$ H C = C H H propene	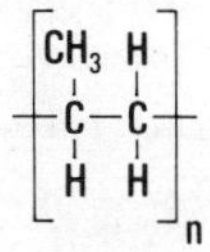 ┌ CH$_3$ H ┐ C—C └ H H ┘$_n$ polypropene

(a)   Which one of the monomers is a hydrocarbon?

(b)   The molecular formula of propene is C_3H_6. Write the molecular formula of chloroethene.

(c)   Write in the table the structural formula of polychloroethene.

(d)   What similarity in structure exists in the three monomers?

(e)   What colour change would be observed if propene gas were bubbled through a solution of bromine?

(f)   Ethene (C_2H_4) can be polymerised under different conditions to form either low or high density polyethene. Both forms of polyethene can be easily moulded using heat and/or vacuum methods.

Low density polyethene is cheaper to produce but has a lower melting point and is less strong than high density polyethene.

(i) What is the usual industrial source of ethene?

(ii) In which form of polyethene are the chains of atoms more closely packed? Give a reason for your answer.

(g)   Washing up bowls used to be made of steel coated with paint. They are now often made of polyethene.

(i) Give *two* reasons why polyethene is more suitable than painted steel for this purpose.

(ii) Give a reason why high density polyethene is more suitable than low density polyethene for this purpose.

(h)   Addition polymers such as polyethene and polypropene are very difficult to dispose of.

(i) Why are these polymers difficult to dispose of?

(ii) One possible method of disposal is burning. Name two possible products of combustion of polyethene and polypropene.

(i)   The table below contains information about four materials in household refuse.

Material	Added to water
Polymers	Float on water
Iron	Sinks in water
Aluminium	Sinks in water
Paper	Floats on water

Paper, however, sinks in water when it is thoroughly wetted.

Assuming household refuse is a mixture only of polymers, paper, iron and aluminium, how could

(i) iron be removed from the refuse

(ii) polymers be removed from the refuse?

(j)   It is impossible at present to separate pure polyethene from household refuse. Usually the mixture of polymers is melted and made into cheap blocks for lining walls.

(i) What properties of addition polymers are important in making and using these blocks?

(ii) What would be the economic advantage of being able to separate pure polyethene from household refuse?

[LEA spec (B), 2]

†15   In the UK all the ethanol used for industrial and medical purposes is obtained from ethene whereas in the West Indies and elsewhere in the world fermentation processes are used.

(a)   Describe and explain the main chemical reactions by which the ethanol is produced commercially,

(i) from ethene

(ii) by fermentation.

(b)   The fermentation processes being developed in the West Indies are creating much interest because the sugar raw material is a renewable resource. Explain how such a resource is better than the resource from which ethene is obtained in the UK.

(c)   Describe, giving an equation and stating conditions and observations, how ethanol may be oxidised in the laboratory.

(d)   What is meant by microbiological oxidation of ethanol? Why is this of importance to wine producers?   [*NISEC* spec 3]

†16   (a)   Ethane and ethene are both hydrocarbons. Explain what is meant by the term *hydrocarbons*.

(b)   Write the structural formulae of ethane (C_2H_6) and ethene, (C_2H_4), showing **all** the covalent bonds by lines.

(c)   Ethane is the second member of the homologous series of alkanes. Give the names and formulae of the first and third members of this series.

(d)   Petrol, the fuel used in car engines, is a mixture of hydrocarbons. One of the hydrocarbons present in petrol is octane, C_8H_{18}, which burns completely in oxygen according to the equation.

$$2C_8H_{18} + 25O_2 \rightarrow 16CO_2 + 18H_2O$$

(i) Calculate the volume of oxygen that must be available if $1000 \ cm^3$ of octane vapour are burned completely, all volumes being measured at the same temperature and pressure.

(ii) This process is *exothermic*. Explain the meaning of this term in terms of the energy conversion taking place.

(iii) What mass of water vapour is produced when 114g of octane are completely burned? (Relative molecular masses: water = 18, octane = 114.)

(e)   Suggest reasons why

(i) a black solid collects in the exhaust pipe which leads the fumes away from a car engine

(ii) it is dangerous to run a car engine in closed garage.

[*LEA* spec (A), 3]

ENERGY IN CHEMICAL REACTIONS. FUELS

CONTENTS

15.1 ENERGY IN CHEMICAL REACTIONS

1. ALL CHEMICAL REACTIONS INVOLVE ENERGY CHANGES

There is always a change in energy when a chemical reaction takes place. The energy is normally in the form of *heat*. (Other forms of energy may be involved, e.g. when chemicals produce electrical energy in a battery, or light energy from a flame, or sound energy from an explosion.) Some reactions *give out* energy to the surroundings. These are called **exothermic** reactions. Some reactions *take in* heat from the surroundings. These are called **endothermic reactions**. Some reactions involve only a small energy change, so a change in temperature is not always obvious.

Exothermic reactions	Endothermic reactions
Energy given out to the surroundings. The chemicals and the container increase in temperature.	Energy taken in from surroundings. Chemicals and container fall in temperature.

2 EXAMPLES OF EXOTHERMIC REACTIONS

(a) THE BURNING OF FUELS

Fuel + air/oxygen $\rightarrow$ products (e.g. $CO_2 + H_2O$)+heat energy
Fuels could include coal, natural gas, petrol, ethanol, etc.

(b) RESPIRATION

Food (fuel) + air/oxygen $\rightarrow$ products (e.g. $CO_2 + H_2O$ + energy
　　　　　　　　　　　　　　　　in mammals,
　　　　　　　　　　　　　　　　CO_2 and
　　　　　　　　　　　　　　　　C_2H_5OH in
　　　　　　　　　　　　　　　　yeasts)

(c) THE REACTION BETWEEN ANHYDROUS SALTS AND WATER

E.g. anhydrous copper(II) sulphate+water$\rightleftharpoons$hydrated copper(II) sulphate+heat (p233). Reactions of this kind are **reversible** (note the $\rightleftharpoons$ sign). The reaction can 'go' from left to right, but it can also 'go' from right to left. If the reaction is reversed, the energy change must also be reversed. In going from left to right, the above reaction is exothermic – heat is given out. If the change is from right to left, heat energy has to be *supplied* to dehydrate the salt. The reverse reaction is therefore endothermic.

Another example of the reversing of an energy change is a simple cell (p99). Chemicals are used up in making electrical energy in a cell or battery. Some batteries can be recharged. Electrical energy then has to be *put in* to the battery to reform the original chemicals.

(d) THE REACTION BETWEEN CONCENTRATED SULPHURIC ACID AND WATER

(see p311).

(e) NEUTRALISATION REACTIONS

When an acid reacts with a base, the reaction is a neutralisation. A salt and water are formed (p183). These reactions are always exothermic.

3 EXAMPLES OF ENDOTHERMIC REACTIONS

(a) PHOTOSYNTHESIS

This important reaction (p208) *takes in* energy from sunlight.

(b) DISSOLVING SALTS IN WATER

Most salts take in energy when they dissolve in water, unless they are anhydrous. In other words, they take heat energy from the water when they dissolve, and so the temperature of the solution goes *down*. You may have measured temperature changes of this kind, e.g. by dissolving ammonium chloride or potassium nitrate in water.

4 THE $\triangle H$ CONVENTION

Energy changes are measured as the *difference* between the energy content of the starting materials (the reactants) and that of the final materials (products). Energy changes are given the symbol $\triangle H$.

$$\triangle H = \text{ENERGY OF PRODUCTS} - \text{ENERGY OF REACTANTS}$$

In an exothermic reaction, when heat is given out, the reactants contain more energy than the products. As the energy content of the chemicals goes *down* during an exothermic reaction, $\triangle H$ in such cases is **negative** (see Fig 15.1). **A negative sign** in front of $\triangle H$ means that the reaction is **exothermic**.

Similarly, endothermic reactions have a **positive** value for $\triangle H$. In these reactions, energy is taken in so that the products contains more energy than the reactants (see

Fig 15.1 Exothermic
reaction, $\triangle H$-ve

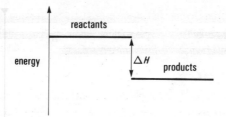

Fig 15.2). **A positive** sign (or no sign) in front of $\triangle H$ means that the reaction is **endothermic**.

Fig 15.2 Endothermic
reaction, $\triangle H$+ve

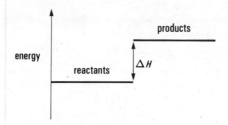

Energy changes are measured in joules or kilojoules. 1kJ = 1000 J. Approximately 4.2 joules (or, more accurately 4.18 joules) are needed to raise the temperature of 1g of water through 1°C.

Quite often, the value for $\triangle H$ is given with a chemical equation. For example,

$$N_2 + 3H_2 \rightleftharpoons 2NH_3 \quad \triangle H = -92.4 \text{ kJ mol}^{-1}$$

This energy change refers to the number of moles used in the equation. In this example, it means that when one mole of nitrogen reacts with three moles of hydrogen to form two moles of ammonia, 92.4 kJ of energy are given *out*. Note that as the sign in front of $\triangle H$ is negative, the reaction is exothermic and heat is given *out*. If the reaction is reversed, $\triangle H$ will be positive, but have the same value.

5 BOND-MAKING AND BOND-BREAKING

In every chemical reaction, some bonds are broken and some new ones are made. This happens because the atoms 'swap partners'. For example in the reaction

$$CuO + H_2 \rightarrow Cu + H_2O$$

we can rewrite this to show the bonds between the particles:

$$Cu\text{-}O + H\text{-}H \rightarrow Cu + H\text{-}O\text{-}H$$

We can see that the following bonds change in the reaction:

Bonds which break	New bonds which are made
bond between Cu and O bond between H and H	2 bonds between H and O bonds between copper atoms in copper metal

Energy is taken in when bonds are broken. **Bond-breaking** is **endothermic** ($\triangle H$ positive). We can see evidence for this in simple reactions. Heat energy is needed to cause calcium carbonate to break down into the oxide and carbon dioxide:

$$CaCO_3 \rightarrow CaO + CO_2.$$

There are many other examples where heat is needed to break down a compound into simpler substances, e.g. cracking (p366). Heat energy is needed to break bonds in all these cases.

The opposite is true when new bonds are formed. When new bonds are made, heat energy is given out. **Bond-making** is **exothermic**. You may have measured temperature changes in reactions where precipitates are formed. Here bonds are being made, between ions in solution which join to form a solid. You will have noticed that heat energy is given out in such reactions.

So what makes a reaction exothermic or endothermic? In *any* reaction, some bonds are broken *and* some are made. The final effect depends upon the energy changes of these different steps in the reaction. If more energy is given *out* (in the formation of new bonds) than is *taken in* (by the breaking of bonds), the reaction as a whole will be exothermic. The opposite is true if it is endothermic.

6 ARE EXOTHERMIC REACTIONS SPONTANEOUS?

Many pupils believe that exothermic reactions should 'just happen', without any help, because they give out energy once they start. In fact, there are many common examples where this does not happen. Petrol is a highly flammable liquid, but it has to be given a 'burst' of energy (a spark or a flame) before it will burn. Once it starts to burn, it then gives out a great deal of energy. In this example, and in the ones given below, some energy is needed to *start* the reaction. Then, once started, the reaction produces far more energy than was needed to start it. The end result is that the reaction as a whole is exothermic, and heat need not be supplied once the reaction has started. (You may have discussed this idea in more detail by referring to **activation energy**; revise if necessary.)

Paraffin in a dish will not burn if touched by a flame. If the paraffin is warmed gently, a flame will then ignite it.

Magnesium metal will not apparently react with oxygen until it is heated. Once it starts to react, a great deal of energy, as heat and light, is given out.

A mixture of iron filings and sulphur will not react until heated. Once started, the reaction is exothermic. The mixture glows. It produces more than enough heat to continue the reaction without further help.

7 FLASH POINTS AND IGNITION TEMPERATURES

If you have discussed these terms, make sure that you understand them.

8 STORAGE OF FLAMMABLE LIQUIDS

The hazard sign for 'flammable' is shown on p175. You will have seen this sign on labels of bottles and perhaps on road tankers. There are important regulations about how flammable liquids are stored and transported, and you may have discussed these. At least make sure that you understand the safety precautions which apply to the use of flammable liquids in the laboratory.

9 EXPERIMENTS ON ENERGY CHANGES

You have probably done experiments in which you mixed solutions and then had to measure the temperature change. You may have done this both for endothermic and exothermic reactions. In order to obtain accurate results, you may have done the following.

(a)   Use a plastic bottle for the container. This is a poor conductor of heat, and so heat energy does not escape from the bottle, or enter it from outside.

(b)   Leave the solutions out in the laboratory for some hours before the experiment, so that they start at the same temperature.

(c)   Stir the mixture during the reaction.

(d)   Use a thermometer with an 'easy to read' scale, and perhaps one marked in 0.1°C.

You may have done calculations on energy changes. Suppose the results of an experiment show that when $50 cm^3$ of substance A reacts with $50 cm^3$ of substance B in an insulated container, $630 J$ of energy are produced. The two solutions each have a concentration of 0.1M (p294). What is $\triangle H$ for the reaction?

$$50 \ cm^3 \ of \ 0.1 \ M \ solution \ contains \ \frac{50}{1000} \times 0.1 \ moles = 0.005 \ moles$$

The reaction was between 0.005 moles of each substance. If one mole of each substance had been used, the energy change would have been

$$\frac{1}{0.005} \times 630 \ J = 12\,600 \ J = 12.6 \ kJ$$

$\triangle H$ for the reaction is 12.6 kJ mole^{-1}

Note the need to calculate $\triangle H$ in J or kJ *per mole*.

If you have done other types of calculation on energy changes, revise them carefully. For example, a few syllabuses include the calculation of energy changes involved in a change of state, e.g. **heats of vaporisation**, and the significance of high and low values.

15.2 FUELS

A fuel is a substance used to provide energy. Most fuels are *burned* to provide *heat* energy. The energy given out may be used directly as heat (for warmth or for cooking), or to operate machines (as in a car) or to make electricity. Our food is also a fuel, which we use to provide our bodies with energy. You may have discussed examples of how energy can be changed from one form into another: the **principle of the conservation of energy**. If so, make sure that you understand it.

PROBLEMS OF THE PAST, PRESENT AND FUTURE

1 THE INCREASING DEMAND FOR ENERGY

You have probably discussed how our need for energy has increased tremendously since the Industrial Revolution. The developed countries now use more energy than ever before. Reasons include transport (cars, buses, lorries, trains, aircraft, ships, etc.), for everyday living (TV, stereo, washing machines, etc.), for keeping warm (heaters and central heating), and for making things in industry (iron and steel, cars, clothing, etc.). To understand the changes which have taken place you should try to compare a typical day now, and all the things you might use in a day, with what it might have been like 150 years ago. We cannot continue to use increasing amounts of energy. Much of it comes from fossil fuels, and these cannot last for ever. We need time to develop alternative sources of energy.

2 PERSONAL ATTITUDES

In the past we have been careless about our use of energy. Few people thought that one day coal would be used up. The same attitude was there when petroleum was developed. Some early steam engines were only 1% efficient, and most of the heat from a coal fire was wasted up the chimney, but it did not seem to matter. We are now developing a more responsible attitude. We are beginning to realise that every time we burn some petrol, or coal, or gas, we are using up in seconds something which has taken millions of years to form, and which cannot apparently be replaced.

Fig 15.3 shows how energy is used in a typical year in Britain.

Fig 15.3 Use of energy in the UK (typical year)

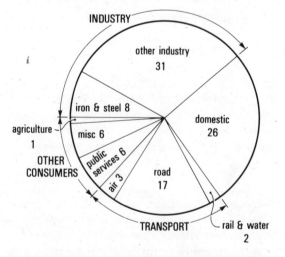

A significant proportion is used in the home, so we can *all* help. You have probably discussed points such as:
(*a*)   better insulation of house walls,
(*b*)   better roof insulation,

(*c*)　　using the 'waste' heat from power stations and factories,

(*d*)　　developing more efficient machines, power stations and transport. Make sure that you understand these and other ways of saving energy. Remember – the more energy we save, the longer our fossil fuels will last, and the more time we have to develop alternatives.

3 THE FUTURE

The basic problem

In 1984, the use of energy in Britain was as follows: oil 43.3%; coal 25.3%; natural gas 24.5%; nuclear power 6.9%. (Further supplies of oil and natural gas are also used for 'non-energy' purposes, such as making plastics, hydrogen and organic chemicals.) Coal reserves in Britain are expected to last until the year 2300 if used in Britain alone. It is expected that oil and gas will be used up in the next century. If coal is used on a larger scale as the oil and gas supplies dwindle, coal will be used up more quickly.

FUTURE AIMS

MORE EFFICIENT GENERATING OF ELECTRICITY

Electricity is a clean and versatile form of energy. It can produce heat, light and power, is instantly available, produces no waste, and is supplied to almost every home. It allows appliances to be portable because of the use of sockets or batteries. Most sources of energy in the future are likely to be developed into ways of generating electricity. The conversion of chemical energy into electricity must also become more efficient. One tonne of coal, 0.6 tonnes of oil and $700m^3$ of natural gas provide roughly the same amount of heat energy when burned at a power station, but only 40% of this energy 'reappears' in electricity.

THE NEED TO FIND AN ALTERNATIVE FUEL FOR TRANSPORT

For all its advantages, electricity is not at present useful as a transport fuel except for short journeys (e.g. battery driven cars and milk floats), and rail transport. This may change as better batteries or fuel cells are developed. The problem remains that something must replace petrol and diesel as transport fuels in the future. Other possibilities are hydrogen and ethanol. If either of these could be produced cheaply, on a large scale, and used safely, they would have the extra advantage that they produce no pollutants when they burn.

3 THE NEED TO USE COAL TO HELP PRESERVE OIL AND GAS

This is not easy. It is almost impossible to extract coal from the ground at a rate quick enough to replace oil. (We cannot pump coal out of the ground.) Also, working with coal is a dirty operation. This is particularly true when coal is processed to make smokeless fuels, organic chemicals and coal gas. The extra environment problem is that any use of coal is likely to put some sulphur dioxide into the air (p212) and it is much more difficult to 'desulphurise' a *solid* such as coal, than with liquids or gases. It is also far more difficult to transport coal than gas or oil. Many of these problems may be overcome with improved technology.

4 THE NEED TO DISCOVER NEW STOCKS OF OIL AND GAS

The rate of discovery of new supplies has slowed down. There will be further discoveries, but the danger is that as they become more and more difficult to find, more energy could be spent on finding them and developing them than can be recovered from them!

5 DEVELOP NEW SOURCES OF ENERGY

See Section 15.4, p369.

15.3 THE FOSSIL FUELS

These are fuels which have been formed from dead animals or plants by a decay process which has taken millions of years. The three main ones are coal, natural gas and petroleum (crude oil).

1 PETROLEUM (CRUDE OIL)

THE RAW MATERIAL AND ITS SEPARATION INTO FRACTIONS

Petroleum is a complicated mixture of many hydrocarbons. It is taken to an oil refinery, where it is processed into useful substances. At one time oil refineries were built near to where petroleum was produced, but now they are built in regions where the products can be used directly, and the raw material is taken to them. (You may need to remember some areas where petroleum, natural gas and coal are found. You may have discussed also the potential pollution problem caused by spillage of oil during transport.) An oil refinery is an enormous, complex site, where the raw material is processed into a vast range of products, from fuels to plastics and organic chemicals.

The crude oil is first desulphurised (p212) and then distilled. (The sulphur content of crude oil varies according to the place of origin; oil from the Middle East has a higher sulphur content than oil from America for example.) Some of the main oil-producing areas are shown in Table 15.1 This also shows how oil supplies have varied with new discoveries.

Table 15.1: World 'proven' crude oil reserves

(Figures in thousands of tonnes. The % figures refer to the total world reserves.)

	1947	1955	1960	1973	1984
Western Europe	13700 –	172700 0.7%	235900 0.6%	2190580 2.5%	3305680 3.4%
Middle East	3924800 41.5%	17318400 66.7%	25091100 61.5%	47967430 55.4%	54612970 56.6%
Africa	– 	2600 –	1109500 2.7%	9219980 10.7%	7608290 7.9%
North America (including USA)	2964100 31.4%	4454800 17.1%	4834700 11.8%	6600000 7.6%	5500000 5.7%
Latin America	1486300 15.6%	2125000 8.2%	3433200 8.4%	4334410 5.0%	11413080 11.8%
Far East and Australasia	178000 1.9%	411000 1.6%	1494000 3.7%	2138530 2.5%	2538330 2.6%
Russia and China	911000 9.6%	1484000 5.7%	4589400 11.3%	14109560 16.3%	11520550 12.0%
Total reserves	9477900	25968500	40787800	86560490	96498900

Information supplied by BP: BP Statistical Review of World Energy.

Distillation takes place in a special **fractionating tower**. This works on the same principle as a fractionating column in the laboratory (p80) but is much larger and more complicated. The oil is 'boiled' inside the tower. Vapours rise up the tower. The temperature gradually falls as

Fig 15.4 Fractional distillation of crude oil

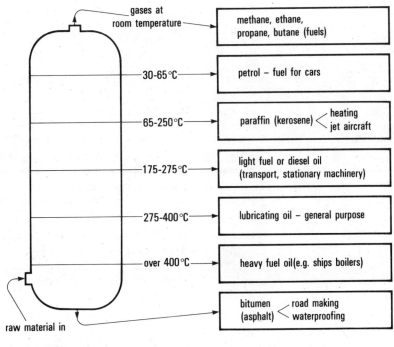

(details of tower not shown)

the vapours rise, and as each substance cools down it eventually changes back into a liquid (**condenses**). The fractions are collected at different heights within the tower, and can be run off. Each fraction is not a pure substance, but is simply a mixture of chemicals which boil within a certain temperature range. Each fraction can be given further fractional distillations to separate it into pure chemicals if needed. The main fractions, and some of their uses, are shown in Fig 15.4.

You may have done a simple experiment to separate crude oil into fractions in the laboratory. If you have done this experiment, make sure that you understand how it works. Also revise the differences between the fractions which you obtained. You probably compared their **viscosity** (thickness, or ability to pour), their colour, their boiling points, how easy it was to light them, and the kind of flame they produced. Some typical results are shown in Table 15.2.

Table 15.2: Typical results of the fractional distillation of crude oil in the laboratory

Note that in *principle*, the only difference between the laboratory experiment and the method used in industry, is that in the laboratory we allow the different fractions to escape one-by-one from the top of the 'tower' (test tube) as the temperature is increased. In industry, the different fractions are collected at different heights (temperatures) within the tower.

Fraction number	Boiling range (°C)	Colour	Viscosity	Flammability
1 (similar to petrol)	30–75	colourless	very low (flows easily)	Very flammable. Burns with clean flame
2 (similar to paraffin)	75–120	colourless or pale yellow	fairly low	Flammable. Yellow flame, some smoke
3 (similar to light oil)	120–170	yellow	slightly viscous	More difficult to ignite. Yellow flame, more smoke
4 (similar to lubricating oil)	170–220	dark yellow/brown	more viscous	Difficult to ignite. Very smoky flame. Carbon formed

CRACKING

Of the fractions produced from crude oil, the most useful are the 'lighter' ones. These are the gases and low-boiling point liquids which have fairly small molecules and are formed near the top of the tower. These are needed in large quantities for making liquid fuels (petrol, paraffin) and for making organic chemicals. Unfortunately, the 'heavier' fractions are also produced in large amounts but these have fewer uses. Small quantities are used for lubricating oils, etc. but the amounts used are very small indeed compared with the need for petrol. (We might change the oil in a car only once per year, but we may add petrol to it each week.) These excess quantities of the heavier fractions are not wasted: they are processed further by **cracking**.

In cracking, the heavier fractions are *briefly* heated to a high temperature (e.g. 900°C), usually mixed with steam and a catalyst.

Carbon-carbon bonds inside the molecules break and the large molecules split up into much smaller, lighter molecules. This produces further supplies of the much-needed lighter molecules for petrol, etc. It also has another advantage. The cracking also makes molecules with carbon-carbon double bonds. These **unsaturated** molecules like the **alkenes** (p333) are important as the starting points of many plastics (p337) and other organic chemicals.

THE EFFECT OF SUPPLY AND DEMAND

As supplies dwindle, the economics of the petroleum industry will no doubt change. In the very early days, before the car was invented, petrol was an inconvenient byproduct and it was often burned off. The main fraction needed in those days was paraffin for lamps, etc. The invention of the petrol engine then created a demand for petrol, and an increased demand for lubricants obtained from the heavier fractions. The balance changed yet again when the 'plastics age' started, and cracking was introduced. This changed some of the heavier molecules into the smaller, unsaturated molecules needed for making plastics. At the same time, it produced more of the petrol-type molecules needed for the ever increasing number of cars. Cracking also produced many simple organic chemicals which had previously been made from coal. What is important today may become unimportant tomorrow. New priorities will have to be faced in the future. It may be necessary, for example, to use petroleum only as a source of organic chemicals which cannot be made by other methods, rather than using it as a source of fuels.

2 NATURAL GAS

Natural gas and crude oil are often found together, because they are formed by a similar process. However, crude oil is a mixture of many hydrocarbons, but natural gas contains only one main hydrocarbon, **methane**, CH_4. The gas supplied to homes and factories in Britain is now natural gas, but until the early 1970s it was **coal gas**. Natural gas has several advantages over coal gas: it is non-toxic, and it produces more heat from an equal volume. Also, it does not have to be manufactured, and it requires very little processing. It is only treated to remove sulphur, and a special substance is added to give it a smell so that leaks can be detected.

Piped gas is a very convenient and clean fuel. As supplies of natural gas are used up, there will still be the need for some kind of piped gas. This could be hydrogen perhaps, or we could once again produce gas from coal. In order to avoid having to convert all gas-cookers and fires for burning coal gas again, research is taking place into making **synthetic natural gas** from coal. This is very similar to natural gas, and applicances would not have to be converted.

3 COAL

Coal is the end product of a series of stages in which dead plant material has rotted. The first stage is the formation of **peat**, which is usually found near the surface as it has not gone through the temperature and pressure changes needed to form coal. There are different kinds of coal (e.g. anthracite, bituminous, lignite), depending on these temperature and pressure changes. Coal contains a variety of chemicals which are not used efficiently if it is burned directly as a fuel. Coal is therefore processed to produce valuable substances such as organic chemicals, plastics and fertilisers, as well as smokeless fuels such as coke and coal gas. The smokeless fuel and coal gas are *clean* fuels, and they can then be burned without wasting all the chemicals which the original coal contained. You may have done an experiment to process or 'improve' coal. The process is called **destructive distillation**. Revise the details if you have seen an experiment of this type. Unfortunately, although this processing of coal seems to have many advantages, it is a very 'dirty' process, and it causes environment problems such as smoke, pollution gases and a very unpleasant smell for people living near to the factory. Also, although smokeless fuels discharge less smoke and tar than by burning the same mass of coal, they produce more sulphur dioxide.

IMPROVING COAL – A SUMMARY

If coal is heated to a high temperature with little or no air present, it does not burn. Instead, it splits up into some very useful substances (see Fig 15.5).

Fig 15.5 Improving coal

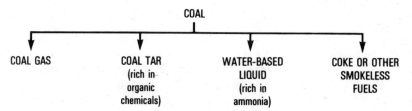

A typical coal gas contains about 50% hydrogen, 30% methane, 8% carbon monoxide, and smaller quantities of other gases, mainly hydrocarbons. The carbon monoxide makes coal gas poisonous.

By far the most important use of coal in Britain is at power stations, where it is burned to produce steam which then drives turbines to produce electricity. Some is also processed as described above, the main purpose being to produce coke for industry (e.g. making iron, p134) and smokeless fuels for use in the home.

4 COMPARING THE FOSSIL FUELS

You should be able to make sensible comments about the advantages and disadvantages of the three fossil fuels, and of the electricity which they are often used to make. For example, some of the advantages/disadvantages of electricity are given on p363. Some points about coal have been mentioned in the previous section, and a few more are given below. You should be able to make similar points about oil and gas. Remember, when making these comparisons, that these fuels are used for other things as well as fuels. Remember also that although the disadvantages of coal may be more obvious, the others have disadvantages too, and coal also has advantages!

SOME PROBLEMS IN USING COAL

1 Has to be mined by hand or machine; gas and oil simply 'flow out' once discovered. Much slower rate of production for coal.
2 Mining causes the land to 'move' or settle – houses and roads are damaged by subsidence.
3 Much solid waste formed by mining – has to be dumped somewhere (p134).
4 Raw coal is the 'dirtiest' fossil fuel. Also difficult to desulphurise.
5 Not convenient to transport or store.

15.4 OTHER SOURCES OF ENERGY. FUELS OF THE FUTURE

1 CHOOSING A FUEL

Any reaction which gives out energy could, in theory, be used as a fuel system. There are thousands of exothermic reactions, including the many examples of substances burning in air to give out heat energy. However, very few substances are actually used as fuels. These are some of the questions we should ask when considering a substance as a possible fuel.

(a)   Occurs naturally, or made artificially? If made, is it expensive, do we use energy in making it?

(b)   If found naturally, is it in large deposits (easy to use) or is it scattered in small, well-separated deposits (difficult to use)?

(c)   If it occurs naturally, is there plenty of it?

(d)   Can it be transported and stored easily?

(e)   When it burns, are pollutants formed? If yes, can it be purified easily and cheaply before burning? Can the impurities which are removed be used for anything else?

(f)   Is *solid* waste formed when it burns? Could this be used, or does it have to be disposed of?

(g)   Does a certain mass or volume of the substance produce as much, or nearly as much, heat as the same mass or volume of other substances used as fuels?

(h)   Is the substance toxic, or difficult to handle?

(i)   How versatile would the fuel be? Can it be used only in special circumstances (e.g. a rocket fuel) or could it be used more widely?

(j)   Can the substance be made, or found, near to transport services?

(k)   Is it easy to ignite?

(l)   Is it **renewable** or **non-renewable**? A renewable fuel is one which is available all the time, and will continue to be available for a very long time. Solar energy is an example of a renewable fuel, as are wind energy and tidal power. Timber is also a kind of renewable fuel because we can grow more trees, although we may not be able to grow them fast enough. Other forms of **biomass** (p372) are renewable. Fossil fuels are non-renewable. Obviously, a substance is more attractive as a fuel if it is renewable.

2 SOLAR ENERGY

Energy from the sun is an attractive form of energy. It is renewable, clean, pollution-free, and the annual supply of solar energy on this planet is more than 5,000 times greater than the total amount of energy that we need. Photoelectric cells can change solar energy into electricity, but at the moment this is only possible on a small scale. The problem remains, therefore, of using solar energy in a cheap and practical way. Solar energy also has other problems. The amount of sunlight which reaches ground level varies a great deal, especially in winter. Winter is the time when we make our greatest demand for electricity. Also, there is no sunlight during the night! Solar energy is thus incapable of producing energy all the time. Its main appeal is as a *supplementary* source of energy, especially for domestic heating.

3 BATTERIES

See p41. Note also the kind of battery used in a car. The main attraction is as a *portable* power supply. Not useful on a large scale. Some can be recharged (by using electricity from another source) but others stop when the chemicals are used up. This can be inconvenient.

4 TIDAL POWER

A barrage is built across a suitable estuary. Water-powered turbines are built in to the barrage. As the tide flows in, the turbines are turned one way, and generate electricity. As the tide flows out, the turbines are turned the other way and again produce electricity. Obviously, tidal power is renewable, but there are problems. Only estuaries with a good tidal range are suitable. It is extremely expensive to build the barrage. The generation of electricity is not constant; it rises and falls according to the tidal flow, and peak output varies from day to day. Each scheme provides only a small proportion of the total energy demand. Tidal power is best considered as a supplementary source of electricity, but on the credit side it does not take up valuable land and it does not create any pollution.

5 WIND POWER

Wind has been used as a source of energy throughout history, in windmills, sailing ships, etc. Now it is being considered as a way of generating electricity. Its attractions are that it is renewable, it is likely to be more active in winter when we need most energy, and it is pollution free. Its disadvantages include: not constant (many calm days); large wind machines needed; and many of them, which would use up a lot of land; each machine quite expensive compared with the electricity it could generate. Best considered as a supplementary source of energy.

6 GEOTHERMAL ENERGY

The centre of the earth consists of molten material at a very high temperature. The temperature gradually falls from the centre to the crust. It is possible to extract hot water from below the crust (this happens naturally in some parts of the world). It is also possible to extract heat directly from underground rocks. This idea is attractive; there is enough heat energy in the top 10 km of the crust in Britain alone to be equivalent to the energy obtainable from 50,000 million million tonnes of coal. Unfortunately, this energy is spread 'thinly' and it is very difficult to extract. This method is still at a very early stage. If technology improves, it could be very useful.

7 NUCLEAR POWER, HYDROELECTRIC POWER

For nuclear power see p46. Nuclear fuel is non-renewable, although supplies will last for a very long time. You should be able to describe the principle of hydroelectric power, and to understand that it is not used very much in Britain. Fast-flowing rivers or large 'drops' from mountainous regions are needed.

8 FUEL CELLS

These are an improvement on the traditional battery. They work in the same kind of way, because a chemical reaction in the cell is used to produce electricity. An important difference is that the 'chemicals' in a fuel cell are supplied continuously to the cell, so that the cell does not stop working, unlike a battery. The 'chemicals' are often gases or liquids, and a steady flow into the cell is easy to achieve. Fuel cells are not portable because of the fuel supply system, and they can only provide fairly low currents, but they are very efficient, can be cheap to run, and are usually pollution free.

9 FUSION

Nuclear power is produced by **fission**: atoms break down into smaller atoms and liberate energy. It is also possible for small atoms to *combine* to make larger ones, and again energy is produced. This kind of atomic reaction is called **fusion**. Fusion is the source of energy in the sun. The energy obtainable from a single fusion is far greater than that from a single fission.

The fusion fuel would be two different isotopes of hydrogen. These would combine to form an atom of helium. In theory, fusion could supply almost limitless energy, and the waste products would be easy to dispose of, unlike those from fission (p46). However, the technological problems are enormous. We can produce fusion; a hydrogen bomb works on the same principle. However, the temperatures needed to cause fusion in a hydrogen bomb are produced by an 'ordinary' atomic bomb. These temperatures are of the order of a hundred million °C. The problems of exposing the fusion fuel, safely, to a temperature as high as this for just a second or so, and then of using safely the enormous energy produced, have not yet been solved.

10 BIOMASS

One renewable source of fuels which is attracting a great deal of attention is **biomass**. This name is used for a variety of organic waste materials (e.g. garden compost, industrial refuse, manures) and energy crops (sugar cane, special plants, or even trees). It is estimated that roughly half of the world's population relies upon some form of biomass for heating and cooking. The traditional way of using such material is to burn it. Modern methods use biomass more efficiently, and these are being developed on a larger scale. Biomass can be made into solid, liquid or gaseous fuels by a variety of processes. Examples of modern applications include:

(i) Cow or pig dung can be broken down by bacteria in specially designed tanks to produce a gaseous fuel consisting of approximately 70% methane and 30% carbon dioxide.

(ii) Industrial and household waste dumped in special pits can produce large volumes of methane as it decomposes with bacterial help.

(iii) Single-stem trees can be grown rapidly to produce wood and wood-thinnings. Other forms of vegetation, special crops, and even plants which grow in water are all being investigated as potential sources of fuels. In many parts of the world, the burning of timber is an important source of energy. There is concern, however, that we are felling trees faster than we are growing them (p209).

(iv) Sugar cane can be grown solely for fermentation of sugar, to produce ethanol, either for direct use as a fuel, or for blending with petrol.

CHECK LIST ▶

REMEMBER THAT SOME OF THESE POINTS MAY NOT BE RELEVANT FOR THE PARTICULAR SYLLABUS YOU ARE FOLLOWING.

YOU SHOULD UNDERSTAND THE FOLLOWING POINTS.
1 ▶ Endothermic, exothermic reactions; $\triangle H$, +ve and −ve values.
2 ▶ Bond-making, bond-breaking processes, the energy changes they produce.
3 ▶ Flash points, ignition temperatures.
4 ▶ Experiments on energy changes.
5 ▶ Calculations on energy changes.
6 ▶ Fuels: problems of the future, what properties are needed in a fuel.
7 ▶ Petroleum: distillation, main fractions, cracking.
8 ▶ Natural gas and coal.

9 ▶ 'Improving coal' (destructive distillation).
10 ▶ Alternative energy sources, according to your syllabus.
11 ▶ Calculations on energy changes during change of state.

SPECIMEN EXAMINATION QUESTIONS

SEE GENERAL NOTE BEFORE QUESTIONS ON pp49 AND 50.
REMEMBER THAT YOU MAY BE ALLOWED TO USE A DATA
BOOK IN THE EXAMINATION.

1   Crude oil can be separated into different fractions because each fraction has a different
  A boiling point   B density   C melting point   D solubility

2   Which one of the following is *not* a fossil fuel?
  A Biogas   B Coal   C Natural gas   D Oil
                 [*SEG* spec (Alt), 1]

3   Cracking of a hydrocarbon mixture results in the
  A   formation of small molecules from larger ones
  B   combustion of the hydrocarbons
  C   formation of ethanol
  D   formation of polythene
  E   separation of the hydrocarbon into groups of substances with
similar boiling-point.   [*LEA* spec (A), 1]

4

$$X = \begin{array}{c} H \;\; H \\ | \;\;\;\; | \\ C = C \\ | \;\;\;\; | \\ H \;\; H \end{array} \; ; \qquad Y = \begin{array}{c} H \;\; H \;\; H \;\; H \;\; H \;\; H \\ | \;\; | \;\; | \;\; | \;\; | \;\; | \\ -C-C-C-C-C-C- \\ | \;\; | \;\; | \;\; | \;\; | \;\; | \\ H \;\; H \;\; H \;\; H \;\; H \;\; H \end{array}$$

When Y is made from X, the reaction is called
  A cracking   B hydrolysis   C oxidation   D polymerisation
    E reduction   [*LEA* spec (B), 1]

5   (*a*)   Name one example of
           (i) a solid fuel,
           (ii) a liquid fuel,
           (iii) a gaseous fuel.
    (*b*)   Fossil fuels all contain carbon.
           (i) Write a word equation for the burning of carbon in a
plentiful supply of air.
           (ii) Write a symbol equation for the same reaction.
                    [*NEA* spec (A), 1]

Questions **6–12** are concerned with fuels and their uses. The PIE chart
in Fig 15.6 shows the amounts of different fuels consumed in Amazonia during 1975.

6   Which of the fuels A to E in the diagram is **not** a fossil fuel?

7   The element present in all these fuels is
  A carbon   B chlorine   C helium   D neon   E sodium

8   In 1975, Amazonia's reserves of petroleum, bituminous coal and
anthracitic coal were as follows:

	Available reserves in millions of tonnes
Petroleum	1000
Bituminous Coal	920
Anthracitic Coal	140

If the amount of fuel consumed each year stays the same, the fuel(s) still available for use in the year 2000 will be

A   all three
B   both types of coal
C   petroleum only
D   bituminous coal only
E   none of them

9 The table below gives the amount of heat energy that is released by 1 tonne of each fuel when it is burned in air.

	Energy released per tonne (arbitrary units)
Wood	4
Natural gas	41
Anthracitic coal	25
Bituminous coal	22
Petroleum	12

Fig 15.6 Chart for questions 6–12

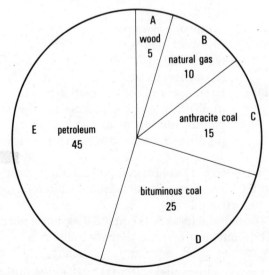

all figures quoted are in millions of tonnes

Natural gas burns more easily than the other fuels. This is most probably because

A   gases always burn better than solids and liquids

B   the other fuels contain many substances which do not burn easily

C   gases occupy a greater volume than do liquids and solids

D   natural gas contains mostly methane

E   gases mix better with the air, and therefore burn more quickly

10   The fuel which produced the most energy overall in 1975 was

A   wood

B   natural gas

C   anthracitic coal

D   bituminous coal

E   petroleum

11   In an effort to conserve its fuel reserves and reduce pollution, Amazonia decided in 1978 that all new motor cars should use ethanol (CH_3CH_2OH) instead of petrol.

The gas that would **not** be found coming out of the exhausts of new cars in 1979 is

A   carbon dioxide

B   carbon monoxide

C   nitrogen

D   sulphur dioxide

E   water vapour

12   Ethanol can be made by fermenting glucose ($C_6H_{12}O_6$) as described in the equation below.

$$C_6H_{12}O_6(aq) \xrightarrow{yeast} 2CH_3CH_2OH(aq) + 2CO_2(g)$$

The mass of glucose needed to make 2 moles of ethanol is (Relative atomic masses: C = 12, H = 1, O = 16.)

A   4g

B   88g

C   92g

D   180g

E   360g   [*LEA* spec (B), 1]

13   The graph (in Fig 15.7) shows the main fuels used to supply Britain's energy during the last fifty years.

Which conclusion can be made from this graph?

A   Solid fuels are not as important as a source of energy as they used to be.

B   There is no future for the mining industry in Britain.

C   Our supply of crude oil will run out by the year 2000.

D   Nuclear fuels will never supply much of Britain's energy.

[*NEA* spec (B), 1]

Fig 15.7 Graph for
question 13

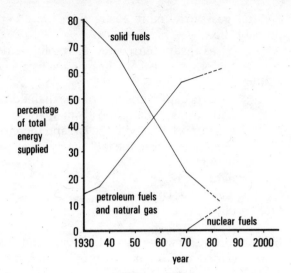

+14   A mixture of methane and carbon dioxide, with traces of other gases, may be made by fermentation of cow dung. The mixture is known as biogas.

(a)   (i) Explain why biogas can be used as a fuel.

(ii) Name one other fuel that can be produced by fermentation.

(iii) Write an equation for the complete combustion of the fuel you mentioned in (ii).

(b)   Devise a method for estimating the percentage by volume of carbon dioxide in biogas.

(c)   Biogas contains 32% by mass of methane. The equation for the complete combustion of methane is shown below.

$$CH_4 + 2O_2 \rightarrow CO_2 + 2H_2O$$

Relative atomic masses: H 1, C 12, O 16.

(i) Calculate the mass of methane in 1 kg of biogas.

(ii) Calculate the mass of CO_2 produced by the complete combustion of this mass of methane.

(iii) The formula mass in grams (one mole) of carbon dioxide has a volume of 24 dm^3 under normal laboratory conditions. Calculate the total **volume** of CO_2 produced by the combusion of 1 kg of biogas.

(d)   (i) State **two** ways in which energy is released during the explosion of mixtures of methane and air.

(ii) Explain why mixtures of methane and air do not usually burn without being ignited.   [*SEG* spec 3]

15   The graph (Fig 15.8) gives information about fuels.

(a)   Use the graph to help you answer the following questions.

(i) Which fuel should last the longest?

(ii) Which fuel is being used up fastest?

Fig 15.8 Graph for
question 15

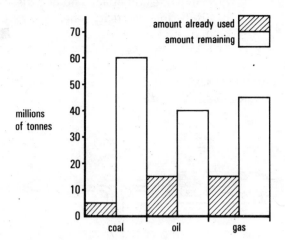

(iii) How would the motor industry be affected if all the oil reserves were used up?

(b)   Coal is used to produce electricity in power stations, but is being replaced by nuclear fuels. For nuclear power stations compared to coal burning ones, give

(i) **one** advantage

(ii) **one** disadvantage

(c)   One method proposed for the production of electrical energy in the future is by harnessing wave power. The diagram (Fig 15.9) shows waves making a plastic unit 'bob' back and forth turning a spindle. The spindle is attached to a generator in the power station.

Fig 15.9 Diagram for
question 15(c)

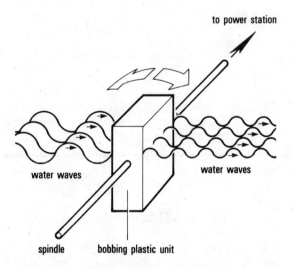

(i) Give **one** source from which the waves get their energy.

(ii) Give **two** reasons why plastic is preferred to steel for the bobbing units.

(iii) Give **one** advantage and **one** disadvantage of this system of producing electricity when compared with methods using coal, oil and gas. [*MEA* spec 2]

16 For over a hundred years the gas supplied to houses and factories for use as a fuel was coal gas. The diagram (Fig 15.10) represents a laboratory scale model of the process used for making coal gas which is called destructive distillation.

Fig 15.10 Diagram for question 16

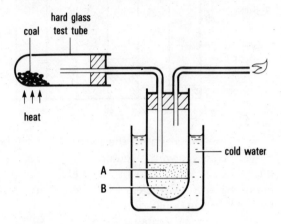

When coal is heated as shown, out of contact with air, a colourless Liquid, A, and a black sticky Liquid B, are collected in a cooled receiver. The coal gas can be burned as it leaves the tube at C and it burns with a smoky flame.

(*a*)   What is the liquid B called?

(*b*)   Mention one substance which can be obtained from B and give a use for it.

(*c*)   The liquid A turns red litmus blue. What type of substance causes such a change?

(*d*)   What remains in the hard glass test-tube at the end of the process?

(*e*)   Give **one** important use for this product.

Northern Ireland does not have any access to the newer type of gas, natural gas, but there are plentiful supplies in the North Sea.

(*f*)   What hydrocarbon does natural gas mostly consist of?

(*g*)   Name two other hydrocarbon gases which are also used as fuels.

(*h*)   What types of hydrocarbon are the gases you have named in (*g*)?

One type of fuel has recently been found in very large quantities in Northern Ireland.

(*i*)   Name this fuel and describe how it differs from ordinary coal.

(*j*)   If the fuel is mined what will it mostly be used for?

Substances such as coal, oil and natural gas are all known as 'fossil' fuels.

(*k*)   Explain what is meant by the name 'fossil' fuel.

(*l*)   At room temperature coal is solid, oil is liquid and natural gas is gaseous. What does this tell you about the molecules of the substances which each contains?

(*m*)　　These fuels are used for more than just burning. From each of them a whole range of chemicals can be made and from some of these chemicals (called monomers) polymers are produced. Explain what we mean when we say that a chemical process changes a monomer into a polymer. [*NISEC* spec 2]

17　This question is about the formation of alcohol (ethanol) from sugars and its possible use as an alternative to petrol as a fuel for car engines.

One source of sugars is sugar cane which is crushed and the juices mixed with yeast. The mixture is allowed to stand for two or three days at around 30°C.

The liquid product is then fractionally distilled, most of the ethanol being in the middle of three fractions.

(*a*)　　Name **one** other crop which is a useful source of sugars.

(*b*)　　The equation for the reaction which changes the sugar glucose into ethanol in the presence of yeast is given below.

$$C_6H_{12}O_6(aq) \rightarrow 2\,C_2H_5OH(aq) + 2\,CO_2(g)$$

(i) What does the symbol (aq) indicate about the glucose?

(ii) What is the purpose of the yeast in the reaction?

(ii) Why is this reaction **not** speeded up if the mixture is boiled?

(iv) Give the name of the process which converts glucose into ethanol in this way.

(v) Why is the same reaction important in bread-making?

(*c*)　　One of the advantages of ethanol over petrol is that, unlike petrol, ethanol is a *renewable energy source*.

Explain the meaning of the term *renewable energy source*.

(*d*)　　What other possible advantages might ethanol have over petrol as a fuel for car engines?

(*e*)　　Methylated spirits is a mixture of ethanol (about 90%) and methanol (about 10%) together with a small quantity of purple dye.

Explain why the ethanol is treated in this way before being sold as 'meths'. [*SEG* spec (Alt), 2]

†18　The label on a bottle containing a brand of 'Health Drink' reads as follows:

> *Ingredients: Glucose, vitamin C, flavouring essence (including caffeine), fruit acid, lactic acid, preservative, carbon dioxide.*

> *Carbohydrate content (as monosaccharide) 19.3 g per 100 cm³.*

> *Energy content 340 kJ per 100 cm³.*

(*a*)　　What colour would a piece of universal indicator paper become when dipped into the drink?

To check the 'energy content', 10 cm³ of the health drink were heated on a water bath to evaporate all the water in the drink.

(b)   Why was the health drink sample heated on a water bath instead of directly over a bunsen burner?

The solid residue from the evaporation was placed in a crucible and the apparatus shown (Fig 15.11) was set up.

Fig 15.11 Diagram for question 18 (c)–(e)

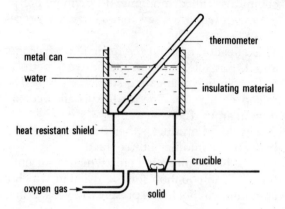

500 cm^3 of water were placed in the metal can and its initial temperature recorded. The supply of oxygen was turned on and the solid ignited. The temperature of the water was recorded again once all the solid had burned.

Readings   Initial temperature of water = 19.6°C
                    Final temperature of water = 34.6°C

(c)   Why was a metal can used to hold the water rather than a glass beaker?

(d)   Calculate the amount of heat (in kJ) absorbed by the water in the can. (4.2 J of heat is needed to raise the temperature of 1 g of water by 1°C).

(e)   (i) Use your answer from (d) to estimate the 'energy content' of 100 cm^3 of the health drink.

(ii) Give **one** reason, other than heat loss to the air, why the 'energy content' measured by the experiment is different from that quoted on the label.

(f)   The Heat of Combustion of glucose ($C_6H_{12}O_6$) is −3200 kJ/mol.

Fig 15.12 Diagram for question 18 (f)

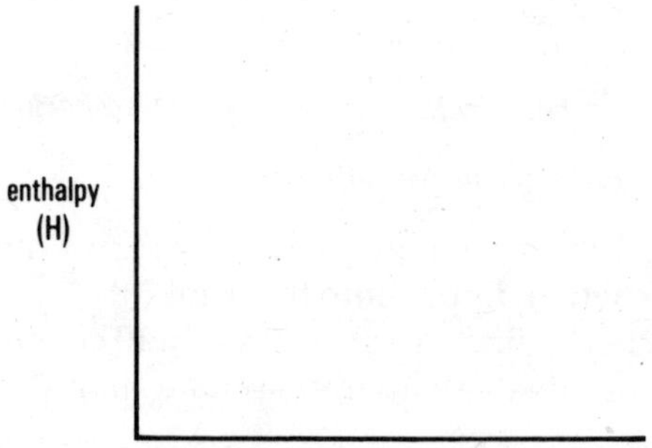

enthalpy
(H)

(i) Write a balanced equation for the complete combustion of glucose.

(ii) Draw an enthalpy level diagram (see Fig 15.12) to show the change in heat energy when glucose burns.

(g)   Why is it useful for energy content values to be printed on many foods?   [*SEG* spec (Alt), 3]

†19 Glucose, $C_6H_{12}O_6$ is a white crystalline solid and is an example of a carbohydrate. By the process of fermentation, an aqueous solution of glucose can be converted into a mixture of ethanol, C_2H_5OH, and water. Ethanol is a colourless liquid which boils at 78°C. It may be converted into the unsaturated hydrocarbon, ethene, C_2H_4, by passing ethanol vapour over heated aluminium oxide. Ethene is a gas at room temperature and is not soluble in water.

(a)   Explain what is meant by the following:
(i) Carbohydrate
(ii) Hydrocarbon
(iii) Unsaturated

(b)   Complete and label the diagram (Fig 15.13) of the apparatus you would use for preparing and collecting a sample of *ethene* free from ethanol vapour.

(c)   The heat given out when 1 mole of ethanol is burned is 1380 kJ mol^{-1}. Calculate the fuel value of ethanol in kJ per gram.
    (Relative molecular mass of ethanol = 46.)

(d)   When a mole of propanol, C_3H_7OH is burnt 2017 kJ of heat energy is given out. Explain why this is different from the value for ethanol.

(e)   Give one example of an important compound formed by addition polymerisation and the monomer from which it is formed.
                    [*LEA* spec (B), 3]

†20 The diagram (Fig 15.14) shows what happens inside a petrol engine.

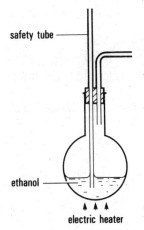

safety tube

ethanol

electric heater

Fig 15.13 Diagram for question 19

Fig 15.14 Diagram for question 20

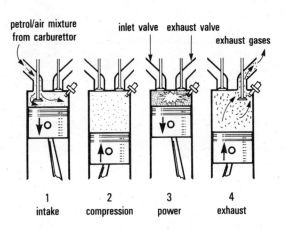

petrol/air mixture from carburettor   inlet valve exhaust valve   exhaust gases

1 intake   2 compression   3 power   4 exhaust

Petrol vapour (mainly hydrocarbons) and air are drawn in to the piston chamber. The mixture is squeezed together by the piston and then exploded by a spark. The explosion pushes down the piston and this gives the engine power.

(*a*)　　What is meant by the term hydrocarbon?

(*b*)　　One of the substances in petrol is heptane (C_7H_{16}). When one mole of heptane is *completely* burned in air 4800 kJ of energy are released.

(i) Write a word equation for the complete burning of heptane.

(ii) Write a symbol equation for this reaction.

(*c*)　　One litre of petrol contains about 70 grams of heptane. What is the *maximum* amount of energy which could be released by burning 70 grams of heptane?

(*d*)　　Why is this amount of energy not produced when 70 grams of heptane is burnt in a car engine?

(*e*)　　Using ideas about particles, explain why an explosion pushes down the piston.

(*f*)　　The names, boiling points and structures of four hydrocarbons of formula C_7H_{16} are shown in the table below.

Name	Boiling point (°C)	Structure
heptane	98	
3-methylhexane	92	
2-methylhexane	90	

Name	Boiling point (°C)	Structure
2,2-dimethylpentane	79	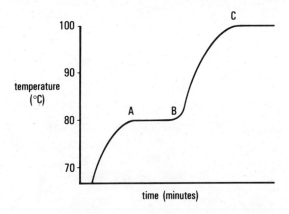

(ii) What is the name given to molecules which have the same formula but different structures?

(ii) What is the connection between the structure of these substances and their boiling points?

(g)   A mixture of heptane and 2,2-dimethylpentane was separated by distillation. The graph below (Fig 15.15) shows the temperature of the vapour entering the condenser over a period of time.

Fig 15.15 Graph for question 20

(i) Why is the graph flat between A and B?

(ii) Comment on the composition of the vapour entering the condenser between times B and C.   [NEA spec (B), 3]

†21   The list below shows some processes which are used in industry: cracking, fermentation, polymerisation.

Using **one** example from industry in each case, describe briefly how each process may be used to manufacture a product useful in everyday life.   [LEA spec (A), 3]

SPEEDS OF REACTION. TWO MORE IMPORTANT RESOURCES: SALT AND LIMESTONE

CONTENTS

16.1 SPEEDS (RATES) OF REACTION

Some chemical reactions take place very slowly, e.g. the rusting of iron. This reaction is so slow that we cannot see anything happening for at least a day or so. Some reactions are very fast, e.g. explosions. Many reactions take place at speeds somewhere in between these two extremes.

There are times when it is useful to be able to *slow down* a reaction, e.g. the 'setting' of concrete, or a decay **process** in food, or a reaction which is normally explosive. (If you have studied **food preservatives**, revise your notes.) There are also times when it is very useful to be able to *speed up* a reaction, e.g. the 'setting' of a glue, or an industrial process. In industry, it is important to be able to make a particular substance *as quickly as possible.* We cannot afford to wait for a slow reaction to take place. Chemists therefore need to know how to speed up or slow down chemical reactions. The main ways of doing so are by

(*a*)   changing the temperature,
(*b*)   changing the concentration of the substances,
(*c*)   changing the particle size if solids are used,
(*d*)   changing the pressure if gases are used, and
(*e*)   using a catalyst.
Light also affects the speed of some reactions.

1 HOW CONCENTRATION CHANGES AFFECT THE SPEED OF A REACTION

There are three main types of experiment used to show this.

(a) USING THE REACTION BETWEEN A DILUTE ACID AND SODIUM THIOSULPHATE SOLUTION

When a dilute acid is mixed with sodium thiosulphate solution, the two colourless solutions react. A precipitate of sulphur is formed. This white/yellow solid makes the liquid go cloudy. The cloudiness increases as the reaction continues.

DILUTE ACID +   SODIUM   →SULPHUR + OTHER
                  THIOSULPHATE   PRODUCTS
                  SOLUTION

The two solutions are normally mixed in a conical flask which is placed over a mark (e.g. a pencilled cross) on a piece of paper. The mark gradually 'disappears' when looked at through the flask, as the cloudiness increases. The reaction time is the time taken between mixing the solutions and the 'disappearance' of the mark.

Suppose that we want to use this experiment to find out how the concentration of a solution affects the speed of reaction. In this experiment, and in all reactions like it, we must keep all the **variable** things *constant* except for the variable we are investigating. For example, the variables in this experiment are:

(i) the volume of acid,
(ii) the volume of sodium thiosulphate solution,
(iii) the particular acid;
(iv) the temperature of the two solutions,
(v) the concentration of the acid,
(vi) the concentration of the sodium thiosulphate,
(vii) the container they are mixed in; and
(viii) the person making the decision about when the reaction is over.

The variable we are investigating is the concentration of one of the solutions. Usually, we vary the concentration of the sodium thiosulphate solution. Everything else must remain unchanged each time we do the experiment. We might do the experiment five times, and the only thing we change each time is the concentration of the sodium thiosulphate solution. The following table shows typical mixtures used.

| | Temperature of solutions | Volume of acid | Concentration of acid | Volume of sodium thiosulphate soln kept at total of $50cm^3$ but different concentrations used | | |
				Vol. sodium thiosulph. soln	vol water	total vol
Exp 1	Fixed (e.g. 20°C)	$5\,cm^3$	fixed	$10cm^3$	$40cm^3$	$50cm^3$
Exp 2	as above	$5cm^3$	as above	$20cm^3$	$30cm^3$	$50cm^3$
Exp 3	as above	$5cm^3$	as above	$30cm^3$	$20cm^3$	$50cm^3$
Exp 4	as above	$5cm^3$	as above	$40cm^3$	$10cm^3$	$50cm^3$
Exp 5	as above	$5cm^3$	as above	$50cm^3$	$0cm^3$	$50cm^3$

All the other variables mentioned earlier are also kept constant in each experiment. The experiment shows that **the speed of a reaction is faster if the concentration of one or more of the chemicals is increased**. In the example above, the fastest reaction would be experiment 5.

(b) THE REACTION BETWEEN CALCIUM CARBONATE AND A DILUTE ACID, BY A WEIGHING METHOD

When a dilute acid is added to calcium carbonate (limestone), a reaction takes place. There is 'fizzing', and the gas carbon dioxide is given off. As the gas *escapes* from the mixture, the mixture loses mass;

it weighs less. If the mixture loses weight rapidly, then the speed of the reaction is fast. If the mixture loses mass slowly, then the speed of the reaction is slow. The reaction can be used to investigate how changes affect its speed. The main variables are:

(i) the mass of calcium carbonate;

(ii) the particle size of the calcium carbonate (whether it is powdered, or in lumps, etc);

(iii) the particular acid;

(iv) the volume of acid;

(v) the concentration of the acid; and

(vi) the temperature.

If we wish to use this reaction to investigate how the concentration of the acid affects the speed, we repeat the experiment several times, with the concentration of the acid changing each time. All the other variables must be fixed each time. The mixture is placed in a flask which stands on a balance. The acid is added last, and the timing then starts. (A plug of loose cotton wool is normally placed in the neck of the flask to prevent any spray escaping.) The mass of the flask and its contents is taken every half-minute. The results are used to plot a graph, as shown in Fig 16.1. If the experiment is done three times, three different sets of readings can be plotted on one piece of graph paper, as in the figure. A typical mass of calcium carbonate would be 5 g. The concentration of the acid might be varied by having 30cm^3 each time, but having different proportions of water and acid (as was done for the concentration of sodium thiosulphate in the table on p.388).

Fig 16.1 Investigating the speed of a reaction

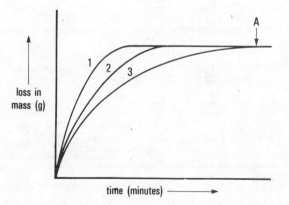

loss in mass (g)

time (minutes) ⟶

Note that the mass *lost* each half-minute is plotted on the graph. This is the same as the mass of carbon dioxide given off each half-minute. You must understand what the shapes of the lines on the graph tell us. The *faster* the speed of a reaction, the *steeper* the line on the graph. If the reaction is rapid, mass is lost rapidly as the gas escapes. The line for the reaction with the highest concentration of the acid should be the steepest line (line 1 in Fig 16.1). This tells us that **increasing the concentration** of a substance **increases the speed of reaction.**

Note

(i) Graphs like the ones in Fig 16.1 show that the speed of a chemical reaction is usually fastest at the *beginning*. The steepness of the line lessens as time goes on. At the beginning of the reaction, the reagents are in their most concentrated form. After this they are gradually used up as they react, and their concentration falls. The speed of the reaction therefore falls as the reaction continues. Eventually the reaction *stops* when one of the reagents is used up. This is when the graphs become horizontal in Fig 16.1 (position A).

(ii) Notice that the three lines on the graph *all* become horizontal at the same 'loss of mass' (marked A). They reach this point at different times, however. This is because the three experiments all used the *same mass of* calcium carbonate, and there was plenty of acid (an **excess**) each time. The same *final* mass of carbon dioxide must be formed, therefore. The experiments only differ in the time taken to form this fixed mass of carbon dioxide.

(c) THE REACTION BETWEEN A METAL AND AN ACID, USING A SYRINGE TO COLLECT THE GAS

(This method could also be used in the previous reaction, using the syringe to collect the carbon dioxide.)

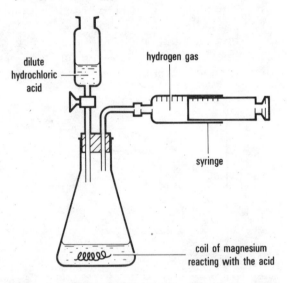

Fig 16.2 Investigating the speed of a reaction between magnesium and a dilute acid

When a metal such as magnesium reacts with sulphuric or hydrochloric acid, hydrogen gas is given off. This can be collected in a syringe, as shown in Fig 16.2 The *volume* of the hydrogen is noted every half-minute. The results are plotted on a graph as in Fig 16.3. Compare this graph with Fig 16.1, and make sure that you understand the differences.

If you have understood the earlier work in this chapter, you should be able to work out the experimental details and likely results for yourself. Try these steps:

(*a*)　　write down a list of all the variables in this experiment;

(*b*)　　decide which of these you would need to change in order to

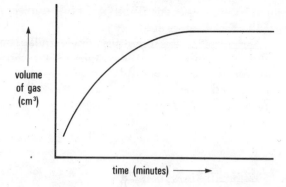

Fig 16.3 The results of an experiment in which the volume of gas is plotted against time

investigate how a change in concentration would affect the speed of the reaction;

(c)   draw a table showing how you would do the experiment three times;

(d)   copy out Fig 16.3 and add two more lines to show what you would expect to find when the results would be plotted; and

(e)   label the line which would be for the most concentrated solution C, the one for the lowest concentration W, and the other one M (for medium).

2 HOW CHANGES IN TEMPERATURE AFFECT REACTION RATES

A typical experiment used to investigate the affect of temperature is the one described in 1(a), p387. This time all the variables are fixed *except the temperature* of one of the solutions. Usually, the temperature of the sodium thiosulphate solution is varied. Make sure that you understand how to do the experiment. The results show that **increasing the temperature increases the speed of a reaction.**

Note that it is possible to cool solutions as well as heating them. For example, one of the solutions could be cooled in an ice bath. Note also that there is no point in trying to start each experiment at a temperature chosen in advance. For example, there is no point in deciding to heat one of the solutions to exactly 50°C, because as soon as you add the other solution the temperature will no longer be 50°C (unless you also take the trouble to warm up the other solution in the same way). It is far simpler to heat one of the solutions to approximately the temperature you need, then add the other, start timing, stir with thermometer, and note the exact temperature of the mixture.

3 HOW CHANGES IN PARTICLE SIZE AFFECT THE SPEED OF A REACTION

(Changing the particle size is sometimes called changing the **surface area.**) This can only affect a reaction if at least one of the reacting substances is a *solid*. For example, in the reaction described in 1(b), p388, the calcium carbonate is a solid. We could use different kinds of 'particle size' for the calcium carbonate. We could use it in a finely divided state (a powder); we could use it in small pieces, or large pieces. The more finely divided a substance is, the greater its surface area. Make sure that you understand how to investigate this, fixing all the variables except one.

Experiments like this show that a **finely divided solid reacts more rapidly than the same solid in the form of large pieces.** (The **greater the surface area of a solid, the more rapidly it reacts.**) If the results are plotted on a graph as for 1(b), p388, the steepest line will be the one for the most finely divided solid.

4 WHY DO THESE CHANGES AFFECT THE SPEED OF A REACTION?

(a) CONCENTRATION CHANGES

A solution contains dissolved chemicals. The dissolved particles move about in the liquid. The substances in the solution can only react when the different particles collide. In 10cm^3 of a concentrated solution there are more dissolved particles than in 10cm^3 of a dilute solution of the same substances. The particles in a concentrated solution collide more often, and therefore they react more quickly.

(b) TEMPERATURE CHANGES

All particles have some kinetic energy. The particles move – they may vibrate, rotate, or move from place to place, depending on how much kinetic energy they have. If the temperature is increased, the particles gain more kinetic energy. They then move more rapidly, and collide more frequently. A reaction therefore speeds up as the temperature is increased.

(c) PARTICLE SIZE

A finely divided substance has a greater surface area with which to react. This means that more of it is exposed to another substance than if the same solid was in 'lump' form. For example, if a cube of sugar is placed in a hot liquid, the liquid only makes contact with the outer surfaces of the cube. All of the sugar *inside* the cube (i.e. most of the sugar) does not at first touch the liquid.

5 HOW A CATALYST AFFECTS THE SPEED OF A REACTION

A **catalyst** is a substance which *alters the speed* of a reaction. It does not appear to take part in the reaction itself. A catalyst seems just to 'sit there' and cause the reaction to go faster.

A typical reaction used to show this is the laboratory preparation of oxygen (p216). If hydrogen peroxide solution is heated, it splits up to produce oxygen. Manganese(IV)oxide, a black powder (MnO_2) can be used as a catalyst for the reaction. If a small amount of the catalyst is added to the hydrogen peroxide solution, the same reaction takes place but *instantly*, without heating. The catalyst does not change itself; it just causes the hydrogen peroxide solution to react more quickly. You may have used other reactions to show the effects of catalysts. Make sure that you understand any experiment you have used in this way.

Enzymes are catalysts found in living things. They help reactions to take place more easily in our bodies. Without enzymes, these same reactions would take much longer, or they would need to occur at much higher temperatures, or with more concentrated solutions. Living things cannot stay alive at high temperatures, and they cannot normally use concentrated solutions. Enzymes are more sensitive than ordinary catalysts (p341).

Note that in order to prove that something is a catalyst for a particular reaction, we should do all of these:

(i) show that the reaction takes place more rapidly with the catalyst than without it;

(ii) show that the same products are formed when the catalyst is used as are formed without it;

(iii) show that the catalyst itself does not react to produce the products; and

(iv) show that the catalyst is still there, unchanged in mass, at the end of the experiment.

6 HOW LIGHT AFFECTS THE SPEED OF SOME REACTIONS

Light is a form of energy, just as heat is. Light affects the speed of some reactions, but there are only a few reactions in which the effect is obvious. One of the examples, however, is one of the most important reactions in the world: photosynthesis (p208). Photosynthesis only takes place in sunlight.

Another useful example is the way in which light causes silver salts to change colour. Silver chloride, silver bromide and silver iodide all darken when exposed to light. This reaction is used in photography. Films and photographic papers are covered with a special layer which contains silver salts. When light is allowed on to the film (e.g. when a photograph is taken), the silver salts go darker. A picture is formed, depending on different amounts of light reaching the film. When the film is *developed* the picture is made more obvious and permanent.

Another example is the way in which the halogens react with hydrogen. Fluorine, the most reactive member of the group, explodes with hydrogen when the two are mixed, even in the dark. Hydrogen fluoride is formed. Chlorine can be mixed safely with hydrogen in the dark or in weak light. If sunlight, or any bright light, is exposed to the mixture, however, it explodes, forming hydrogen chloride.

7 HOW THESE IDEAS ARE USED IN INDUSTRIAL REACTIONS

Also Contact Process for H_2SO_4

See P310 —

In industry, it is important to speed up a reaction if possible, so that the products can be made quickly. In most of the industrial reactions you have studied, we make use of these different ways of speeding up reactions. For example, in the Haber Process to make ammonia (p314) a *high temperature* is used, and a *catalyst*, and the gases are under pressure which makes them *more concentrated*. Each of these speeds up the reaction. You should be able to understand how these ideas are used with *any* industrial reaction you have studied. (A few syllabuses include the understanding of **equilibrium**, and how changes of temperature, etc. **change the equilibrium position.** If you have discussed these ideas, and applied them to industrial reactions, make sure that you understand them.)

16.2 THE SALT AND LIMESTONE INDUSTRIES

General points about industry have been made in various sections of the book: pollution (pp210–43); the use of energy (p98); the choice of site for a factory (p133); the need to recycle substances (p138); and ways of speeding up reactions (previous section). Several industrial reactions have been studied in more detail. For each of these processes you should be able to make sensible comments about all of these general points, especially if you are given information about a process and are asked to comment on it. You could, for example, be asked to choose a site for a factory and be given information about the reaction, raw materials, pollution risks, energy factors, and several possible sites.

The chemical industry uses *raw materials*. These are obtained from the world's *resources*. The main resources have been mentioned on p132. Two important resources are sodium chloride (salt) and calcium carbonate (limestone). Whole industries have grown up around these important substances.

1 SODIUM CHLORIDE, NaCl

Sodium chloride is also known as 'common salt', and its solution in water is called *brine*. It is found naturally in many parts of the world. On land it is usually found as *rock salt*. This is impure sodium chloride. You have probably purified some rock salt in the laboratory. Sodium chloride also occurs dissolved in sea water. Rock salt has been formed where 'inland seas' dried up millions of years ago.

Sodium chloride is extracted from both of these sources. In coastal areas where there are also long, hot sunny days, **salt pans** are used. These are shallow 'tanks' which fill up with sea water at high tide. The water is left behind when the tide goes out. The heat of the sun then evaporates the water, and eventually solid sodium chloride crystallises out, in fairly pure form.

On land, rock salt can be mined directly. Alternatively, water is pumped down into the rock salt deposits. It dissolves the salt, which is then pumped out as brine. The brine is evaporated to form solid salt. As with any mining operation, there are problems if sodium chloride is extracted directly or as brine. Subsidence is the main problem, although modern mining methods largely overcome this. There is very little solid waste, and so there are no slag heaps as there are near coal mines. Pollution is not a problem, either.

Sodium chloride is a very important raw material. It is used to make chlorine, hydrogen, sodium hydroxide and sodium carbonate. Each of these has a variety of important industrial uses, so we can see that sodium chloride is the starting point of *many* processes. This is why large industries have grown up in any area where sodium chloride is extracted, e.g. in Cheshire and Merseyside. In this area, sodium chloride is available from Cheshire. Calcium carbonate (limestone, see next section) could be obtained from North Wales or the Peak District. Coal is available from the Lancashire coal field. In addition, there were the import/export facilities of a large port (Liverpool), and a local market for many of the products: the Lancashire cotton industry, which uses dyes, bleaches and organic chemicals. The area also has good transport links – the Manchester Ship Canal, rail and road networks. It is easy to understand how a complex industry grew up around the salt deposits of Cheshire. Fig 16.4 shows how many industries can grow up around a supply of sodium chloride, especially if there are good transport facilities, energy supplies, etc.

Fig 16.4 The salt industry

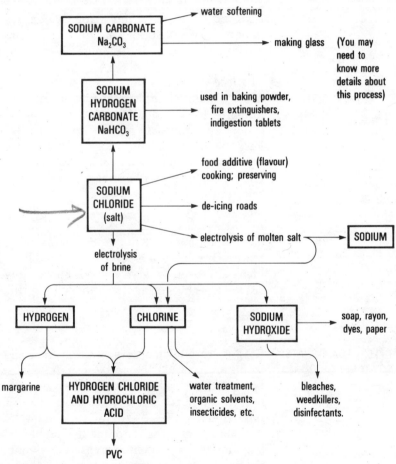

USES OF SODIUM CHLORIDE

(a) The electrolysis of sodium chloride solution (brine)
Three important substances are made by this one reaction (p119).

(b) The electrolysis of molten sodium chloride

This is used to manufacture the metal sodium (p116). Chlorine is also formed, and this is an important byproduct.

(c) De-icing roads in winter

When a solid is dissolved in water, the freezing point of water is lowered. This is like saying that when water is made impure, its melting point is lowered (p84). Rock salt is added to road surfaces in winter (often with extra sand added). The sand and rock particles help to give vehicles a better grip. The salt dissolves in any ice or snow to make the frozen water impure. The melting point of the water is made lower than normal, so it melts even at temperatures *below* 0°C. Normally, ice or snow will melt only when the temperature is above 0°C. This helps to prevent icy roads and accidents.

Unfortunately, this use of salt also causes a problem. Salt causes iron and steel to rust more quickly. Car bodies rust more rapidly if they pick up salt spray from the roads. Cars should be washed more often in winter than in summer, especially underneath the body.

(d) In food

Some sodium chloride is needed in the diet of all animals, including humans. It is needed for some important reactions in the body. We constantly lose sodium chloride from the body, mainly in sweat. People who are likely to lose a lot of salt by sweating (e.g. in long distance running, or by travelling through desert regions) need to take in extra salt, perhaps as salt tablets. Most people obtain enough salt from

(*a*)   cooked food (salt is often added to vegetables before cooking, to improve flavour);

(*b*)   adding small amounts of salt to a meal. It is dangerous to eat too much salt, because this raises the blood pressure. Sodium chloride is also used to *preserve* food. Historically, meat was kept on long sea voyages by storing it in brine or by sprinkling salt on it.

2 CALCIUM CARBONATE, (LIMESTONE), $CaCO_3$

Calcium carbonate occurs naturally in several forms, e.g. chalk, limestone and marble. Huge deposits of limestone are found in many parts of the world. These deposits are found near the surface, so that mining is not necessary. Instead, the limestone is obtained by removing the limestone at the surface and forming a quarry.

Quarries cause environmental problems. Large holes, craters or scars are formed, often in areas of great natural beauty (e.g. the Peak District in Derbyshire). The dust from the quarrying operations (blasting out the rock, and transporting it) settles on nearby trees, fields and houses. Huge lorries are needed to transport the limestone, and these bring their own problems. In addition, people living nearby have to put up with the noise and vibrations from the blasting, which may take place several times per day. Every effort is made to reduce these problems (p134). The process is necessary because calcium carbonate is such an important raw material.

As with sodium chloride, calcium carbonate is the starting point of many industries, and it is used to produce materials which we depend upon in our daily lives (Fig 16.5). This point is emphasised when we remember that many industries grew up in regions where limestones was easily obtained. This is why the steel industry grew in Sheffield. Limestone was available in the nearby Peak District, and coal from the Nottingham/Yorkshire/Derbyshire coal fields. Both of these are important raw materials in iron-making (p134).

Fig 16.5 The limestone industry

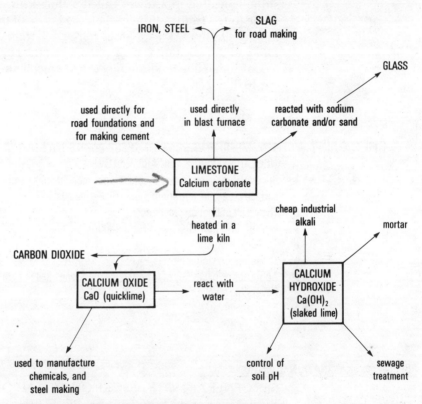

SOME USES AND PROPERTIES OF CALCIUM CARBONATE

(a) General properties as a carbonate of a metal

Its reaction with a dilute acid has been used many times in this book, in making salts, preparing carbon dioxide, and studying speeds of reaction. It has also been mentioned in the control of the pH of soil (p318), and in its natural reaction to form hard water (p234). Its use in the blast furnace to make iron is described on p134.

(b) The decomposition of calcium carbonate in a lime kiln

You may have done a small scale experiment on heating a piece of limestone. Very strong heating is needed to make it decompose. It then gives off carbon dioxide, and forms a coating of the white solid, calcium oxide, CaO. There is nothing to *see* when this happens; the original carbonate and the product are both white.

$$CALCIUM\ CARBONATE \rightarrow CALCIUM\ OXIDE + CARBON\ DIOXIDE$$

$$CaCO_3(s) \rightarrow CaO(s) + CO_2(g)$$

This reaction is performed on a large scale in industry. The limestone is heated in a tower called a **lime kiln**. It is heated by jets of flame (often from natural gas) on the inside of the tower. Air is drawn in at the bottom. Waste gases (air and carbon dioxide) escape at the top, and the calcium oxide is removed at the bottom.

Calcium oxide is commonly called quicklime. It has many uses (see Fig 16.5).

CHECK LIST ▶

REMEMBER THAT SOME OF THESE POINTS MAY NOT BE RELEVANT FOR THE PARTICULAR SYLLABUS YOU ARE FOLLOWING.

1 ▶ Speeds of reaction: experiments, graphs, conclusions involving changes in temperature, surface area, concentration, pressure and catalysts.
2 ▶ The effect of light on reactions.
3 ▶ Equilibrium: how changes in temperature, etc affect the equilibrium position.
4 ▶ The 'salt' industry.
5 ▶ The limestone industry.
6 ▶ Applications/examples of the changes mentioned in 1 in industry.
7 ▶ Reversible reactions.
8 ▶ Food preservatives.

SPECIMEN EXAMINATION QUESTIONS

SEE GENERAL NOTE BEFORE QUESTIONS ON pp49 AND 50. REMEMBER THAT YOU MAY BE ALLOWED TO USE A DATA BOOK IN THE EXAMINATION.

1   A metal was put into excess hydrochloric acid and the volume of gas formed was measured every two minutes. The readings are shown in the table below.

Time (minutes)	0	2	4	6	8	10	12	14	16	18	20	22	24
Volume (cm³)	0	16	26	34	41	47	51	55	58	59	60	60	60

How many minutes did it take for half the metal to react?

    A 4   B 5   C 6   D 10

2 Which one of the following will have the fastest initial rate of reaction?

    A   1 g of marble chips in 200cm^3 of acid at 20°C

    B   1 g of marble chips in 200cm^3 of acid at 40°C

    C   1 g of powdered marble in 200cm^3 of acid at 20°C

    D   1 g of powdered marble in 200cm^3 of acid at 40°C

3 The main reason for using catalysts in industry is that they

    A   increase the yield of the products

    B   raise the temperature of reaction mixtures

    C   remove impurities from reaction mixtures

    D   speed up the rate of formation of the products

                                [*SEG* spec (Alt), 1]

4 The graph (Fig 16.6) shows the total volume of hydrogen produced in the reaction of magnesium ribbon with excess dilute hydrochloric acid over a period of time.

Fig 16.6 Graph for question 4

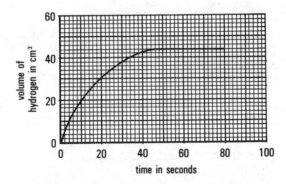

(*a*)   What volume of hydrogen has been produced after 15 seconds?

(*b*)   How long does it take to produce 28cm^3 of hydrogen?

(*c*)   Use the graph to work out the volume of hydrogen produced after 100 seconds.

(*d*)   Sketch on the graph the results you would expect to obtain if the same mass of magnesium were treated with more concentrated acid.   [*SEG* spec 1]

5 Use **one** of the two words **fast** or **slow** to describe the rate of the following reactions.

    a)   (i) The action of sodium on water.

            (ii) The rusting of the steel body of a motor car.

            (iii) The decomposition of hydrogen peroxide using a catalyst.

            (iv) The neutralisation of sodium hydroxide solution with an acid.

    (*b*)   (i) Name the solution formed in (*a*) (i).

            (ii) Name the gas formed and the catalyst used in (*a*) (iii).

(iii) What kind of energy change takes place in (*a*) (iv)?

[*MEA* spec 2)

6 Potassium chloride is the chemical name for an important fertiliser sometimes called 'potash'.

A chemical company is trying to get potash from a mine near Whitby in Yorkshire. Unfortunately the potash is mixed with rock salt. The graph will help you to understand one way in which potash and salt can be separated.

Fig 16.7 Graph for
question 6

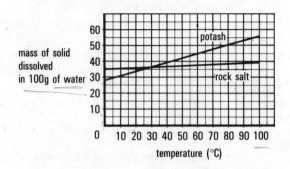

(*a*)   What is the chemical name for rock salt?
(*b*)   Use the graph to find the solubility of potash and rock salt at 100°C and 20°C.

Solubility at	100°C	20°C
potash		
rock salt		

(*c*)   Suggest a method that could be used to separate rock salt from potash.

7 In a discussion on the use of rock salt, two pupils suggested that

ICE MELTS MORE QUICKLY IF ROCK SALT IS ADDED TO IT.

To test their prediction, they did the following experiment (see Fig 16.8):

Step 1 Two funnels were filled with lumps of ice.
     2 Rock salt was added to one of the funnels.
     3 Water from the melting ice was collected in measuring cylinders.
     4 The volume of water was recorded every minute.

(*a*)   State one precaution which should have been taken in Step 1 to make this a fair test.

(*b*)   The volume of water collected from the ice *without* added salt is shown in the table below.

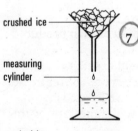

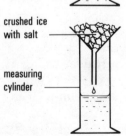

Fig 16.8 Diagram for
question 7

Time (minutes)	1	2	3	4	5	6
Volume of water collected (ml)	2	4	7	9	11	14

Draw a line graph to show how much water was collected as the ice melted and label this line A. (See Fig 16.9).   2 . +2

Fig 16.9 Graph for question 7

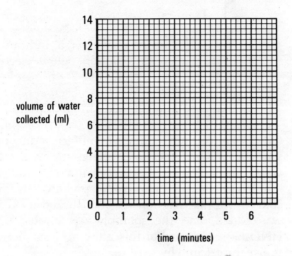

volume of water collected (ml)

time (minutes)

(c)   The volume of water collected in the second measuring cylinder proved that the pupils' prediction was correct. Draw in another line on your graph to show this result and label this line B.   2

(d)   Why does ice melt more quickly when rock salt is added?   2

(e)   Give one *disadvantage* of using salt on icy roads.   1

[*NEA* spec (A), 1]   10

8   Sodium chloride can be obtained from a solution of sodium chloride by evaporation.

(a)   Draw a labelled diagram to show how a solid sample of sodium chloride could be obtained by evaporation in the laboratory.

(b)   During the later stages of the evaporation, the solution often starts to spit. Give one way of reducing this spitting.

(c)   In some Mediterranean countries, sodium chloride is obtained from sea water by evaporation. Large, shallow lakes of sea water are left to evaporate.

(i) What is the source of energy used for evaporation?

(ii) Why are large shallow lakes better than smaller deeper lakes?

(iii) Why is this process *not* economical in Great Britain?

(d)   Electrolysis of a concentrated, aqueous solution of sodium chloride produces hydrogen and chlorine gases at the electrodes.

(i) What is an aqueous solution?

(ii) Name the gas produced at each electrode

Positive electrode . . . .

Negative electrode . . . .

(iii) Complete the diagram (Fig 16.10) to show how electrolysis of a sodium chloride solution could be carried out in the laboratory.

Show how the gases produced could be collected.

Fig 16.10 Incomplete
diagram for question 8

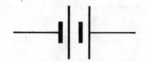

(iv) A few drops of Universal indicator were added to the sodium chloride solution before electrolysis. The solution changes from green (pH 7) to purple (pH 11) during the electrolysis. From these observations, it can be concluded that a solution of sodium chloride is .... and the solution after electrolysis is 		[*LEA* spec (B), 2]

†9 Quicklime (calcium oxide) is manufactured by heating limestone in a limekiln. When quicklime, straight from the kiln, is shaken with water, an alkaline solution of calcium hydroxide is formed.

A solution of calcium oxide, prepared in this way, was filtered. 25.0 cm^3 of this solution was transferred to a conical flask, indicator was added, and the solution was titrated with 0.050 mol/dm^3(l) HNO_3(aq). 16.2 cm^3 of this nitric acid solution was needed to neutralise the calcium hydroxide.

(*a*)	Write an equation for the reaction between quicklime and water.

(*b*)	Describe, stating precautions, how you would transfer the calcium hydroxide solution to the conical flask.

(*c*)	Most common indicators can be used in this titration. Name one and describe its colour change.

(*d*)	Which piece of apparatus would be used to measure the 0.050 mol/dm^3 HNO_3(aq)?

(*e*)	Calculate the concentration of the calcium hydroxide solution
	(i) in mol/dm^3 (mol/l),
	(ii) in g/dm^3 (g/l)

(*f*)	Calculate the mass of calcium oxide which dissolved to give 10.0 cm^3 of the calcium hydroxide solution.

(*g*)	Calculate the minimum mass of limestone needed to produce 2.8 kg of quicklime.

†10	(*a*)	Outline one method for the industrial production of hydrogen.

(*b*)	Write a symbol equation for the conversion of hydrogen to ammonia and state the conditions employed in industry for this conversion.

(*c*)	Hydrogen is usually prepared in the laboratory by collecting the gas given off when zinc reacts with sulphuric acid. This reaction was investigated using the apparatus shown (Fig 16.11).

In a first experiment, the acid was added to the zinc and the volume of hydrogen was noted every 15 seconds. In a second experi-

Fig 16.11 Diagram for
question 10

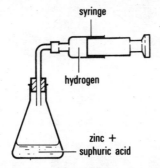

ment, five drops of copper sulphate solution were added to the zinc
before the addition of the sulphuric acid, but otherwise the experiment was the same. The results obtained were plotted graphically
and are shown in Fig 16.12.

Fig 16.12 Graph for
question 10

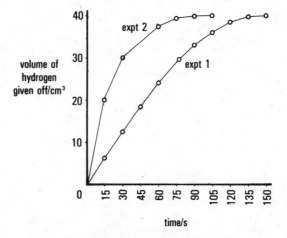

(i) What can you tell from the different curves resulting from
the two experiments?
(ii) Suggest a possible explanation for the difference between
the graphs.
(iii) Describe an experiment which you would use to see
whether or not your suggested explanation in (ii) is correct.
(iv) Outline two other experiments to investigate more fully
the reaction between zinc and sulphuric acid, and indicate
the results that you would expect.   [*NISEC* spec 3)

ANSWERS TO QUESTIONS IN 'CHECK YOUR UNDERSTANDING'

CHAPTER 1 ATOMIC STRUCTURE AND BONDING. RADIOACTIVITY AND NUCLEAR POWER

QUESTIONS ON p24

1 I Br 2Br 2I.
2 H_2O, SO_2, Cl_2, I_2, Br_2, H_2SO_4, HNO_3.
3 (*a*) Zn
(*b*) 2Cu
(*c*) N_2
(*d*) CO
(*e*) $2N_2$.
4 Chlorine, sulphur, oxygen, hydrogen, nitrogen. They are all atoms of non-metals. (Hydrogen usually forms positive ions, but it can form negative ions also.)

QUESTIONS ON p26

1 (*a*) 3
(*b*) 8
(*c*) 10
(*d*) 13
(*e*) 19.
2 (*a*) 5
(*b*) 6
(*c*) 10
(*d*) 16
(*e*) 20.
3 (*a*) 5
(*b*) 7
(*c*) 14
(*d*) 16
(*e*) 18.
4 (*a*) $^{23}_{11}Na$
(*b*) $^{24}_{12}Mg$
(*c*) $^{35}_{17}Cl$.

5   (a)   argon
       (b)   nitrogen
       (c)   F+He; Li+O; N+Be; C+B (four pairs).

6   (a)   Should be eight neutrons+eight protons in nucleus
       (b)   Second energy level has a maximum of eight electrons; should be six in third energy level
       (c)   Atoms are neutral. Diagram shows 12 protons (positive) but only 11 electrons (negative).

7   See Fig 11.1 (p253) for details of energy levels.

QUESTIONS ON p30

1   (a)   and
       (d)   could not exist. Mass numbers must be whole numbers for an individual atom. We cannot have 0.5 protons or neutrons, for example.

2   80.

3   79.6.

4   D and E.

QUESTIONS ON p39

1   Both have 18 electrons, but the nucleus decides what the 'parent' atom is; argon atom has 18 protons, chlorine ion has 17 protons (as does a chlorine atom).

2   (a)   ionic
       (b)   formed by joining a metal with a non-metal
       (c)   sulphur chloride and carbon dioxide (both non-metal+non-metal).

3   (a)   C
       (b)   B
       (c)   A

4   (a)   covalent
       (b)   formed by joining two or more non-metals
       (c)   calcium fluoride+potassium oxide (both ionic).

5   (a)   covalent
       (b)   two or more non-metals
       (c)   ionic
       (d)   high
       (e)   ionic
       (f)   yes.

6   (a)   Should be H-O-H. (Oxygen has a combining power of two and each H atom can only have a combining power of one).
       (b)   Diagram shows *double* covalent bond, resulting in nine electrons in outer energy levels. Should be single covalent bond, which results in eight electrons in outer energy levels.

7   (a) WX_3 covalent
       (b)   ZX ionic
       (c) X_2 covalent

(d)   none (noble gas).

8 (a)   Contains two double covalent bonds,

    (b)   four single covalent bonds,

    (c)   a triple covalent bond,

    (d)   a double covalent bond between the carbon atoms, and four single covalent bonds to hydrogen.

QUESTIONS ON p43

1 The formulas are all included in Chapter 7.

2 (a)   Should be $Al(OH)_3$

    (b)   should be $FeCl_3$

    (c)   should be MgO

    (d)   the bracket is not necessary.

3 First column: 2;2;2;1;2;3;. Second column: 2;2;1;2;2;2. Third column: $CuSO_4$; CuO; $Cu(OH)_2$; Cu_2O; $FeSO_4$; $Fe_2(SO_4)_3$.

4 (a)   should be iron(III);

    (b)   sodium cannot have combining power 2 – always 1;

    (c)   should be $Fe(NO_3)_2$.

QUESTIONS ON p48

1 0.125 g (⅛ g).

2 (a)   becomes 4 less

    (b)   becomes 2 less.

3 (a)   no change

    (b)   increases by 1.

4 (a) $^{228}_{88}X$ $^{228}_{89}Y$ $^{228}_{90}Z$

    (b)   isotopes.

CHAPTER 2 THE KINETIC THEORY. STATES OF MATTER

QUESTIONS ON p61

1 (a)   solid

    (b)   gas

    (c)   gas

    (d)   solid

    (e)   liquid.

2 (a) $NaCl(s)$

    (b) $NaCl(aq)$

    (c) $NaCl(l)$

    (d) $NaCl(g)$.

3 Pressure higher at noon. Temperature higher.

4 A substance has to melt *before* it can boil.

5 (a)   diffuse more quickly

    (b)   diffuse much more quickly.

6 (a)   B

(b)   E
(c)   D
(d)   B and C
(e)   · none
(f)   E
(g)   B.

7   (a) H_2
(b)   HCl
(c) N_2.

8   N_2 and CO.

9   Air pressure is very low.

10   (a)   Level would go down in side joined to porous pot. Hydrogen diffuses *into* the pot faster than air diffuses *out*, therefore pressure inside pot rises.
(b)   Water level rises in same side, as opposite happens.
(c)   Changes happen in reverse order, as CO_2 diffuses more slowly than air.

11   Escaping steam forces all air out of flask. Cloth causes steam to condense to water, creating partial vacuum in flask. Water inside boils even though temperature is less than 100°C, as pressure is much less.

CHAPTER 3 ELEMENTS, COMPOUNDS AND MIXTURES. PURIFICATION

QUESTIONS ON p72   1   (a)   element
(b)   compound
(c)   mixture of elements
(d)   mixture of compounds
(e)   mixture of two elements and a compound
(f)   compound
(g)   mixture of elements and compounds
(h)   element
(i)   mixture
(j)   mixture
(k)   compound
(l)   mixture
(m)   element.

2   Sulphur – the others are metals.

3   No – only a few are, e.g. iron, cobalt.

4   Use a magnet, or 'dissolve' the iron in warm, dilute acid.

5   HCl is a compound – it has totally different properties from the elements within it.

6   B.

7   Glass and plastics are not elements, and do not belong in the table.

QUESTIONS ON p82

1. (a)   sand is insoluble in water
   (b)   Sugar dissolves
   (c)   immiscible with what?
   (d)   filtrate will contain both dissolved solids.
2. (e)   is the best answer; (a) would also work, but difficult to obtain pure salt and pure water by distillation – better to distil to obtain some pure water, hen crystallise the rest of solution to obtain salt.
3. Examples such as using a strainer or sieve.
4. Liquid X.
5. The liquids are immiscible.
6. (a)   3
   (b)   B
   (c)   distil.
7. (a)   A and E
   (b)   A,B,C,E
   (c)   B,C,D,G
   (d)   F
   (e)   It is a mixture of B,C and E
   (f)   It is a mixture of B and D.
8. A   fractional distillation;
   B   chromatography;
   C   evaporation.
9. (a)   filtration
   (b)   distillation
   (c)   separating funnel.
10. (a)   Distillation
    (b)   Use a magnet
    (c)   Dissolve the iron in warm, dilute acid (hydrochloric or sulphuric), filter off the copper
    (d)   Add water, warm, stir. Sodium chloride dissolves, calcium carbonate insoluble. Filter off calcium carbonate, wash, dry. Crystallise sodium chloride from filtrate.
    (e)   Add lots of water until all calcium has reacted. Filter off the copper, wash, dry.
    (f)   Same method as in (d) – copper sulphate soluble in water, calcium sulphate insoluble.

QUESTIONS ON p85

1. Use a liquid which boils much higher than 140°C, not water.
2. Atmospheric pressure higher or lower than normal.
3. Air pressure could be higher than normal. The liquid might not be water.
4. (a)   Water expands on freezing
   (b)   Antifreeze makes the water 'impure' and so lowers its melting point.

5 Salt dissolves, making water 'impure'. Melting point of water made lower than 0°C. When temperature falls to 0°C, water stays in liquid form. No ice formed.

6 Could be *slightly* impure C, or impure D or E.

CHAPTER 4 THE ACTIVITY SERIES

QUESTIONS ON p100

1 (a) T
  (b) F
  (c) F
  (d) F
  (e) T
  (f) F.
2 C, A,B, D.
3 (a) Gases less soluble in hot water than in cold
  (b) Hydrogen – reaction between iron and very hot water.
4 Low down.
5 D, B,C,A.
6 (a) F
  (b) F
  (c) T
  (d) T.

CHAPTER 5 ELECTROLYSIS

QUESTIONS ON p115

1 Any six metals, or five metals plus carbon in the form graphite.
2 Ions within it are not free to move around.
3 W_2Y and XZ.
4 NaOH, KBr.
5 Non-metals.
6 (a) negative (cathode),
  (b) gain
  (c) 2
  (d) $Cu^{2+} + 2e^- \rightarrow Cu$.
7 (a) positive (anode),
  (b) lose
  (c) 1
  (d) $2Cl^- - 2e^- \rightarrow Cl_2$.
8 (a) chlorine *molecules*
  (b) $+3e^-$
  (c) $-e^-$.
9 B.
10 (a) copper metal at negative electrode (cathode), bromine at the positive (anode); colour of solution fades.

(b)   hydrogen gas at cathode, iodine at anode; solution changes to alkaline sodium hydroxide.

(c)   potassium metal at cathode, bromine at anode, no change.

(d)   copper at cathode, oxygen at anode, solution changes to nitric acid and colour fades.

11   Blue colour fades as copper ions are discharged. Solution gradually becomes sulphuric acid, because hydroxide ions also discharged.

12   (i) happens because two electrons leaving the cathode discharge 1 H_2 molecule, and two electrons entering the anode discharge 1 Cl_2 molecule.

      (ii) chlorine is more soluble in water than hydrogen, so some of the gas 'disappears' into solution.

CHAPTER 6 OXIDATION AND REDUCTION. METALS AND ALLOYS. RECYCLING AND CORROSION

QUESTIONS ON p131

1   Ca oxidised (gains oxygen).

2 Fe_2O_3 reduced (loses oxygen), CO oxidised (gains oxygen).

3   C oxidised (gains oxygen), H_2O reduced (loses oxygen).

4   CuO reduced (loses oxygen), H_2 oxidised (gains oxygen).

5   Cu oxidised (loses electrons).

6 Ag^+ reduced (gains electron), Mg oxidised (loses electrons).

7 $FeSO_4$ contains Fe^{2+} ions. These are oxidised (by loss of electron) to Fe^{3+} ions in Fe_2O_3.

8   Fe oxidised to Fe^{2+} ions (in $FeSO_4$) by loss of electrons; Cu^{2+} ions in $CuSO_4$ reduced to Cu atoms by gaining electrons.

9   Cl atoms in Cl_2 reduced to Cl^- in KCl by gaining electron; Br^- ions in KBr oxidised to Br atoms in Br_2 by losing electron.

10   Na atoms oxidised to Na^+ in NaCl by loss of electron; Cl atoms in Cl_2 reduced to Cl^- ions in NaCl by gaining electron.

QUESTIONS ON p141

1   Iron has to be separated from other elements *joined* to it, because it is found as a *compound*.

2   (a)   Stage 1

      (b)   (i) has to be dumped or disposed off,

              (ii) could produce sulphur dioxide gas, which would cause pollution

      (c)   reduction

      (d)   metals near top of series much more difficult to separate from their ores

      (e)   answers in text

      (f)   energy.

3   Examples include copper (wiring) and lead (battery).

4   (a)   oxygen

      (b)   allows coke to burn to produce heat, and reacts with coke to form reducing agent, CO

(c)   removes impurities as slag

(d)   carbon

(e)   carbon, sulphur, phosphorus reduced, other metals may be added

(f)   (i) F

(ii) F

(iii) T

(g)   answers in text.

5   (a)   NaCl occurs naturally, NaOH has to be manufactured. NaCl also produces chlorine, important commercial gas. Electrolysis of NaOH also produces H_2O, which would interfere with the reaction and react with the sodium

(b)   NaOH has a lower melting point than NaCl – less energy

(c)   Adding calcium chloride to lower the melting point.

QUESTIONS ON p146

1   Second student correct; water contains *dissolved* oxygen.

2   More exposure to wet weather, longer times for metal to dry out, salt used on roads increases rate of rusting.

3   (a)   bathroom or kitchen – plenty of water vapour around

(b)   living room – warm, dry.

4   (a)   galvanising

(b)   grease or oil

(c)   galvanising

(d)   paint.

5   Expensive to buy; would last very long time, people would therefore buy cars less frequently.

6   (a)   plated with tin,

(b)   two different metals (iron, tin) in contact and bathed by electrolyte (e.g. fruit juice). Tin less reactive than iron, therefore iron corrodes rapidly.

7   Gloss paint is oil-based, but emulsion is *water* based.

CHAPTER 7 GENERAL PROPERTIES OF METALS AND THEIR COMPOUNDS. TESTS FOR 'UNKNOWN' SUBSTANCES

QUESTIONS ON p169   1   (a)   chlorine

(b)   oxygen

(c)   carbon dioxide.

2   (a)   magnesium

(b)   potassium

(c)   copper

(d)   sodium

(e)   zinc

(f)   aluminium

(g)   iron

      (*h*)   lead.

3 (*a*)   copper oxide
      (*b*)   magnesium hydroxide
      (*c*)   iron(II) oxide
      (*d*)   calcium carbonate
      (*e*)   anhydrous copper(II) sulphate
      (*f*)   calcium chloride
      (*g*)   copper(II) sulphate
      (*h*)   sodium hydroxide.

4 (*a*)   copper(II) oxide
      (*b*)   sodium carbonate
      (*c*)   aluminium sulphate
      (*d*)   copper(II) hydroxide
      (*e*)   iron(II) chloride
      (*f*)   iron(III) chloride
      (*g*)   magnesium nitrate.

5 (*a*)   nitric
      (*b*)   hydrochloric
      (*c*)   sulphuric.

6 (*a*)   calcium carbonate, calcium sulphate
      (*b*)   sodium and potassium
      (*c*)   nitrates
      (*d*)   none
      (*e*)   all except for sodium and potassium carbonates.

7 (*a*)   all forms of calcium carbonate
      (*b*)   all alloys.

8 (*a*)   F
      (*b*)   T
      (*c*)   F.

9 (*a*)   iron(III)
      (*b*)   copper.

10 (*a*)   Aluminium carbonate does not exist. Use aluminium oxide or hydroxide+dilute sulphuric acid. (Metal should not be suggested – protected by oxide layer.)

      (*b*) $CuSO_4$ is soluble so cannot be precipitated. Use copper(II) oxide, hydroxide, or carbonate+dilute sulphuric acid. (Metal cannot be used – too low in Activity Series.)

      (*c*)   There is no reaction between a chloride and a dilute acid. The mixture of ions would produce both zinc sulphate and zinc chloride if crystallised. Use either zinc metal, or the oxide, hydroxide, or carbonate with dilute sulphuric acid.

      (*d*)   Calcium carbonate is insoluble, so cannot be in solution. Calcium sulphate is insoluble salt, so prepare by precipitating it by mixing any soluble calcium compound (e.g. the chloride or nitrate) with any soluble sulphate (e.g. sodium sulphate).

      (*e*)   Copper metal will not react with typical dilute acids – too low in activity series. Prepare as in (b) but with hydrochloric acid instead of sulphuric.

CHAPTER 8 ACIDS, BASES AND SALTS. pH AND NEUTRALISATION

QUESTIONS ON p187

1 (*b*) is true.

2 Copper(II) oxide, potassium hydroxide, magnesium oxide, calcium hydroxide.

3 (*b*) an insoluble base.

4 (*a*) salt+water
   (*b*) +carbonate → +water
   (*c*) → copper(II) chloride+water
   (*d*) carbon dioxide+sodium sulphate+water
   (*e*) +hydrochloric acid.

5 (*a*) pH slowly rises until reaches 7, then stays at 7 even when more base added
   (*b*) pH slowly rises, reaches 7, then continues to rise as more alkali added.

6 copper(II) sulphate, copper(II) chloride, sodium nitrate.

7 (*b*) acid+alkali, and
   (*d*) precipitation, and (*f*)

8 (*a*) nitric acid+sodium carbonate
   (*b*) nitric acid+sodium hydroxide.

9 (*a*) calcium nitrate and sodium carbonate
   (*b*) silver nitrate and sodium chloride
   (*c*) barium nitrate and sodium sulphate
   (*d*) copper(II) nitrate and sodium carbonate.

10 hydrochloric acid: 1; sodium chloride: 7; lemon juice: 5; calcium hydroxide: 8.

11 (*a*) T
    (*b*) T

12 Yes, $CuCO_3$; No; Pb^{2+} NO_3^- Zn^{2+} Cl^- yes $PbCl_2$; Cu^{2+} Cl^- Zn SO_4^{2-} no; Cu^{2+} Cl^- Ag^+ NO_3^- yes AgCl; H^+ SO_4^{2-} Ca^{2+} Cl^- yes $CaSO_4$; potassium carbonate lead(II) nitrate yes $PbCO_3$; Na^+ I^- Pb^{2+} NO_3^- yes PbI_2.

13 see p179.

14 $CuO(s)+2HCl(aq) \rightarrow CuCl_2(aq)+H_2O(l)$
    $Cu(OH)_2(s)+H_2SO_4(aq) \rightarrow CuSO_4(aq)+2H_2O(l)$
    $CaCO_3(s)+2HCl(aq) \rightarrow CaCl_2(aq)+CO_2(g)+H_2O(l)$
    $Mg(s)+2HCl(aq) \rightarrow MgCl_2(aq)+H_2(g)$
    $Na_2CO_3(s$ or $aq)+2HNO_3(aq) \rightarrow 2NaNO_3(aq)+CO_2(g)+H_2O(l)$

CHAPTER 9 WORKING WITH GASES. THE AIR. OXYGEN AND HYDROGEN

QUESTIONS ON p201

1 air, CO_2, H_2, N_2, O_2.

2 CO, H_2S.

3 H_2.

4 CO_2.

5 NH_3.

6   Cl_2, SO_2.

7   SO_3.

8   NO_2.

9   (a)   water should *enter* the bottle; long and short tubes in first flask should be other way round; drying agent should be *concentrated* sulphuric acid; copper metal should fill tube so air has to pass *through* it; 'nitrogen' should not be collected over water, which wets it again; the two flasks should be exchanged, so that the air is not made 'wet' again by the sodium hydroxide *solution* after being dried.

     (b)   first samples will not have passed through all stages of the apparatus.

     (c)   noble gases.

10   Heat glass wool – steam formed – steam forces air out of slit – heat copper – no air inside tube, and no air can enter – copper does not oxidise.

11   acid rises to meet solid; gas made by reaction; gas can be collected through tap; when tap closed, gas collects inside 'bulb', pressure rises; acid forced out of bulb; reaction stops, but bulb is still full of gas ready for use; when tap opened, gas escapes, acid rises, reaction continues.

QUESTIONS ON p215

1   CO_2 + water vapour.

2   Glucose also contains oxygen.

3   (a)   C + H

     (b)   Sulphur

     (c)   Oxygen

     (d)   Carbon dioxide, water (steam), and sulphur dioxide

     (e)   Carbon

     (f)   Carbon monoxide. Formed when oxygen supply is inadequate.

4   (a)   Carbon dioxide

     (b)   nitrogen

     (c)   a noble gas or nitrogen

     (d)   helium.

5   (a)   busy road tunnels

     (b)   South Pole

     (c)   E

     (d)   Higher concentration of cars, etc. – lead compounds in exhaust gases.

6   Clouds form a 'blanket' which helps to stop cooling by loss of heat through infra red rays.

7   Oxygen is more soluble in water than the other gases in air.

QUESTIONS ON p221　**1**　(*a*)　If any air still in apparatus, mixture of O_2+H_2 might explode.

(*b*)　When H_2 *mixed* with O_2, it explodes, not burns, if ignited.

(*c*)　When sample did not 'pop' as flame applied, must be pure H_2, therefore safe to light jet.

2　If tube opened while still hot, oxygen in the air might react with the hot metal to reform the original oxide.

3　Any two oxides of metals near top of Activity Series, e.g. sodium oxide, potassium oxide, calcium oxide, magnesium oxide.

CHAPTER 10　WATER. SOLUTIONS. WATER POLLUTION

QUESTIONS ON p238　**1**　Might not be pure water – could be any liquid *containing* water.

2　All three samples must have the same volume – not clear if this was done.

3　(*a*)　B

(*b*)　both hard, A more hard than C.

4　Running hard water constantly supplies new calcium compounds which react with soap – never forms good lather. In fixed volume, once calcium compounds used up, soap then works normally.

5　For softening water, *positive* ions only need to be exchanged.

6　(*a*)　(i);

(*b*)　(ii);

(*c*)　(i).

7　(*c*)

QUESTIONS ON p242　**1**　(*a*)　no temperature given

(*b*)　only true for solids; gases opposite effect.

2　(*a*)　approximately 55 g/100 g water

(*b*)　approximately 30 g/100 g water

(*c*)　approximately 28°C

(*d*)　approximately 38°C

(*e*)　approximately ½ of 62 g = 31 g.

3　(*a*)　32 g/100 g water at 40°C

(*b*)　10 g/100 g water at 25°C

(*c*)　30 g/100 g water at 30°C.

4　(*a*)　10 g/100 g water at the temperature of the experiment

(*b*)　14 g/100 g water at the temperature of the experiment.

5　(i) exact volume of water not known

(ii) less than 28 g actually dissolved

(iii) temperature not given.

6　Gases are less soluble in warm water, so more would pass through for collection.

7　Approximately 20 g

CHAPTER 11 THE PERIODIC TABLE. STRUCTURE

QUSTIONS ON p261
1 (a) H,N
   (b) A,I
   (c) C,K
   (d) I
   (e) G.
2 (a) solid
   (b) metal
   (c) no
   (d) no
   (e) yes.
3 C,E,F,A,G,B,H,D.
4 (a) 5
   (b) 5
   (c) 2.
5 (a) W,Y and X,Z
   (b) A,B and C,D.
6 GCl_3.
7 A metal, B non-metal, C metal, D non-metal.
8 (a) 2
   (b) K,H,J.
9 (a) 5
   (b) O,M,N.
10 D,B,C,A.
11 D.
12 (a) D and A
   (b) C and H.
13 At will not react with sodium iodide solution. Iodine should displace astatine from potassium astatide.
14 (a) metals (ions smaller than atoms)
   (b) A.
15 (a) A,D
   (b) B
   (c) D and C (A and C nearly as good)
   (d) B
   (e) E
   (f) C
   (g) (i) A^+
      (ii) C^-
   (h) B,C. BC_4.
16 (a) hydroxide of Z
   (b) H_2
   (c) 2,8
   (d) (i) H_2
      (ii) Cl_2.

QUESTIONS ON p271

1 hydrogen.
2 graphite.
3 sulphur.
4 sodium.
5 diamond.
6 giant ionic.
7 (a) metal
  (b) molecular (simple)
  (c) giant ionic
  (d) graphite – giant atomic.
8 (i) D
  (ii) A
  (iii) E
  (iv) C
  (v) B
  (vi) D
  (vii) D
  (viii) D.
9 (a) giant ionic
  (b) particles must escape from surface
  (c) all particles (ions) bonded strongly together – cannot escape
  (d) simple molecular
  (e) bonds between molecules easily broken – some molecules can escape.

CHAPTER 12 EQUATIONS. THE MOLE

QUESTIONS ON p280

1 40.
2 17.
3 94.
4 98.
5 58.5.
6 63.
7 160.
8 18.
9 286.

QUESTIONS ON p281

1 sodium chloride+carbon dioxide+water.
2 zinc sulphate+water.
3 copper(II) nitrate+water.
4 zinc sulphate solution+copper metal.
5 bromine+potassium chloride solution.

6   calcium oxide.
7   calcium chloride+hydrogen.
8   copper metal+water (steam).
9   copper(II) carbonate+sulphuric acid.
10   zinc metal+hydrochloric acid.
11   (*a*) (*b*) (*c*) and (*d*) – all of them.

QUESTIONS ON p283	Answers are given on p284, where the correctly balanced equations are used in some calculations.

QUESTIONS ON p284

1   18 g
2   80 g.
3   8 g.
4   62 g.
5   40 g.
6   The acid is in excess, by 3.5 g.

QUESTIONS ON p285

1   (i) 14 g
            (ii) 11 g.
2   11.7 g.
3   16 g.

QUESTIONS ON p288

1   (*a*)   64 g
    (*b*)   65 g
    (*c*)   56 g
    (*d*)   24 g
    (*e*)   32 g.
2   (*a*)   16 g
    (*b*)   5.6 g
    (*c*)   6 g
    (*d*)   32 g
    (*e*)   49 g.
3   (*a*)   18 g of carbon
    (*b*)   7 g of nitrogen
    (*c*)   both the same.

QUESTIONS ON p288

1   (*a*)   2 g
    (*b*)   71 g
    (*c*)   28 g

	(d)	17 g
	(e)	63 g
	(f)	100 g
	(g)	62 g
	(h)	94 g.
2	(a)	149 g
	(b)	20 g
	(c)	40 g
3	(a)	0.5 moles
	(b)	2.0 moles
	(c)	0.5 moles.

QUESTIONS ON p290

1	(a)	24 litres
	(b)	48 litres
	(c)	12 litres
	(d)	2.4 litres.
2	(a)	12 litres
	(b)	24 litres
	(c)	120 litres
	(d)	2.4 litres
	(e)	6 litres.
3	(a)	17 g
	(b)	7 g
	(c)	0.28 g.

QUESTIONS ON p290

1	(a)	$Zn(s) + 2HCl(aq) \rightarrow ZnCl_2(aq) + H_2(g)$
	(b)	2.4 litres.
2	0.6 litres.	

QUESTIONS ON p292

1	(a)	Ca 40%, C 12%, O 48%
	(b)	Cu 40%, S 20%, O 40%
	(c)	C 75%, H 25%
	(d)	K 39%, H 1%, C 12%, O 48%.
2	(a)	Na 16.08%, C 4.2%, O 16.78%, water 62.94%
	(b)	Fe 20.14%, S 11.51%, O 23.02%, water 45.32%.
3	(a)	21.21%
	(b)	35%.
4	Contains much more nitrogen for a given mass of solid.	

QUESTIONS ON p293

1 $CaCl_2$
2 (a) $MgCl_2$
   (b) $CuSO_4$
   (c) $CN_2O_3H_8$, which is $(NH_4)_2CO_3$
   (d) CH_4.

QUESTIONS ON p293 1 (a) C_2H_6
   (b) H_2O_2
   (c) CH_5N (the actual compound, which you will not know, is CH_3NH_2).

QUESTIONS ON p294 1 0.1 mole/l or 0.1M.
2 0.4 moles.
3 0.05 moles.
4 2.0 g.

QUESTIONS ON p296 1 (a)   0.12 moles/l or 0.12M
   (b)   3.75 moles/l or 3.75M
   (c)   1.0 moles/or 1.0M.

CHAPTER 14 ORGANIC CHEMISTRY. PLASTICS

QUESTIONS ON p345   The following parts are the 'odd ones out' in each question.
1 C (which is false).
2 E (which is false).
3 D (false).
4 C (false).
5 B (false).
6 C (false).
7 A (false).

PERIODIC TABLE
OF ELEMENTS

Group	1	2							
	1 **H** Hydrogen 1 — 1								
	7 **Li** Lithium 3 — 2)1	9 **Be** Beryllium 4 — 2)2							
	23 **Na** Sodium 11 — 2)8)1	24 **Mg** Magnesium 12 — 2)8)2							
	39 **K** Potassium 19 — 2)8)8)1	40 **Ca** Calcium 20 — 2)8)8)2	45 **Sc** Scandium 21 — 2)8)9)2	48 **Ti** Titanium 22 — 2)8)10)2	51 **V** Vanadium 23 — 2)8)11)2	52 **Cr** Chromium 24 — 2)8)13)1	55 **Mn** Manganese 25 — 2)8)13)2	56 **Fe** Iron 26 — 2)8)14)2	59 **Co** Cobalt 27 — 2)8)15)2
	85.5 **Rb** Rubidium 37 — 2)8)18)8)1	88 **Sr** Strontium 38 — 2)8)18)8)2	89 **Y** Yitrium 39 — 2)8)18)9)2	91 **Zr** Zirconium 40 — 2)8)18)10)2	93 **Nb** Niobium 41 — 2)8)18)12)1	96 **Mo** Molybdenum 42 — 2)8)18)13)1	[99] **Tc** Technetium 43 — 2)8)18)14)1	101 **Ru** Ruthenium 44 — 2)8)18)15)1	103 **Rh** Rhodium 45 — 2)8)18)16)1
	133 **Cs** Caesium 55 — 2)8)18)18)8)1	137 **Ba** Barium 56 — 2)8)18)18)8)2	139 **La** Lanthanum 57 — 2)8)18)18)9)2	178.5 **Hf** Hafnium 72 — 2)8)18)32)10)2	181 **Ta** Tantalum 73 — 2)8)18)32)11)2	184 **W** Tungsten 74 — 2)8)18)32)12)2	186 **Re** Rhenium 75 — 2)8)18)32)13)2	190 **Os** Osmium 76 — 2)8)18)32)14)2	192 **Ir** Iridium 77 — 2)8)18)32)15)2
	[223] **Fr** Francium 87 — 2)8)18)32)18)8)1	[226] **Ra** Radium 88 — 2)8)18)32)18)8)2	227* **Ac** Actinium 89 — 2)8)18)32)18)9)2						

Lanthanide / Actinide series and key:

139 **La** Lanthanum 57 — 2)8)18)18)9)2	140 **Ce** Cerium 58 — 2)8)18)20)8)2	141 **Pr** Praseodymium 59 — 2)8)18)21)8)2	144 **Nd** Neodymium 60 — 2)8)18)22)8)2	[147] **Pm** Promethium 61 — 2)8)18)23)8)2	150 **Sm** Samarium 62 — 2)8)18)24)8)2
227* **Ac** Actinium 89 — 2)8)18)32)18)9)2	232 **Th** Thorium 90 — 2)8)18)32)18)10)2	[231] **Pa** Protactinium 91 — 2)8)18)32)20)9)2	238 **U** Uranium 92 — 2)8)18)32)21)9)2	[237] **Np** Neptunium 93 — 2)8)18)32)23)8)2	[242] **Pu** Plutonium 94 — 2)8)18)32)24)8)2

Key:

Atomic mass

Symbol

Name

Atomic number

Electronic structure

[ ] This is the mass number of the isotope with the longest known half life of the element indicated
* This is the mass number of the most stable or best known isotope of the element indicated

OF ELEMENTS

3	4	5	6	7	0

					4 **He** Helium 2 — 2

| 11 **B** Boron 5 — 2)3 | 12 **C** Carbon 6 — 2)4 | 14 **N** Nitrogen 7 — 2)5 | 16 **O** Oxygen 8 — 2)6 | 19 **F** Fluorine 9 — 2)7 | 20 **Ne** Neon 10 — 2)8 |
| 27 **Al** Aluminium 13 — 2)8)3 | 28 **Si** Silicon 14 — 2)8)4 | 31 **P** Phosphorus 15 — 2)8)5 | 32 **S** Sulphur 16 — 2)8)6 | 35.5 **Cl** Chlorine 17 — 2)8)7 | 40 **Ar** Argon 18 — 2)8)8 |

59 **Ni** Nickel 28 — 2)8)16)2	64 **Cu** Copper 29 — 2)8)18)1	65 **Zn** Zinc 30 — 2)8)18)2	70 **Ga** Gallium 31 — 2)8)18)3	73 **Ge** Germanium 32 — 2)8)18)4	75 **As** Arsenic 33 — 2)8)18)5	79 **Se** Selenium 34 — 2)8)18)6	80 **Br** Bromine 35 — 2)8)18)7	84 **Kr** Krypton 36 — 2)8)18)8
106 **Pd** Palladium 46 — 2)8)18)18	108 **Ag** Silver 47 — 2)8)18)18)1	112 **Cd** Cadmium 48 — 2)8)18)18)2	115 **In** Indium 49 — 2)8)18)18)3	119 **Sn** Tin 50 — 2)8)18)18)4	122 **Sb** Antimony 51 — 2)8)18)18)5	128 **Te** Tellurium 52 — 2)8)18)18)6	127 **I** Iodine 53 — 2)8)18)18)7	131 **Xe** Xenon 54 — 2)8)18)18)8
195 **Pt** Platinum 78 — 2)8)18)32)17)1	197 **Au** Gold 79 — 2)8)18)32)18)1	201 **Hg** Mercury 80 — 2)8)18)32)18)2	204 **Tl** Thallium 81 — 2)8)18)32)18)3	207 **Pb** Lead 82 — 2)8)18)32)18)4	209 **Bi** Bismuth 83 — 2)8)18)32)18)5	[210] **Po** Polonium 84 — 2)8)18)32)18)6	[210] **At** Astatine 85 — 2)8)18)32)18)7	[222] **Rn** Radon 86 — 2)8)18)32)18)8

152 **Eu** Europium 63 — 2)8)18)25)8)2	157 **Gd** Gadolinium 64 — 2)8)18)25)9)2	159 **Tb** Terbium 65 — 2)8)18)27)8)2	162.5 **Dy** Dysprosium 66 — 2)8)18)28)8)2	165 **Ho** Holmium 67 — 2)8)18)29)8)2	167 **Er** Erbium 68 — 2)8)18)30)8)2	169 **Tm** Thulium 69 — 2)8)18)31)8)2	173 **Yb** Ytterbium 70 — 2)8)18)32)8)2	175 **Lu** Lutetium 71 — 2)8)18)32)9)2
[243] **Am** Americium 95 — 2)8)18)32)25)8)2	[247] **Cm** Curium 96 — 2)8)18)32)25)9)2	[249] **Bk** Berkelium 97 — 2)8)18)32)27)8)2	[251] **Cf** Californium 98 — 2)8)18)32)28)8)2	[254] **Es** Einsteinium 99 — 2)8)18)32)29)8)2	[253] **Fm** Fermium 100 — 2)8)18)32)30)8)2	[256] **Md** Mendelevium 101 — 2)8)18)32)31)8)2	254* **No** Nobelium 102 — 2)8)18)32)32)8)2	[257] **Lr** Lawrencium 103 — 2)8)18)32)32)9)2

INDEX